16.95

Term-time

M

WITHDRAWN

New Directions in
Educational Psychology
1. Learning and Teaching

New Directions in Educational Psychology
1. Learning and Teaching

Edited and
Introduced by

Noel Entwistle
University of Edinburgh

 The Falmer Press

(A member of the Taylor & Francis Group)
London & Philadelphia

UK   The Falmer Press, Falmer House, Barcombe, Lewes, East Sussex,
            BN8 5DL

USA   The Falmer Press, Taylor & Francis Inc., 242 Cherry Street,
            Philadelphia, PA 19106-1906

First published 1985

Library of Congress Cataloging in Publication Data

Main entry under title:
New directions in educational psychology.

  Includes bibliographies and indexes.
  Contents: v. 1. Learning and teaching.
  1. Educational psychology—Addresses, essays, lectures.
2. Learning, Psychology of—Addresses, essays,
lectures.   3. Learning—Addresses, essays, lectures.
I. Entwistle, Noel James.
LB1055.N495   1984   370.15   84-15801
ISBN 0-905273-72-9 (v. 1)
ISBN 0-905273-71-0 (pbk. : v. 1)

Typeset in 10½/12 Plantin by
Imago Publishing, Thame, Oxon

*Printed in Great Britain by Taylor & Francis (Printers) Ltd,
Basingstoke*

Contents

Contents

Acknowledgements

The Publishers are grateful to the following for permission to reproduce copyright material.

Dr David Ausubel for extracts from his book *Educational Psychology: A Cognitive View*.

The editor and publishers of the *British Educational Research Journal* for BENNETT, S.N. and RUTTER, M. (1980)

The editor and publishers of the *British Journal of Educational Psychology* for:

HEWISON, J. and TIZARD, J. (1980)

TIZARD, J. and SCHOFIELD, W. (1982)

The editor and publishers of *Educational Analysis* for:

EYSENCK, H.J. (1982)

MESSICK, S. (1982)

NISBET, J. (1982)

The editor and publishers of *Scottish Educational Review* for:

SIMPSON M. and ARNOLD B. (1982)

Lawrence Erlbaum Associates for:

GINSBURG, C. (1981)

Goldsmiths' College for:

ENTWISTLE, N.J. (1983)

Charles Merrill Publishing Co. for:

ROGERS, C. (1969)

National Foundation for Educational Research in England and Wales for:

BADGER, E. (1981)

Ohio State University for:

BLOCK, J. (1980)

Open University Enterprises Ltd for:

GIBBS, G. (1981)

A.P. Watt Ltd for:

DONALDSON, M. (1979)

General Editor's Preface

'Psychology is a science, and teaching is an art: and sciences never generate arts directly out of themselves,' wrote William James at the turn of the century in his classic work, *Talks to Teachers on Psychology*, adding, 'An intermediary, inventive mind must make the application, by using its originality.'[1]

It is in the spirit in which William James proceeded to show how psychology could be of help to teachers that this volume of articles has been compiled by Noel Entwistle, who is Professor of Education at Edinburgh University, and a former Editor of the *British Journal of Educational Psychology*. It is nicely empirical in the best tradition of psychology applied to education and teaching, of which there have been many distinguished contributors in this country, in Europe and in the United States.

Not only does this collection of articles show that educational psychology is alive and well, it also shows its sensitivity to the concerns of the teacher in the school. In particular, this book* addresses the nature of the learning process, the experience of learning and psychology in learning and assessment in a way which, without being prescriptive, suggests to educators what choices and conditions might well make more effective the tasks they seek to perform.

The roll call of contributors to this book is considerable: each is an acknowledged authority in his or her field.

They address such diverse concepts and topics as human ability, learning and its relation to heredity and environment, learning and meaning, cognitive styles in learning, and the role of the computer in learning. In fact, the articles collected together provide both an excellent introduction to the psychology of learning and teaching and a powerful teaching resource for those engaged in teaching the psychology of education.

* A second forthcoming volume will address issues of behaviour and motivation in schooling and teaching.

General Editor's Preface

As did William James, an American and a distinguished philosopher and psychologist, so did Edward Thring,[2] a distinguished headmaster of Uppingham School, writing a decade earlier, see that one of the key issues in teaching was, as he put it '... a simple one, simply stated, without any circumlocution. It is this, how to reach the mind of each boy.' This remains still the case and still the aspiration of every teacher. This collection of articles is part of the continuing contribution which psychology makes to this endeavour.

Philip H. Taylor
University of Birmingham
June 1984

Notes

1 JAMES, W. (1899) *Talks to Teachers on Psychology*, London, Longmans, Green.
2 THRING, E. (1883) *The Theory and Practice of Teaching*, Cambridge, Cambridge University Press.

Foreword

This book contains a set of articles which is intended to illustrate some of the new directions in educational psychology which are relevant to teaching and learning mainly in schools, but also in colleges, universities and continuing education. The choice of a relatively small number of articles to represent these new directions is a hazardous enterprise for the editor. The final choice will inevitably be seen as reflecting some idiosyncratic preferences, and even prejudice. It may be useful to explain how the final choice was made.

The first step was to decide how much knowledge of technical terms and research methodology could be taken for granted. As the book is intended mainly for students training to be teachers, or taking degrees in education, and for teachers on in-service courses with little detailed knowledge of psychology, it was decided to look for articles which made few demands of this type, but also to select a few more technical articles. This decision immediately restricted the number of suitable papers quite drastically. Most of the articles in academic journals of educational psychology are written for fellow researchers, and are written in a style inaccessible to most teachers. The use of jargon and complex statistical analyses make the majority of these articles very difficult to follow. Of course there are also, occasionally, articles on educational psychology in the educational press and in teachers' journals, but these generally lack detail, or fail to reflect the most recent research findings. It was therefore decided to look for well-written review articles. A thorough search of the literature, however, identified only a small number of such articles. In the end it seemed best to invite colleagues involved in current research on learning and teaching to write some articles specially for this book. That proved to have the considerable advantage of ensuring that the very latest research findings could be included. The editor is extremely grateful to these authors who were prepared to write articles specifically for this book.

1
Psychology Applied to Teaching and Learning

Contributions of Psychology to Learning and Teaching

Noel Entwistle
University of Edinburgh

The claim that psychology has direct relevance to the practice of education has been insistent and regularly reiterated since the writings of William James and John Dewey at the turn of the century. In the elegant logic of their British contemporary James Ward, the argument ran thus.

> It is not hard to show in a general way that a science of education is theoretically possible, and that such a science must be based on psychology and the cognate sciences. To show this we have, indeed, only to consider that the educator works, or ought to work, upon a growing mind, with a definite purpose of attaining an end in view. For unless we maintain that the growth of mind follows no law; or, to put it otherwise, unless it be maintained that systematic observation of the growth of (say) a hundred minds would disclose no uniformities; and unless, further, it can be maintained that for the attainment of a definite end there are no definite means, we must allow that if the teacher knows what he wants to do there must be a scientific way of doing it. (Ward, 1926, p. 1)

The logic of this argument cannot be faulted, but Ward, and generations of psychologists since, have sought in vain to identify simple 'laws' of learning which would convert education into an applied science firmly rooted in the findings of psychological research. It is not that simple laws cannot be found. Indeed they have been found — at regular intervals. But what confuses and irritates the teacher is that the principles of learning pronounced by the theorists are often seen to be contradictory in their implications for education, and in any case the 'laws' have usually been derived from experiments with types of learning very different from those encountered by pupils or students in the classroom. Thus teachers remain to be convinced, logic or not, that psychology has much of relevance to offer. How might a present-day James Ward mount an argument for using 'psychology and the cognate sciences' to guide the practice of education? The argument might be mounted along the following lines.

> Education takes place in a social context. The organisation of education, and even what is taught, is powerfully influenced by social and political forces. The school or college exists and conducts its educational efforts within that network of external pressures. The interpretation of the effects of those influences is broadly the domain of sociology. Psychology is concerned with establishing principles for guiding our understanding of people's behaviour, their mental processes, and their emotional responses, within the social world of everyday experience. Educational psychology aims at guiding teachers' and students' understanding of behaviour within the specific contexts where learning and teaching take place. The principles of learning established have thus to be derived from a systematic investigation of the methods of presenting ideas and information regularly adopted by teachers, or the strategies used by students in undertaking the academic tasks they have been given. As teachers have a wide variety of contrasting pedagogical aims, educational psychologists must seek to provide a range of guidelines from which to match learning principles and educational objectives for defined groups of students. It is only at this level of practicality and specificity that psychology can realistically claim to inform educational practice. But current research is aiming to provide just such a range of guidelines. Educational psychology is no longer pretending to offer immediate solutions to classroom problems; it is beginning to offer the teacher more precise ways of considering the options available in a particular learning context, and of making systematic and informed choices.

This remains a strong claim for the relevance of educational psychology, probably too strong for the theories of learning and teaching currently available. It does, however, limit the range of evidence considered relevant to that which has demonstrable ecological validity — which derives from a context similar to that of the classroom. This limitation does not exclude the consideration of findings from experimental research or of more general theories of cognitive processes. But implications for education cannot be accepted without contextual reinterpretation of the theories or empirical evidence derived from the everyday activities of learner and teacher.

Areas of Social and Political Concern

In considering what new directions might be identified in educational psychology as applied to learning and teaching, perhaps the first step is to recognize that researchers are themselves influenced by social and political pressures. In the past psychologists have invested substantial effort in the areas of most immediate public concern — for example, the attempts at refining techniques of allocating children to appropriate schools within a tripartite system in post-war Britain. The problems of selection were investigated, but as part of a strong theoretical interest in the nature of individual differences, particularly intelligence.

What are the current issues which may attract psychologists' attention? The current parallel with transfer at 11+ would be accountability, which has recreated a demand for accurate standardized assessment of scholastic achievements. But there is an equally strong pressure against reliance on single scores to describe pupils' attainments. The term 'score' carries with it an impression of precision — like the number of runs from the bat, say, or the tally from three darts. Such scores are generally readily derived from accepted rules, but interpretation of the rules can sometimes lead to disagreement — tempers aroused by a puff of dust on a tennis court, for example. In examinations there are similar rules, and marking schedules or multiple choice questions can provide 'scores' which are widely accepted as fair. But all too often such scores are subsequently used as if they were absolute values. Educational psychologists would probably prefer to use a term such as 'attainment estimate' (with an indication of an associated range of measurement error) where numbers are used to describe the outcome of learning. Yet many psychologists would be opposed even to this approach to assessment: they would argue instead for a profile of scores which expressed the variability of performance across a range of carefully defined skills or topics. There are considerable ideological disputes between the proponents of these different ways of describing academic achievements, and educational psychologists will continue to push forward along rather different paths to improve techniques of assessment.

Accountability can be found in quite different forms, too. Schools are being asked to justify their overall performance in terms of examination results, but also in terms of the preparation of pupils for employment and home life. Relevant to this pressure is the research on 'school effects' which seeks to describe those differences between schools that may affect not just attainment, but also truancy and indiscipline. Parents are another group whose 'effects' are being reconsidered. How much responsibility should parents have for their children's education, and how should it be exercised? The issues of choice of schools or voucher-systems do not usually concern psychologists, but they are interested in helping parents in their crucial role of educators in the home. The early education of children by their parents is thus an area of developing concern for psychologists.

If we look for other growth points, the most obvious issues would bring together the problems of unemployment, increased leisure and community education into the general concern about ways of encouraging lifelong learning among adults no longer within the formal educational system. The psychology of adult learning, particularly in an informal setting, has had little attention in the past — but its importance is beginning to be recognized. Arrangements for 'open learning' and 'distance learning' are being actively discussed and implemented, but systematic research into these areas is lagging behind the development work. There will also be a growing recognition that education must reconsider its attempts to ensure equality of opportunity. It will be necessary to ensure, for example, that the education of women escapes from the snares of sexual stereotyping, and that ethnic minorities are not unthinkingly pressed into inappropriate cultural moulds. Psychology can help teachers to understand the nature of differences in gender, race, or cultural background.

Another concern is the impact of information technology on education. Already microcomputers are being introduced into schools, and psychologists will be expected to contribute to an understanding of the types of learning to be embodied in their programs. Before long, large bodies of information will be directly transferred between central and local computers through telephone or television links. Psychologists will have to consider the organizational principles involved in devising effective presentation and retrieval strategies — and how teachers can adjust their teaching styles to cope with the wider variety of resources available in the schools. At present, computer programs have tended to follow, all too readily, the learning principles embodied in programmed learning, or to be based on the belief that the modes of thinking implicit in computer programming will be easily transferred to other areas of the curriculum. There is an urgent need for psychologists to investigate the types of learning fostered by different forms of computer program.

Most of the issues discussed in this section are addressed, directly or indirectly, in the articles collected in this book (particularly in Section 4). But inevitably some possible trends are not covered, through limitations in space, questions of balance, or lack of currently available articles. In 'reading the tea-leaves' in this way, the impossibility of predicting new areas of concern becomes clear. For example, the issue of accountability arose in the Callaghan administration, and remains to the forefront of current Conservative thinking — but a shift in political power at the next election could bring another set of issues into prominence. Political fashions cause periodic perturbations in the priorities given to particular educational aims and practices, and to some extent psychological research has to follow them.

Theories of Learning and Teaching

Whatever government is in power, however, the central concern of teachers will remain the activities which take place in the classroom. The methods of teaching being used in schools reflect mainly traditional beliefs about how pupils learn and what objectives are most important at different age levels. But these methods have been influenced to some extent by certain prominent psychological theorists and their interpreters (or misinterpreters).

In the 1950s Skinner's ideas on conditioning led to a surge of commercial interest in programmed learning. The specific educational proposals which derived from Skinner's principles of learning have had only modest continuing impact, but newer ideas in the behaviourist tradition are still being tried out — for example, mastery learning and the tutorial modes of computer-assisted learning. The 1960s will perhaps be seen, in retrospect, as the period when Piaget's ideas belatedly came into prominence. His developmental theories, backed up by the skilful arguments of Bruner, had a considerable impact on the work of primary classrooms — mainly through the concepts of 'activity' and 'readiness'. Yet many of the interpretations of Piaget had rather little direct connection with the theories of genetic epistemology, often showing closer links with the ideas of Dewey and Montessori.

In the 1970s two main directions can be traced. The first comes from the work of Ausubel and other cognitive or constructivist psychologists. Their concern was with the way people 'constructed meanings' from the information they received through their senses. They tended to emphasize the importance of structure in presenting information to children, and to use models of memory processes and concept development to justify their suggestions. The second direction is represented by Rogers and psychologists in the humanistic or phenomenological mould. They are concerned with the worth of the whole individual and in using education to ensure freedom for the full development and expression of the personality.

What, then, of the 1980s? Which directions will learning theorists be taking? This set of readings has been selected on the assumption that the most crucial shift in emphasis will be towards various interactionist theories. It is notable that all the other theories derived implications for teachers or for the activities of the learner from evidence and contexts remote from the classroom. The ideas of both behaviourists and cognitive psychologists came from simple experimental studies where the material learnt, and the carefully controlled manipulations of the conditions, made extrapolation to the classroom hazardous in the extreme. The psychologists who argued from an interest in individual differences based their conclusions on elaborate statistical analyses of test scores from large-sample surveys: the individual learner vanished from their view.

Piaget started his work with observations of individual children, but his subsequent ideas were influenced by his training as a biologist and his developing interest in formal logic. The experiments he developed were then guided by his theory, rather than by the types of thinking and learning in which teachers are mainly interested. Finally, Rogers based his ideas on his experiences as a psychotherapist — or learning in the ideal one-to-one situation.

All these theorists have captured an aspect of human learning of continuing importance, but none of them has given an adequate description of learning in the classroom. As psychologists gradually accept the importance of the social context, and recognize that the types of learning carried out in classrooms depend on a complex interaction between pupil, teacher and the contents and requirements of the learning task, so teachers will be provided with ideas which are closer to their own experiences. The research findings will then be more recognizable as descriptions of a common reality, more acceptable, and more applicable to day-to-day work in the classroom.

To develop such theories educational psychologists will have to draw data of varying types from the classrooms themselves. They will have to observe in detail the learning activities of the pupils and systematically interpret them in relation to the teacher's actions and the pupils' perceptions of what they are supposed to be doing. Older pupils, and students, can provide direct information of their own learning strategies, aided by various techniques designed to 'exteriorize' the internal processes they are trying to report.

The future of the psychology of learning and teaching is certainly not likely to involve grand general theories of elegant simplicity. The developing interactionist theories are more likely to be of direct use to the teacher, but they will also be intellectually demanding in their complexity. Children's learning will be seen as depending on the particular learning milieu, the teacher's intentions and ways of teaching, and the pupil's capabilities, motivations and personality — all interacting together to explain different outcomes of learning. The potential utility of the interactionist theories may be easy to justify logically, but we have yet to see whether they can be presented to teachers in ways which make them practically useful.

This view of future trends in learning and teaching is a personal one. It seemed important, therefore, to present an alternative viewpoint. Dennis Child has just completed his term as editor of the *British Journal of Educational Psychology*, and so is in an ideal position to judge future trends from the articles currently being submitted to him for consideration.

References

WARD, J. (1926) *Psychology Applied to Education*, Cambridge, Cambridge University Press.

Educational Psychology: Past, Present, and Future*

Dennis Child
University of Leeds

On being asked to explore new directions in educational psychology, I soon discovered that two modes of travel were available to me. Both were treacherous, highly speculative and littered with my prejudices about education and psychology. One route (on foot) was to take the existing roads, many scarcely half made up, and build on these in the hope of arriving at some future destinations. The other (by air) involved indulging in speculative leaps of fantasy about how the educational world might look in, say, the next century and guessing about the part, if any, which psychology might play in reaching that world. Of course, both of these are largely doomed to failure. History teaches us that fashions come and go in educational psychology, of which only a small residue of ideas becomes incorporated as educational practices.

My approach has been to couple together present indications with future prospects, and also to trace some historical perspectives which I think might be pointers to the future. I have then tried to link these to guesses about future developments which would make demands of an educational system and to which psychology might contribute. What I have to say relates almost entirely to formal educational settings, although I recognize the important part played by the study of educational influences at home, work or play.

You will also quickly detect that within these formal educational settings my major concern is with the quality and quantity of learning, be it intellectual, social, moral or whatever. The central *activity* of a formal educational system in the primary, secondary or tertiary sectors, is the stimulation and advancement of learning especially, but not exclusively, of an intellectual kind. The motives and purposes for which learning is undertaken will vary with place and with time, but each generation of

* This is a slightly edited version of 'Psychology in the Service of Education: A Review', an inaugural lecture delivered at the University of Leeds on 12 December, 1983.

teachers will still be faced with a similar range of fundamental problems of how to expedite and enhance learning in a formal arrangement in such a way as to enable the learner, in time, to be self-sufficient.

This is one of the major concerns of educational psychology. It seeks to discover, by studying the mental, physical, social and emotional behaviour of people, the factors which influence the quality and quantity of learning. Ideally the subject offers to replace trial and error notions and practices with systematic knowledge derived from studies of learners, teachers and the environments in which they operate.

There are, of course, wider issues of concern to other social scientists in education such as the impact of social institutions on individuals or more specific topics such as pupils' family backgrounds, school subcultures, the role of the headteacher and so on. But as far as teachers are concerned these topics become of particular interest when they illuminate the day-to-day problems of learning and teaching.

Historical Perspective

Let me first say a little about the origins and growth of the subject.

Some form of psychology has been taught throughout the period from the introduction of teacher-training colleges in the 1840s. At first, any psychology was embedded in philosophy. Major questions about the mind, consciousness, memory, perception, the senses, etc. were resolved from the security of an armchair. Indeed, in some colleges at first there were no theory papers in education. The examinations were in practical teaching or subjects taken to a more advanced level by the trainees, such as, English, mathematics, Latin, Greek, and so forth. The emphasis on raising the academic level of the students seems obvious when you recall that the minimum age of entry to college was 15 and that a student could qualify at 18 for teaching in the equivalent of our junior schools. Many had not gone much further than the junior school curriculum, particularly those who started as pupil-teachers at the age of 12 and then entered college at 15.

During the period up to 1900, at which time the first textbooks in educational psychology began to appear, the curriculum saw the introduction of methods of teaching elementary and class subjects, 'training' the senses and the memory, and devising extraordinary programmes about the order in which the so-called 'faculties' of children developed. The rest dealt with the occasional famous educator (particularly Locke), registers, the Education Code, physical health and notes on lessons. The interesting thing here is that despite the tremendous growth and success in the application of scientific method in the natural sciences, the study of human behaviour by methods of introspection and anecdotal case study persisted and the 'inner states of mind' continued to be described either in terms of the ancient faculty theory or associationism, or both. School subjects were seen as the medium by which intellectual powers could be enhanced. This became known as 'mental' or 'formal' discipline and enshrined the notion that certain subjects provided training in desired mental activities, or 'faculties', and the effects of these mental exercises were general. Latin was said to improve the memory and verbal accuracy; mathematics developed reasoning ability and concentration; science developed powers of observation. Latin declensions and Euclidean theorems were said to exercise the mind like a muscle. Lower down the system where the 3Rs prevailed, the methods of teaching involved group chanting and drill and exercises for the senses. Rote learning would not only stamp in facts, but would provide valuable exercises for the hypothetical structures to do with learning.

The chief beneficiaries of alternative child-oriented perspectives of such educational thinkers as Pestalozzi, Herbart and Froebel were infant or kindergarten children. For the rest, the *school subject* was the focus of attention.

From the turn of the century to the present time I detect three shifts of emphasis forming a gradual accumulation of concerns in educational psychology. These concerns relate to the roles played in the learning process by, first, the subjects being taught, as I have just suggested, second, the learner, third, the teacher and much more recently the educational context. It is important to emphasize the cumulative nature of these interests. All have been considered over the period mentioned, but with varying degrees of attention.

Before saying a little more about these changes of interest, I want to speculate about the possible reasons for the change of direction at the turn of this century. In the closing decades of the nineteenth century, two immensely important developments took place which completely changed the approach and direction of psychology and consequently its contribution to educational issues. One was Darwin's theory of evolution and the origin of species; the second was the increased significance attached to scientific method especially applied to animal and human behaviour. Pinpointing two developments in this way oversimplifies the complexity of the tides of fashion which washed over the country in the late nineteenth century. But the lasting and wide-ranging effects of these two factors were quite crucial in changing the philosophy of teaching alongside the growing reality of compulsory education for all.

It seems to me that the two major implications of Darwin's work for psychology were the importance which became attached to, firstly, the notion of progression from animal to human and within humans from birth to death, and secondly, the interaction between the animate and the inanimate, that is, between animal and environment, in the process of survival.

The first gave substance to the use of animals in experiments as a source of information about human behaviour. The logic was that if humans were one end product of the progression in the development of the animal kingdom then the study of these less complex, more controllable representatives of the animal kingdom should reveal the basic ingredients of human behaviour — thus *animal psychology*. Also the study of transitions, both physical and mental, from childhood to adulthood became popular, reversing the Victorian notion of children as homunculi. Darwin himself was deeply interested in this subject and kept careful diaries of children's development — thus *child development*.

The second influence arising from the notion of compatibility between inherent characteristics and environmental circumstances gave encouragement to three kinds of development in psychology. The study of inherent characteristics of 'internal factors' gave birth to *instinct and need theories* which became fashionable in educational psychology during the first half of this century. Freudian *psychoanalysis* was also very much influenced by this aspect of Darwin's theory. On the other hand, external or environmental circumstances as sources of systematic study were espoused by the *behaviourists* from the beginning of this century.

The rapid growth of studies, particularly in child development, animal psychology and behaviourism was encouraged by the second influence mentioned before, that is, the application of scientific method to the study of human behaviour. The scientific study of those attributes which enabled humans to survive, particularly intellectual attributes, inevitably led educational psychologists to search for those qualities which might influence the motivation and academic performance of children. Our predecessors in education became confident that in time laws of human behaviour would be established and used for the benefit of human interests such as education. So strong was this belief that professors of education were prepared to speculate in their inaugural lectures. So things haven't changed very much, although I hope I am a bit nearer the target than the following quotation:

> The last twenty years have witnessed a great development which bids fair to revolutionise our whole educational procedure.... It is not impossible that our children's children [*that's us!*] will witness the evolution of a body of human sciences not less systematic and comprehensive than the knowledge of physical science which we now possess....

This was from the inaugural lecture of Professor Bompas Smith, Manchester, 1913. To be fair to him, he also said the following which illustrates one change which came about:

> ... in our work as teachers we must recognise the individual point of view and interests of each boy and girl. All education must be based upon sympathetic insight into the minds of those we teach. We must not treat them simply as units with attributes which for practical purposes are the same. If this principle were always followed we should not find children of four sitting on benches for

five hours a day spending most of their time on lessons in reading, writing and arithmetic. . . .

The functionalist view generated by Darwinism inspired the search for human capacities which correlated with success and gave rise to the mental testing movement. This, coupled with the growth in the study of child development and the first fruits of scientific method applied to human behaviour brought about a remarkable transformation in teacher training around the turn of the century. The focus was now firmly fixed on the child as learner and the impact of psychological findings on education during the first half of this century was substantial. One only need compare the curriculum, materials and practices in classrooms at the turn of the century with those prevailing in, say, 1950 to appreciate that those fifty years were golden years for educational psychology in terms of influence. A few examples should suffice as reminders of the contribution.

The design and application of intelligence and school achievement tests is most often associated with the 11+ exam. But another, equally significant, development was the school psychological service and the use it made of these and other standardized tests in the detection of learning and behaviour *problems*. It was the age of norms when those far above or far below average in academic performance were offered abnormal provision in grammar or special schools. Some account was taken of children's varying levels and rates of performance by streaming and setting and organizing timetables so that shorter periods occurred in order to have distributed rather than massed practice. Research on the senses and perception, particularly during the two world wars, had an effect on the use of visual and auditory materials, including improvements in textbook presentation. The growth of teaching aids during this time was impressive, based on the belief that all the senses should play a part in learning, and so on — there are many more examples.

Although interest in the school subject as the means of training the mind had declined, questions about the appropriateness and presentation of subjects at certain ages, and progression in the level of difficulty of concepts within a subject were still being asked. Graded reading and number books began to appear, based largely on the work of researchers in educational psychology. Alternative forms of assessment and evaluation made their appearance, chiefly in America at this time because of the upsurge in multiple choice techniques and the beginnings of programmed learning.

Thus far, variation in the performance of children was placed squarely on their shoulders. Poor performance was put down to lack of effort or lack of ability on their part. What about the teachers? The fact is that the teacher's role, both in terms of personal qualities *and* details of the task of teaching, was almost ignored up to the 1950s. As editor of the *British Journal of Educational Psychology*, I commissioned a cumulative index from 1930 to 1980. It's a most instructive document on the changing interests in the subject over that period. Entries relating to teachers occurred six times in the first twenty-five years (1930–54) and twenty-seven times in the last twenty-five years (1955–80). These researches include teacher personality, selection, expectations of teaching as a career or of their pupils, their attitude to various aspects of school life and so on. Some of the earliest research looked into the qualities of merit in teachers as seen by pupils. It stretches back to 1896, but it is thinly scattered in the literature. All the findings on this topic to the present come to much the same conclusion — that pupils like teachers to keep order, have a laugh, explain clearly and interestingly, have something to say, be fair and friendly. I'm sure this list won't surprise anyone.

But there are two things to notice about these research topics. The first is that most of them are isolated from *classroom practices*. The commonest research techniques involved questionnaires which were completed in the staffroom or at home. Little was done until about ten or so years ago on the actual instructional techniques and their effects on pupil performance. The second thing to notice is that most of the attributes examined are for the most part unchangeable. Personality, attitudes, expectations, sense of humour or friendliness are fairly stable in an individual. These are the reasons, I suspect, why this line of investigation has had next to no impact on educational practices.

The fourth and most recent shift of emphasis casts the net of interest even wider to include the educational context within which teaching occurs. Hargreaves (1977) concludes that:

> in the last ten years psychologists, social psychologists and sociologists of education have all converged on the classroom as an important area for educational research. . . . [Much of this research] employs a range of well established concepts to analyse classroom life, such as attitude, self-image, role expectation, as well as newer concepts such as self-fulfilling prophecy and hidden curriculum . . . one common theme throughout the literature is what teachers and pupils expect of one another and how they perceive one another.

Other examples of contextual research are those of Bennett (1976) and the ORACLE project at Leicester (1980). In these, one major concern has been the importance of the context generated by the teacher's style. Style in these researches refers largely to the organizational or managerial preferences of teachers in their classrooms which are categorized in various ways such as formal, informal, group instructors, individual monitors, class enquirers, and so on. Correlations between these contexts and pupil performance were also explored — and the conflicting and inconclusive results have been a source of enjoyment for those who like to argue the toss between formal and informal arrangements in classrooms.

There are two things to notice about these contemporary lines of investigation. Firstly, they do occur *in situ* — in the classroom where the learning is actually taking place. It has helped to remind us that the classroom is a unique educational environment with its own particular problems and solutions. Secondly, and unfortunately I believe, these contextual researches have concentrated on the overtly organizational and affective styles of teachers almost to the exclusion of their instructional and cognitive styles. I am thinking here particularly of the characteristic ways in which teachers unfold areas of knowledge for curriculum planning and execution. Along with a number of other recent researches they are anthropological in the methods used. Of necessity they are descriptive and do not purport to be diagnostic or prescriptive.

Whilst I am amongst the first to accept the worthwhile nature of this line of research in providing more parts for the jigsaw portraying classroom life, I am doubtful as to how much these second- and third-order influences account for differences in the performance of children and to what extent they are, in any case, susceptible to modification. Such stable attributes as teachers' personalities, affective style, or their attitudes to authority or misbehaviour are, I believe, pretty well impervious to adaptation. Like Benjamin Bloom, who has popularized the ideas of 'mastery learning', I think that we have to concentrate on those aspects of life in classrooms which can be manipulated to the benefit of pupils.

The Present Position

Whatever the reasons, it is clear to me that the contribution of educational psychology research over the last twenty years has been less significant than in the first half of the century. It is interesting to note that those contributions which have made an impact in the last twenty years relate once again to the task of teaching, and to analyzing subjects and the developing child. Of late this has become an interactive model, particularly in junior school curricula. For example, the norm-referenced aspects of Piaget's work on children's cognitive development and Gagné's hierarchical theory on the organization of subject content and presentation have been extensively plundered and applied by subject specialists to give a highly productive and well-oiled industry in curriculum design. Schools Council schemes, Nuffield Science and Maths, Science 5–13, language, literacy and communications programmes, social and vocational schemes, to mention a few, have sprung into being.

So far in the development of educational psychology the prevalent models have been static ones. Norm-referenced tests of attainment, intelligence, development, etc. have provided snapshot evidence, one frame in the reel of life if you like, which tells us by how much a child might differ from children of his or her own age, without telling us how the difference comes about. For example, two children with arithmetic ages say two years less than their chronological ages as determined by an arithmetic achievement test, or two adolescents with the same low mark in an O-level, may have very different problems. These problems cannot be determined without a more sophisticated analysis of the specific skills called for by the tests. We have still a long way to go in designing exploratory devices from which diagnoses and corresponding programmes can be formulated. We have theories *describing* intellectual development, but not theories for *assisting* intellectual development. Measures from static models identify problems in retrospect. They give few directions for the solution of those problems.

This is a current dilemma for the professional educational psychologists in their work on children's learning difficulties and in giving advice on how to cope. The recent Education Act of 1981 on special educational needs highlights the increasing importance placed on the LEA educational psychologists' role in identification *and* advice about provision. Circular 1/83, which is an advisory document on how the Act might be implemented, makes it very clear that in addition to analyzing a child's learning difficulties, there must also be a diagnosis of the special needs for different kinds of approaches, facilities and resources. The burden of responsibility for these provisions has also been placed on teachers in the normal state system. I quote: 'The teacher . . . is in a key position to observe [a pupil's] response in the classroom, to recognise the child who is experiencing difficulties in learning, and to try out different approaches to help meet the child's needs.' As I have tried to indicate, I am not convinced that we have the wherewithall to fulfil this latter demand.

This much more dynamic model, placing the teacher in the role of manager of change by progressively adjusting instructional methods to suit each child is, I submit, one obvious growth point in the future and I shall return to it later. It's not a new idea. The second quotation from Bompas Smith hinted at it and Plowden, for another, has said it. But it is not in general a reality in schools. One of the most consistent criticisms contained in the recent HMI reports of primary and secondary education was that brighter children are not stretched enough. Similarly, less able children need more specifically tailored content and method to suit their needs. The reasons are that teachers have neither the time nor the opportunity to give the individual attention needed.

Professional educational psychologists are heading in the same direction. The following quotation captures the essence of their views:

> In terms of professional practice the shift in emphasis is quite distinct: the psychologist's appraisal of a child and his difficulties is now much more in terms of the means of achieving change, rather than burrowing into the past or into the psyche in pursuit of causes and explanations. . . . The heart of educational psychology must be the theory and technology of change and this takes the psychologist a long way from being a mere clinician. (Gillham, 1978)

The Future

The time has come for me to step out on to the plank and make some speculations about the future contribution of psychology to education. Earlier I said that we had theories *describing* learning and intellectual development, but few theories for *assisting* learning and intellectual development. The reason is that the former are descriptive and therefore much easier to live with than the latter which are prescriptive. It requires confidence and conviction that we have something positive to say about learning and teaching which will improve levels of performance, and this *is* the direction in which we shall head. Teaching will become more diagnostic. Learning will become more clearly directed towards greater self-sufficiency in the learner. The history of the learner, such as home influences, early schooling, life experiences, will be examined more closely for its contribution to later learning. Syllabuses and subjects will be dismantled and scrutinized for improved methods and sequences of presentation. More stress will be placed on those aspects of learning and teaching which are alterable and not static. If you agree with even some of these observations, then the next step is inevitable. *We will have to develop theories or models of instruction* and I want to concentrate now on some aspects of these models.

Some people get 'up tight' about the term 'instruction' because it seems to convey a mechanical, dehumanizing, 'do this or else', approach to learning and teaching. That would be a gross distortion of the way it is used by educational psychologists. I believe there are six major features which any theory of instruction must specify and all of them are sensitive to individual differences. I want to give a brief elaboration of these in order to summarize what I see as the main lines of development into the next century. The six specifications are:

1   the cognitive predisposition of the learner — that is, the knowledge, skills and abilities which a learner brings to a task and which would influence performance;
2   the affective predisposition of the learner — that is, the interests, attitudes and self-concept brought to a task;
3   how a body of knowledge needs to be structured in order for efficient and effective learning by individuals to take place;
4   the sequencing and best methods of presenting that body of knowledge;
5   the reinforcement mechanisms necessary to ensure continued interest such as rewards, incentives, feedback; and
6   evaluation of pupil performance and the system used.

To help in summarizing the advances which might be generated from these specifications, I have adapted a diagram from Bloom (1976) (see Figure 1).

Figure 1   Bloom's model of instruction

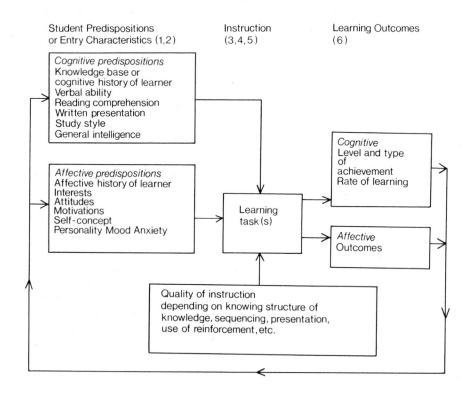

Student Predispositions or Entry Characteristics (1,2)   Instruction (3,4,5)   Learning Outcomes (6)

Cognitive predispositions
Knowledge base or cognitive history of learner
Verbal ability
Reading comprehension
Written presentation
Study style
General intelligence

Affective predispositions
Affective history of learner
Interests
Attitudes
Motivations
Self-concept
Personality Mood Anxiety

Learning task(s)

Cognitive
Level and type of achievement
Rate of learning

Affective
Outcomes

Quality of instruction depending on knowing structure of knowledge, sequencing, presentation, use of reinforcement, etc.

Source: Based on Bloom, B.S. (1976) *Human Characteristics and School Learning*, McGraw-Hill.

Entry Predispositions

The first two characteristics represent what are called 'student entry characteristics' or 'predispositions'. In plain language they are about the history of the learner prior to the task in hand which will be of relevance to that task. Three, four and five, about structuring of knowledge, sequencing of presentation and reinforcement mechanisms, are incorporated into the central part of the diagram under 'instruction'. Learning outcomes are about the effects of learning and must involve evaluation of some kind. Note also that the outcomes become part of the history of the learner and that is why the model is cyclical.

Incidentally, Bloom also suggests that we should concentrate on those aspects which are *alterable*. Entry variables such as general intelligence and personality, whilst they give useful background knowledge, are fairly stable and we should concentrate on the other predispositions which can be modified for the benefit of the learner. The numerical, verbal, reading, writing, communication skills of the young are inescapably and profoundly affected by child-rearing practices. We have a lot to learn about early home and school influences and of discovering ways of improving these skills by capitalizing on this critical early period. Studies in paediatrics and the physiology of early child development will make significant contributions to educational psychology.

We have only a hazy idea of how a child assimilates and organizes knowledge and how this process in turn will affect decision-making and problem-solving. How do previous experiences, and the generalizations formulated from them, impinge upon new experience? Research on this question is being conducted, for example, by Rosalind Driver (1983). She is looking at the ways in which children develop specific ideas and concepts in science and how these compete with the accepted generalizations in science. Whether we like it or not, it seems that children formulate their own laws of nature from their experiences and these may be in competition with those presented by the science teacher. This illustrates very clearly the importance of studying the entry characteristics of pupils from their learning history and of finding ways of unravelling false notions and replacing them with methods for finding more acceptable notions. In current teaching, I wonder how many teachers are confident that they know, prior to the learning tasks they set, exactly what content and skills will be required for maximum understanding and performance of the learners? My belief is there is a tremendous job to be done in this respect.

I have also listed 'study style' on Figure 1. By this I mean the characteristic and unique ways in which an individual tries to cope with the learning process. We each of us have favoured tactics and strategies which we bring to study. How efficient are they? Could they be improved? Is the teaching compatible with our favoured strategies? And so on. Most of the research in this field has been concerned with secondary and higher education (Marton in Sweden, Biggs in Australia, Entwistle in the UK). Most of this work gives useful descriptive glimpses of student methods or characteristics. Biggs, for example, gives several amusing thumb-nail sketches of methods of study: e.g. the 'minimax' method in which the student learns only the bare essentials for a pass, hoping to obtain the maximum mark for a minimum output. There is also the 'opportunist' type who carefully studies the prejudices of a teacher and feeds these back in essays. Unfortunately, the study methods of students in higher education are probably so well ossified that there is little chance of encouraging modifications for improved performance. Yet at the important end of the system, in junior schools, we almost completely ignore training in study methods. We wrongly assume that effective methods of study are automatically picked up as children progress through the system. We need detailed researches of how study skills grow and how to teach them to the individual's best advantage.

The central importance of interest and motivation to pupil or student performance is self-evident. Yet we have a long way to go in trying to comprehend and do something about the credibility gap which exists between pupils, teachers, parents and society as to the place of a formal system of education in the life-chances of an individual. Selling the system gets harder as one reaches the final two years of secondary school life, especially to those with little hope of obtaining O-levels or good CSEs. There will have to be a considerable shift in syllabus content and design as changing patterns of work and leisure, individuals' expectations and technological advances bite deeper and deeper into our present way of life. Unfortunately, society inadvertently generates in the young expectations which the educational system can rarely fulfil. Whilst I think there will be progress in the ways I've described, there has also to be an air of reality about what can be achieved with pupils in the first years of life.

Instruction

The central portion of Figure 1, Instruction, places great demands on the teacher as a manager of learning. The aspiration of teachers should be to lead learners to a point where they, the pupils, can help themselves. This is becoming increasingly more important as our knowledge base rapidly increases. Information retrieval and self-help are growing in significance. The cheap miniaturization of equipment suitable in educational settings will have a marked effect on educational provision in both the curriculum and teaching arrangements *in some subjects*. The design of software requires a deep knowledge of the structure of a subject and teachers will need to know more about how to unwrap their areas of knowledge for presentation in a variety of ways. The ready availability and cheapness of home computers for which educational software is now available means that parents are becoming more conscious of the role of such machines in education.

The simulation of human thinking and action in the form of artificially intelligent systems may have something to offer to teachers. Our inventions are often extensions of ourselves. Telescopes and microscopes are extensions of our eyes, amplifiers our ears, tools and vehicles our limbs. Robotics combines some of these senses and is taking the routine out of some manufacturing industries. Apart from the obvious impact this will have on our work and leisure activities in the future, the study of artificial intelligence must in time have some messages for the analysis and presentation of subject matter, and provide additional knowledge about the human being as a learner.

In the next century, self-sufficiency will be the order of the day. This is becoming increasingly apparent in a society where knowledge in discovering 'know-how' is at a premium. There will be a growing and successful pressure for individualization in learning. The research scenario will be one of facilitating those aspects which have to do with the uniqueness of learning for each person. Of course, the convention of classroom teaching of large groups will be here for a long time to come, but skills in adapting an ever-increasing range of facilities and opportunities for personalized learning will need to be developed.

Against the trend of thinking in educational psychology at present, I happen to believe that the influence of Applied Behavioural Analysis (the new term for behaviour modification) will become substantial. The principles involved in designing software had their origins in behaviourism. But a second line of development is in the treatment of disruptive children in normal classrooms, and I feel confident that any useful advice on this subject would be gratefully received by the teaching profession. I am told by cognitive psychologists that their chief interest is in *how* people process *internally* in acquiring, modifying, manipulating, using or storing knowledge. They focus on the inner person for information processing and this is a very important development in recent years. Behaviourists tell me that as behaviour is primarily learned and based on an individual's reactions with his or her environment (including teachers), the important thing is to know how to control that environment to get the desired effects. Their concern is with the *external* influences on humans. As an eclectic in psychology I find both these propositions and their implications useful in the classroom. The teaching profession would be ill-advised to ignore helpful findings from either of these sources.

To enhance the quality of instruction we shall need to influence the teacher in training. The catch-phrases and methods seeping into the system at present seem to be pointing in the directions I've outlined. A few examples are (1) flexi-programmes and adaptive tutoring which are designed to be adjusted to the needs of particular children by using either reproduced materials, video or microprocessor; (2) courses for students on instructional craft knowledge; (3) the use of simulation exercises using close circuit or recorded TV programmes; (4) the more extensive use of recorded teaching episodes — sometimes called micro-teaching; (5) courses in diagnostic techniques and social skills. In some public sector training institutions which I have visited for the CNAA, some of these innovations are beginning to replace some parts of the conventional psychology and sociology of education syllabuses.

Learning Outcomes

In a sense, learning outcomes need to be considered alongside entry predispositions, because one needs to know the destination before being able to choose an appropriate route.

Evaluation is an essential part of the process of learning. The development of skills and tools which enable teachers to make accurate diagnoses and treatment of individual children's problems is crucial and is badly in need of research.

Two particularly interesting growth points are error analysis and the effects of high and low achievement on future performance — called attribution theory. In a nutshell, to what do we attribute our success or failure in a given task? If we believe that failure was within our control we are more likely to react adversely than if it was beyond our control. If it happens often enough, motivation and self-image of academic achievement decline and performance suffers.

Of more interest to me is error analysis. It has become an important contribution from the researches of the APU (Assessment of Performance Unit) in mathematics, science and English. Trends in the nature and direction of children's incorrect responses to problems is beginning to reveal information which could have much to tell us about the appropriateness of materials, methods of presentation of content, the design of questions, the 'virtuous' errors which children make, and so on.

Each learner has unique characteristics and learning problems. One of the teacher's main tasks is to identify those characteristics and problems (diagnosis) and create appropriate learning conditions (treatments) which will enable that individual to reach required levels of competence.

Clearly, there is ample credible work still to be done by educational psychologists. The more practical and relevant this work can be, the better. All disciplines need a theoretical base and research of this kind is important. But the time is overdue for us to convert more of this theory into practical outcomes. Educational psychology, like most academic disciplines, has always had three main functions. Two we are very familiar with, that is the creation and transmission of knowledge. But the third tends to be under-valued, that is the *application* of knowledge. Medicine, Dentistry and Engineering, for example, have long had this tradition. Educational psychology needs to recognize the importance of this third function — applying psychology in the service of education.

References

BELL, S. (1900) 'A study of the teacher's influence', *Ped. Semin.*, 7, p. 493.

BENNETT S.N. (1976) *Teaching Styles and Pupil Progress*, London, Open Books.

BIGGS, J.B. (1978) 'Individual and group differences in study processes', *Brit. J. Educ. Psychol.*, 48, pp. 266–79.

BLOOM, B.S. (1976) *Human Characteristics and School Learning*, New York, McGraw-Hill.

BOMPAS SMITH, H. (1913) *Education as the Training of Personality*, inaugural lecture delivered at Manchester University.

BOOK, W.F. (1905) 'The high school teacher from the pupils' point of view', *Ped. Semin.*, 12, p. 488.

BRITISH JOURNAL OF EDUCATIONAL PSYCHOLOGY (1982) Cumulative Index 1930–80.

DRIVER, R. (1983) *The Pupil as Scientist?* Milton Keynes, Open University.

EDUCATION ACT (1981) An Act to Make Provision with Respect to Children with Special Educational Needs, London, HMSO.

EDUCATION CIRCULAR 1/83 (1983) Assessments and Statements of Special Educational Needs, London, HMSO.

ENTWISTLE, N. and RAMSDEN, P. (1983) *Understanding Student Learning*, London, Croom Helm.

GILLHAM, W. (1978) *Reconstructing Educational Psychology*, London, Croom Helm.

HARGREAVES, D.G. (1977) 'The process of typification in classroom interaction: Models and methods', *Br. J. Educ. Psychol.*, 47, pp. 274–84.

HARTLEY, J.R. (1980) 'Computer Assisted Learning', in SMITH, H.T. and GREEN, T.R.G. (Eds), *Human Interaction with Computers*, London, Academic Press.

HARTLEY, J.R. (1981) 'An appraisal of computer assisted learning in the United Kingdom', in RUSHBY, N. (Ed.), *Selected Readings in Computer Based Learning*, London, Kogan Page.

KRATZ, H.E. (1896) 'Characteristics of the best teacher as recognised by children', *Ped. Semin.*, 3, p. 413.

MARTON, F. and SÄLJÖ, R. (1976) 'Qualitative differences in learning. I: Outcome and process; II: Outcome as a function of the learning', *Brit. J. Educ. Psychol.*, 46, pp. 4–11, 115–22.

ORACLE research at Leicester University. GALTON, M. *et al.* (1980) *Inside the Primary School*; GALTON, M. and SIMON, B. (Eds) (1980) *Progress and Performance in the Primary School*, London, Routledge and Kegan Paul.

TOUGH, J. (1976) *The Development of Meaning: A Study of Children's Use of Language*, London, Allen and Unwin.

TOUGH, J. (1976) *Listening to Children Talking*, Schools Council Communication Skills in Early Childhood project, London, Ward Lock.

TOUGH, J. (1977) *Language and Learning in Early Childhood*, London, Heinemann.

2
Learning Processes and Individual Differences

Introduction

New trends in thinking about learning and teaching have often had their roots in earlier theories, as we have seen in the previous section. The development of educational psychology has seen the enthusiastic adoption of new ideas about learning, followed by an equally strong rejection. It seems as if teachers have been looking to research for a panacea, and as if psychologists have been all too ready to supply their own idiosyncratic 'cure-all'. The ideas are often presented by the theorists with a great deal of rhetoric, which 'converts' some educationalists but also antagonizes others. Teachers are thus presented with a confusing variety of what seem to be contradictory implications for education.

It is easier to accept this welter of contrasting views if it is recognized that each psychological theory is partial and essentially metaphorical. The theorist is presenting a model, saying implicitly that it is *as if* learning is like this or that. But what is really being said is that either some aspect of learning, or learning under certain conditions, has these metaphorical connections. The metaphor helps us to see parallels, to understand abstract ideas in terms of more concrete experience, but it can never cover the whole range and variety of learning experiences. If we abandon the search for a panacea, and the parallel search for theories of general validity, what are we left with? We have to conclude that each theory will fit with some educational philosophies more closely than others; that each theory will have more useful applications to a particular age-range, subject area, or teaching style. Then we will be able to accept the variety of theories of learning as a menu from which to select, rather than as a multiple choice question where the 'right' answer has to be found. Inevitably this leads us towards interactive theories, but with an even broader implication. Not only do we need to consider ways of matching teaching styles to the differing preferences and skills of the pupils, but we shall also be selecting theories of learning which provide ways of converting our educational aims into effective pedagogical practice.

This section thus presents a variety of theories about learning, but mainly at this stage well-established theories. As happens in psychology these theories have passed the stage of enthusiastic endorsement. The limitations have now become clearer, and there is a danger of rejecting the theories outright because of those limitations. However, if we accept all theories of learning as having a limited range of applicability, then it is easier to recognize the aspects of the established theories which remain useful and at least partially valid. The starting point is individual differences — with Hans Eysenck arguing the case for the inheritance of both intelligence and personality. He also presents evidence which indicates that discovery methods are preferred by extraverts, while computer-assisted methods are more effective with introverts. The implications suggest the need for matching the characteristics of pupils with appropriate teaching techniques — a theme which is taken up by Peter Tomlinson later on.

The educational implications of this emphasis on the inheritance of intelligence are not explored by Eysenck, but teachers have worried about the possible effects on subsequent school attainment of accepting the inevitability of a relatively fixed intellectual capacity. John Nisbet sees an important change in thinking about the nature of ability — a change from singular to plural and from consistency to variability. Instead of concentrating attention on a global trait — intelligence — educational psychologists are more interested now in the range of specific abilities which underlie intelligence. They are also alert to the educational implications of the fact that abilities develop — can be changed by educational experiences, no matter what proportion of intelligence is considered to be inherited. The fact of change is an encouragement to teachers to find ways to develop both ability and educational achievements.

The ideas of Piaget come in for critical scrutiny in the following two articles. Herbert Ginsburg reminds us that Piaget had very little to say about specific practical implications of his theory for education. Ginsburg re-examines that theory, and cautiously reappraises the claims that have been made in its name. Margaret Donaldson is more forthright. She attacks the conclusions Piaget drew from some of his best-known experiments, by showing how changes in the procedures can produce importantly different results. Her argument is that Piaget's empirical findings have led teachers seriously to underestimate the power of children's thinking, when that thinking is done in terms of situations and language which is already familiar to them.

The extracts from David Ausubel's well-known textbook are used to illustrate a constructivist theory as applied to education. As Ausubel's own writing is used, the ideas are presented persuasively without contrary argument. But there has been recent criticism of his theory, particularly about the utility, or otherwise, of 'advance organizers' in providing a structure in anticipation of new information. The specific ways in which knowledge is reconstructed in the memory are also in dispute. For the teacher, however, the theoretical arguments are less important than the main message presented by Ausubel — that above all we should discover first what a pupil already knows, and then decide what programme of instruction is likely to encourage reconstruction of knowledge — and so the development of understanding. The message is deceptively simple: but Ausubel's assimilation theory is altogether more complex and has much of value for the secondary teacher whether or not the detail of the theory proves to be accurate.

To follow the historical development of theories of learning outlined earlier, the ideas of Carl Rogers should have been introduced at this point. But as his experiential or humanistic research is within a very different tradition, it seemed more sensible to present it as the starting point of the following section on 'The Experience of Learning'.

The final two articles present a first look at interactionist theories in which both the characteristics of the learner and the educational context are given equal prominence. Samuel Messick reviews applications of current cognitive psychology within education before mounting an argument for the importance of recognizing, and coping with, the existence of preferred ways of learning (cognitive styles). He urges the necessity of matching learning with teaching methods in ways which encourage flexibility in thinking, but sees self-matching as being the only practicable approach. Peter Tomlinson is also concerned with the problems of 'match' and describes two approaches to those problems — aptitude-treatment interactions and conceptual systems theory. He also presents some recent British research which indicates that interactionist ideas are beginning to influence educational psychology on both sides of the Atlantic.

The articles by Ausubel and Messick are both difficult, as they introduce many technical terms and use abstract and formal language. They do, however, provide a good introduction to the type of cognitive psychology applied to education in the United States.

Heredity and Environment:
The State of the Debate*

H.J. Eysenck
Institute of Psychiatry, University of London

It would probably be true to say that many people are rather tired of the 'debate' about the relative influence of heredity and environment on intelligence and educational abilities, and on personality. A recent book by Eysenck and Kamin (1981) sets out the positions of those who, like the writer, believe that the phenotype (that is, the actually observed behaviour) is determined both by biological and social factors, the relative importance of which can be studied along several divergent lines, all of which give rather similar results, and those who like Kamin believe that environment is all, and that there is no acceptable evidence for any contribution by hereditary factors. The book is written at a popular level and, as far as the evidence for genetic factors is concerned and the possibility of assessing the relative contributions of biological and social factors, the writer's recent book on *The Structure and Measurement of Intelligence* (Eysenck, 1979) should be consulted, with Fulker's (1981) article on the genetic architecture of personality taking up the same theme in relation to non-cognitive aspects of behaviour.

Recent work, both in the United States and by the Birmingham School in this country, has concentrated not so much on heritabilities as on the unravelling of the genetic architecture of the phenotype, whether this be IQ test scores, personality test scores, or whatever. Such analyses involve a distinction between additive genetic variance and such factors as dominance versus recessivity, assortative mating, epistasis, etc., on the genetic side, the distinction between within-family and between-family environmental factors on the environmental side, and the recognition of two different types of interaction between the genetic and the environmental determinants of behaviour. These various factors can be estimated or measured by using a variety of different techniques, explained in some detail in Eysenck (1979) and Fulker (1981), but too technical to be discussed in detail here. Each

* This is a shortened version of the article which appeared in *Educational Analyis*, 4, 2, 1982, pp. 7–16.

method, of course, has its weaknesses, and can be criticized; what is important to note, however, is that these different methods give very similar results, which are mutually reinforcing in a very impressive manner. Examples of such agreement will be given later; the existence of such agreements encourages the research worker to believe that the estimates of heritability, and so forth, which he may arrive at, although of course subject to a margin of error still uncomfortably large, are probably not too far from a reasonably accurate assessment of the situation.

When we look at the evidence, we find that the results for intelligence and personality are similar in some ways, but very different in others. For both we find a high degree of additive genetic variance, amounting to something like two-thirds of the total variance, and even higher when allowance is made for the errors of measurement usually involved in this type of work. Thus heredity plays an impressively large part in the causation of individual differences in both cognitive and non-cognitive types of behaviour. However, in the case of intelligence, dominance and assortative mating play a very important part. Assortative mating, that is, the marriage of like with like, is very marked as far as intelligence is concerned, but is almost completely absent as far as personality is concerned; for such variables as extraversion-introversion, neuroticism, or psychoticism, cor-relations over husbands and wives seldom depart much from zero and hardly ever exceed 0.2. This may be contrasted with intelligence, where correlations of above 0.5 are quite common. Similarly, there is little evidence of *dominance* in the personality field, whereas, for intelligence, directional dominance is very pronounced and almost total. These are important differences.

On the environmental side, two-thirds of the variance is contributed by between-family environmental differences, that is, differences in socio-economic status, schooling, upbringing, etc., which distinguish one family from another; only one-third of the variance is contributed by within-family environmental factors, that is, those which differentially affect children brought up within the same family. The position is quite different with respect to personality, where within-family factors are all-important, and there is little if any evidence of between-family environmental influences (Loehlin and Nichols, 1976; Eaves and Eysenck, 1975, 1977). Thus we find important differences, as well as similarities, in the biometrical genetical analysis of cognitive and noncognitive behaviour.

The Evidence for the Inheritance of Intelligence

Modern investigations of biometrical genetical analysis essentially use the methods of analysis of variance, and proceed by postulating certain models and then testing the adequacy of the model against empirical data, whether derived from twin studies, from adoption studies, from intra- and inter-family correlational studies, from regression analysis, from inbreeding depression, from heterosis (hybrid vigour), or whatever. It is data of this kind which furnish the analyst with the necessary material for his analyses. It is important to recognize the essential restrictions this puts on the interpretation of the results achieved; heritability estimates, for instance, are population statistics, and cannot be applied to individuals. Thus to state that 80 per cent of the total variance of differences in intelligence in a given population are due to genetic causes cannot be taken to read that for a particular person 80 per cent of his IQ is so determined; the figure applies to the population as a whole, and might of course be higher or lower in a different population, at a different time. Similarly, the existence of such a high heritability does not preclude the possibility of environmental factors, not present in the given population, having powerful effects on the phenotype in some other population.

Let us now consider two examples of the use of empirical material for elucidating statistical properties relevant to genetic analyses of certain approaches, and let us also look at the relevance of criticisms made of these approaches. The first source of data to be surveyed is the study of twins. We can look at MZ (identical) twins brought up in isolation, or we can look at the differences between MZ and DZ (fraternal) twins. In the case of MZ twins brought up in isolation, we can attribute any observed differences to the environment. In the case of the comparison between MZ and DZ twins, we can attribute any differences in similarity between the groups to genetic factors, because this is the only way in which they differ systematically. This is the general paradigm which has given rise to a great deal of work; what about the objections and criticisms?

An obvious criticism of the design using MZ twins brought up in isolation is that the twins are not allocated at random to different families, but that usually the socio-economic status of the two families will be rather similar, and that, often, the twins are not separated at birth but after several years of living together. These criticisms would seem quite meaningful until it is realized that the empirical evidence does not support either. As far as separation is concerned, studies of twins separated at various stages of their careers have shown that, if anything, the separated twins are more alike when separated early rather than later; this indicates the inapplicability of this particular criticism. When it comes to separated twins being brought up in families rather similar in socio-economic status, etc., the evidence indicates that this criticism is applicable, but we can estimate the importance of this factor by looking at children (such as cousins) also brought up in rather similar types of families, but less closely related as far as heredity is concerned. Such comparisons indicate that MZ twins are very much more similar than cousins or other groups brought up in families of similar socio-economic status and, consequently, we can correct the observed figures from MZ twins brought up in separation to take into account this particular criticism.

Let us now turn to a comparison between MZ and DZ twins. Here the criticism is usually made that MZ twins are treated more alike than are DZ twins by their parents, and that this may cause the greater similarity between them with respect to IQ. There are two powerful arguments against this. In the first place, Loehlin and Nichols (1976) have looked carefully at the degree of similarity of upbringing involved, and have found that the degree of similarity of IQ is completely unrelated to the degree of similarity of upbringing. In the second place, it has been possible to look at families where the parents erroneously believed their twins to be MZ or DZ, when in actual fact they were the opposite; it was found that this made no difference to similarities in IQ. We may thus consider these criticisms to be misapplied also.

Next we may consider one further point, which indicates the degree to which criticism of the genetic position is often very much *ad hoc* and contradictory. Criticism of the MZ-DZ comparison fastens on very minute environmental manipulations, such as dressing the MZ twins alike, and declares these to be so important in the genesis of IQ differences that they are made responsible for the tremendous differences between MZ and DZ twins. Yet in criticizing the MZ isolation studies, the same critics disregard the much more important differences brought about by bringing up these two children in entirely different homes, and explain the observed similarities in terms of socio-economic status similarities between the two homes. This illustrates one of the major weaknesses of the environmentalist approach, namely a refusal to state testable hypotheses and apply these uniformly to all the available data. No such hypotheses are available, and those which have been put forward to account for individual results are mutually contradictory.

Let us now turn to another phenomenon often used in the analysis of genetic data; namely, genetic regression. As Galton has already shown, of physical or mental traits which are inherited less than 100 per cent showed regression to the mean, in the sense that children of parents above or below the mean on a given trait are also above or below the mean, but less so than their parents; they have regressed to the mean. The writer has suggested that this is a powerful indication of genetic determination of individual differences in IQ (Eysenck, 1973), but critics have replied that it is merely a consequence of the imperfect correlation between parents and children. How can we resolve this contradiction?

It is true that, given the correlation between parents and children of roughly 0·5 and given that parents and children have roughly the same mean and standard deviation of IQ, then regression to the mean follows, and has all the statistical properties observed. But, of course, correlations require causal analysis; what is it that produces the correlation between two events in the first place, and to what extent is the observed correlation expected on the grounds of a given theory? Let us first look at the environmental theory. What is required to be explained is that the children of very high IQ parents have themselves IQs which are *lower* than that shown by the parents, by quite a sizeable margin, whereas the IQs of children who have a very low IQ, have IQs *higher* than their parents, also by a substantial margin. This surely is not what would be expected on the grounds of a theory which attributes overwhelming importance to environmental factors — such as socio-economic status, number of books in the home, pressure for education, etc. — all of which would be found more readily in the homes of the children of high IQ parents, and would be missing in the homes of low IQ parents. What the environmentalist hypothesis would lead us to expect would be that the children of very high IQ parents should have, if anything, higher IQs than their parents (many of whom grew up in homes of lower socio-economic status than they themselves are able to furnish for their children), whereas the children of very low IQ parents, being deprived with respect to all these environmental advantages to an extent even greater than was true of their parents (many of whom dropped in the social scale as a consequence of their low IQ), would therefore have, if anything, lower IQs than their parents.

Thus, we would expect, not two generations of equal IQs and identical variance, but rather two populations of equal IQs but increasing variance. This is not what is in fact observed, and thus requires an explanation which is not forthcoming in environmental terms. Furthermore, the observed correlation should be much higher if the environmentalist hypothesis were correct; why it is so low requires explanation. Thus the environmentalist would have great difficulties in explaining the observed facts in terms of an environmentalist model.

The geneticist has no such difficulties, because genetic theory predicts not only the occurrence of regression, but also its extent, given the degree of heritability. Not only do we find that the genetic explanation predicts the empirical results observed, but also gives a close quantitative prediction, whereas environmental hypotheses are non-existent, and would, if anything, give totally different predictions. Thus we can see that the objections made to regression analysis of genetic data are quite untenable, and cannot be taken seriously.

Individual Differences and Education

It would seem to be a necessary (and testable) consequence of the genetic hypothesis that the phenotypic behaviours observed under the heading of cognitive abilities and personality traits should be firmly anchored in anatomical, physiological and biochemical reality. Evidence on the personality side favouring this view has been provided by Eysenck (1967, 1981a), and recent work on the relationship between the averaged evoked potential on the EEG and IQ has strongly supported this view on the cognitive side (Eysenck, 1981b). Using a group of over 200 school children representing a reasonably normal sample as far as Wechsler IQs are concerned, Hendrick-

son used the evoked potential measure specially developed in our laboratories and based on certain theoretical formulations (Hendrickson and
Hendrickson, 1980) to show a correlation between the two measures of
(0·84.) This is as high or higher than the correlations between orthodox IQ
tests, and further evidence has been furnished on adult samples using other
IQ tests such as the Matrices. In view of the very high heritability and
replicability of EEG measures of this type and the very high correlation with
IQ measures, it can hardly be doubted that findings such as these add
strongly to an interpretation of IQ differences as being largely mediated by
genetic factors.

There is no doubt that individual differences must play a very prominent
part in deciding on the type of education that is suitable for a given child.
This is almost axiomatic with respect to intelligence; it has been less debated
in relation to personality, but the evidence there is equally clear. As the
writer has shown elsewhere (Eysenck, 1978), in a detailed review of the
literature concerning the interrelationships of education and personality,

*Figure 1. Regressions of Residual Arithmetic Achievement on Introversion-Extraversion for
Different Ratios of Reward to Punishment.*

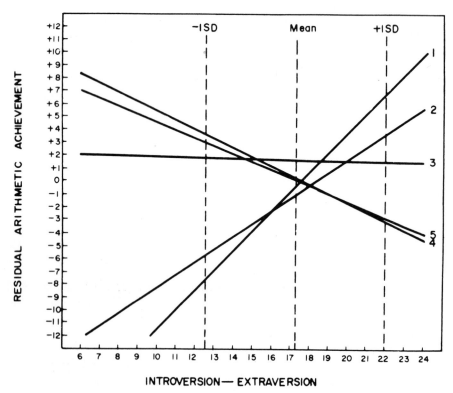

Note: The lines, representing classrooms, are numbered 1 to 5, indicating, from highest to
lowest, their placement in the rank-order of reward-punishment ratios.

there is little evidence of the superiority of one type of educational methodology (for example, the discovery method, or computer-assisted education) as opposed to any other, but there is good evidence for the importance of interaction factors. Thus discovery methods are liked by, and aid achievement of, extraverts as opposed to introverts, and computer-assisted methods are liked by, and aid achievement of, introverts as compared with extraverts. When it is realized that these temperamental variables have a strong genetic component, it becomes all the more important to acquaint teachers with the facts, and to make it possible for them to incorporate in their teaching methods the knowledge thus acquired.

To take but one example, Gray (1973), on the basis of neurological and psychological studies, has demonstrated that introverts respond better to pain, extraverts better to positive rewards, and McCord and Wakefield have shown that in the classroom introverts respond with greater achievement to blame, extraverts to praise (McCord and Wakefield, 1981). Figure 1 shows the cross-over effect for extraversion-introversion and achievement for different amounts of reward and punishment, and Figure 2 shows how to use scores on extraversion, psychoticism and neuroticism, to determine the appropriate use of reward or punishment. Obviously much more research is required to determine the degree to which results of this type can be extended to other types of pupils, to other countries, and to other subject

Figure 2.   Use of E, P and N to Determine Appropriate Use of Reward or Punishment

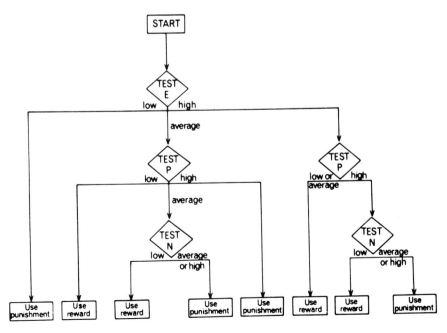

matters, but the large literature surveyed by Eysenck (1978) makes it clear that the main effects of different teaching methods are seldom significant, whereas interaction effects are very large and can be predicted in terms of personality theory. Thus the findings concerning the strong genetic component in both cognitive and non-cognitive aspects of phenotypic behaviour have clearly important consequences in the classroom and it is important that teachers should be aware of them, and should be acquainted with the best ways of using this information. Wakefield (1979) has shown how the scientific findings distributed over many academic journals can be simplified and codified to apply to individual teaching situations, and it seems that any improvement in our teaching methods will have to take account of facts such as these, and apply methods based on the available scientific evidence.

References

EAVES, L. and EYSENCK, H.J. (1975) 'The nature of extraversion: A genetical analysis', *Journal of Personality and Social Psychology*, 32, pp. 102–12.

EAVES, L. and EYSENCK, H.J. (1977) 'Genotype — environmental model for psychoticism', *Advances in Behaviour Research and Therapy*, 1, pp. 5–26.

EYSENCK, H.J. (1967) *The Biological Basis of Personality*, Springhill, C.C. Thomas.

EYSENCK, H.J. (1973) *The Measurement of Intelligence*, Lancaster, MTP.

EYSENCK, H.J. (1975) *The Inequality of Man*, London, Maurice Temple Smith.

EYSENCK, H.J. (1978) 'The development of personality and its relation to learning', in MURRAY-SMITH, S. (Ed.), *Melbourne Studies in Education*, Melbourne, Melbourne University Press, pp. 134–81.

EYSENCK, H.J. (1979) *Intelligenz, Struktur und Messung*, Berlin, Springer.

EYSENCK, H.J. (1980) *The Causes and Effects of Smoking*, London, Temple Smith.

EYSENCK, H.J. (1981a) *A Model for Personality*, London, Springer.

EYSENCK, H.J. (1981b) 'The psychophysiology of intelligence', in SPIELBERGER, C.D. and BUTCHER, J.N. (Eds), *Advances in Personality Assessment*, Hillsdale, Lawrence Erlbaum.

EYSENCK, H.J. and KAMIN, L. (1981) *The Intelligence Controversy*, New York, Wiley (published in Great Britain as *Intelligence. The Battle of the Mind.* London. Macmillan).

FULKER, D. (1981) 'The genetic and environmental architecture of psychoticism, extraversion and neuroticism', in EYSENCK, H.J. (Ed.), *A Model for Personality*, New York, Springer.

GRAY, J. (1973) 'Causal theories of personality', in ROYCE, J. (Ed.). *Multivariate Analyses and Psychological Theory*, New York, Academic Press.

HENDRICKSON, D.E. and HENDRICKSON, A.E. (1980) 'The biological basis of individual differences in intelligence'. *Personality and Individual Differences*, 1, pp. 3–33.

LOEHLIN, J.C. and NICHOLS, R.C. (1976) *Heredity, Environment and Personality*, London, University of Texas Press.

MCCORD, R. and WAKEFIELD J. (1981) 'Arithmetic achievement as a function of introversion-extraversion and teacher presented reward and punishment', *Personality and Individual Differences*, 2, pp. 145–52.

SCHENK, J. (1979) *Die Persönlichkeit des Drogenkonsumenten*, Toronto, Verlag für Psychologie.

WAKEFIELD, J. (1979) *Using Personality in Individualized Instructions*, San Diego, Edits.

Changing Views on Ability*

John Nisbet
University of Aberdeen

Watching the professionals on television, in athletics, golf, tennis or music, one asks oneself, 'What is it they have that I don't? Why can't I perform like this?' There are many excuses: we do not practise, have never had expert coaching, perhaps missed opportunities at a crucial young age, lack the qualities of competitive personality; but deep down we accept that it is because they have talent that we lack. What then is the secret of their exceptional ability? Physique, coordination, reaction speed, fluency, perception — any or all of these may be involved, but we are left with the feeling that there is some essential difference of ability which divides us from them. Ability is an inference: it cannot be observed directly. Ability is a concept inferred to explain a consistent superiority in performance through a series of related tasks. Thus, in education, pupils are seen as having ability in mathematics or art or languages. This is the simplest level of meaning, in which ability is used to explain present performance, as affected by training and experience. But some people learn faster or better than others even with identical training or equivalent experience. Such a capacity for acquiring skill tends to appear consistently through a series of different learning tasks: the person who is good at learning one thing tends to be good at learning quite different things. This is a second and more general meaning of ability, and it too is a hypothetical construct, this time at two removes from observable performance.

But if ability in the first of these two meanings — say, ability in solving crossword puzzles, or in solving quadratic equations — can be improved by appropriate training, experience and practice, perhaps ability of the second kind can also be learned, or at least improved by appropriate teaching. Learning how to learn, if it can be done, depends on being introduced to appropriate strategies, and also on the possession of important prerequisites. For example, if you speak a primitive language with few abstract

* This article appeared in *Educational Analysis*, 4, 2, 1982, pp. 1–5.

words, you will not learn to handle abstract ideas; if your language lacks a number scale, being limited to 'one, two, many', you will not learn mathematics. What these prerequisites are, we do not precisely know; but they impose a limitation on the scope for developing ability.

We often hear it said that the aim of education is 'to develop whatever abilities a child may have'. This assumes that the abilities are already there in some form or other. In Freudian manner, we speak as if the latent talents lie waiting to be discovered — and one need only bring them to light for them to flourish. Perhaps if we took up some activity we have never tried before — lacrosse, fencing, marathon running, oil-painting — we might discover in ourselves a unique talent. Alas, undiscovered potential ability is unlikely to be realized at our age: we have already made our commitment, and the skills we have limit our capacity for acquiring any quite different ones. For example, if we were to try to learn to speak Arabic, we would find it difficult; yet it is remarkable how many young and inexperienced Arabs succeed in learning it without difficulty. The point is obvious: in one sense we all have the potential ability to speak Arabic, but if we had been born in Arabia, some of us would have more difficulty than others in learning English. The confusion lies in the concept of 'potential ability'. Our potential ability now to learn a new skill like computer technology is affected by our previous experience with mathematics and the strategies of learning which we have acquired. The potential abilities of 16-year-olds may be more open, but some show more promise than others.

The fact of individual differences in ability is one of the incontrovertible findings of psychology. The source of these differences remains an unre-solved problem; and if we try to argue in terms of differences in potential ability, the problem is unresolvable. Within families there is often a wide range in the level of performance of children, and since the children have had much the same upbringing, parents attribute this to differences in the children's ability. Why these differences occur within families is a major question for environmentalists to answer, but it can be readily explained if a genetic component is assumed. However, if instead of looking within families we study differences between cultures, the influence of experience is clear to see. Margaret Mead's (1930) Manus are schooled as babies to the hazards of the sea, and acquire an ability in water, swimming and handling canoes, beyond anything most of us can aspire to. With us, the management of machinery is a basic element in our way of life: the intricate handling of a five-ton lorry on a motorway is graded by the Registrar General as only a semi-skilled occupation. Of course, some Manus are more adept than others in handling canoes in stormy waters; and there are good drivers and others not so good. Scholastic performance is no doubt affected similarly by cultural differences, but they are less easy to detect. Each culture has its basic competences which are open to all (or nearly all, barring injury), and it is in competitive situations that the concept of ability is seen as important.

While there is incontrovertible evidence of relatively stable individual differences in ability, other theories describe the developmental *changes* which can be observed in intellectual performances. Over time children develop increasingly complex sets of cognitive abilities, which may be described in terms of Piagetian stages. Here again we have a hypothetical construct which implies a relatively stable and internally consistent set of abilities, but available to a child only over a particular period of time. Later on, a more sophisticated set of abilities becomes available through maturation and appropriate environmental stimulation.

Recent research has, however, shifted the focus of attention away from the relative *stability* of individual differences to the importance of the remaining *variability*. For example, Piaget tended to dismiss the observed differences in performance between tasks intended to be equally difficult. But if these differences are examined, it becomes clear that they are affected by the nature of the particular tasks provided. Indeed it is becoming clear that the performances from which the existence of stages are inferred are also dependent on the experimental conditions — the form of question asked, the language used, the rapport between child and experimenter and so on. If this is true of Piagetian experiments then we should also expect similar differences in performance between children at the same overall intellectual level in the tasks set by teachers. Thus, some of the more recent research on learning has been looking at these differences in performance within the natural setting of the school or university. The focus on variability produces yet other hypothetical constructs, such as 'approach to learning' or 'style of learning'. These constructs are again derived from the analysis of performance, but create a tension with the assumptions traditionally associated with the meaning of ability. How is it possible to allow stability and variability to coexist as apparently contradictory characteristics of the same concept?

These preliminary observations are intended to demonstrate that ability is a hypothetical construct, an intervening variable whose importance we infer from observing differences in performance and learning. Thus any debate about ability is a debate about theories. Underlying theories, often hidden and implicit, are important because they determine the models we use to interpret our perceptions. We impose a structure, and that structure affects the meaning we derive and the action we take. Applying this to learning problems:

In the nineteenth century, a child's failure to learn was seen as a moral lapse, due to carelessness or lack of effort. The psychometrists of the twentieth century introduced a different model, in which learning was determined by the child's quantity of intelligence. In the 1950's another model became popular, explaining difficulties in learning as environmental, in terms of culture or early childhood experiences or social conditions. It is only recently that we have begun to look for an explanation in terms of the actual

teaching itself. Is the subject-matter properly ordered and appropriately matched to the learner's stage of development? Do the
methods fit the mental equipment which the learner brings to the
task? (Davies and Nisbet, 1981)

The last twenty years or so have seen major developments in theories of
learning, involving new interpretations of the concept of ability. But most of
those who are directly concerned with schools and teaching — teachers,
administrators, policy-makers, parents, even the pupils and students themselves — still rely on the old models, particularly the idea of a built-in
intelligence as the prime determinant of learning. The 'schemata' of
contemporary cognitive psychology provide an explanation of this resistance
to new concepts. Teachers use the theories and constructs of a generation
ago, now firmly established as a 'commonsense' model of intelligence, to
explain why some pupils learn more readily. Politicians use the same model
to decide what proportion of an age-group should go to university. The
framework they use selects and interprets evidence to test and confirm their
assumptions and, since the framework is a relatively strong one (or
otherwise it would not have survived at all), there is usually plenty of
supporting evidence. Contrary evidence also fits the framework and chal-
lenges the theory, but evidence which does not fit readily into any available
framework tends to escape notice.

In recent years, however, alternative frameworks have been advocated
with growing assertiveness. Some of these make quite forceful claims. For
example, Bloom (1976), amplifying the tenets of mastery learning, contends:

> Much of individual differences in school learning may be regarded
> as man-made and accidental rather than as fixed in the individual at
> the time of conception.... What any person in the world can learn,
> almost all persons can learn if provided with appropriate prior and
> current conditions of learning.

('*Prior* ... conditions' rather begs the question, implying not that everyone
actually has the potential ability, but that anyone *might* have had the
potential ability if the whole of his life had been arranged differently.)
Others, especially some educational technologists, tend to see learning as
essentially unproblematic, implying that if only we had enough research and
resources, the right material, the appropriate method and sufficient time, we
could teach everybody everything. Bruner (1965) bravely suggested the
hypothesis that 'any subject can be taught effectively in some intellectually
honest form to any child at any stage of development.' But he put it forward
as a hypothesis, not as an article of faith:

> Its value is that it directs attention to the subject-matter of
> instruction, its structure and form, and to the intellectual powers of
> the learner, his stage of development and his cognitive frames of

reference, and to the interaction between these, namely the process of education [the title of the book from which the quotation is taken]. (Nisbet, 1982)

The contribution of recent work in cognitive psychology and learning stops short of such dramatic claims. But it does compel us to re-examine the concept of ability which is central to our assumptions about education. Lovell (1980) distinguishes two main directions of recent work on learning, unfortunately rather difficult to reconcile: the Piagetians and the 'skill integrationists' such as Bruner, Cronbach, Gagné and Ausubel.

The Piagetian contribution is well known: popular interpretation of Piaget's stages reflect what Lovell calls 'internal age-related restrictions on learning'. This viewpoint is reminiscent of older theories of innate intelligence. The other group represents the environmentalist side of the controversy: humans are active and assign meanings to the tasks they encounter, creating from previous experience schemata and cognitive styles which are crucial to the processes of learning and development.... To the followers of Ausubel and Gagné, the metaphor for knowledge creation is the production line: assemble the necessary components and the product will appear.... To the disciples of Piaget, knowledge is an exotic bloom which has its own proper season. (Davies and Nisbet, 1981, summarizing Lovell, 1980)

There are of course many other tributaries which contribute to this current of theory. Though the examples given above are drawn from cognitive psychology, parallel developments can be seen in information theory, or in theories of language. The Bullock Report (1975), for instance, demonstrates in its underlying (but seldom explicit) theoretical base the application of ideas such as these to the teaching of reading and, beyond this, to the development of children's ability to handle problems and abstract ideas: 'A word that names an object is, for a young child, a filing pin upon which he stores successive experiences of the objects themselves.'

Most practitioners, if they reflect on their work, are unashamedly eclectic in their borrowings from theory. All theories can be useful if they help in thinking about education, and if they make practitioners aware of aspects which they would otherwise have missed. Indeed, one of the themes in current writing about teaching and learning is that there is a virtue in the variety of interpretations. Entwistle (1981) describes this as 'the most insistent message derived from the research literature':

There can be no single 'right' way to study or 'best' way to teach. People differ so much in intellectual abilities, attitudes and personality that they adopt characteristically different approaches to learning.... No one of these approaches could be 'right' for more than a small proportion of people.

The relevance of recent work in cognitive psychology is that it has moved away from preoccupation with the measurement of ability, from studies of prediction and selection, and instead focuses attention on the process of learning. It treats ability as a construct, and aims to trace the elements which contribute to, or limit, its growth. The study of ability in these terms is of central importance for an understanding of children's potential and their learning processes, and thus for education.

References

BLOOM, B.S. (1976) *Human Characteristics and School Learning*, New York, Harper.

BRUNER, J. (1965) *The Process of Education*, Cambridge, Mass., Harvard University Press.

BULLOCK REPORT (1975) *A Language for Life*, London, HMSO.

DAVIES, G.M. and NISBET, J. (1981) 'Cognitive psychology and curriculum development', *Studies in Science Education*, 8, pp. 127–34.

ENTWISTLE, N.J. (1981) *Styles of Learning and Teaching*, Chichester and New York, Wiley.

LOVELL, K. (1980) 'The relevance of cognitive psychology to science and mathematics education', in ARCHENHOLD, W.F. *et al.* (Eds). *Cognitive Development Research in Science and Mathematics*, Centre for Studies in Science Education, University of Leeds.

MEAD, M. (1930) *Growing Up in New Guinea*, Harmondsworth, Penguin (1942).

NISBET, J. (1982) 'The present state of studies in educational psychology', in HIRST, P. (Ed.), *Educational Theory and Its Central Disciplines: A Contemporary Review*, London, Routledge and Kegan Paul.

Piaget and Education*

Herbert P. Ginsburg,
University of Rochester

Piaget's theory of genetic epistemology has been extended beyond its intended domain to deal with problems of education. At first many of these applications involved the *direct teaching* of Piagetian concepts like conservation. An example is provided by Kohlberg and Mayer (1972) who believe that the very aim of education is the promotion of the Piagetian stages and that therefore the curriculum should focus on them. Subsequently, other applications have taken a different form, involving the use of general principles derived from Piaget's theory to guide educational practice. As Sinclair (1976, p. 1) puts it:

> I'm not sure that much can be done with applications of Piaget's theory in a detailed way by the Piagetian psychologist.... As you know there are absolutely no practical applications in the work of Piaget with respect to education. All one can do is to talk about some general principles, some hints and some cautions.... Piaget has very little to say with respect to specific problems such as how to teach reading and writing, and various other educational techniques.

Hence, it is necessary to limit oneself to a consideration of general principles derived from Piaget.

In all attempts at applying a theory to practical concerns and at extending its principles from one domain to another, there may arise problems of legitimacy and validity. Can the principles discovered in one area be used to provide a valid explanation of phenomena in another? Is the application a legitimate one? With respect to the extension of Piaget's theory to education, issues of this sort need to be examined most closely for several reasons. One is that the applications have concrete effects on the lives of

* This article appeared originally as Chapter 18 in SIGEL, I.E. *et al.* (Eds) (1981) *New Directions in Piagetian Theory and Practice*, Hillsdale, Lawrence Erlbaum.

many children; we need to be sure that the interventions are helpful. Another is that the Piagetian approach to education has become something of a faddish movement; clear analysis of the issues is especially warranted so as to avoid dogmatism. Piaget himself has taken a cautious attitude towards educational applications of his theory.

The aim of this chapter is therefore to achieve a clearer understanding of the relations between Piaget's theory and educational practice. The goals are to describe the theory's contributions and limits, to identify misapplications of the theory, and to outline important educational issues which remain to be solved. I shall argue that the literal approach to applying Piaget — e.g., the direct teaching of Piagetian concepts — is a mistake. A more reasonable strategy involves a focus on Piagetian principles which can furnish overall guidance for educational practice. But this approach also has its limits: the Piagetian principles are of a general nature, can be misapplied, and are not easily extrapolated to the classroom context. And there is a more serious difficulty: the very nature of Piaget's theory sets strong limits on its potential contribution to education. In particular, the theory has little to say about cultural knowledge, individual differences, the social context of education, and certain modes of learning prevalent in the classroom. This of course is no criticism of Piaget's theory itself. Although it already deals with an incredibly wide range of phenomena, the theory cannot be expected to concern itself with everything. Given the limits of the theory, a truly Piagetian approach to education requires innovative research going beyond Piaget's particular focus on genetic epistemology.

To develop these arguments, we shall review a number of commonly held propositions concerning the applications of Piaget's theory to educational practice. These propositions are grouped into several categories. First, we consider two relatively literal applications of Piaget's theory: curriculum development, and testing. Next we consider somewhat broader applications in the areas of: learning, and limits and opportunities. Finally we consider areas where the theory has fundamental limitations with respect to education, namely individual differences and academic knowledge.

Curricula

One major approach involves the derivation of curricula from Piagetian theory. Kohlberg and Mayer (1972) propose essentially that school curricula can be derived directly from the Piagetian stages. According to Kohlberg and Mayer, the aim of education is to promote the kind of development described by Piaget. What better way to do this than to teach the Piagetian stages? Taking this approach, Kamii (who has subsequently changed her position) has developed a 'program of preschool intervention related to each of the chapter headings of Piaget's books: space, time, causality, number...' (p. 488).

This approach is misguided for several reasons. First, in the vast majority of children, at least in Western cultures, the preoperational and concrete-operational stages develop in a spontaneous fashion, and therefore do not need to be taught. There is some debate about whether this is true of formal operational thought as well. Our view is that there is no clear evidence indicating the lack of spontaneous development of formal operations in Western adolescents (Ginsburg and Koslowski, 1976; see also Piaget, 1972). Whatever may be true of adolescents, it seems clear that for Western elementary school children, instruction in Piagetian subject matter is likely to be unnecessary. Second, it makes little sense to provide instruction in a topic like conservation since it is intended only as an index for tapping deeper thought structures. The training programs may inculcate only the surface manifestations and not the underlying structure. As Sinclair (1971, p. 1) puts it: 'Piaget's tasks are like the core samples a geologist takes from a fertile area and from which he can infer the general structure of a fertile soil; but it is absurd to hope that transplanting these samples to a field of nonfertile soil will make the whole area fertile.' Third, the aims of education should not be limited to — and perhaps should not at all include — the promotion of the Piagetian thought structures. Surely education must stress the transmission of the cultural wisdom and basic social values. It is not at all clear that Piaget himself would endorse Kohlberg and Mayer's 'Piagetian' model.

It is therefore necessary to take a more modest approach in which one attempts to adjust particular curricular materials in line with the child's understanding as described by Piaget. Thus, if a physics curriculum is to be introduced, it behoves the curriculum developer to take into account the child's informal knowledge of physics and his related thought processes. Although rare, work of this type, as for example conducted by Shayer (1972), has great potential for education. A curriculum at least partially based on the psychology of the child is apt to be more effective than one which is not. On the other hand, there is some danger in this approach as well. One must not allow the Piagetian conception of thought in a given area fully to determine one's approach to it. For example, Piaget's view of scientific reasoning in adolescence places heavy stress on the hypothetico-deductive method. Although useful, that is not all there is to science. A curriculum based entirely on such an approach would ignore a good deal that characterizes the essence of scientific activity, for example, exploration, the formation of hypotheses by analogy and intuition, the role of luck and serendipity. Obviously, future research should concentrate on expanding our knowledge of the child's spontaneous understanding of the various subject matter areas — science, mathematics, etc. The more we know about the child's informal reasoning in these areas, the better are we able to design effective curricula in them. We shall return to this topic later when we consider *academic knowledge*.

In brief, an attempt to base education on the teaching of the Piagetian stages is an unfortunate misapplication of the theory. A more useful approach is the modification of the curriculum in line with knowledge of the Piagetian stages, without, however, placing undue emphasis on them and without allowing them to circumscribe one's approach. More research is needed on the nature of the child's informal knowledge of the various subject matter areas.

Testing

There seem to have been two major approaches to applying Piaget's theory to the question of testing. One approach is to standardize the various Piagetian tests in order to be able to administer them to large numbers of children. The purpose of this is of course not to measure academic accomplishment — the achievement tests are intended for that — but to obtain a psychometrically reliable portrait of the child's cognitive structures, in Piagetian terms. This approach is misguided for two reasons. One is that it is not clear that knowledge of the Piagetian thought structures helps us a great deal in understanding the child's academic work. If one is going to test children in the schools, it would seem more relevant to find out how they go about doing addition than whether they conserve number. A second reason is that, even if one has an interest in measuring the Piagetian thought structures, standardized testing is an inferior method for assessing them. Piaget's clinical method is deliberately unstandardized since that is a superior way to explore the subtleties of the child's cognitive structure. The rationale for the clinical method (for an early account see Piaget, 1929) is straightforward and sensible. Tapping the child's competence requires subtle and sensitive procedures, tailored to the peculiarities of each individual child. Pursuing the idiosyncracies of the child's solution processes requires flexibility in approach. The clinical method, used properly, accomplishes these purposes well; standardizing the procedure only serves to vitiate its power. Perhaps the major gain for standardization is a false sense of scientific respectability.

A second application of Piaget to testing involves retaining both the clinical method and the Piagetian content as well. Sometimes teachers are encouraged to use the clinical method as applied to problems like the conservation of number. Such demonstrations may make an important impression on teachers, showing them that the child's thought can be distinctive. At the same time, the contribution of orthodox clinical interviewing is limited because of its failure to go beyond the Piagetian content, and to address itself directly to the teachers' concerns.

In brief, the standardization of Piagetian tests is not beneficial as it focuses too narrowly on Piagetian phenomena and because it deliberately abandons the strengths of the clinical method. The demonstration of Piagetian phenomena via the clinical method may be of some utility to teachers in illustrating the distinctiveness of the child's thought, but it does not speak directly to their needs. In education, we do not need more standard tests, nor even clinical interviews concerning Piagetian subject matter. Instead we need to exploit the great advantages of the clinical method in order to engage in the direct exploration of children's academic knowledge. It may be helpful for teachers to appreciate children's distinctive reasoning on the conservation tasks: but it would be even more useful for them to observe, via the richness of the clinical method, the unusual patterns of reasoning displayed by young children as they grapple with ordinary school arithmetic. Future work on testing needs to explore the uses of the clinical interview procedure with respect to uncovering the structure of academic knowledge.

Learning

One can derive from Piaget's theory several principles concerning children's learning and understanding.

1 Learning and understanding as active processes. According to Piaget, learning is not simply imposed by environmental forces. Learning is not shaping. The child takes an active role in his own learning. He assimilates environmental events into his own cognitive structures. The result is an active system of knowing. Knowledge is constructed by the child: 'to understand is to invent.'

These psychological principles have been extended to the educational setting. Piaget's theory provides a general rationale for active approaches which have existed for many years, stemming from Rousseau, Pestalozzi, and Froebel. The logic is simply that to know something in depth requires that one rediscover the matter for oneself. The teacher may guide the student in the direction of rediscovery, but the active learning involved in the rediscovery is itself crucial. If knowledge is active reconstruction, then active methods of education are required. We see then that in this case Piaget's contribution is to provide a psychological rationale for an already existing educational approach which is certainly a useful alternative to traditional education, with its heavy stress on passive learning.

At the same time, the educator must recognize that the Piagetian rationale is a general exhortation, itself solving no educational problems. It needs to be supplemented by specific techniques deriving from the art of the teacher. Further, there are possibilities for mischief in the application of the Piagetian ideas. One involves the misinterpretation of Piaget's notion of active learning. For example, some writers place undue stress on the role of concrete activity. Ginsburg and Opper (1969, p. 221) maintain that: 'Children, especially young ones ... learn best from concrete activities.' Further, 'the teacher should not teach, but should encourage the child to learn by manipulating things.' These undoubtedly well-meaning authors exaggerate. The important Piagetian idea is activity, not necessarily physical, concrete activity. Important for learning are active engagement and commitment, not necessarily actions on things. As Piaget (1970, p. 68) puts it: '. . . it has finally been understood that an active school is not necessarily a school of manual labor. . . . The most authentic research activity may take place in the spheres of reflection, of the most advanced abstraction, and of verbal manipulations (provided they are spontaneous and not imposed on the child . . .)'.

More important than simply misinterpretation is a limitation in Piaget's theory. It fails to provide an adequate account of receptive learning. We should not forget that education has a *legitimate* receptive side as well. Indeed Piaget (1970, pp. 137–8) feels that: 'Memory, passive obedience, imitation of the adult, and the receptive factors in general are all as natural to the child as spontaneous activity.' One of the many legitimate aims of education is to promote receptive learning. By necessity, students must engage in some 'rote learning', such as learning the names of the states, memorizing addition facts, learning the chemical elements, acquiring foreign vocabulary, etc. All this is not the only aim of education, or even the most important one: but receptive learning cannot be avoided. Further, Piaget points out that for learning of this type, the teaching machine and various forms of programmed instruction may be extremely efficient and useful. Yet, while receptive learning or 'learning in the narrow sense' is a basic part of education, Piaget has no good theory of it. He simply has not been interested in this type of learning, so that if you wish to understand the teaching of vocabulary or some other aspect of receptive learning you must go to other theorists.[1]

In brief, Piaget's theory provides the theoretical underpinnings for an active approach to education. But it suggests no specific techniques, is liable to misinterpretation, and does not provide much understanding of receptive learning which is basic for education.

2 Cognitive conflict and equilibration. Another proposition derived from Piaget's theory is that cognitive development is promoted when there is a moderate degree of discrepancy between the child's cognitive structure and some new event which he encounters. This notion has been expressed in various forms within Piagetian theory. Piaget's early work on infancy proposed that moderate novelty tends to attract the infant's interest and hence promotes learning. In later work, Piaget has stressed cognitive conflict as promoting the equilibration process. Certainly Piaget's notion of the role of cognitive conflict gives a different perspective from behaviorists' approaches to learning. The strategy of deliberately jarring the student's cognitive structure and thereby enhancing active learning is an important idea for education.

At the same time, there may be a number of difficulties with the notions of cognitive conflict and equilibration as applied to education. First, the Genevans would be the first to admit that equilibration theory is itself not yet fully developed. It has only been in the past decade that Genevan research has extensively focused on problems of cognitive conflict and equilibration. Equilibration theory itself requires further elaboration.

Second, the proper applications of equilibration theory to school learning are unclear. No doubt, the informed pursuit of cognitive conflict is at least on some occasions a useful model for education. But we do not really know for which circumstances this model is most appropriate and for which circumstances other models are required. Does all school learning involve cognitive conflict? Is equilibration theory a useful approach to reading, for example, which involves some memorization of whole words, and some abstraction of orthographic rules? In other words, while the notion of equilibration may be informative with respect to the development of those cognitive structures of concern to Piaget, it is not clear to which aspects of school learning the notion of cognitive conflict might apply.

Third, and even more fundamentally, whereas the notion of cognitive conflict may be a key notion for educators in many areas, identification of the precise nature of educational conflicts is hardly guaranteed by knowledge of the Piagetian structures. Thus, a student's cognitive conflict in the area of history, for example, may in no way involve the concrete operations or any other Piagetian cognitive structure. If this is so, identification of the precise nature of the conflict requires a theory of the cognitive structures which in fact are involved in school learning. Unfortunately, as we shall see later, such a theory is almost entirely lacking, and Piaget's theory of cognitive structures is not an adequate substitute for such a theory.

In brief, Piaget's principle of cognitive conflict offers a useful educational alternative to receptive teaching procedures. But the theory of equilibration is only in its formative stages; the areas of application of the model to academic knowledge are unknown; and identification of the precise nature of educational conflict is not guaranteed by knowledge of Piagetian structures.

3 Self-directed learning. Piaget's theory proposes that sensorimotor and cognitive structures develop in a spontaneous and self-directed fashion. The child takes a major role in directing the course of cognitive development: the latter does not depend on instruction. No doubt, self-directed learning is a real phenomenon. As Piaget has demonstrated most convincingly in the case of infancy, children *can* learn on their own. The coordination of schemes, for example, is not taught; it is learned spontaneously and parents are often quite oblivious of it.

Piaget's theory of spontaneous, self-directed development of cognitive structures has often been generalized to education in the form of an exhortation to allow children to engage in extensive self-directed learning. For example, Ginsburg and Opper (1969, p. 224) state that children '...

should be allowed considerable freedom for their own learning.' They state further that, 'If left to himself the normal child does not remain immobile; he is eager to learn. Consequently it is quite safe to permit the child to structure his own learning' (p. 225). In arguing against adult controlled teaching, writers sometimes point out an analogy with speech. Without instruction, children in all cultures learn to speak. If such natural learning were replaced by formal instruction in school, there would no doubt be disastrous results. Arguments of this sort have been used to justify some long-standing practices of progressive education. Thus Piagetians often support the 'open classroom' approach, popularized in the British infant school, in which children are assumed to control a good deal of their own learning.

Although Piaget's theory demonstrates that self-directed learning *can* take place in the natural environment — and indeed in that setting may be the prevalent mode of learning — there is once again a problem of goodness of fit when the psychological principle is applied to the educational setting. The model of self-directed learning was originally designed to explain such phenomena as the development of cognitive structures or sensorimotor schemes. We cannot know a priori whether self-directed learning does characterize some or all academic situations. This is an empirical matter. Unfortunately, little evidence exists concerning the issue. Informal observation of open classrooms suggests that under some circumstances self-directed learning can take place in school and can predominate there. At the same time, it is also obvious that self-directed learning does not always occur and that other forms of learning appear to be successful in some situations. For example, some forms of receptive learning may have to be imposed on children and it may be that only after such an imposition takes place is self-directed learning possible. Music teachers often report that young children have to be *forced* to play an instrument before they can spontaneously appreciate it. Another example involves minority education. In the 1960s it was reported that some poor black inner-city children who failed miserably in ordinary public schools achieved a high degree of success when they attended extremely structured and militaristic, authoritarian schools run by Black Muslim groups. Presumably these children benefited from the discipline and structure.

All this is to say that the freedom to learn principle may be effective in some cases and may even be an ideal to which education should aspire. Yet, common experience teaches us that the principle does not apply under all circumstances. Piagetian theory does not concern itself with the nature of these circumstances. The theory does not attempt to disentangle the social, ecological, and political factors which seem to play a major role in determining whether self-directed learning is possible in a given school situation. Those who attempt to apply Piagetian theory must become aware of the realities of the schools; but to learn about these realities, they must look beyond Piaget's theory.

4 Factors influencing development. Piaget proposes that several factors influence development: maturation, physical experience, logicomathematical experience, social experience, and equilibration. We have already dealt with equilibration, and there is nothing much to say about the role of physical maturation, except that it is important but poorly understood. Now we consider the other factors, physical experience, logicomathematical experience, and social experience.

In the case of *physical experience*, Piaget points out that individuals sometimes obtain knowledge of the world through direct perceptual experience with external objects and the consequent abstraction of properties from them. This is usually classified as perceptual learning, as in the theory of J.J. Gibson (1966). Piaget (1971, p. 266) further points out that physical experience involves 'a vast category of knowledge'. Surely, in schools, physical experience may be very important in some areas. In the case of science, for example, it is often important for children to 'mess around' with objects (to use David Hawkins', 1974, phrase) in order to obtain through physical experience — through perceptual learning — a 'feel' for objects' properties. In mathematics, it is important for children to observe the behaviour of numbers. Yet, while perceptual experience is both extensive and important for education, Piaget's theory has tended to slight it. His theory focuses on thought, not perception, and has been unsuccessful in offering an explanation of the means by which individuals manage to abstract knowledge directly from the real world. As a result, Piaget's theory has virtually nothing to say about this aspect of education, just as it has little to offer concerning the mechanisms of receptive learning.

The notion of *logicomathematical experience* is unique, and I think very valuable, in Piaget's theory. The idea that the individual learns from reflecting on his own actions on the world gives a new perspective to learning. In the case of mathematics, for example, the child may, after considerable activity, learn something about *his own actions* with respect to number, and this may be an important acquisition. The perspective afforded by the notion of logicomathematical experience seems to be an extremely useful one for teachers. The only problem with it is that since it is unique we have little insight concerning the aspects of educational activity to which it applies.

Social experience can have several senses in Piaget's theory. It may refer to the role of language, to the effect of peers, and to that of adults. Consider each in turn.

For Piaget, *language* generally plays a secondary role to thought. Because the child's thought is distinctive, his language therefore bears distinctive meaning. Such an emphasis is extremely useful for education, since it prods teachers to listen with the 'third ear' to what children say, and to go beyond teaching by mere verbalisms, in accordance with the mistaken belief that children simply learn by listening.

From his early work in the 1920s and 1930s on egocentrism and moral judgment, Piaget has stressed the facilitating effect of *peer interaction* on cognitive development. In general, the view is that the conflict of opinions generated through peer interaction is instrumental in promoting decentration, and hence development in general. The recent experimental work of Murray (1972) supports this view, showing that peer disagreements seem to promote development in reasoning concerning conservation.

In general, the Piagetian view on peer interaction seems to have some value. Surely it is wasteful for children to spend a good portion of their time in school observing a vow of silence. Surely debate, the exchange of ideas and intellectual conflict are all to the good in many classroom situations. At the same time, we must recognize the obvious fact that peer interaction has many dimensions, and does not always promote intellectual growth. Peers interact with one another in many ways, and sometimes this interaction involves the transmission of values which are antithetical both to genuine intellectual activity and to school learning (the two do not always coincide!). On some occasions, the promotion of learning among teenagers may require less peer interaction and more contact with appropriate adult models. All this is to say that in the context of education the social psychology of peer interaction must obviously go far beyond the Piagetian analysis.

With respect to *adult influence*, Piaget feels that it has an important role in the promotion of intellectual development. The adult can help to structure a situation so that the child is able to assimilate it effectively. The adult can intervene in the course of events so as to produce a moderate degree of intellectual conflict within the child. Piaget's position is similar to that of John Dewey who felt that the adult has a distinctive responsibility in the educational process, mainly to devise situations in which the child can engage in active learning. In this regard, Piaget (1970) reports a visit he paid to an open school run by Susan Isaacs. Piaget found the school interesting but somewhat undisciplined and felt that the adults should have taken a more active role in structuring the situation for the children.

The principle of adult influence is a most useful emphasis for the teacher. Yet Piaget does not go beyond a very general and well-meaning position. Piaget has nothing further to say on the role of the teacher; he has no theory of instruction. Indeed in Piaget's enormous corpus of writing on child development, one can find virtually no mention of the role of the adult. One exception to this is in the case of moral judgment, where Piaget reports, somewhat plaintively, that as a parent he was unable despite his best efforts to advance his daughter beyond a primitive stage of moral judgment. Because Piaget's almost exclusive emphasis has been on the child, he has virtually nothing to say about teaching.

In brief, a number of factors influence development, among them physical experience, logicomathematical experience and social experience. Although Piaget acknowledges the importance of physical experience, his theory has little to say concerning the perceptual learning it entails and hence can contribute little to the understanding of vast areas of education.

The notion of logicomathematical experience is promising, but its sphere of application is uncertain. In the area of social experience, Piaget's view of language encourages in teachers a sensitivity to the unique meanings of children's speech; his conception of the beneficial effects of peer interaction is useful but limited; because of his almost exclusive concentration on children, Piaget has little to say concerning teaching.

Limits on Learning and Opportunities

To some extent Piaget's theory has a pessimistic side with respect to education. One principle states that because of the nature of his current stage of intellectual development, the child is limited in what he can learn. Thus, in the stage of concrete operations, he may not be able to engage in certain forms of scientific reasoning. Or, in the preoperational stage, he may not be able to understand certain basic mathematical concepts. In general, this must be true. Everyone knows that you cannot teach a baby to speak or a young child to do the calculus. It is certainly useful for the teacher to be alert to aspects of the child's thought processes which might make it difficult for him to assimilate a certain body of material.

Yet there is a serious danger in the Piagetian position. Some Piagetians have adopted too zealous a view of the child's limitations. It is a common belief, for example, that the preoperational child cannot engage in 'abstract thought' or that he cannot perform any useful scientific activity. These are misconceptions. The young child is capable of mental representation from the age of about 18 months, and indeed sometimes thinks *too* abstractly, as when he overgeneralizes the meaning of words. Piaget himself is careful to point out intellectual strengths in the preoperational child, as in the case of the early understanding of functional relations. Similarly, there is a good deal that the young child can do with respect to science, whose scope should not be limited to the kind of hypothetical reasoning Piaget attributes to adolescents. It is even more incorrect to suppose that the preoperational child or even the concrete operational child is not yet 'ready' for reading since his thought structures are so primitive. Obviously 3- and 4-year-old children can learn to read — this is a common observation — and it is by no means clear that the structures of preoperational or concrete operational thought set any kinds of limits on basic reading. In brief, there is some validity to the Piagetian principle that the nature of the young child's thought limits his learning. But this principle has been applied indiscriminately, with the unfortunate effect of restricting the range of educational experiences for the young child.

Piagetian theory displays an optimistic side as well. According to Piaget, the spontaneously developed thought structures existing at various stages make it possible for the child to assimilate various aspects of school material. These thought structures form the cognitive basis for academic knowledge. Because the child approaches many areas of academic study with spontaneously developed and relatively powerful 'intuitions', the task for education is to make connections among the child's intuitions and the formalizations which are taught in school. As Piaget (1970, p. 47) puts it: 'The pedagogic problem ... still subsists in its entirety: that of finding the most adequate methods for bridging the transition between these natural but nonreflective structures [that is, the child's spontaneously developed but unaware intuitions] to conscious reflection upon such structures and to a theoretical formulation of them.' There is thus a particularly Piagetian form of consciousness raising: in presenting formalizations, the teacher must make an effort to exploit the child's intuitions. As Freud put it in a somewhat different context, 'Where id was there ego shall be.'

Pursuing this analysis, Piaget claims that children should not have as much difficulty as they do with school mathematics, since it is more or less an elaboration of what they already know. As Piaget (1970, p. 44) puts it: '... it is difficult to conceive how students who are well-endowed when it comes to elaboration and utilization of the spontaneous logicomathematical structures of intelligence can find themselves handicapped in the comprehension of a branch of teaching that bears exclusively upon what is to be derived from such structures.'

The notion of drawing on the child's spontaneous intuitions and relating them to what is taught in school is a key idea for education. Piaget makes an important contribution in stressing that a basic strategy for education should consist in bridging the gap between spontaneous and cultural knowledge. Yet the Piagetian analysis cannot carry us very far in this direction because the theory pays scant attention to two areas which we shall consider next, namely *individual differences* and *academic knowledge*.

Individual Differences

In many of his works, Piaget takes pains to point out that there exist individual differences in children's rate of attainment of the various cognitive structures. In the Piagetian scheme such individual differences may result from variations in any of the factors promoting development — maturation, physical experience, etc. Such differences may also appear in the rates of development displayed by entire cultures.

Although the theory acknowledges the existence of individual differences — how could it not? — Piaget has little interest in them. His concern is with the 'general human mind' of Wundt, with the development of common structures of knowledge. Hence Genevan theory and research have paid scant attention to individual differences in rate of attainment of the various stages. Moreover, the theory has virtually ignored other individual differences. The theory does not concern itself with such variables as impulsiveness, intellectual conscientiousness, persistence, commitment, creativity. These are all individual difference characteristics at the heart of intellectual activity. To observe that Piaget's theory fails to deal with them is no criticism, merely a statement of fact: the theory cannot be expected to solve all psychological problems.

At the same time, this gap in Piaget's theory limits its relevance for the classroom. Individual differences are at the heart of education. To a large degree, education is or should be concerned with developing meaningful forms of learning for individuals who differ in important ways. To some extent, these important characteristics may include individual differences in rates of attainment of the Piagetian stages. Perhaps some topics in mathematics will come easier to the 7-year-old who is in the period of concrete operations than to one who is preoperational. But it is likely that other individual differences — those not discussed by Piaget — are at least equally important for education, and may well be more important than rate of attainment of the Piagetian stages. For real children in classrooms, what matters is creativity, intelligence, cognitive style and intellectual motivation. A deep understanding of these factors is vital for the effective conduct of everyday education. Yet these are factors concerning which Piaget's theory has virtually nothing to say.

Piagetian Thought Structures and School Knowledge

It is usually assumed that educators should be sensitive to the child's intellectual status as described in terms of Piagetian thought structures. There is some validity to this notion. A teacher should be aware of the concrete operational child's one-to-one correspondence or of the formal operational child's capacity for hypothetico-deductive reasoning. To some extent, the structures described by Piaget are informal intuitions which can serve as a foundation for formal instruction and hence the teacher can profit from knowledge of them. The open question, however, is this: In what ways do the Piagetian structures *account for* the nature of academic cognition? To what extent can the concrete operations *explain in detail* the child's performance in algebra or in reading?

It is becoming evident that the explanatory power of the Piagetian structures with respect to academic knowledge is weak. For example, in the case of adolescent science, as we have pointed out below, the Piagetian theory deals with the details of hypothetico-deductive reasoning. Yet this is only one part of the scientific enterprise. Similarly in the case of mathematics, Piagetian theory deals with some fundamental notions of one-to-one correspondence and equivalence, but does not have a great deal to say about the child's uses of counting or the details of his problem-solving techniques in algebra. In particular, Piaget's theory does not deal with knowledge which is symbolized and codified. Thus, it does not seem very productive to use Piagetian notions in developing models for reading, either at the level of 'decoding' (the technical aspect of reading), or at the level of comprehension. In brief, although Piaget's theory may explicate some fundamental structures of thought, it does not concern itself with, and therefore cannot be directly applied to, basic aspects of academic knowledge in particular, and culturally derived thought in general. Whereas the theory gives insight into such informal 'intuitions' as one-to-one correspondence, it does not deal explicitly with the cultural elaborations of these intuitions. Hence the effort to bridge the gap between intuition and formalization is hindered.

Why does Piaget's theory not pay more attention to cultural forms of knowledge? Piaget (1970, p. 137) sees education as a dialectic process involving interaction between child and society. 'To educate is to adapt the child to an adult social environment, in other words, to change the individual's psycho-biological constitution in terms of the totality of collective realities to which the community consciously attributes a certain value.' The culture attempts to transmit to the child its wisdom, its modes of thought, knowledge, and values. On his part, the child attempts to assimilate the cultural wisdom and eventually to contribute to it, to modify it. In the case of mathematics, for example, over the course of centuries the culture has developed codified, written procedures and explicit, symbolized principles, a cumulative legacy which the educational system attempts to inculcate in the child. This accumulated wisdom is powerful and can serve the child well once it is assimilated into his cognitive structures. This having been done, the child is then in a position to make original contributions to the culturally derived body of knowledge.

Although apparently recognizing the central role of the 'collective realities' — the cultural wisdom — Piaget's theory does not contribute a great deal to understanding them. As a genetic epistemologist, Piaget has been concerned mainly with the development of fundamental but non-cultural forms of knowledge. Thus he is interested in the notion of one-to-one correspondence, not with written algebra. Piaget focuses on ideas and modes of thought operating outside the school context, not within it. Another way of putting it is to say that Piaget is interested in biologically-based forms of knowledge, not socially-based forms. Piaget (1971, p. 268) maintains that:

> We are omitting [from consideration] the modes of metaphysical and ideological knowledge because they are not kinds of knowledge in the strict sense but forms of wisdom or value coordinations, so that they represent a reflection of social life and cultural super-structures rather than any extension of biological adaptation. By this we do not mean to dispute their human importance; it simply means that the problems are quite different and are no longer the direct province of biological epistemology.

Thus, Piaget's theory has focused on 'biological epistemology', on the basic Kantian categories of thought, and has slighted social knowledge.

If education is in good measure concerned with acculturation — the transmission of the accumulated wisdom of a culture — then Piaget's theory is limited in its explanatory power with respect to academic knowledge. At the very least we can say that it is not clear that there is a strong relation between the Piagetian structures and the kinds of thought processes involved in school learning. To a large extent the question is an empirical one, since we have very little knowledge concerning the thought processes actually employed in academic learning. A productive approach, I think, is for those with a Piagetian orientation to undertake direct investigations of academic cognition in order to determine whether the Piagetian notions are indeed useful, or whether new accounts need to be developed. For education, knowledge of the Piagetian thought structures is only a preliminary first step.

Conclusions

Piaget's theory yields several principles providing both deep understanding of children and general guidance for the educational enterprise. The principles serve as a basis for a progressive approach to education. At the same time, we must recognize that the theory may be misinterpreted: sometimes this results in too literal and rigid an application of Piaget's views. Much more importantly, we must also understand that Piaget's is a specialized theory, failing to consider many issues crucial for education. In particular, because Piaget is a genetic epistemologist, whose theory focuses on the development of what he considers to be the basic categories of the general human mind — on biologically-based, Kantian categories — he has little to say about the acquisition and nature of culturally-based forms of knowledge, the forms inculcated by schooling.

Considering these limitations in Piaget's theory, it seems fair to say that we sometimes rely too much on Piaget, and the result is detrimental to the understanding and practice of education. Too often, we say to teachers that Piaget wants us to look at the child, but then all we show them is what Piaget has seen. We demonstrate the child's distinctiveness through his inability to conserve, but we cannot describe his unique approach to addition. While preaching a child-centred view, Piagetians too often assume a Piaget-centred view.

An effective contribution to education requires utilizing the Piagetian framework to go beyond Piaget. Such an approach requires, among other things, attempts to understand self-directed learning within the social context of the classroom and the ecological setting of the school in the larger society. It requires a direct focus on the structures of academic knowledge in particular and cultural knowledge in general. It requires the use of flexible methods to investigate cognitive structures of direct relevance to education. In these ways can we begin to understand the education of the child.

Herbert P. Ginsburg

Acknowledgment

The writer wishes to thank the following colleagues for their helpful comments on the paper: Kathy Hebbeler, Jane Knitzer, Leon Levy, Barbara Means, Ellin Scholnick, Marilyn Wang.

Note

1 The irony is that modern experimental psychology views receptive learning as very much an active process. For example, memory of nonsense syllables involves active organizational strategies. Even rote learning is no longer seen as the stamping in of associations onto a passive learner.

References

GIBSON, J.J. (1966) *The Senses Considered as Perceptual Systems*, Boston, Houghton Mifflin.

GINSBURG, H. and KOSLOWSKI, B. (1976) 'Cognitive development', *Annual Review of Psychology*, 27, pp. 29–61.

GINSBURG, H. and OPPER, S. (1969) *Piaget's Theory of Intellectual Development: An Introduction*, Englewood Cliffs, N.J., Prentice-Hall.

HAWKINS, D. (1974) *The Informed Vision*. New York, Agathon Press.

KOHL, H. (1967) *36 Children*. New York, New American Library.

KOHLBERG, L. and MAYER, R. (1972) 'Development as the aim of education', *Harvard Educational Review*, 42, pp. 449–96.

MURRAY, F.B. (1972) 'Acquisition of conservation through social interaction', *Developmental Psychology*, 6, pp. 1–6.

PIAGET, J. (1929) *The Child's Conception of the World*, London, Routledge and Kegan Paul.

PIAGET, J. (1970) *The Science of Education and the Psychology of the Child*, New York, Orion Press.

PIAGET, J. (1971) *Biology and Knowledge*, Chicago, University of Chicago Press.

PIAGET, J. (1972) 'Intellectual evolution from adolescence to adulthood', *Human Development*, 15, pp. 1–12.

SHAYER, M. (1972) 'Conceptual demands in the Nuffield O-level physics course', *School Science Review*, 186, pp. 26–34.

SINCLAIR, H. (1971) 'Piaget's theory of development: The main stages' in ROSSKOPF, M.F. *et al.*, *Piagetian Cognitive-Developmental Research and Mathematical Education*, Washington, D.C. National Council of Teachers of Mathematics.

SINCLAIR, H. (1976) in O'BRIEN, T.C. *Implications of Piagetian Research for Education: Interview with E.M. Hitchfield*, St Louis, Teacher's Center.

VYGOTSKY, L.S. (1962) *Thought and Language*, Cambridge, Mass., MIT Press.

The Mismatch between School and Children's Minds[*]

Margaret Donaldson
University of Edinburgh

Visitors to infant schools often comment that most of the children are excited, happy, and eager to learn. But if they were to continue their visit to upper primary or secondary classrooms they would find many pupils who are unhappy, unresponsive and bored. Yet from infancy all normal human beings show signs of a keen desire to learn — a desire that does not appear to depend on any reward apart from the satisfaction of achieving competence and control. This desire is still strong in most children when they enter school. How is it that something that starts off so well regularly ends up so badly? Why do many children learn to hate school?

The answer cannot be that most children are stupid after the age of 7, nor can it be that teachers enjoy making children miserable. Recent research into the nature of children's language and thinking can help us to see what goes wrong.

It is now clear that we have tended both to underestimate children's competence as thinkers and to overestimate their understanding of language.

The underestimations are in large measure a result of the theories of the most influential of all students of child development, Jean Piaget. From his experiments with young children he concluded that until the age of about 7, though competent in practical skills, children are extremely limited thinkers.

The overestimation of children's understanding of language is, in part, a result of the theories of linguist Noam Chomsky. In the 1960s Chomsky (1965) caused a wave of excitement among psychologists by drawing attention to the significance of one simple fact: children who are only 2 or 3 years old can utter complicated sentences *that they have never heard before.*

Since these sentences generally conform to the rules of syntax, the children must, in some sense, know them. And even sentences that are not

---

[*] This article appeared in *Human Nature*, March 1979, pp. 61–7.

fully correct by adult standards still show that rules of some kind are at work in their construction. In fact the errors frequently reveal rules, as when 'bringed' is used instead of 'brought'. We can be fairly sure that children who say 'bringed' have not heard adults say it. They must have generated the form for themselves by applying the rule for forming past tenses in weak verbs in English.

The implications of these facts presented psychologists with a highly challenging question: How is it possible for a young child to master such a complex system of rules? There seemed to be only two possibilities: the child either has remarkable skills as a thinker, or some very special skills as a language learner. Chomsky argued for the second of these explanations. He proposed that human beings are endowed with a highly specialized faculty for learning language, which he called a language-acquisition device. This idea enjoyed widespread popularity for a while, and at least part of the reason was that the other explanation seemed implausible. There was evidence around — weighty, respectable evidence obtained by careful systematic study and experiment — that appeared to imply that the young child is not much of a thinker.

Observations and Children's Logic

Yet there was other evidence, freely available but largely neglected, that pointed to a different conclusion. Anyone who talks with young children seriously and attentively knows that they say a great many thoughtful and seemingly intelligent things. The curious thing is that while so much attention was being paid to the grammatical sophistication of children's speech, very little attention was being paid to its meaning.

The following examples are remarks made by very young children (all younger than 5, and some barely 3 years old) as they were listening to stories:

> The nails will tore his trousers. [A prediction about what will happen to a character who is putting nails in his pocket. Uttered in tones of concern.]

> You can't sew a turnip. [A confusion of 'sew' and 'sow'; uttered with scorn.]

> He's got sharp teeth and sharp claws. He must be a wild cat.

These examples are typical. Yet they are remarkable for the awareness of possibility and impossibility, of contingency and necessity revealed. They establish beyond doubt a well-developed ability to make sense of a highly complex world. The impression of good sense gleaned from these isolated remarks becomes even greater when we are aware of the context in which they were made.

Piagetian Theory

The problem is to reconcile these observations with experimental evidence that seems to show that children of this age are quite limited in their ability to deal with possibility, to reason inferentially, and to think intelligently in general. Although the evidence comes from diverse sources, the source that has been the most influential over the past few decades is the work of Piaget and his colleagues in Geneva. The reason for Piaget's great influence is not only his ingenious studies of children, but also the fact that he has woven his findings into a theory of great internal consistency and beauty, so that the mind is dazzled.

Once adopted, a theory tends to make us disregard evidence that conflicts with it. This is true even of a theory that is not very impressive, let alone one like Piaget's. But the most entrenched theory can be dislodged in the face of overwhelming evidence that it is wrong.

In the case of our theories about children's thinking, such evidence has been mounting for some time. Recent research, much of it concerned with the comprehension of language, throws new light on the reasons children can seem so limited as thinkers when they are tackling Piaget's tasks, yet so skilled when we watch them and listen to them in their spontaneous behavior.

In the early days after Chomsky's revolution in the field of linguistics, almost all those who were doing research on child language concentrated on studies of what children said. The reason was simply that the evidence needed in order to work out the rules of grammar that the children in some sense knew and used was evidence about language production. As long as this was the main concern, the question of what children could understand was largely ignored. But over the past few years there has been a marked shift of interest from syntax to semantics, and studies of comprehension have come into their own.

Recent Research Studies

My own interest in language comprehension began in 1968 with a study of the ways in which children interpret the words 'less' and 'more'. For this research we built two large cardboard apple trees, each equipped with six hooks on which beautiful red apples could be hung. Putting different numbers of apples on each tree, we asked which tree had more apples, which less. Then the children were asked to put more (or less) on one tree than on the other. The results surprised us. We had thought it likely that they would understand 'more' better than they understood 'less'. What we found was that the two words appeared to be treated as synonyms. No matter which word we used, we tended to get the same responses — and they were the responses that were correct for 'more'.

This result was provocative in many ways, and it led to a series of further studies. One of these, by David Palermo of Pennsylvania State University, replicated the original results; but others, including research by Susan Carey of MIT, used different methods and cast doubt on the interpretation of these first findings.

My own view now is that we were asking the wrong question. Instead of asking how the children understood the words 'less' and 'more', we should have been looking at their interpretation of the utterances in which these words were used. I was led to see this by the results of a series of further studies, the first of which was still planned as an investigation of the development of word meanings. I wanted to study the children's understanding of words like 'all' and 'some'. Naïvely, as it now seems to me, I hoped to discover the meanings of these words for the children by inserting them in statements like, 'All the doors are shut' or 'All the cars are in the garages', and presenting the statements along with objects that rendered them true or false. What I discovered was that the children seemed to have no single meaning for 'all'. They judged all the doors to be shut if there was no door open, but often they judged all the cars to be in the garages when one car was sitting in full view outside. In the latter case the question they seemed to be considering was not where the cars were but whether all the garages were occupied. So we tried another configuration. We used two rows of garages, one row having four and the other six; and two rows of cars, one with four and one with five. In this study we again looked at the interpretation of sentences with the word 'more' in them.

We were going to ask the children to make a comparison, and we wanted to make it as easy as possible for them, so we arranged the cars one above another on two shelves, with the extra car in one row always projecting on the right-hand side.

When the two rows of cars were presented alone, without garages, most of the children said there were more cars in the row of five than in the row of four. However, we also presented the cars enclosed in garages: four cars in the row of four garages, and five cars in the row of six garages (so that one garage was empty). About one-third of the children now changed their judgments, saying there were more cars in the row of four. Again the question the children appeared to be answering was whether all the garages were filled: this was the thing that seemed to stand out, and no matter what we asked, this was the question they answered. Clearly 'fullness' was what they expected to be asked about.

Conservation Experiments

An important feature of this last experiment was that the task the children were given was, in its logical structure, the same as a Piagetian conservation test. Of all the tests that Piaget devised to reveal the nature of children's thinking in the preschool and early school years, the conservation tests are probably the best known. There are many such tests — tests of conservation of number, weight, volume, and length — but they all make use of the same key elements. Conservation of number will serve as an example.

First, the experimenter shows the child two rows of objects, equal in number and laid out opposite one another in one-to-one correspondence. The child is asked whether there is the same number in the two rows. Unless the child agrees that this is so, the test cannot proceed. In the next step the experimenter destroys the perceptual equivalence of the two rows, by moving the objects in one row closer together, for instance. Usually this action is accompanied by a remark like, 'Now watch what I do', which ensures that the child is paying attention. Once the new configuration is in place, the original question is repeated, usually in the same words. Children who continue to say that the two rows are equal are said to conserve and are called conservers. If they claim that one row now has more objects than the other, they are not conserving and are called non-conservers. According to Piaget, a child's ability or inability to conserve is an indication of his or her stage of mental development.

Clearly the task involving two rows of cars, with and without enclosing garages, has the structure of a conservation task, although it is an unorthodox one. First the child is asked a question that calls for a comparison, then something irrelevant to the meaning of the words in the question is changed, then the original question is asked again.

Some may say that many of the children in our study were not conserving. But *what* were they not conserving? The most plausible and generally applicable notion seems to be that what the children were failing to conserve was their interpretation of the words of the experimenter. The same question was put to them twice, but *in a different context*. Adults would have discounted the shift in context. They would have known that in this kind of formal task they were meant to discount it and to base their replies on the meaning of the words. But perhaps the children did not know they were meant to do this, or perhaps they could not do it because the context was too powerful for them. In either event, it looked as though some non-linguistic feature was strong enough to cause a shift in interpretation of what, for an adult, was a repetition of the same question.

At this stage my attention was drawn to the possibility that part of the reason for the shift in interpretation had to do not with the physical context of the experiment, like fullness of garages or length of rows, but with what the children thought was the intention underlying the experimenter's behavior. I owe this insight to James McGarrigle, (McGarrigle and Donaldson, 1974) who devised an ingenious experiment to test it.

The experiment made use of a number-conservation task and a small teddy bear called Naughty Teddy. The task proceeded in the usual way up to the point where the child agreed that the number in the two rows was the same. But before the experimenter went on to the next stage, Naughty

Teddy would emerge from hiding, swoop over one row, and disarrange it. Once the one-to-one correspondence had been destroyed the child was invited to help put Naughty Teddy back in his box (an invitation that was usually accepted with glee) and the questioning was resumed: 'Now, where were we? Ah yes, is the number in this row the same as the number in this row?' and so on. What happened was that many more children between the ages of 4 and 6 conserved number in the Naughty Teddy version of the task than in the traditional version (fifty out of eighty, compared with thirteen out of eighty).

Egocentricity Experiments

Piaget's account of the reasons for failure cannot deal with this finding. His explanation makes use of several related arguments, putting the emphasis now here, now there. But at the heart of them all is the notion that children fail to conserve because they cannot sufficiently 'decentre', that is, they are not flexible about shifting their point of view. Typically non-conservers are held to 'centre', or concentrate attention, on a particular state or feature, failing to take account either of transformations between states or of other features of the object. They centre on the fact that one row of objects is longer than the other and fail to notice that the latter is more dense. In general, they are believed to centre on the present moment and to make judgments on the basis of how things *now* appear, with no relation to how they were a moment ago.

It is quite possible to fit these arguments to the finding that children will sometimes change their judgments about the numbers of cars in two rows after the addition of enclosing garages. We have only to say that children who do so 'centre on fullness'. However, there seems to be no way to fit them to the findings of the Naughty Teddy study (and these findings have already been replicated twice, by Julie Dockrell of Stirling University and by Irene Neilson of the Glasgow College of Technology). Nothing in Piaget's theoretical account of conservation suggests that it should matter who changes the arrangement of the objects.

But the Naughty Teddy results do fit very well with the idea that non-conserving children fail to answer the experimenter's question in the same way on the second occasion because, for them, it is not the same question. It seems different because it is not sufficiently detached, or disembedded, from the context of what the child believes the experimenter wants.

So disembedding will explain more of the findings than decentring will. But this does not establish that the decentring argument is false. It is possible that the child has difficulty with both decentring *and* disembedding. We must look at other evidence to see whether children are as limited in their ability to decentre as Piaget would have us believe.

In Piaget's view, inability to decentre is a feature of young minds that shows itself in a wide variety of ways. Some of these have already been considered. Another, perhaps the most fundamental, is the inability to appreciate the relativity of one's own point of view in space and time. A simple example of this is the inability to understand that one's own view of an object is not the same as that of someone looking at it from another side.

In a famous experiment, Piaget established that children presented with a three-dimensional model of a group of mountains have great difficulty choosing a picture of how the model would look to a doll viewing it from another position. For the most part, young children given this task choose the picture that shows exactly what they themselves see. It seems, then, that they are notably lacking in mental flexibility, bound by the egocentric illusion that what they see is the world as it really is. If this were true, it would certainly have far-reaching implications for the ability to think and reason.

Recent research has called this conclusion into question. My own thinking on the subject has been influenced by the work of Martin Hughes. Hughes (1975) placed before a group of children a configuration of two walls intersecting to form a cross. At the end of one of the walls he placed a wooden doll, representing a policeman. The children were then given another wooden doll, representing a boy, and were asked to 'hide the boy so that the policeman can't see him.' (The policeman was not tall enough to look over the walls.)

The arrangement made it easy to tell whether the children were able to escape from the domination of their own point of view, and the results were clear. Even 3-year-olds were highly competent at the task. They showed no sign of a tendency to hide the doll from themselves, as would have been predicted from Piaget's theory, and they showed every sign of understanding what the policeman would be able to see from where he stood. Even when there were two policemen, placed so that the only effective hiding place was one where the boy doll was clearly visible to the child, about 90 per cent of the responses from 3 and 4-year-old children were correct.

The policeman task differs in many ways from Piaget's mountain task, but one is particularly significant in light of what we now know. In the policeman task there is an interplay of motives and intentions that is entirely comprehensible, even to a child of 3. For this reason the task makes *human sense* to the children: they understand instantly what it is all about. The verbal instructions are so well supported by the context that no difficulties of disembedding arise. As soon as the doll is handed over, the children's faces light up, they smile, they latch on.

The mountain experiment on the other hand does not make immediate human sense in this way. There is no interplay of motives and intentions, no intelligible context. The task is as disembedded as the one given the American Indian who was asked to translate into his native tongue the sentence, 'The white man shot six bears today.' The Indian was baffled.

'How can I do that?' he asked. 'No white man could shoot six bears in one day.'

Now we can reconcile the disparity between children's skills as thinkers in everyday situations and their limitations when confronted with formal tasks. Most formal tasks are geared to minds that are capable of a high degree of disembedding of thought and language — minds that are able to dispense with the support of human sense — and these tasks make demands of a quite special kind. (For a fuller description of the experiments, see Donaldson, 1978.)

Implications for Schooling

When we first learn to think and to use language, it is within situations where we have purposes and intentions and where we can recognize and understand similar purposes and intentions in others. These humanly meaningful contexts sustain our thinking.

Precisely how they do this is of the greatest theoretical interest, but it is still mysterious. One thing is clear: when thought and language are functioning smoothly in real-life contexts, we are normally aware of the ends to which our activity is directed but not of the mental means that are needed to get there. We do not stop to think about our thinking or about the words we are using.

A formal task interrupts the flow of life. It demands deliberation, mental awareness, and control. It is by definition a thing to be considered out of context. We must set our minds to it. We must accept the premises, respect the constraints, direct our thought. This activity is difficult and, in a sense, unnatural. But that does not mean it should be avoided or abandoned — only that it will not happen spontaneously. We must recognize this fact so that we do not label our children 'stupid' or 'backward' if at first they find it hard.

The ability to take a problem out of context and consider it in its own right is the product of long ages of a particular kind of culture. It is closely linked to the development of literacy because written language, unlike speech, is by its very nature disembedded. Speech is transient, elusive, entangled in happenings. A written page, or a clay tablet, is physically separate and permanent: you can take it with you and go back to it. It is scarcely possible to learn to handle written language without becoming aware of it as a system and as a tool of the mind.

Disembedded intellectual skills underlie all our mathematics, all our science, all our philosophy. It may be that we value them too highly in comparison with other human skills and qualities, but we are not at all likely to renounce them. We have come to depend on them. As schooling progresses, the emphasis on them becomes harder to evade or postpone. The student who can solve problems, as problems, divorced from human sense, is the student who will succeed in the educational system. The better a student is at it, the more awards he or she will receive, and the better that student's self-image will be. But large numbers of students never achieve even a moderate level of competence in these skills and leave school with a sense of failure.

Seen in the context of human history, universal compulsory schooling is a new social enterprise, and it is a difficult one. We should not be surprised or ashamed if we do not yet know how to manage it well. At the same time, if we are going to persist in it, there is urgent need for us to learn to manage it better. We must not forget how grave a responsibility we assume when we conscript children for these long, demanding years of service. And when the outcome is not all that we would wish, we must not resort to blaming this on the shortcomings of the children. Since we impose the demands, it is up to us to find effective ways of helping children to meet them.

Many children hate school because it is a hateful thing to be forced to do something at which you fail over and over again. The older children get, the more they are aware that they are failing and that they are being written off as stupid. No wonder many of our children become disheartened and bored.

What are we to do about it? There is no simple formula, but there are a number of guiding principles.

The first takes us back to the topic of decentring. Although research has shown that children are better at this than Piaget claims, it is true that human beings of any age can find it hard. As adults we often fail to understand the child's point of view. We fail to understand what perplexes a child and why. In *Cider with Rosie*, Laurie Lee gives an account of his own first day at school:

'What's the matter, Love? Didn't he like it at school, then?'
'They never gave me the present.'
'Present? What present?'
'They said they'd give me a present.'
'Well, now, I'm sure they didn't.'
'They did! They said: "You're Laurie Lee, aren't you? Well, you just sit there for the present." I sat there all day but I never got it. I ain't going back there again.'

The obvious way to look at the episode is to say that the child didn't understand the adult. But if we are to get better at helping children, it is more profitable to say that the adult failed to make the imaginative leap needed to understand the child. The story carries a profoundly important moral for all teachers and parents: the better you know something yourself, the greater the risk of not noticing that children find it bewildering.

When Jess Reid of the University of Edinburgh studied children who were learning to read, she found that some did not have the least idea of what reading was. They could not say how the postman knew where to deliver a letter. They did not understand the relationship between the sounds of speech and the marks that we make on paper, or that these marks are a means of communication.

It would help greatly if children told teachers when they felt perplexed. Many do not. But if they are explicitly encouraged to ask questions, they can often do so effectively, and the act of asking helps children become conscious of their own uncertainty.

It is also important to recognize how greatly the *process* of learning to read may influence the growth of the mind. Because print is permanent, it offers special opportunities for reflective thought, but they may not be taken if the reading child is not given time to pause. Once children gain some fluency as readers, we can help them notice what they are doing as they extend their skills and begin to grapple with possibilities of meaning; for it is the thoughtful consideration of possibility — the choice of one interpretation among others — that brings awareness and control.

One final principle is implicit in all that has been said: if we want to help children to succeed at school and to enjoy it, it is not enough to avoid openly calling them failures. We must respect them as thinkers and learners — even when they find school difficult. If we respect them and let them know it, then the experience of learning within a structured environment may become for many more of our children an opening of new worlds, not a closing of prison bars.

References

BRUNER, J.S. (1975) 'The ontogenesis of speech acts,' *Journal of Child Language*, 2, pp. 1–19.

CHOMSKY, N. (1965) *Aspects of the Theory of Syntax*, MIT Press.

DONALDSON, M. (1978) *Children's Minds*, Fontana.

GRIEVE, R. *et al.* (1977) 'On the child's use of lexis and syntax in understanding locative instructions', *Cognition*, 5, pp. 235–50.

HUGHES, M. (1975) *Egocentrism in pre-school children*, Unpublished PhD thesis, University of Edinburgh.

LEMPERS, J.D. *et al.* (1977) 'The development in very young children of tacit knowledge concerning visual perception', *Genetic Psychology Monographs*, 95, pp. 3–53.

McGARRIGLE, J. and DONALDSON, M. (1974) 'Conservation accidents', *Cognition*, 3, pp. 341–50.

MACNAMARA, J. (1972) 'Cognitive basis of language learning in infants', '*Psychological Review*, 79, pp. 1–13.

OLSON, D.R. (1976) 'Culture, technology and intellect, in RESNICK, L.B. (Ed.) *The Nature of Intelligence*, Halstead Press.

Learning as Constructing Meaning*

David Ausubel
City University of New York

Education as the Acquisition of Knowledge and Skills

In setting our academic goals ... we must be concerned with the *ultimate* intellectual objectives of schooling; namely, these are the long-term acquisition of valid and usable bodies of knowledge and intellectual skills and the development of ability to think critically, systematically and independently....

The very nature of education as adequately guided instruction implies knowledgeable selection, organization, interpretation, and sequential arrangement of learning materials and experiences by academically and pedagogically competent persons rather than a trial-and-error process of self-instruction. True, since education does not end when students leave school, they must also be taught to learn by themselves ... [But] acknowledgement of the desirability of students devoting part of the school day to acquiring skills in locating, interpreting, and organizing information by themselves does not in any way relieve the educational establishment of the primary responsibility of structuring subject matter content.

The Principal Kinds of Learning

From the standpoint of enhancing school learning, no theoretical concern is more relevant or urgent in the present state of our knowledge than the need for distinguishing clearly among the principal kinds of learning ... that can take place in the classroom. The most significant way of differentiating among these types of classroom learning is to make two crucial process

* This article comprises reordered extracts from *Educational Psychology: A Cognitive View*, 2nd ed., 1978, published by CBS College Publishing, reproduced by permission of the author.

distinctions that cut across all of them. We can make a distinction between *reception* and *discovery learning* and another between *rote* and *meaningful* learning. The first distinction is significant because most of the understandings that learners acquire both in and out of school are presented rather than discovered. And since most learning material is presented verbally, it is equally important to appreciate that verbal reception learning is not necessarily rote in character and can be meaningful without prior non-verbal or problem-solving experience....

For the most part, large bodies of subject matter are acquired through *reception learning*, whereas the everyday problems of living are solved through discovery learning.... As far as the formal education of the individual is concerned, the educational agency largely transmits readymade concepts, classifications and propositions.... One can justifiably argue that the school is also concerned with developing the student's ability to use acquired knowledge in solving particular problems systematically, independently, and critically in various fields of inquiry. But this function of the school, although constituting a legitimate objective of education in its own right, is less central than its related transmission-of-knowledge function. This is true in terms of the amount of time that can be reasonably allotted to this function, in terms of the objectives of education in a democratic society, and in terms of what can reasonably be expected from most students....

Meaningful learning takes place if the learning task can be related in non-arbitrary, substantive (non-verbatim) fashion to what the learner already knows, and if the learner adopts a corresponding learning set to do so. Rote learning, on the other hand, occurs if the learning task consists of purely arbitrary associations, as in paired-associate ... learning, if the learner lacks the relevant prior knowledge necessary for making the learning task potentially meaningful, and also (regardless of how much potential meaning the task has) if the learner adopts a set merely to internalize it in an arbitrary, verbatim fashion (that is, as an arbitrary series of words)....

A student could learn Ohm's law, which indicates that current in a circuit is directly proportional to voltage. However, this proposition will not be *meaningfully learned* unless the student already has meanings for the concepts of current, voltage, resistance, direct and inverse proportion, *and* unless he or she tries to relate these meanings as indicated by Ohm's law.

One reason why pupils commonly develop a rote learning set in relation to potentially meaningful subject matter is because they learn from sad experience that substantively correct answers lacking in verbatim correspondence to what they have been taught receive no credit whatsoever from some teachers. Another reason is that because of a generally high level of anxiety or because of chronic failure experience in a given subject (reflective, in turn, of low aptitude or poor teaching), they lack confidence in their ability to learn meaningfully, and hence perceive no alternative to panic apart from rote learning.... Moreover, pupils may develop a rote learning set if they are under excessive pressure to exhibit glibness, or to conceal, rather than admit and gradually remedy, original lack of genuine understanding. Under these circumstances it seems easier and more important to create a spurious impression of facile comprehension, by rotely memorizing a few key terms or sentences, than to try to understand what they mean. Teachers frequently forget that pupils become very adept at using abstract terms with apparent appropriateness — when they have to — even though their understanding of the underlying concepts is virtually non-existent.

Types of Meaningful Learning

Classroom learning, we believe, is concerned primarily with the acquisition, retention, and use of large bodies of potentially meaningful information. Therefore it is important that we make very explicit at the outset what is meant by the psychology of meaning and meaningful learning.... The most basic type of meaningful learning, upon which all other meaningful learning depends, is *representational* learning, which involves learning the meaning of single symbols (typically words) or learning what they represent.

Another type of meaningful learning which is prominent in the acquisition of subject matter consists of *concept learning*... We shall define concepts as objects, events, situations or properties that possess certain criterial attributes and are designated by some sign or symbol.... [There are] two methods of concept learning: (1) concept formation, which takes place primarily in young children; and (2) concept assimilation, which is the dominant form of concept learning in school children and adults.

In *concept formation* the criterial attributes of the concept are acquired through direct experience, through successive stages of hypothesis generation and testing and generalization. Thus young children come to know the concept 'dog' through successive encounters with dogs, cats, cows, and so on, until they can generalize these criterial attributes that constitute the cultural concept of 'dog'.... Meanings of signs or symbols for concepts must be acquired gradually and idiosyncratically by each learner. Once initial meanings are established..., new meaningful learning will give additional meaning to the signs or symbols (by *concept assimilation*), and new relationships between previously learned concepts will be acquired (*propositional learning*)....

Concept labels for specific concepts, like 'dog' or 'red', become differentiated further and develop new relationships to (more general) concepts, such as animal or colour, as meaningful learning progresses. Although learners acquire meanings in their own idiosyncratic way, these meanings have sufficient commonality in any given culture to allow use of the symbols to exchange information. If this were not so, schooling or any other form of organized exchange of information would be impossible, and meaningful learning would also be impossible except through discovery learning ... (in reality), as a child's vocabulary increases, new concepts can be acquired through the process of concept assimilation since the criterial attributes of new concepts can be defined by use in new combinations of existing referents available in the child's cognitive structure. While concrete-empirical props may also aid concept assimilation in young children, it is possible to use existing relevant concepts to accelerate the process of defining the criterial attributes of new concepts.... (Hence much emphasis is placed on) the processes and conditions that facilitate concept assimilation.

Assimilation Theory

It is important to recognize that meaningful learning does not mean that new information forms a kind of simple bond with pre-existing elements of cognitive structure. On the contrary, only in rote learning does a simple arbitrary and non-substantive linkage occur with pre-existing cognitive structure. In meaningful learning the very processes of acquiring information result in a modification of both the newly acquired information and the specifically relevant aspect of cognitive structure to which the new information is linked. In most instances new information is linked to a relevant concept or proposition. As a matter of convenience, we will refer to concepts or propositions as relevant *ideas* in cognitive structure. In order to connate that meaningful learning involves an interaction between new information and pre-existing ideas in cognitive structure, we will employ the term *anchorage* to suggest the role of the pre-existing idea.... This process of linking new information to pre-existing segments of cognitive structure is referred to as *subsumption* ... [which is described in terms of] the particular way in which the content of the new proposition is related to the content of relevant established ideas in cognitive structure. The relationship in question may be either subordinate, superordinate, or a combination of the two....

Since cognitive structure itself tends to be hierarchically organized with respect to level of abstraction, generality, and inclusiveness of ideas, the emergence of *new* propositional meanings most typically reflects a *subordinate* relationship of new material to existing cognitive structure. This involves the subsumption of potentially meaningful propositions under more inclusive and general ideas in existing cognitive structure, and this in turn results in the hierarchical organization of cognitive structure.... It is necessary to distinguish two basically different kinds of subsumption that occur in the process of meaningful learning and retention. *Derivative* subsumption takes place when learning material is understood as a specific example of an established concept in cognitive structure or is supportive or illustrative of a previously learned general proposition.... An example would be to recognize that scarlet, aqua, and lavender are names for colours, albeit less common than red, blue or purple.... Under these circumstances, the meaning of the derivative material emerges quickly and *relatively* effortlessly.

More typically, however, new subject matter is learned by a process of correlative subsumption. The new learning material in this case is an extension, elaboration, modification, or qualification of previously learned propositions. It is incorporated by and interacts with relevant and more inclusive subsumers, but its meaning is not implicit in, and cannot be adequately represented by, these latter subsumers. For example, recognition that displaying the (national) flag is an act of patriotism would be a common example of correlative subsumption....

New learning bears a *superordinate* relationship to cognitive structure when one learns an inclusive new (concept or) proposition under which several established ideas may be subsumed ... for example, when children learn that the familiar concepts of carrots, peas, beans, and spinach may all be subsumed under the new term 'vegetable'.

The meaningful learning of new propositions that bear neither a subordinate nor a superordinate relationship to *particular* relevant ideas in cognitive structure ... gives rise to *combinatorial* meanings.... They are potentially meaningful because they consist of sensible combinations of previously learned ideas that can be non-arbitrarily related to a *broad background* of *generally* relevant content in cognitive structure.... This availability of only generally and non-specifically relevant content presumably makes combinatorial propositions less relatable or anchorable to previously acquired knowledge and hence, at least initially, more difficult to learn and remember than subordinate or superordinate propositions....

Most of the *new* generalization that students learn in science, mathematics, social studies, and the humanities are examples of combinatorial learnings, for example, relationships between mass and energy, heat and volume, genic structure and variability, demand and price.... Up to this point we have tried to clarify the differences between meaningful learning and rote learning. The processes of subsumption, superordinate learning, and combinatorial learning are *internal cognitive* processes and hence not part of behaviourist theories of learning. We have emphasized that the acquisition of new information is highly dependent on the relevant ideas already in cognitive structure and that meaningful learning in humans occurs through an *interaction* of new information with relevant existing ideas in cognitive structure. The result of the interaction that takes place between the new material to be learned and the existing cognitive structure is an *assimilation* of old and new meanings to form a more highly differentiated cognitive structure.... The ideas presented up to this point are summarized in Table 1.

During the course of meaningful learning, two important, related processes take place. As new information is subsumed under a given concept or proposition, new information is learned and the subsuming concept or

David Ausubel

Table 1. *Forms of Meaningful Learning as Viewed in Assimilation Theory*

1. Subordinate Learning:
   A. *Derivative*
      subsumption

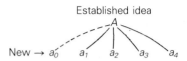

In derivative subsumption, new information a_0 is linked to superordinate idea A and represents another case or extension of A. The criterial attributes of the concept A are not changed, but new examples are recognized as relevant.

   B. *Correlative*
      subsumption

In correlative subsumption, new information y is linked to idea X, but is an extension, modification, or qualification of X. The criterial attributes of the subsuming concept may be extended or modified with the new correlative subsumption.

2. Superordinate Learning:

In superordinate learning, established ideas a_1, a_2, and a_3 are recognized as more specific examples of new idea A and become linked to A. Superordinate idea A is defined by a new set of criterial attributes that encompass the subordinate ideas.

3. Combinatorial Learning:

New idea $A \rightarrow B\text{-}C\text{-}D$

Established ideas B C D

In combinatorial learning new idea A is seen as related to existing ideas B, C, and D but is neither more inclusive nor more specific than ideas B, C, and D. In this case, new idea A is seen to have some criterial attributes in common with pre-existing ideas.

4. Assimilation Theory:

New information is linked to *relevant, pre-existing* aspects of cognitive structure and both the newly acquired information and the pre-existing structure are modified in the process. All of the above forms of learning are examples of assimilation. Most meaningful learning is essentially the assimilation of new information.

---

proposition is modified (refer to Table 1). This process of subsumption, occurring one or more times, leads to *progressive differentiation* of the subsuming concept or proposition. In the assimilation theory of learning presented (here), most of the meaningful learning that occurs could be characterized as involving progressive differentiations of concepts or propositions. For example, the new meanings that would be acquired over time for propositions such as Ohm's law or concepts like democracy or evolution would represent progressive differentiation of these propositions or concepts.

In superordinate or combinatorial learning (see Table 1), established ideas in cognitive structure may become recognized as related, in the course of new learning. Thus new information is acquired and existing elements of cognitive structure may take on new organization and hence new meaning. This recombination of existing elements of cognitive structure is referred to as *integrative reconciliation*. For example, students may know peas or tomatoes as vegetables, but these are classified as fruits in biology. The initial confusion a student may experience is resolved when new combinatorial meanings are learned and the student recognizes that the nutritional classification of foods is not the same as the botanical classification ... integrative reconciliation proceeds best when possible sources of confusion are sorted out by the teacher or instructional materials. ... One attribute of outstanding teachers is that they have sufficient breadth of knowledge and experience ... to aid students to form their individual integrative reconciliations. When students regard a course or a textbook (rarely) as well organized, it is because the meanings of new concepts or propositions are clearly presented, possible conflicts in meanings are resolved, and new integrative reconciliations are facilitated.

Active Reception Learning

The acquisition of meanings through meaningful reception learning is far from being a passive kind of cognitive process. ... In the first place, at least an implicit judgment of relevance is usually required in deciding which established ideas in cognitive structure are most relatable to a new learning task. Second, some degree of reconciliation between them is necessary, particularly if there are discrepancies or conflicts. Third, new propositions are customarily reformulated to blend into a personal frame of reference consonant with the learner's experiential background, vocabulary, and structure of ideas. Finally, if the learner, in the course of meaningful reception learning, cannot find an acceptable basis for reconciling apparently or genuinely contradictory ideas, he or she is sometimes inspired to attempt a degree of synthesis or reorganization of his or her existing knowledge under more inclusive and broadly explanatory principles. The learner may either seek such propositions in more recent or sophisticated expositions of a given topic, or, under certain circumstances, may try to discover them independently. All of this activity (except for the last-mentioned), however, stops short of actual discovery learning or problem-solving. ...

The extent to which meaningful reception learning is active depends in part on one's need for integrative meaning and on the vigorousness of one's self-critical faculty. One may either attempt to integrate a new proposition with *all* of one's existing relevant knowledge or remain content with establishing its relatedness to a single idea. Similarly, one may endeavour to translate the new proposition into terminology consistent with one's own vocabulary and ideational background, or remain satisfied with incorporating it as presented. Finally, one may strive for the acquisition of precise and unambiguous meanings, or be completely satisfied with vague, diffuse notions.

The main danger in meaningful reception learning is not so much that learners will frankly adopt a rote approach, but rather that they will delude themselves into believing that they have grasped genuine meanings when they have *really* grasped only vague and confused sets of empty verbalisms. It is not so much that they do not want to understand, but that they lack the necessary self-critical ability and are unwilling to put forth the necessary active effort in struggling with the material, in looking at it from different angles, in reconciling and integrating it with related or contradictory knowledge, and in reformulating it from the standpoint of their own frame of reference. One may find it easy enough to manipulate words glibly so as to create a spurious impression of knowledgability, and thereby delude oneself and others into thinking that the material is truly understood when it is not.

A central task of pedagogy, therefore, is to develop ways of facilitating an active variety of reception learning characterized by an independent and critical approach to understanding of subject matter. This involves, in part, the encouragement of motivations for and self-critical attitudes toward acquiring precise and integrated meanings, as well as the use of other techniques directed toward the same end. Precise and integrated understandings are, presumably, more likely to develop if:

1 the central unifying ideas of a discipline are learned before more concepts and information are introduced;
2 the limiting conditions of general developmental readiness are observed;
3 precise and accurate definition is stressed, and emphasis is placed on delineating similarities and differences between related concepts;
4 learners are required to reformulate new propositions in their *own* words.

All of these devices come under the heading of pedagogic techniques that promote an active type of meaningful reception learning. Teachers can help foster the related objective of assimilating subject matter critically by encouraging students to recognize and challenge the assumptions underlying new propositions, and to distinguish between facts and hypotheses and between warranted and unwarranted inferences. Much good use can also be made of Socratic questioning in exposing pseudo-understanding, in transmitting precise meanings, in reconciling contradictions, and in encouraging a critical attitude toward knowledge.

Providing Structure for Reception Learning

The assimilation theory of human learning ... not only has value for explaining learning mechanisms as they operate in the classroom but also for guiding school curriculum development, instructional design and evaluation practices. . . .

In order to plan curriculum and design instruction consistent with assimilation theory . . . a primary — and exceedingly difficult — task is to identify *concepts* in any given discipline and to organize these concepts into some hierarchical or relational scheme . . . if we cannot succeed in identifying salient concepts in a field of study, distinguishing among concepts and isolating relatively trivial or subordinate concepts, the result is likely to be that curriculum planning will proceed from an array of topics. The simplest definition we can give for topics is that this is what you find in the table of contents of most books. Sometimes topics are also concepts (for example, 'Cell-Structure and Function' or 'Mercantilism'), but more often they represent a conglomeration of concepts, perhaps with some *logical* coherence but without psychological organization. In other words, it is not possible to show how early instruction on a topic leads to progressively better differentiated concepts. . . . Our own view is that, although it is useful to identify and organize concepts and propositions in any discipline as an aspect of curriculum planning, the relationships between these ideas need not be expressed in a strict, undirectional hierarchy. . . . [Moreover] the *curriculum* plan places primary emphasis on the organization of knowledge in the discipline, whereas the *instructional* plan places primary emphasis on the learner and the kind of entering subsumers the learners have to serve as anchorage for new learning. . . . Even in grade 1, [one] would begin with the most general, most inclusive ideas. These not only would link more easily with the existing concepts of children, but also would serve subsequently as powerful subsumers for anchorage of a wide array of specific new knowledge. The important element from assimilation theory that enters into curriculum planning is that optimal meaningful learning requires progressive differentiation of concepts or propositions in cognitive structure. Therefore these concepts must be the basic elements of our curriculum plan. . . .

Our experience has been that the best programme is made when we begin considering one or two major concepts to be illustrated, as well as motivational issues. For example, we might decide (for motivational reasons) to begin a science course with field study. . . . We may begin to consider one or two major concepts of science that can best be illustrated through (that) field work. . . . We can see that at least initial choice of concepts to be taught (a curriculum decision) can be very much a function of what kind of instructional material may be most meaningful to a given group of students at a certain time of year (instructional planning decisions). However, we cannot ignore the fact that substantial development of one major concept (such as the concept of diversity of living things) cannot be realized until some progress has been made in the development of other major concepts (such as the hierarchical organization of living things). Any arbitrary decisions that would be made in curriculum planning with respect of *sequencing* of concepts to be presented might result in undesirable or unmotivating instructional sequences. Conversely, arbitrary decisions on topics or activities in instructional planning might obviate any chance for concept differentiation or integrative reconciliation. We can schematize this starting dilemma in curriculum and instructional planning as shown in Figure 1.

Of all the possible conditions of learning that affect cognitive structure, it is self-evident that none can be more significant than organization of the material.... The principles of progressive differentiation and integrative reconciliation have been represented throughout as being of central importance in the programming of meaningful subject matter. Optimal utilization of these principles presupposes not only their consistent use in the sequential presentation of subject matter but also the supplementary availability of a hierarchical series of *advance organizers*. These latter organizers provide relevant ideational scaffolding, enhance the discriminability of the new learning material from previously learned related ideas, and otherwise effect integrative reconciliation, generality, and inclusiveness that is much higher than that of the learning material itself. To be maximally effective they must be formulated in terms of language and concepts already *familiar* to the

Figure 1

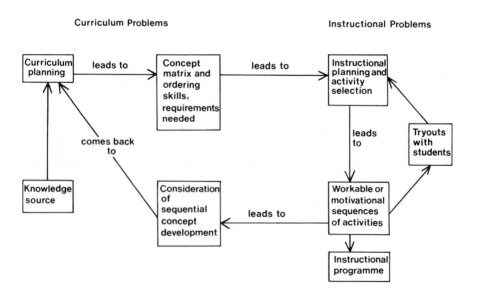

Curriculum Problems   Instructional Problems

learner and use appropriate illustrations and analogies if developmentally necessary.

True organizers, thus defined, should not be confused with ordinary introductory overviews. The latter are typically written at the same level of abstraction, generality, and inclusiveness as the learning material and achieve their effect largely through repetition, condensation, selective emphasis on central concepts, and prefamiliarization of the learner with certain key words....

Generally speaking, therefore, it makes good organizational sense if the presentation of more detailed or specific information is preceded by a more general or inclusive principle to which it can be related or under which it can be subsumed. This not only makes the new information more meaningful and enables the student to anchor most easily forgotten specifics to more easily remembered generalizations but also integrates related facts in terms of a common principle under which they can all be subsumed. In a physics, engineering, or biology course, for example, the general characteristics of *all* regulatory or cybernetic systems should be presented before considering any *particular* regulatory or cybernetic system. The latter, in turn, should be explicitly related to the more general principles, showing how they exemplify them.... This makes for some redundancy; but such redundancy, in turn, greatly reinforces the general principles....

Progressive differentiation of cognitive structure through the programming of subject matter is accomplished by using a hierarchical series of organizers (in descending order of inclusiveness), each organizer preceding its corresponding unit of detailed, differentiated material, and by sequencing the material within each unit in *descending* order of inclusiveness....

(*Comparative*) organizers may also be expressly designed to further application of the principle of integrative reconciliation. They do this by explicitly pointing out in what ways previously learned, related ideas in cognitive structure are either basically similar to, or essentially different from, new ideas and information in the learning task. Hence, for one thing, organizers explicitly draw upon and mobilize all available concepts in cognitive structure that are relevant to and can play a subsuming role in relation to the new learning material. This manoeuvre effects great economy of learning effort, avoids the isolation of essentially similar concepts in separate, non-communicable compartments and discourages the confusing proliferation of multiple terms to represent ostensibly different but essentially equivalent ideas. In addition, organizers increase the discriminability of genuine differences between the new learning materials and seemingly analogous but often conflicting ideas in the learner's cognitive structure....

[In textbooks] it is desirable not only for the material in each chapter to become progressively more differentiated (to proceed from ideas of greater to lesser inclusiveness), but for textbooks as a whole (from one chapter to another) to follow the same organizational plan. The *spiral* kind of organization, in which the same topics are treated at progressively higher levels of sophistication in successive sections, is an extension of the same principle.... There is (also) a progressive increase in scope, depth, complexity, level of abstraction, and level of sophistication at successively higher grade levels, with the earlier acquired knowledge serving as a foundation for the more abstract and complex material introduced later.... Throughout ... it has been repeatedly stressed that the conditions of learning primarily influence the meaningful acquisition and retention of ideas and information by modifying *existing* cognitive structure.... If we had to reduce all of educational psychology to just a single principle, we would say this: 'Find out what the learner already knows and teach him or her accordingly.'

Style in the Interplay of Structure and Process*

Samuel Messick
Educational Testing Service, Princeton

This article addresses a number of interlocking themes in educational research and practice. These include the roles of knowledge and of context in school learning, the role of schooling in the development of cognitive abilities and developed abilities in the processes of school learning, and the role of cognitive styles as characteristic modes of organization and regulation in information processing which afford unifying self-consistency in the manner of learning. There is, as well, the issue of the match between features of instruction and characteristics of the learner. That is, what aspects of method, material, teacher and setting should be matched to which student characteristics, in what ways, for what instructional purposes — and who should decide among the alternatives for the pursuit of whose goals? The question of *what* should be matched is the problem of prescription; the question of *how* to match is a problem of educational technology; while the questions of *purpose* and *locus of choice* raise issues of social values, thereby highlighting the inherently value-laden nature of the educational enterprise. In the main, then, this commentary centres on some of the salient roles in education and learning of knowledge, abilities, context and style — especially as they merge in what Hunt (1961) called 'the problem of the match'.

Abilities and Knowledge in the Structure of Intellect

To speak of processes of learning and intelligence on the one hand and of structures of ability and knowledge on the other is reminiscent of the distinction sometimes attempted between intelligence and intellect. McDougall (1923, p. 379), for example, maintained that, 'intelligence is

* This is a shortened version of the article published in *Educational Analysis*, 4, 1982, pp. 105–21.

essentially the capacity for making new adaptations; it cannot be described in terms of structure. Intellect includes intelligence and much more besides; for "a good intellect" implies good intelligence that works through and by means of rich and well-organized cognitive structure,... which organization is the work of intelligence.... [The more intelligence] is exercised, the more it perfects the instruments through which it works, namely, the cognitive structure of the mind.' My point here is that this cognitive structure of intellect comprises not only acquired *knowledge* structures but acquired *ability* structures. Furthermore, these ability structures, being learned constellations of information-processing components organized by assembly and control processes (Snow, 1980b; Sternberg, 1977), underlie both specific task proficiencies and stable patterns of individual differences across multiple tasks. Through transfer, they also facilitate the learning of new tasks, the acquisition of new knowledge, and the development of more complex abilities. Since the extensiveness and complexity of knowledge structure influences subsequent learning and performance in a field — as witness the large functional differences between experts and novices or experienced and inexperienced students (Glaser, 1981; Hunter, 1982) — and since current knowledge structure is an outcome of earlier learning, a question arises as to the limitations imposed on early learning as a function of the developmental level of the student (Desforges, 1982; Driver, 1982).

Constructivist versus Component Learning Theories

Learning is dependent not just on instructional experiences, as behaviourists maintain, but also on the conceptual representations constructed by the learner. One way in which constructivist theories seem to differ from other learning theories is in the perspective they afford in regard to mediating processes (Messick and Sigel, 1982). Mediating processes in non-constructivist learning theories tend to be viewed as direct links between the stimulus conditions or task requirements on the one hand and effective responses or task performance on the other, whether these are conceptualized as internal chains of implicit stimuli and transformational responses organized through habit family hierarchies (for example, Berlyne, 1965) or as elementary information-processing components organized by means of plans or production systems (Miller *et al.*, 1960; Newell and Simon, 1972). In contrast, mediating processes in constructivist theories tend to be viewed as facilitators or vehicles of task performance rather than as components of task performance. The structure of cognitive operations available to the learner — as in Piaget's stages of concrete or formal thinking — is an example of such a mediating vehicle. Another example of a facilitating vehicle is the level at which such cognitive modes as representational thinking, whether in terms of propositional schemes or visiospatial images, are readily available to the learner.

From the constructivist perspective, effective intervention strategies should attempt to enhance facilitating vehicles which would in turn improve a variety of cognitive performances, as opposed to direct attempts to enhance the components of cognitive performance *per se*, which would be a strategy more consistent with non-constructivist learning perspectives. This is not to say that constructivists would be averse to the direct enhancement of component skills, but rather that both the structure — representational/ knowledge/ability — and the components should be explicitly addressed in instruction. A specific instance of this approach is Sigel's (1970, 1979) instructional strategy of *distancing*, which serves to provide young children with cognitive environments that constantly stimulate them to reconstruct the past, anticipate the future, and take different perspectives on the present as a means of fostering representational thinking. Representational thinking in turn provides a mode of cognition that facilitates the acquisition and assimilation of specific knowledge and skills as well as the formation and reformation of knowledge structures.

Instruction for Structure

When students learn something specific, they frequently also learn something general — that is, they tend to educe general attributes from specific instances and evolve general structures for representing and understanding new specifics. Such structures are not typically under instructional control, however, for they are rarely thought of as educational objectives in their own right. Nor are the development of structuring and restructuring skills or of flexibility in the utilization of multiple structures often conceived as direct educational goals. As a consequence, the students' general structures tend to be basically idiosyncratic, at least in elementary education, being frequently fragmented or overextended or misaligned with reality. Since the structure or organization of knowledge and skills is not often explicitly addressed in instruction, what students *typically* develop by way of structure in school learning is usually taken to be what they *can* develop — as witness the quick prescriptive use by Biggs and Collis (1980) of their structural taxonomy of observed learning outcomes (Desforges, 1982).

Constructivist approaches to instruction, as exemplified by Sigel's (1970, 1979) programmatic focus on representational modes and thinking skills, attempt to address directly the issue of structure in learning. And if the structuring and restructuring of knowledge and skills can be influenced by instruction, then perhaps the cognitive structures that students typically exhibit at a given age — that is, their 'internal age-related restrictions on learning' (Lovell, 1980) — are a function not only of psychological development, as Piaget contends, but of the nature and quality of traditional teaching itself. This raises the question of the degree to which the nature and quality of teaching may impose external restrictions on learning.

Several instances of this concern may be seen in recent papers. For example, Nisbet and Entwistle (1982) point out, 'It is only recently that we have begun to look for an explanation [of children's learning difficulties] in terms of the actual teaching itself.... Do the methods fit the mental equipment which the learner brings to the task?' (Davies and Nisbet, 1981). Desforges (1982, p. 35) opines that 'pupils' capacities to invent abstractions (albeit erroneous ones) raise questions about whether some notions are ever taught at all and about what fragments of concepts pupils have to make sense of in real circumstances. The child's experience of concepts in classrooms may frequently be inappropriate and fragmented, the fragmentation emanating from a number of sources including the teacher's organization and instructions.' One direct consequence of teacher's instructions and emphases, he avers, is that teachers' stress solely on procedural features of tasks leads students to define success as task completion rather than understanding (Anderson, 1981). Moreover, Entwistle (1982) suggests that students' adoption of a meaning orientation or a deep approach in learning is a function of 'good teaching' and freedom of choice, whereas the adoption of a reproducing orientation or a surface approach in learning is a function of heavy workload and lack of choice (Ramsden and Entwistle, 1981). As a final instance, Driver (1982, p. 75) laments that although learning in science apparently requires the restructuring of children's conceptualizations, there are few investigations of this process in action in classrooms. She concludes that 'we may need to pay as much attention to the learner's current ideas and how they change as we do to the structure of knowledge to be taught.'

Developed Abilities as Structures of Enabling Processes

Attention needs to be paid not only to learners' knowledge structures but to their ability structures as well. From my perspective, abilities need to be viewed in terms of both process and structure. On the one hand, abilities are seen as task proficiencies — specifically, as particular constellations of information-processing components that satisfy the requirements of a given task or type of task (Sternberg, 1977), functioning much like subroutines or prior assemblies in computer terms. They develop through repeated performance and practice across similar tasks and gradually attain relative stability through exercise, challenge, and overlearning (Ferguson, 1954, 1956). Note that we are speaking of relative stability, not fixity, and hence of developed abilities — or, more precisely, of developing abilities. They may develop more slowly later in learning for some individuals and earlier and more rapidly for others, but they appear to respond over the long term to education and experience throughout the school years — even such intellective abilities as verbal comprehension and quantitative reasoning which are relatively well crystallized by adolescence (Cattell, 1971; Messick, 1980, 1982). One prominent theory of ability development, for example, maintains that learning leading to the emergence of a particular ability is influenced by prior learning and previously established abilities through mechanisms of transfer (Ferguson, 1954, 1956). 'As the learning of a particular task continues, the ability to perform it becomes gradually differentiated from, although not necessarily independent of, other abilities which facilitate its differentiation' (Ferguson, 1954, p. 110). Furthermore, differential exposure to various task domains leads to differential learning and, hence, to development of different ability patterns in different students and different population groups (Lesser *et al.*, 1965).

On the other hand, abilities are also seen as dimensions of individual differences — specifically, as generalized constellations of information-processing components that form stable patterns of individual differences across multiple tasks or types of tasks. The critical concept bridging process and structure in this formulation is that abilities are stable consistencies *within* individuals (across variations in setting, time, and task) that reliably differentiate *between* individuals. The *intraindividual* pattern of abilities for a particular student is the ability structure of concern for present purposes, and this may or may not include all of the dimensions — or interrelate them in the same way — as in *interindividual* structures of between-person differences. Nevertheless, research on the structure of individual differences does provide many of the dimensions and associated ability measures for characterizing and assessing individual structures (Burt, 1949; Cattell, 1971; Ekstrom *et al.*, 1976; Haskstian and Cattell, 1974; Guilford, 1967). Overall, then, ability structure is conceptualized here as a multidimensional organization of stable assemblies of information-processing components that are combined functionally in task performance, learning, problem-solving and creative production (Messick, 1972, 1973). Although 'global assessments of ability or of competence are not appropriate models for a dynamic educational process', as Clark (1982, p. 59) concludes, I suggest that information about ability structures — that is, individual patterns of multiple abilities — in concert with information about knowledge structures, 'could lead directly to educational decisions on learning strategies or ordering of presentation of material for individual children' (p. 57).

In discussing ability structures, I have gone out of my way to emphasize that these cognitive or intellective abilities develop gradually and experientially through processes of learning and transfer, although I recognize that individual differences in this learning and development may be partly or even largely genetically based, as Eysenck (1982) avows. I stress the developing nature of these abilities in response to education and experience because schooling, especially in the early years, may be instrumental in enhancing their development and effective utilization as opposed to merely building upon them as givens (Hunt, 1961, 1980). Thus, unless one would like to argue that any of us has fully attained the limits of our genotype, there appears to be ample room to reap the benefits of learning, even for students at the low end of ability distributions — and given the restricted nature of instruction in much of special education, perhaps especially for those at the low end (Furneaux, 1982; Heller *et al.*, 1982).

Abilities are enabling processes in the sense that they facilitate task performance and the acquisition and retrieval of knowledge as well as the structuring and restructuring of knowledge (Snow, 1980a, 1980b). They also facilitate the development of more complex abilities — but so do rich and extensive knowledge structures. Highly developed knowledge structures, such as those characterizing experts in contrast with novices, foster cognitive functioning in terms of what Hunter (1982) aptly calls 'adroitly usable patterned complexes'. These complex abilities to perceive and apply patterned relationships and action sequences strongly influence the nature of problem representations, the avoidance of irrelevancies, and the organization of performance and solution processes (Chi *et al.*, 1981; Chiesi *et al.*, 1979; Glaser, 1981; Hunter, 1982; Larkin *et al.*, 1980a, 1980b). Thus, developed abilities influence the acquisition and structuring of knowledge while developed knowledge structures influence the organization and application of abilities, leading to increasingly more complex structures of each.

Context and Style in School Learning

The focus up to this point has been on factors contributing to stability in learning and task performance, but there are also a number of factors contributing to systematic variability in learning and performance. In counterpoint to knowledge and abilities, then, let us next consider the impact of context and style.

The Context of Learning

The first problem here is that we have no systematic way of specifying what constitutes 'context'. Context is not any and all attributes of the environment but, as in discourse, those aspects of the surround that illuminate or add to the meaning of the focal variables and their functioning. What is needed is some form of context analysis — not just behavioural analysis to establish empirical relations between stimulus conditions and response class (S-R analysis), whether or not organismic mediators are taken into account (S-O-R), but functional analysis to conceptualize stimulus conditions and environmental circumstances in terms of the organismic needs and values they serve (O-S-R analysis). Failing this, what is usually offered is a specification of potential sources of context effects (Messick and Barrows, 1972).

One source of potential context effects has already been highlighted — namely, the *intrapersonal influences on learning* of the student's ability and knowledge structures and of personality structure more generally. Students with different patterns of abilities, with different amounts and kinds of prior knowledge, and with different personality traits may respond differentially and selectively to stimulus conditions and learn either to different degrees or in qualitatively different ways, or both. Thus, an individual's existing knowledge and skill, or the lack thereof, can facilitate or interfere with the acquisition and assimilation of new knowledge and skill (Driver, 1982). Similarly, aspects of an individual's motivation and temperament may facilitate or interfere with school learning (Eysenck, 1982).

In addition to the student as context, other sources of potential effects are the *situational influences on learning* deriving from current or prior social and educational experiences. These include the psychoeducational impact of home, family (both status and process variables), school, classroom, programmes, teachers, communication media, community and culture. In effect, these intrapersonal and situational influences, if operative, provide the context *for* teaching, whether or not they are taken into account in teaching.

The Context of Teaching

Other potential sources of differential effects on learning stem from the method, material and manner of teaching and from the circumstances in which it occurs. These include cognitive, stylistic and personality characteristics of the teacher; content features and demand characteristics of materials and tasks; aspects of the physical surround (furnishings, ventilation, lighting, temperature); dimensions of the social setting (classroom, small group, tutorial); and perceptions of the learning climate (evaluative or test-like, spontaneous or game-like, productive or work-like).

Teaching in Context

Still other sources of differential learning effects are the interactive influences stemming from combinations of the previous sources, especially in regard to the nature and degree of match or mismatch between the context of teaching and the student's intrapersonal and situational context of learning. The problem of the match will be discussed in more detail shortly, but for the moment let us briefly entertain a particularly optimistic scenario. If teachers were fully aware that they are teaching in a multifaceted context of interactive influences and if their teaching were flexible enough and they had resources enough, perhaps they could modify the match to optimize learning during the course of teaching. That is, in contrast to using prior assessment of scholastic achievement (Tobias, 1976) or intellective abilities and other functional characteristics of learners (Cronbach and Snow, 1977) in order to predict optimal instruction, we might use responses to current instruction to predict optimal instruction. And since responses to *optimal* instruction in turn may be indicative of what is really meant by functional characteristics of learners — that is, the way students function at their best under optimal conditions — this approach might yield not only alternative teaching strategies, but alternative assessment strategies as well (Feuerstein, 1979, 1980; Vygotsky, 1962, 1978). Better yet, we could attempt to tailor instruction to measured functional characteristics of learners and then use current responses to such instruction to fine tune or adaptively revise the system. As we shall see, this tailoring may involve not only systematic matching but deliberate mismatching so as to foster conceptual change and flexibility, thereby reducing the extent to which learning is context-bound. Such efforts might facilitate the development of generalizable modes of learning that cut across and transcend contexts when necessary and appropriate.

Styles as Organizing and Regulating Processes

Much of our concern over context effects pertains to variability in individual performance across situations, times and tasks and to the possibility that individuals from different family or cultural backgrounds might perform differently if the task conditions were altered. This latter point mirrors Cole's dictum that 'cultural differences reside more in differences in the situations to which different cultural groups apply their skills than in differences in the skills possessed by the groups in question' (Cole and Bruner, 1971, p. 874; Cole *et al.*, 1971). In addition to variability in individual performance *across contexts*, another source of systematic learning differences is variability *across individuals* in the manner or form of learning and performance, which broaches the question of differential modes or styles of learning and of cognition more broadly.

Cognitive styles are usually conceptualized as characteristic modes of perceiving, remembering, thinking and problem-solving, reflective of information-processing regularities that develop in congenial ways around underlying personality trends (Messick, 1976c, 1979, 1981). They are inferred from consistent individual differences in ways of organizing and processing information and experience. They appear to serve as high-level heuristics that organize more specific strategies, propensities and abilities into functional patterns characteristic of the individual. They function in part as controlling mechanisms determining an individual's characteristic regulation and control of attention, impulse, thought and behavioural expression in diverse areas (Gardner *et al.*, 1959; Gardner *et al.*, 1960; Klein, 1958, 1970).

In contrast with abilities, which refer to the content and level of cognition (the questions of What? and How much?), cognitive styles refer to the manner or form of cognition (the question of How?). In further contrast with abilities, which are unipolar and value directional (high amounts of ability are always preferable to low amounts and are uniformly more adaptive), cognitive styles are bipolar and value differentiated (each pole of a style dimension has different adaptive implications for cognitive functioning) (Messick, 1976c, 1981; Witkin and Goodenough, 1981). Cognitive styles also typically embrace personalistic and not merely cognitive consistencies, as in the instance of field independence versus field dependence, where the field-independent person is characterized as analytical, self-referent and impersonal in orientation and the field-dependent person as global, socially sensitive and interpersonal in orientation (Witkin, 1978; Witkin and Goodenough, 1981). Descriptions of other cognitive styles, such as scanning versus focusing, levelling versus sharpening, cognitive complexity versus simplicity, converging versus diverging, reflection versus impulsivity, and risk-taking versus cautiousness, appear in Messick (1970, 1976c), Kogan (1971), and Goldstein and Blackman (1978), along with discussions of relevant research.

A distinction is commonly made between cognitive styles and cognitive strategies — the former being spontaneously applied without conscious consideration or choice in a wide variety of situations and the latter reflecting decisions among alternative approaches as a function of task requirements, problem content and situational constraints (Bruner *et al.*, 1956; Shouksmith, 1970). Moreover, cognitive strategies are often selected, organized and controlled in part as a function of larger-scale, more general cognitive styles — as in the relationship between holist versus serialist strategies and the more general styles of comprehension learning versus operation learning (Pask, 1976). In comparison to styles, which tend to be stable and relatively pervasive across diverse areas, strategies are likely to be more amenable to change through instruction and training. It may indeed be possible for individuals not only to learn to use a variety of problem-solving and learning strategies that are consonant with their cognitive styles, but also to learn to shift to less congenial strategies that are more effective for a particular task.

Accumulating research evidence indicates that at least some cognitive styles variously influence how students learn, how teachers teach, how students and teachers interact, and how educational and vocational choices are made (Kogan, 1971; Witkin *et al.*, 1977). On this latter point, cognitive styles — by virtue of the differential adaptiveness of each pole of a style dimension — are especially useful in guidance because of the positive aspects of the message, regardless of which end of a cognitive style a student leans toward (Witkin, 1974). Since each pole of a cognitive style has adaptive value under different circumstances, attention has also been given to the possibility of effectively utilizing the positive features of both ends — as in Pask's (1976) 'versatile' learners who combine comprehension learning and operation learning, in Hudson's (1966) 'all-rounders' or intellectual 'labiles' who combine converging and diverging, and in the 'bicognitive' development of both field independence and field sensitivity espoused by Ramirez and Castañeda (1974).

This suggests that an important educational goal should be to develop and enhance flexibility in modes of thinking — to the degree possible, to convert cognitive styles into cognitive strategies, as it were, which could then be selectively and appropriately applied in learning and performance as a function of varied task requirements — thereby reducing to some extent the restrictiveness and preemptiveness of habitual thinking. As always, however, we must also consider and evaluate the potential dangers and trade-offs in such an enterprise — efforts to foster multiple modes of cognition may hamper some students from soaring in the unfettered application of their predominant style (Messick, 1970).

The Problem of the Match

This issue of trade-offs is the essence of the problem of the match between functional characteristics of learners on the one hand and the methods and materials of instruction and the conditions of learning on the other (Messick, 1976a). Of primary concern in deciding upon the match is the educational purpose to be served. Snow (1970, 1976) proposed two heuristic bases for matching, one as a means of compensating for learner weaknesses and the other of capitalizing on learner strengths. Compensatory matches are designed to circumvent the debilitative effects of learner deficiencies or disturbances without trying to remove or improve them, whereas capitalization matches ignore such deficiencies while exploiting what the student is already capable of doing well. Salomon (1972) elaborated these two principles and articulated a third, namely, corrective matching to eliminate learner weaknesses through remediation. In addition to these compensatory, capitalization and corrective matches, there are also challenge matches, which in actuality are mismatches — that is, a deliberate attempt is made to create conflict between instructional components and learner characteristics in order to challenge learners to change, to become more flexible, to increase the variety of strategies and modes of functioning in their repertoires (Messick, 1976b).

The complexity of the problem of the match is well illustrated by simply addressing the question of which instructional purpose to serve, granting that the complexity increases enormously with the questions of what to match and how — that is, when we confront the problems of prescription and of educational technology. But consider the intricacies of just asking what the purpose of the match should be? Lewis (1976, p. 307) attempts to short-circuit this problem with the following advice: 'In general, I am greatly in favour of helping students to develop their strengths.... In fact, there are only two circumstances in which I would seriously worry about a student's weaknesses. The first circumstance would arise if I detected in the student a weakness that was holding back the development of a strength. The second circumstance arises in connection with weaknesses that are sufficiently grave to have some enduring social stigma attaching to them, ... [such as] the inability to read and write.'

Unfortunately, the decision is more complicated than Lewis' advice implies, even granting that the detection of weaknesses that hold back strengths may not be a straightforward matter. For example, there is some evidence that if one looks only at immediate subject matter achievement, the elaboration of instruction to reduce the student's information-processing burden is beneficial for the less able learners but suboptimal for the most able; furthermore, it appears best to match the form in which instruction is elaborated, say verbally versus graphically, to the learner's relative strengths. Yet if retention is considered, minimally-elaborated instruction appears best, especially for highly able students, and it would seem better to mismatch the form of elaboration with the student's ability profile (Snow, 1980a). One possible reason for this is that 'retention requires cognitive organization, cognitive organization requires actual mental work, and active mental work for any given individual is prompted most by instruction that is incomplete for that particular individual' (Snow, 1980a, p. 56).

This is consistent with other research suggesting that, if students have the ability to educe and discover things for themselves, the form of instruction should encourage them to do so because in the long run their achievement will be stronger, better integrated with prior knowledge structures, and more transferable as a result (Egan and Greeno, 1973; Greeno, 1978, 1980). But what of students who do not have the ability to do things for themselves? This research suggests that one should be very careful about providing them consistently with the kind of instructional help they apparently need most — 'To conclude from this that low prior ability learners should be given a formula or rule learning treatment on the grounds that this produces the "most" learning for them would consign them to developing technical facility ... at the expense of general understanding and transferability' (Snow, 1980a, p. 50).

The finding of such aptitude-treatment interactions leads naturally to attempts to tailor instructional programmes to types of learner characteristics, if not directly to the individualization of instruction (Cronbach and Snow, 1977). This is important because, as Snow (1976, p. 292) proclaims in his Parkinsonian law of conservation of instructional effectiveness. 'no matter how you try to make an instructional treatment better for someone, you will make it worse for someone else.' Worse still, there is a particularly perverse corollary to Snow's law: 'No matter how you try to make an instructional treatment better in regard to one outcome, you will make it worse in regard to some other outcome' (Messick, 1976a, p. 266). Trade-offs are apparently intrinsic to the instructional enterprise, which is what makes the prospect of matching a problem.

Choices need to be made in each instance, although they are usually made by default, about the particular instructional purposes to be served or the particular learning outcomes sought — acquisition, retention, generalization and transfer, structuring and restructuring of knowledge, strategy selection, flexibility — as well as about *what* to prescribe for *whom* and *how* to effect the match. There is also the fundamental question of *who* should decide among the alternatives for the pursuit of *whose* social goals. Thus, even if the technical problems of prescription and implementation were solved, which is far from the case, and we had sufficient means available, we would still be faced with the challenge of choice among ends.

Although teachers and experts in instructional technology probably should have major prerogatives in deciding about desired learning outcomes in the short run and about what to match and how, they probably should not have complete discretion in these matters because that might foreclose some options regarding long-range goals, in which the student's stake should prevail. In attempts to resolve this issue of where the locus of choice should be, the notion of self-matching to educational treatments has emerged as a viable strategy, even in elementary education but especially for higher education (Glaser, 1973, 1977; Hunt, 1975; Messick, 1976b). This would of course require some appropriate educational groundwork to facilitate the development of self-management skills, self-directed learning, and informed student choice.

The major difficulty with self-matching is in the area of self-assessment, particularly in the extent to which students are able to distinguish between the instructional treatments or environments they need and those they want. But this might be addressed by developing a system in which students could directly sample various learning options or instructional modes so that they could, with some guidance, base relatively long-term commitments — course-long not school-long or life-long — on short-term experiences (Glaser, 1973; Hunt, 1975). The very existence of instructional options and freedom of choice might have beneficial educational effects. Critical to the success of self-matching is the flexibility afforded by provisional choice and the willingness of educators to vest in the student major responsibility for determining means as well as ends. As Hunt (1975, pp. 224–5) phrased it, 'Educational arrangements in which the student is entirely responsible for matching himself to an educational environment raise basic questions about the nature of student needs and who is to define them. Whatever one's stance on this issue, it seems clear that more attention should be paid to the question of how students can learn to make more appropriate choices.' Such choices about the context of learning and teaching would seem to be fundamentally recursive in that they depend on the student's developed structures of abilities, knowledge, and style and aim to enhance or transform these structures in a continual process of future choice.

References

ANDERSON, L.M.(1981) 'Student responses to seatwork: Implications for the study of students', Cognitive Processing, paper presented at the annual meeting of the American Educational Research Association, Los Angeles.

BERLYNE, D.E. (1965) *Structure and Direction in Thinking*, New York, Wiley.

BIGGS, J. B. and COLLIS. K.F. (1980) 'The solo taxonomy', *Education News*, 17.

BRUNER, J.S. (1956) *A Study of Thinking*, New York, Wiley.

BRUNER, J.S. (1966) *Studies in Cognitive Growth*, New York, Wiley.

BURT, C. 1949, 'The structure of the mind: A review of the results of factor analysis'. *British Journal of Educational Psychology*, 19, pp. 100–11; 176–99.

CATTELL, R.B. (1971) *Abilities: Their Structure, Growth, and Action*, New York, Houghton Mifflin.

CHI, M.T.H. *et al.* (1981) 'Representation of physics knowledge by experts and novices', *Cognitive Science*, 5, pp. 121–52.

CHIESI, H.L. *et al.* (1979) 'Acquisition of domain-related information in relation to high and low domain knowledge', *Journal of Verbal Learning and Verbal Behavior*, 18, pp. 257–73.

CLARK, M.M. (1982) 'Young children', *Educational Analysis*, 4, 2, pp. 55–9.

COLE, M. and BRUNER, J.S. (1971) 'Cultural differences and inferences about psychological processes', *American Psychologist*, 26, pp. 867–76.

COLE, M. *et al.* (1971) *The Cultural Context of Learning and Thinking*, New York, Basic Books.

CRONBACH, L. J. and SNOW, R.E. (1977) *Aptitudes and Instructional Methods*, New York, Wiley.

DAVIES, G.M. and NISBET, J. (1981) 'Cognitive psychology and curriculum development', *Studies in Science Education*, 8, pp. 127–34.

DESFORGES, C. (1982) 'In place of Piaget: Recent research on children's learning'. *Educational Analysis*, 4, 2, pp. 27–41.

DRIVER, R. (1982) 'Children's learning in science', *Educational Analysis*, 4, 2, pp. 69–79.

EGAN, D. E. and GREENO, J.G. (1973) 'Acquiring cognitive structure by discovery and rule learning', *Journal of Educational Psychology*, 64, pp. 85–97.

EKSTROM, R.B. *et al.* (1976) *Manual and Kit of Factor-Referenced Cognitive Tests*, Princeton, N.J., Educational Testing Service.

ENTWISTLE, N. (1982) 'Approaches and styles: Recent research on students' learning', *Educational Analysis*, 4, 2, pp. 43–54.

EYSENCK, H.J. (1982) 'Heredity and environment: The state of the debate', *Educational Analysis*, 4, 2, pp. 7–16.

FERGUSON, G.A. (1954) 'On learning and human ability', *Canadian Journal of Psychology*, 8, pp. 95–111.

FERGUSON, G.A. (1956) 'On transfer and the abilities of man', *Canadian Journal of Psychology*, 10, pp. 121–31.

FEUERSTEIN, R. (1979) *The Dynamic Assessment of Retarded Performers: The Learning Potential Assessment Device, Theory, Instruments, and Techniques*, Baltimore, Md., University Park Press.

FEUERSTEIN, R. (1980) *Instrumental Enrichment: An Intervention Program for Cognitive Modifiability*, Baltimore, Md., University Park Press.

FURNEAUX, B.(1982) 'Special education', *Educational Analysis*, 4, 2, pp. 81–5.

GARDNER, R.W. *et al.* (1959) 'Cognitive control: A study of individual consistencies in cognitive behavior', *Psychological Issues*, 1, Monograph 4.

GARDNER, R.W. *et al.* (1960) 'Personality organization in cognitive controls and intellectual abilities', *Psychological Issues*, 2, Monograph 8.

GLASER, R. (1973) 'Educational psychology and education', *American Psychologist*, 28, pp. 557–66.

GLASER, R. (1977) *Adaptive Education: Individual Diversity and Learning*, New York, Holt, Rinehart and Winston.

GLASER, R. (1981) 'The future of testing: A research agenda for cognitive psychology and psychometrics', *American Psychologist*, 36, pp. 923–36.

GOLDSTEIN, K.M. and BLACKMAN, S. (1978) *Cognitive Style: Five Approaches and Relevant Research*, New York, Wiley.

GREENO, J. G. (1978) 'A study of problem solving', in GLASER, R. (Ed.), *Advances in Instructional Psychology*, Vol. 1, Hillsdale, N.J., Erlbaum.

GREENO, J.G. (1980) 'Some examples of cognitive task analysis with instructional implications', in SNOW, R.E. *et al.* (Eds), *Aptitude, Learning and Instruction, Vol. 2: Cognitive Process Analyses of Learning and Problem Solving*, Hillsdale, N.J., Erlbaum.

GUILFORD, J.R. (1967) *The Nature of Human Intelligence*, New York, McGraw-Hill.

HASKSTIAN, A.R. and CATTELL, R.B. (1974) 'The checking of primary ability structure on a broader basis of performances', *British Journal of Educational Psychology*, 74, pp. 140–54.

HELLER, K. *et al.* (1982) *Placing Children in Special Education: A Strategy for Equity*, Washington, D.C, National Academy Press.

HUDSON, L. (1966) *Contrary Imaginations*, New York, Schocken Books.

HUNT, D.E. (1975) 'Person-environment interaction: A challenge found wanting before it was tried', *Review of Educational Research*, 45, pp. 209–30.

HUNT, J.McV. (1961) *Intelligence and Experience*, New York, Ronald Press.

HUNT, J.McV. (1980) *Early Psychological Development and Experience*, Worcester, Mass, Clark University Press.

HUNTER, I.M.L. (1982) 'Acquiring complex abilities', *Educational Analysis*, 4, 2, pp. 17–25.

KLEIN, G.S. (1958) 'Cognitive control and motivation', in LINDZEY, G. (Ed.), *Assessment of Human Motives*, New York, Holt, Rinehart and Winston.

KLEIN, G.S. (1970) *Perception, Motives and Personality*, New York, Knopf.

KOGAN, N. (1971) 'Educational implications of cognitive styles', in LESSER, G.S. (Ed.), *Psychology and Educational Practice*, Glenview, Ill., Scott Foresman.

LARKIN, J.H. *et al.* (1980a) 'Expert and novice performance in solving physics problems', *Science*, 208, pp. 1335–42.

LARKIN, J.H. *et al.* (1980b) 'Models of competence in solving physics problems', *Cognitive Science*, 4, pp. 317–45.

LESSER, G.S. *et al.* (1965) 'Mental abilities of children from different social-class and cultural groups, *Monographs of the Society for Research in Child Development*, 30, 4, Serial No. 102.

LEWIS, B. (1976) 'Aptitude-treatment trivialities', in MESSICK, S. (Ed.), *Individuality in Learning: Implications of Cognitive Styles and Creativity for Human Development*, San Francisco, Jossey-Bass.

LOVELL, K. (1980) 'The relevance of cognitive psychology to science and mathematics education', in ARCHENHOLD, W.F. *et al.*, *Cognitive Development Research in Science and Mathematics*, Leeds, Centre for Studies in Science Education.

McDOUGALL, W. (1923) *Outline of Psychology*, New York, Scribners.

MESSICK, S. (1970) 'The criterion problem in the evaluation of instruction: Assessing possible, not just intended, outcomes', in WITTROCK, M.C. and WILEY, D.W. (Eds), *The Evaluation of Instruction: Issues and Problems*, New York, Holt, Rinehart and Winston.

MESSICK, S. (1972) 'Beyond structure: In search of functional models of psychological process', *Psychometrika*, 37, pp. 357–75.

MESSICK, S. (1973) 'Multivariate models of cognition and personality: The need for both process and structure in psychological theory and measurement', in ROYCE, J.R. (Ed.), *Multivariate Analysis and Psychological Theory*, New York, Academic Press.

MESSICK, S. (Ed.) (1976a) *Individuality in Learning: Implications of Cognitive Styles and Creativity for Human Development*, San Francisco, Jossey-Bass.

MESSICK, S. (1976b) 'Personal styles and educational options', in MESSICK, S. (Ed.), *Individuality in Learning: Implications of Cognitive Styles and Creativity for Human Development*, San Francisco, Jossey-Bass.

MESSICK, S. (1976c) 'Personality consistencies in cognition and creativity', in MESSICK, S. (Ed.), *Individuality in Learning: Implications of Cognitive Styles and Creativity for Human Development*, San Francisco, Jossey-Bass.

MESSICK, S. (1979) 'Potential uses of noncognitive measurement in education,' *Journal of Educational Psychology*, 71, pp. 281–92.

MESSICK, S. (1980) *The Effectiveness of Coaching for the SAT: Review and Reanalysis of Research from the Fifties to the FTC*, (ETS RR 80–8), Princeton, N.J., Educational Testing Service.

MESSICK, S. (1981) 'The controversy over coaching: issues of effectiveness and equity', *New Directions for Testing and Measurement*, 11, 21–53.

MESSICK, S. and BARROWS, T.S. (1972) 'Strategies for research and evaluation in early childhood education', in GORDON, I. (Ed.), *Early Childhood Education*, Chicago, National Society for the Study of Education.

MESSICK, S. and SIGEL, I. (1982) 'Conceptual and methodological issues in facilitating growth in intelligence', in DETTERMAN, D.K. and STERNBERG, R.J. (Eds), *How and How Much Can Intelligence Be Increased?* Norwood, N.J. Ablex.

MILLER, G.A. *et al.* (1960) *Plans and the Structure of Behavior*, New York, Holt.

NEWELL, A. and SIMON, H.A. (1972) *Human Problem Solving*, Englewood Cliffs, N.J. Prentice-Hall.

NISBET, J. and ENTWISTLE, N. (1982) 'Changing views on ability', *Educational Analysis*, 4, 2, pp. 1–6.

PASK, G. (1976) 'Styles and strategies of learning', *British Journal of Educational Psychology*, 46, pp. 128–48.

RAMIREZ. M. and CASTANEDA, A. (1974) *Cultural Democracy, Bicognitive Development and Education*, New York, Academic Press.

RAMSDEN, P. and ENTWISTLE, N.J. (1981) 'Effects of academic departments on students' approaches to studying', *British Journal of Educational Psychology*, 51, pp. 368–83.

SALOMON, G. (1972) 'Heuristic models for the generation of aptitude-treatment interaction hypotheses', *Review of Educational Research*, 42, pp. 327–43.

SHOUKSMITH, G. (1970) *Intelligence, Creativity and Cognitive Style*, New York, Wiley-Interscience.

SIGEL, I.E. (1970) 'The distancing hypothesis: A causal hypothesis for the acquisition of representational thought', in JONES, M.R. (Ed.), *Miami Symposium on the Prediction of Behavior, 1968: Effect of Early Experiences*, Coral Gables, Flo., University of Miami Press.

SIGEL, I.E. (1979) 'On becoming a thinker: A psychoeducational model', *Educational Psychologist*, 14, pp. 70–8.

SKEMP, R.R. (1982) 'Mathematics as an activity of our intelligence', *Educational Analysis*, 4, 2, pp. 61–7.

SNOW, R.E. (1970) 'Research on media and aptitudes', *Bulletin of the Indiana University of Education*, 46, pp. 63–91.

SNOW, R.E. (1976) 'Aptitude-Treatment interactions and individualized alternatives in higher education', in MESSICK, S. (Ed.), *Individuality in Learning: Implications of Cognitive Styles and Creativity for Human Development*, San Francisco, Jossey-Bass.

SNOW, R.E. (1980a) 'Aptitude and achievement', in SCHRADER, W.B. (Ed.), *New*

Directions for Testing and Measurement — Measuring Achievement: Progress over a Decade (Proceedings of the 1979 ETS Invitational Conference), San Francisco, Jossey-Bass.

SNOW, R.E. (1980b) 'Aptitude processes', in SNOW, R.E. *et al.* (Eds) *Aptitude, Learning and Instruction, Vol. 1: Cognitive Process Analyses of Aptitude*, Hillsdale, N.J., Erlbaum.

STERNBERG, R.J. (1977) *Intelligence, Information Processing, and Analogical Reasoning: The Componential Analysis of Human Abilities*, Hillsadle, N.J., Erlbaum.

TOBIAS, S. (1976), 'Achievement treatment interactions', *Review of Educational Research*, 46, pp. 61–74.

VERNON, P.E. (1973) 'Multivariate approaches to the study of cognitive styles', in ROYCE, J.R. (Ed.), *Multivariate Analysis and Psychological Theory*, New York, Academic Press.

VYGOTSKY, L.S. (1962) *Thought and Language*, Cambridge, Mass., MIT Press.

VYGOTSKY, L.S. (1978) *Mind in Society: The Development of Higher Psychological Processes*, Cambridge, Mass., Harvard University Press.

WITKIN, H.A. (1974) 'A cognitive-style perspective on evaluation and guidance', *Proceedings of the 1973 Invitational Conference on Testing Problem — Measurement for Self-Understanding and Personal Development*, Princeton, N.J, Educational Testing Service.

WITKIN, H.A. (1978) *Cognitive Styles in Personal and Cultural Adaptation*, Worcester, Mass., Clark University Press.

WITKIN, H.A. and GOODENOUGH, D.R. (1981) *Cognitive Styles: Essence and Origins — Field Dependence and Field Independence*, New York, International Universities Press.

WITKIN, H.A. *et al.* (1977) 'Field-dependent and field-independent cognitive styles and their educational implications', *Review of Educational Research*, 47, pp. 1–64.

Matching Learning and Teaching: The Interactive Approach in Educational Psychology

Peter Tomlinson
University of Leeds

The interactive approach has emerged as a major theme in educational psychology over the last decade or so, most clearly on the North American scene. But its roots go back a good deal further, both in the form of theoretical ideas and of the traditional intuitions of practising teachers. This chapter will take advantage of this fact in presenting the interactive approach: the topic will be introduced via the intuitive and often implicit versions that can be discerned in everyday teaching, then I shall outline some of the systematic notions developed recently. This will lead naturally into some examples of interactive research and teaching applications, with particular references to Hunt's work on the matching of teaching strategy with learners' conceptual levels. The chapter will round off with a brief consideration of some of the broader applications and implications of this approach in education.

In educational terms the essence of this approach may be summed up as the view that *effective teaching depends not just on any single factor, but on the interplay (interaction) of many features in the teaching situation*: such as the nature of the topic, kind of teaching strategy used, age, ability, motivation, previous experience of the pupils, similar aspects of the teacher, available resources, and possibly even such specific factors as time of day. Like most powerful insights, this one sounds obvious when stated: we tend to recognize it as part of 'common sense', i.e., something we can all take for granted. 'Commonsense theories' tend, precisely by virtue of their everyday informality, not to be coherent and systematic, but, nevertheless, if we listen carefully to teachers' everyday talk we can note certain well-established intuitive versions of interactionism, however general or fragmentary, positive or negative.

At the broad, positive end examples are: 'different kids learn in different ways' and 'So is this the best way of teaching topic X? Well, it depends...'; more negatively: 'How does he expect me to teach a class of such mixed ability and background?' and 'What works for one doesn't necessarily work for another.' More fragmented, but still with strong interactive implications, are such statements as 'all children are different' — in respect, presumably, of the approaches from which they will profit most. Something very similar is also implied by the saying that 'all education is special education': namely that the particular characteristics of learners should always be taken into account, not just when they are highly exceptional. Whilst any teaching situation will involve a great many features that might influence the effectiveness of the teacher's efforts to do his job, i.e., promote learning and interest, a summarizing theme that emerges is that these varied features eventually group under two headings: the nature of the learner and the nature of the teaching. Their interplay is crucial. In other words, what one gets by way of teaching outcome depends both on what the learner is like and on what the learner gets. It is noteworthy in this context that in Stones' and Anderson's (1972) survey amongst teachers, student-teachers and college tutors the most important objectives of teaching educational psychology in teacher training were held to relate to ability to adapt teaching to varying pupils and situations.

The traditional concern of psychology has been with the individual: the individual's behaviour, motivation, perception and thought, learning processes, and so on. But the need to see the individual essentially in interaction with his surroundings has been stressed by a number of distinguished psychologists. In terms of general approaches to behaviour, for example, Lewin (1951) offered the principle that 'behaviour (B) is a function of the person's (P) interaction with his environment (E), which he summarized in the quasi-mathematical form $B = f(P,E)$. In terms of research emphasis, Cronbach pointed out in his important 1957 presidential address to the American Psychological Association that there was a pressing need to combine the two main approaches or 'disciplines' in scientific psychology, the experimental and the correlational. This would allow one to gauge not just 'what works', but 'what works for whom'.

It should be noted that this interactive stance may be applied, in principle, to any psychological theory concerning the nature of processes within the person. We have here not so much a theory as a 'metatheory', so called because the approach goes beyond, is more general than, particular psychological process theories. Having said this, some psychological theories are more obviously interpretable interactively than others; Hunt and Sullivan (1974) review various educational psychological views in terms of their interactive potential. Equally, it is possible to investigate particular combinations of teaching approach and pupil characteristic without reference to the sort of general framework being introduced here. Riding's chapter in a recent collection (Wheldall and Riding, 1982) illustrates such a pragmatic focus.

Aptitude-Treatment Interactions

The development of interactive approaches in educational psychology has followed a number of parallel strands which have led, as we shall see, to a broadly similar position. In North American circles the approach has, typically, been more explicit and systematic, with a development of ideas and corresponding jargon. In Britain our more 'pragmatic-intuitive' emphasis on getting to grips with real-life teaching in all its messy complexity may make us reticent about explicit formulation of systematic ideas, but our focus on the classroom has brought interactive themes to varying levels of awareness. In this section I shall therefore look at the Transatlantic scene, dealing first with the major facets of *aptitude-treatment interaction (ATI)* research and then the parallel *matching models* approach of David Hunt's group, illustrating some of the general issues by reference to his particular research focus. We will then draw out some of the interactive strands in recent British educational psychology in readiness for an appraisal of the implications and applications of the approach in a final section of the chapter.

Having called for the integrated study of causal influences and individual differences, and then more specifically of individual variation in aptitude in relation to different instructional methods (Cronbach, 1967), Lee Cronbach and his colleague Richard Snow practised what they were preaching by surveying the educational research literature for studies demonstrating interaction effects and by presenting a systematic treatment of the ideas and research methods implied by the interactive approach. Their 1977 handbook, *Aptitudes and Instructional Methods*, is a contribution of massive thoroughness, and has recently been brought up to date (Snow *et al.*, 1980). The methodological treatment goes to very advanced levels, but the central notion is that of an *aptitude-treatment interaction* (ATI). This is most directly conveyed through graphical representation (see Figures 1 and 2). It will be seen that in each figure the teaching outcome effects (vertical axis) for two hypothetical teaching approaches (treatments) vary according to pupils' scores on the aptitude dimension portrayed on the horizontal axis. In other words, the interaction of aptitude level and treatment type has a significant effect. In Figure 1 the interaction is termed *disordinal* because the relative effectiveness of teaching types A and B is reversed according to whether a pupil is high or low on the aptitude. Figure 2 portrays an *ordinal* interaction, in which the difference between approaches A and B varies according to aptitude level of recipient, but not to the extent of significantly reversing their effectiveness.

Obvious though an interactive approach may be, early reviews of research left the impression of two main setbacks to it. First, the occurrence of significant ATIs seemed rather rare, especially disordinal ATIs. Second, when ATI effects were found, they did not appear reliable; that is, there was difficulty in replicating them (Tobias, 1981).

Peter Tomlinson

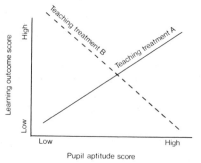

Figure 1: Example of a Disordinal Interaction

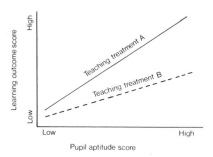

Figure 2: Example of an Ordinal Interaction

The response of the interactionists has been instructive, nevertheless. Cronbach and Snow (1977) offer some complex methodological arguments for their view that critics such as Bracht had been too narrow in their criteria. With writers such as Hunt (1975) they also make the more basic general point that different types of teaching process will only result in differing effectiveness when the receiving pupils vary in characteristics that relate to the particular teaching/learning *processes* involved. For whilst the measurement of individual qualities and differences had been the traditional focus of the correlational or psychometric branch of psychology, its tests were designed more for classification of individuals on the basic of their products than for understanding how they might go about task processes (Ferguson, 1976; Eysenck, 1967a). It is not surprising, therefore, that the relevance of IQ scores to classroom teaching has been problematic for generations of teachers. One cannot, in other words, simply throw together the two traditional disciplines of academic psychology in the hope of producing useful interactive findings for teaching. Rather, one will need to seek 'new aptitudes' (Glaser, 1972, 1977), i.e., personal characteristics that might affect engagement in the sorts of processes that are varied by differing teaching methods. This new line of investigation of 'aptitude processes' in ATI circles is now proceeding apace (cf. Snow *et al.*, 1980), utilizing a number of methodological techniques of multivariate statistical analysis originally developed in the individual differences testing approach.

A second insight of relevance both to the apparent rarity of early ATI findings and to their unreliability has been the realization that if it was naive to look at just one kind of causal factor, such as teaching method, in order to discover what one presumed would be best for everyone, then it is going little further to make allowance also for just one form of individual characteristic in the pupils which might modify the treatment effects. Effective outcome might depend on what sort of person (aptitude level) is receiving what kind of teaching (treatment), yielding an aptitude-treatment interaction. But the success of that particular aptitude-treatment combination might depend also on the type of subject or task being taught, yielding a three-way aptitude-treatment-task interaction (ATTI). More generally, there may be a number of individual pupil qualities that interact with each other and with a number of features of the teaching treatment, to produce results that will be hard to pin down unless many aspects of an investigation can be monitored and held constant. In Lewin's (BPE) terms, the *behaviour* or outcome may depend on the interplay of multiple aspects of the *person* (including aspects of their ability, motivation, processing styles, and so on) with multiple features of the educational *environment* to which they are exposed (teaching methods and style aspects, teacher temperament, topic, resources, etc.).

This broader notion of interaction has now become firmly embedded in North American educational psychology, as is evidenced, for instance, by its being one of the major recurring themes in the recent review edited by Farley and Gordon (1981). We have thus progressed from the relatively simple notion of an interaction between person and environment to the idea that was presented in commonsense terms at the outset of this chapter, namely that teaching effectiveness depends on the interplay of a wide variety of features of the teaching situation. These may range from stable characteristics of the pupils, teachers and their actions, to transient and unpredictable events of considerable power; thus Friday afternoons with 4D may tend to be bad, but even with 4D they are occasionally enjoyable!

Complete individualization means matching a whole range of specific aspects of a pupil; the more aspects, the more difficult the matching. But individualization need not be all or none. Any inroad we can make into the complexity, any extent to which we can begin to match necessary features of a pupil or group of pupils has to be welcomed, including relatively simple ATI effects. Which leads us to ask what findings the approach has thrown up. In fact, these are not easy to summarize: Cronbach's and Snow's (1977) survey is exhaustively detailed and the interested reader will also find Tobias' (1981) chapter and its references useful in taking the topic further. Here I must limit myself to an illustration of major examples: first, the systematic and sustained work of David Hunt and his Toronto group on matching models in education, and second, some British versions of the approach.

Conceptual Systems Theory

If the ATI version of interactionism takes its themes from research methodology, the parallel development of David Hunt's matching models approach has, as its name perhaps suggests, been a more positive movement. Hunt has long been advocating the direct application of the Lewin $B=f(P,E)$ approach to education (Hunt, 1966, 1971, 1976; Hunt and Sullivan, 1974). That is, if the outcome effects of teaching (Lewin's B) are likely to depend on the interplay between the pupil's characteristics (P) and the nature of the teaching or educational environment (E) to which they are exposed, then this should make us concerned to discover what kinds of learner characteristic may have such effects, and to adapt our teaching accordingly. The good teacher, by definition, is one who has somehow achieved such a capacity; but we need to understand what is going on as clearly as possible, not least so that we can train other teachers effectively. We need, in other words, 'matching models of teaching'.

Hunt's own researches have concentrated on the educational interaction aspects of a personal characteristic called *conceptual level* (CL). This is a notion deriving from *conceptual systems theory*, originally put forward by Harvey, Hunt and Schroder (1961). This cognitive approach to personality arose out of personal construct theory as formulated by George Kelly, under whom both Hunt and Schroder had studied. Of central concern in conceptual systems theory is the degree of complexity and flexibility of a person's outlook, particularly on social and personal decision-issues. It is not only a personality theory of individual differences but also a developmental theory, for it proposes that (under appropriate circumstances) individuals will proceed through the following levels of conceptual complexity during adolescence and beyond. These levels relate to the ways in which information and perspectives are integrated in everyday problem-solving; although they have been variously labelled by workers in this tradition, the following presentation uses Hunt's original notation:

Level 0: Lack of systematic thinking about an issue; tendency to react blindly, either aggressively or defensively by withdrawal/denial; sole concern with own immediate wants.

Level 1: Single perspective outlook, often of an absolute, all-or-none type. Tendency to compartmentalize, minimize conflict, depend on external sources for certainty/correctness.

Level 2: Awareness of alternative perspectives on an issue, often with some emphasis on plurality of viewpoints, indeterminacy of issues and own individuality of outlook.

Level 3: Awareness of alternative perspectives, but with the further capacity to compare them on the basis of common features and purpose, yielding insight into nature and need of compromise and adaptability; often an emphasis on mutuality of different personal perspectives.

Level 4: The capacity to compare and link not just particular sets of outlooks amongst themselves, but whole systems of thinking involving radically different assumptions.

Some readers will recognize these levels as very similar to those of the recently presented SOLO taxonomy (see pp. 290–2, this volume) for the qualitative assessment of learning (Biggs and Collis, 1982). A fuller introduction and further references on CL are available in Tomlinson (1981a), but even from the above bare outline it will be seen that these different conceptual levels involve increasingly complex ways of taking account of and integrating information. Indeed, CL is typically assessed by using a manual on which one has been trained to score responses to such paragraph openers as 'What I think about rules . . .', 'When I'm not sure . . .', 'When someone disagrees with me. . . .' Schroder's (1967) work demonstrated that such CL scores predict complexity of problem-solving processes in realistic situations. That young people follow this order of stages insofar as they develop interpersonal perspectives during the teenage years has been shown in various ways, most recently by a six-year longitudinal study by the present writer (Tomlinson, 1981b). This study also confirmed that considerable variation in CL is to be found at any particular age and that progress beyond level 2 is relatively rare.

CL is thus a clear case of a process-related personal attribute: it involves a person's disposition to see regularities, make distinctions, draw together strands and relationships, in a word, to cope with the structures in information. As such, it appeared to Hunt that a learner's CL might be likely to interact with the amount of structure inherent in a teaching method he received. Those low on CL do not appear to generate much of their own structuring, so they ought to profit from having more features of learning content formulated and presented explicitly by the teacher. On the other hand, high CL individuals might not only not need such a degree of 'spoonfeeding', they might actually be put off by it. At the beginning of the 1970s, therefore, prompted by the hitherto inconclusive debates concerning discovery versus traditional teaching approaches, Hunt and his colleagues began investigating the interaction of learner CL with variations in teaching structure. A very thorough review of CL-based studies has recently been provided by Miller (1981), and Hunt and Sullivan (1974) survey the early work, which on the whole confirmed the hypothesized interaction. A study conducted by myself with David Hunt (Tomlinson and Hunt, 1971) may serve as an illustration.

In this small-scale study a social science concept was taught to groups of secondary school pupils using three approaches varying in degree of structure provided by the teaching material. In the strongest form of structuring learners were provided first with a definition of the concept, followed by examples embedded in a continuous prose narrative. In the intermediate structure condition, they were first presented with the narrative and invited to seek ('discover') recurring instances of a common type of experience (the examples) before being provided with the definition also. In the low structure condition they were given the narrative text only (though they were briefly exposed to the definition after they had used the examples-only text). Although as is typical in this sort of study, the more structured treatment showed a superior effect on immediate post-tests of concrete elements, a one-week post-test on a composite of different kinds of learning indicator showed results of the form depicted in Figure 3. This pattern represents an ordinal interaction between CL and teaching method structure: high CL pupils profited equally well from all three types of teaching approach, whereas low CL pupils did significantly worse on intermediate and low structure. They did do as well as high CL pupils when provided with high structure in the form of definitions preceding example material. Other studies by members of Hunt's group showed similar results, which served to underline the naîvety of expecting there to be 'one best method' for everyone, the establishment of which might have settled the discovery-traditional debate.

Studies such as these have led Hunt and his group to develop a number of ideas and implications in their matching models interactive approach. A central pair of concepts are *congruent and developmental matching*. On the basis of the above sort of finding, we would want to try to directly match low CL learners' needs by providing more structured teaching, i.e., approaches which are congruent with their characteristics. We would be doing this in

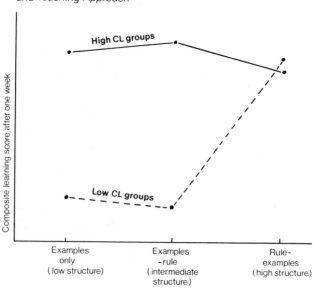

Figure 3: Concept Learning Scores as a Function of Pupil CL and Teaching Approach

Source: Based on Tomlinson and Hunt (1971)

order to teach, i.e., change their capacity, in something other than CL. On the other hand, it might be thought that such congruent matching might actually tend to hold the person at his or her low CL. Whilst this raises many issues and distinctions that cannot be gone into here, it serves to highlight the need for a concept of developmental matching. For when we are dealing with a personal characteristic which may itself develop, then we may wish to foster such development precisely by not framing things in terms of the current level, but by providing an approach likely to promote developmental progress, e.g., by 'stretching' the person towards the next stage up. Conceptual systems theory levels and Piagetian stages would constitute examples of such characteristics. We may on occasions need to engage in developmental matching before going on to some form of congruent matching, perhaps in the sense of first ensuring that a given subskill level is present before teaching a further aspect of a complex domain using a congruent approach.

It will be noticed that the interactive way of looking at individual characteristics is more positive and 'dynamic', i.e., process-oriented, than the traditional test-score approach, with its tendency to become the basis for a permanent labelling of the learner. Hunt underlines this view by suggesting that we should see pupil qualities as their 'accessibility characteristics' which teaching must match if it is to effectively reach them.

In recent years (e.g., 1976) Hunt has been investigating the implementation of a matching approach in school settings. As he points out, many aspects of matching are known to teachers at least intuitively; a major need is to develop a plausible vocabulary for expressing these notions and further informing them by relevant insights from ATI-type research. Thus, for instance, one practical implication of an interactive matching approach is that teachers should develop skills of perceiving relevant features of the pupil as well as those of flexibly adapting their approach to suit such features. As Hunt puts it, teachers need to 'read' and 'flex'. This may take place at very many levels of unit in the teaching process, from an immediate answer to a pupil's question (where one is trying to answer *his* particular question), through to broader strategy issues such as the sort of approach to a subject to use with lower 4D this term. The question of pupil grouping thus becomes an obvious issue in a matching approach, but for once it may be informed by relevant, instruction-related theory, rather than simply by social tradition or individual assumption regarding the classification of pupils. An early study by Hunt (1966), for instance, showed that homogeneous grouping (i.e., 'streaming', 'tracking') by CL produced classes which differed systematically in such respects as their classroom behaviour style and mode of approaching group discussion and questioning.

Like any good educational theory, the conceptual systems matching approach can and should be used reflexively: the model is applicable not just to subject teaching in school and college, but also to the training of teachers and even the training of teacher-trainers. As Hunt (1976) argues, the interactive approach provides a framework which can unite educational practitioner and psychologist in a common search for insight and skill development.

British Versions of Interactionism

The status of interactive notions on the British scene perhaps reflects our general tendency to distrust systematic 'grand theory' in favour of a sometimes unorganized, though often sensitive, awareness of the subtle complexities of a topic. Thus, whilst there have been (1) various educational practices and issues that have implied an interactive awareness and (2) some major British research on personality differences that might imply a matching style of application, nevertheless, (3) work informed explicitly by these themes has been forthcoming only in the relatively recent past. I now want briefly to illustrate these three categories.

Practices and Issues

Major British educational issues over the last few decades have included the across-schools question of selecting pupils at 11+ years of age and the within-school issue of streaming versus mixed ability grouping. In both cases there would appear to be some underlying assumptions of an interactive/matching nature. However, in both cases the model appears to be rather crude and narrow. Selection at 11+ seems to involve 'cobbling together' applications of Cronbach's two disciplines, namely individual difference testing (IQ and other standardized tests) and differing educational treatment; indeed, a leading British writer went so far as to describe it as a case where 'an advanced technology of mental testing has been used to some degree to prop outdated social distinctions' (Butcher, 1968). At any event, the implicit model of both 11+ segregation and ability-based streaming often appears to go no further than the crudely commonsensical 'some kids are duller, so they need to be taught at a slower rate, others are brighter and can be taught more (of the same) and faster.' Unfortunately the opposition, i.e., proponents of mixed ability teaching, sometimes seem to hold equally naive (though opposite) assumptions. Examination of the issues and relevant literature reveals, of course, that there is far more to it than this, but here I must content myself with the comment that it is unfortunate that what interactionism we have found in these perennial British concerns has limited itself to congruent matching of product-assessed ability, with all the social-motivational problems of self-esteem and labelling that this is known to bring. Taking a process-related approach might have more useful educational matching applications, though as we shall see in the following subsection, British educationalists have not necessarily derived such lessons from process-related research on interaction.

Personality Differences

At least two major areas of British educational psychological research have yielded interactive patterns of results. In the 1960s there were a number of British studies (see, for instance, Naylor, 1972, for a summary) indicating on the whole that extravert pupils achieved more at primary school, whilst in secondary and higher education it is introverts that fare better. Post-primary changes in predominant teaching approach, atmosphere and study demand would seem to be interacting with pupil personality disposition. Although Eysenck has long advocated an interactive approach in the area of social learning (cf. Eysenck, 1967b) I know of no moves to apply the matching model implications of the above findings, for instance, in the form suggested by Eysenck himself, of 'streaming' on the rather neutral but relevant basis of extraversion-introversion of pupil (and/or of teacher, one might add). In another area, namely the domain of sex-differences, there does, however, seem to be an emerging awareness of some of the subtle interactions that affect differential academic achievement by girls and boys in varying subjects, together with a corresponding consideration of appropriate matching in school provision (Shaw, 1980).

Research on Interactions

This brings us to British work of an explicitly interactive type. Here one can discern strands corresponding to what I earlier introduced as, on the one hand, a more specific person-environment or ATI/BPE kind of approach, and on the other hand, a more generalized interactionism which sees teaching outcomes as depending on a constant and extended interplay of all sorts of factors in the educational context, including persons and processes.

The clearest and most systematic example of the former strand must be the work of Pask (see Daniel, 1975). Working largely in the area of programmed learning (which has long shown concern for matching instruction to learner), Pask has formally set out an interactive or, as he puts it, 'conversational' theory of instruction and he has extensively studied the matching of instructional approach to preferred strategies, or styles, of learning in terms of the distinction between *holists* and *serialists*. Essentially, holists (or 'comprehension learners') take an approach which stresses the overall picture and the relation of particular learning content items to it and each other, whilst serialists ('operation learners') build up their knowledge bit by bit. Whilst these different styles of approach have their different strengths and weaknesses, Pask finds that they will lead to equally effective learning when congruently matched by the teaching approach (holist teaching for holists, serialist teaching for serialists). Moreover, in various studies in which mismatched conditions have been included, clear disordinal interactions occurred, with the mismatched learners being severely disrupted.

Other instances of interactive research designs have recently been summarized by Riding (1982), describing the adaptation of teaching to pupils' *visualizing* vs *verbalizing* styles of representation and to their degree of *field-dependence/independence*, i.e., capacity to distinguish elements from their context (cf. Witkin *et al.*, 1977). Relating these to the personality dimension of extraversion-introversion, Riding also raises the question which we saw earlier as having been revitalized by North American ATI work, namely the interrelations amongst the various pupil characteristics we might assess and match instructionally.

Finally, one of the healthier emphases in recent British educational research has been the attempt to get to grips with what actually takes place in schools and classrooms. Following his earlier work on teaching styles, for instance, Neville Bennett has turned with Charles Desforges to look at the ways in which infant school teachers actually attempt to match the tasks they set to the children in their classes (see pp. 161–172, this volume).

Broader Implications

In this concluding section I want to draw together some of the broader points that have been implied more or less directly hitherto. Interactive educational psychology would seem to carry various advantages, both as an *approach* framed either at the general level of an openness to any number of possible interacting factors or in its minimal form of interactions between person-environment, or learner-teaching treatment. It could also be seen as a *data resource*, insofar as this type of research informs us of particular interactions that could be used as a basis for matching. These advantages may be seen within the classroom and in terms of developments in educational psychology.

Classroom Implications

General thinking about education and curriculum stands to be informed in various ways stemming from the explicit recognition and communication of the complex subtleties of real-life schooling situations. As such, it should help combat various stereotypes and simplistic polarizations, including: (1) the *'child-centred versus subject-centred'* dichotomy — for an interactive formulation reminds us that there is always *both* a recipient and a topic in teaching and that interacting features of both are likely to be important in affecting outcome and reaction; (2) *the need for individualization* — the foregoing material will hopefully have shown that this is not an all-or-none issue, though there may well be a trade-off aspect involved. That is, the more features of a particular situation (pupil, topic, teacher, etc.) one takes into account, the more difficult it is to actively match them in an effective interaction: the more features noted, the more obvious the uniqueness of the task. On the other hand, some degree of matching may make a great difference, so that discovering just one aspect of variation amongst one's pupils which interacts with different teaching approaches may allow a relatively simple but effective adaptation in one's actual offering; (3) *grouping and streaming* — the matching models approach looks at this as a potentially positive tool in adapting to individuals' needs and as such orients us towards pupil characteristics which relate differentially to teaching approaches, i.e., process-related qualities which we may be able to match by adapting the teaching process. Such qualities should avoid the features of negative labelling previously found with streaming solely by ability. The concept of developmental matching is also important in this more positive approach to pupil grouping.

Developments in Educational Psychology

Educational psychology stands to gain from an interactive perspective in various ways. (1) It is more likely to become more *realistic and useful* through grasping the complexity of real-life situations, rather than, say, by encapsulating itself in fragmented attention to innumerable specific issues generated by 'pure theory' in terms of artificial experimental contexts. Indeed, an interactive approach is necessary in applied psychology in order to prevent the various pure sub-branch applications from 'cancelling each other out'. (2) The interactive or BPE approach can likewise offer a *useful framework for the presentation of educational psychology* (see Tomlinson, 1981a). Not only does such a framework allow a systematic interrelating of the various subtopics in an educational psychology course; it tends to do so effectively in its own terms. That is, since most teachers have at least an implicit conception of teaching interaction, then using such an approach allows us to follow the recommendation of much modern theory, namely, to start where the learner is and teach thus adaptively. (3) Finally, in common with other work drawing attention to the complexities of real teaching situations (e.g., Doyle, 1979), an interactive awareness points up *the need for adequate theories of human learning* to inform the acquisition of what are thereby seen to be complex skills of flexible, intelligent teaching. Whilst an interactive meta-theory is compatible with many particular psychological theories, the modern psychology of skill can cope particularly well with its complex but realistic demands (Tomlinson, 1981a; Hunt and Sullivan, 1974).

References

BIGGS, J.B. and COLLIS, K.F. (1982) *Evaluating the Quality of Learning: The SOLO Taxonomy*, New York, Academic Press.

BUTCHER, H.J (1968) *Human Intelligence: Its Nature and Assessment*, London, Methuen.

CRONBACH, L.J. (1957) 'The two disciplines of scientific psychology', *American Psychologist*, 12, pp. 671–84.

CRONBACH, L.J. (1967) 'How can instruction be adapted to individual differences?' in GAGNÉ, R. (Ed.) *Learning and Individual Differences*, Columbus, Merrill.

CRONBACH, L.J. and SNOW, R.E. (1977) *Aptitudes and Instructional Methods: A Handbook for Research on Interactions*, New York, Irvington.

DANIEL, J.S. (1975) 'Learning styles and strategies', in ENTWISTLE, N.J. and HOUNSELL, D.J. (Eds) *How Students Learn*, Lancaster, Institute for Research and Development in Post-Compulsory Education.

DOYLE, W. (1979) 'Making managerial decisions in the classroom', in DUKE, D.L. (Ed.) *Classroom Management. 78th Yearbook of the N.S.S.E. Part II*, Chicago, University of Chicago Press.

EYSENCK, H.J. (1967a) 'Intelligence assessment: Theoretical and experimental approaches', *British Journal of Educational Psychology*, 37, pp. 81–98.

EYSENCK, H.J. (1967b) *The Biological Bases of Personality*, Springfield, Thomas.

FARLEY, F.H. and GORDON, N.J. (Eds) (1981) *Psychology and Education: The State of the Union*, Berkeley, McCutchan.

FERGUSON, G. (1976) *Statistical Analysis in Psychology and Education*, 4th ed., New York, McGraw-Hill.

GLASER, R. (1972) 'Individuals and learning: The new aptitudes', *Educational Researcher*, 1, pp. 5–13.

GLASER, R. (1977) *Adaptive Education: Individual Diversity and Learning*, New York, Holt, Rinehart and Winston.

HARVEY, O.J. *et al.* (1961) *Conceptual Systems and Personality Organisation*, New York, Wiley.

HUNT, D.E. (1966) 'A conceptual systems change model and its application to education', in HARVEY, O.J. (Ed.) *Experience, Structure and Adaptability*, New York, Springer.

HUNT, D.E. (1971) *Matching Models in Education*, Toronto, OISE.

HUNT, D.E. (1975) 'Person-environment interaction: A challenge found wanting before it was tried', *Review of Educational Research*, 45, pp. 209–30.

HUNT, D.E. (1976) 'Teachers are psychologists too: On the application of psychology to education', *Canadian Psychological Review*.

HUNT, D.E. and SULLIVAN, E.V. (1974) *Between Psychology and Education*, Hinsdale, Ill., Dryden Press.

LEWIN, K. (1951) *Field Theory and Social Science*, New York, Harper.

MILLER, A. (1981) 'Conceptual matching models and interactional research in education', *Review of Educational Research*, 51, pp. 33–84.

NAYLOR, F.D. (1972) *Personality and Educational Achievement*, Sydney, Wiley.

PERVIN, L.A. and LEWIS, M. (Eds) (1978) *Perspectives in Interactional Psychology*, New York, Plenum Press.

RIDING, R. (1982) 'Adapting instruction for the learner', in WHELDALL, K. and RIDING, R. (Eds) *Psychological Aspects of Learning and Teaching*, London, Croom Helm.

SCHRODER, H.M. *et al.* (1967) *Human Information Processing*, New York, Holt, Rinehart and Winston.

SHAW, J. (1980) 'Education and the individual: Schooling for girls, or mixed schooling — a mixed blessing?' in DEEM, R. (Ed.) *Schooling for Women's Work*, London, Routledge and Kegan Paul.

SNOW, R.E. *et al.* (Eds) (1980) *Aptitude, Learning and Instruction*, 2 vols, Hillsdale, N.J., Erlbaum Associates.

STONES, E. and ANDERSON, D. (1972) *Educational Objectives and the Teaching of Educational Psychology*, London, Methuen.

TOBIAS, S. (1981) 'Adaptation to individual differences', in FARLEY, F.H. and GORDON, N.J. (Eds) *Psychology and Education: The State of the Union*, Berkeley, McCutchan.

TOMLINSON, P.D. (1981a) *Understanding Teaching: Interactive Educational Psychology*, London, McGraw-Hill.

TOMLINSON, P.D. (1981b) 'Interactive educational matching and conceptual systems theory: A longitudinal study of conceptual level development'. Paper read to the Education Section Annual Conference, British Psychological Society, Oxford, 1981.

TOMLINSON, P.D. and HUNT, D.E. (1971) 'Differential effects of rule-example order as a function of learner conceptual level', *Canadian Journal of Behavioral Science*, 3, pp. 237–45.

WHELDALL, K. and RIDING, R. (Eds) (1982) *Psychological Aspects of Learning and Teaching*, London, Croom Helm.

WITKIN, H.A. *et al.* (1977) 'Field-dependent and field-independent cognitive styles and their educational implications', *Review of Educational Research*, 47, pp. 1–64.

3
The Experience of Learning

Introduction

While the previous two sections have taken us through recent developments in educational psychology, the new directions introduced so far have emerged mainly from criticisms of previous established theories. In the remaining two sections, the new directions are being established by pioneering research within the classroom or in relation to classroom concerns. It is here, above all, where we shall find the major growth points in thinking about educational psychology as it influences teaching and learning.

The distinguishing feature of the articles in this section is that they reflect the realizations that learning takes place in a social context and that one important way of understanding more about the processes of learning is to ask the students to explain what they are doing and why. The articles thus place great emphasis on *process*, on learning strategies and how these are influenced by the teacher and by the institutional environment. Many of the authors are explicitly critical of an educational system which forces students to adopt methods of learning which are designed more to cope with the demands of teacher or syllabus than to reach a better understanding of the world or to develop useful skills.

These criticisms reflect the experience of many of the pupils who find schooling 'boring'. Carl Rogers can be seen as the founding father of this new way of investigating learning in the classroom, although his ideas have been mainly extrapolated from his early work as a psychotherapist. Thus, although his thinking about education has had a profound influence, its roots are to be found mainly in his interviews with clients.

Some of his suggestions will thus have an idealistic ring to them when heard by teachers facing classes of thirty, rather than an individual client. His explorations of 'encounter groups' have also informed this thinking about education. But here again the intensity of the experiences provoked is difficult, and perhaps even dangerous, to achieve in everyday schooling. His experiences led Rogers to be extremely critical of formal education, but that criticism has to be seen within its philosophical perspective — a view of the purpose of education, mainly in terms of personal development, which would probably be shared by only a minority of teachers.

Guy Claxton sees important advantages in using encounter sessions in helping students become more aware of the role feelings and emotions play in learning — particularly in learning to be a more effective person — or teacher. He stresses above all the devastating effects on pupils of the prolonged experience of failure, and shows how experiential learning can help children and students to come to terms with their uncertainties and anxieties. The culprit, as with Rogers, is the school — or at least its current emphasis on intellectual achievement. 'School is a major cultural transmitter of the mistaken beliefs that personal worth is related to success on the one hand and to the ability to hide and control feelings ... on the other.'

The third article contains a short review of research on student learning. It is in this area that experiential research has flourished most conspicuously with the exploration of students' own reports of their reasons for studying, of their intentions, and of the strategies they adopt to meet lecturers' demands. This research effort has been led in the USA by William Perry who has described the ways in which students gradually develop the awareness that most knowledge is relative, that understanding is personal. 'Theories become, not "truth" but metaphors ... and there will be areas of great concern in which reasonable people will reasonably disagree.' In Europe an equivalently influential series of research studies has been stimulated by the ideas of Ference Marton in Gothenburg. He has pointed up the overwhelming importance of a student's intention in understanding the subsequent learning process. Like Perry he is also concerned to emphasize the implications for education of the fact that every learner reconstructs knowledge within a personal framework. Here there are echoes of Ausubel's ideas, but without the rather mechanical model of memory and impersonal treatment of the learning process. All these ideas apply to both youngsters and adults. But in the article by Entwistle the ideas are related to the needs of adults, particularly to those who are returning to formal education after many years away from it. As our population ages, the importance of recurrent education will grow, and the need to understand the specific educational interests and problems of adults will become even more acute.

One of the needs of adult learners, and of many younger ones, is 'learning to learn'. Graham Gibbs attacks traditional 'how to study' courses, and draws on recent research on learning to show how students can be helped to become more purposive in their approaches to studying. He finds, as a side effect, that teachers gain insights from conducting study skill workshops, often realizing for the first time how their assessment demands may be distorting the types of learning they want their students to adopt.

It is this theme that Charles Desforges develops in relation to very young children. Teachers often provide contradictory messages for children in what they exhort them to do (for example, write imaginatively) and what they reward (neatness). Pupils react to praise: this is the powerful currency of any interpersonal encounter. By observing and questioning children in the classroom, by emphasizing the *ecology* of learning, the inescapable conclusion is that 'the pupil tries to deliver what the teacher is predicted to reward.'

Traditionally 'reading', and particularly the early stage of learning to read, has been a major interest of educational psychologists. Hazel Francis manages to continue that tradition while reinterpreting the process in terms of the pupil's own experience. It becomes clear that some pupils come to school with little idea that written words are connected with spoken language. Until that realization dawns — or is taught — the process of learning to read is a meaningless exercise in rote learning and guesswork. Progress in the early stages of both reading and writing may depend, more than most teachers realize, on making the tasks personally meaningful to the individual pupil.

The articles in this section may have suggested that most children and researchers are critical of the effects of schools. But there is also a positive side to school and to child-rearing. In the final article Béla Kozéki looks at motivation and identifies sources of reward and satisfaction at school and in the home. Parents, teachers and peers all shape a pupil's developing motivational style. Schools provide affective, cognitive and moral rewards, but in different proportions. The burden of Kozéki's argument, like many other contributors to this section, is that schools should not overemphasize the intellectual components of learning to the detriment of the emotional or the moral. Kozéki also reminds us of the joint responsibilities of parents and teachers in the educational process — which leads us on to the final section.

Freedom to Learn*

Carl Rogers

In my view education should evoke *real* learning . . . *not* the lifeless, sterile, futile, quickly forgotten stuff which is crammed into the mind of the poor helpless individual tied to his seat by ironclad bonds of conformity! I am talking about LEARNING — the insatiable curiosity which drives the adolescent boy to absorb everything he can see or read about gasoline engines in order to improve the efficiency and speed of his 'hot-rod'. . . .

Learning, I believe, can be divided into two general types, along a continuum of meaning. At one end of the scale is the kind of task psychologists sometimes set for their subjects — the learning of nonsense syllables. To memorize such items as *baz, ent, nep, arl, lud*, and the like, is a difficult task. Because there is no meaning involved, these syllables are not easy to learn and are likely to be forgotten quickly.

We frequently fail to recognize that much of the material presented to students in the classroom has, for the student, the same perplexing, meaningless quality that the list of nonsense syllables has for us. . . . Large portions of his curriculum are, for him, meaningless. Thus education becomes the futile attempt to learn material which has no personal meaning. Such learning involves the mind only. It is learning which takes place 'from the neck up'. It does not involve feelings or personal meanings; it has no relevance for the whole person.

In contrast, there is such a thing as significant, meaningful, experiential learning. When a toddler touches the warm radiator he learns for himself the meaning of the word 'hot', he has learned a future caution in regard to all similar radiators; and he has taken in these learnings in a significant involved way which will *not* soon be forgotten. . . .

Let me define a bit more precisely the elements which are involved in such significant or experiential learning. *It has the quality of personal*

* This article comprises extracts from *Freedom to Learn*, 2nd ed., 1979, Columbus, Ohio, Merrill.

involvement — the whole person in both his feeling and cognitive aspects being *in* the learning event. *It is self-initiated.* Even when the impetus or stimulus comes from the outside, the sense of discovery, of reaching out, of grasping and comprehending, comes from within. *It is pervasive.* It makes a difference in the behaviour, the attitudes, perhaps even the personality of the learner. *It is evaluated by the learner.* He knows whether it is meeting his need, whether it leads toward what he *wants* to know, whether it illuminates the dark area of ignorance he is experiencing. The locus of evaluation, we might say, resides definitely in the learner. *Its essence is meaning.* When such learning takes place, the element of meaning to the learner is built into the whole experience.

I believe that all teachers and educators prefer to facilitate this experiential and meaningful type of learning, rather than the nonsense syllable type. Yet in the vast majority of our schools, at all educational levels, we are locked into a traditional and conventional approach which makes significant learning improbable if not impossible. When we put together in one scheme such elements as a *prescribed curriculum, similar assignments for all students, lecturing* as almost the only mode of instruction, *standard tests* by which all students are externally evaluated, and *instructor-chosen grades* as the measure of learning, then we can almost guarantee that meaningful learning will be at an absolute minimum.

The change I would most like to see is a shift in emphasis from teaching to learning — from the teacher to the learner. I wish to begin ... with a statement which may seem surprising to some and perhaps offensive to others. It is simply this: Teaching, in my estimation, is a vastly over-rated function. Having made such a statement, I scurry to the dictionary to see if I really mean what I say. Teaching means 'to instruct' ... 'to impart knowledge or skill' ... 'to make to know'. Here my hackles rise. I have no wish to *make* anyone know something. 'To show, guide, direct'. As I see it, too many people have been shown, guided, directed. So I come to the conclusion that I *do* mean what I said. Teaching is, for me, a relatively unimportant and vastly overvalued activity....

I see *the facilitation of learning* as the *aim* of education, the way in which we might develop the learning man, the way in which we can learn to live as individuals in process. I see the facilitation of learning as the function which may hold constructive, tentative, changing, *process* answers to some of the deepest perplexities which beset man today.

But do we know how to achieve this new goal in education ... ? We know ... that the initiation of such learning rests not upon the teaching skills of the leader, not upon his scholarly knowledge of the field, not upon his curricular planning, not upon his use of audiovisual aids, not upon the programmed learning he utilizes, not upon his lectures and presentations.... No, the facilitation of significant learning rests upon certain attitudinal qualities which exist in the personal *relationship* between the facilitator and the learner.... First of all is a transparent realness in the facilitator, a willingness to be a person, to be and live the feelings and thoughts of the moment. When this realness includes a prizing, a caring, a trust and respect of the learner, the climate for learning is enhanced. When it includes a sensitive and accurate empathic listening, then indeed a freeing climate, stimulative of self-initiated learning and growth, exists. The student is *trusted* to develop....

Individuals who hold such attitudes, and are bold enough to act on them, do not simply modify classroom methods — they revolutionize them. They perform almost none of the functions of teachers.... They are catalyzers, facilitators, giving freedom and life and the opportunity to learn, to students.

Yet the traditional school continues to be far removed from this approach to education.

Experiential Learning and Education

Guy Claxton
Chelsea College, University of London

'From a very early age I have been aware that I was searching for something of 'greater significance'. I was aware that I was learning according to the school system i.e. the facts, but that there was a great deal of learning I was not doing. I did not know what exactly it was or how to do it, but just knew I wasn't doing it. . . .

'My life and interpersonal relationships have always seemed lacking something. Although my work (art) is extremely important to me, it still failed somehow in providing me with whatever it was I needed. I suppose what I have been looking for is warmth, approval, ultimately a feeling of being accepted, loved and wanted just as I am inside, me with all my lousy failings. . . .

'I left home as early as possible, 18, desperately trying not to need. I would never open up — I still can't cry without feeling terribly guilty, desperately trying to stifle the feeling. In fact there are a whole range of feelings I stifle, the important one being caring, allowing myself to care. I can care about anyone freely and deeply when I know I'm in no danger of being hurt. As soon as there is the remotest chance of being rejected, I immediately stop the feeling. This permeates to all levels of my life, even to such things as who rings who first in a relationship. . . .

'Having these inner feelings and trying to suppress them, I consequently moulded myself into what I thought was a strong person. Now I'm stuck with the image I have made for myself. I am trying desperately to break it down and let the real me out, but it's so difficult. . . .

'The thought of the Encounter session struck terror into me as I'd heard 'rumours'. I think my basic fear was of being revealed as the weak, inadequate, pathetic me. The one who is terrified of being alone in the dark at night, the one who regularly contemplates ending it all when the going gets rough. I have always wanted to tell someone how it is with me, and I knew that this might be the time when I would break down and reveal all. Well, with the aid of 2 Martinis I got there, nerves jangling. I have never regretted going. The weekend was the most important event of my life.

'I have always felt alone and isolated. That weekend it went. And in fact hasn't been back in quite the same way since, although I still slump every now and then. But I have grown stronger in a real way — inside. I feel more confident and run from difficult situations far less often. To me this sort of real contact is vital in the world — the world where we're constantly judged, misunderstood, evaluated, labelled. All packed up shiny and bright on the outside and rotten inside. In the space of one weekend I got nearer to what I've been trying to learn for as long as I can remember.'

This quotation says a lot about what experiential learning is. It is common enough for people who have been through similar learning experiences to give such accounts (see, for example, Rogers, 1971). But this particular one is unusual in two respects. First, this is not a 'patient' speaking, not someone who has sought therapy, but an intelligent, attractive, seemingly competent and successful young woman doing a Post-Graduate Certificate in Education (PGCE) course in London, outwardly a student just like all the other students. Second, the quotations come not from a private letter or conversation, but from an assessed essay she wrote and submitted as part of the course. Out of her experience of 'experiential learning' has come, as well as strength to be more 'real' in her own life, the courage to share her hidden self with the world at large. In writing this piece of course-work, too, she had given up the bright and shiny act.

This chapter is an attempt to explain what experiential learning is, what its theoretical roots are, what techniques and methods it employs, and what its place is, if any, in teacher training and in education as a whole. What Tricia says gives a feel for it. The rest of the chapter reviews details, rationales and misgivings.

What Does Experiential Learning Do?

Experiential learning refers to a quite specific process, that of *re-learning to experience oneself*. It is not about learning *through* experience: many other branches of psychology, such as the 'learning theory' of the behaviourists (e.g., Skinner, 1974), deal with that. It is not about changing the way one conceptualizes or pigeon-holes what one sees — that is the province of 'perceptual learning' and 'concept formation'. Nor is it about how infants come to know their world. That is 'perceptual development' (Bower, 1977). Experiential learning is to do with the recovery of the ability to permit into conscious awareness, and to accept, aspects of a person's experience that they have been denying or shying away from.

The theoretical foundations of experiential learning were laid at the beginning of the century by Freud (Wollheim, 1971) and Jung (Storr, 1973); the walls erected by Rogers (1961), Perls (1972) and Maslow (1968) and the roof put on by Wilber (1981), Laing (1971) and Watts (1973). Interestingly the building has grown to resemble a Buddhist temple more than a concrete and glass laboratory. And it is buttressed much more by personal accounts of first-hand experience, largely from the field of psychotherapy, than by experimental research, though the latter exists. Its neighbours are philosophy, literature and religion, not cognitive science or statistics (which is not necessarily bad company: for not all knowledge comes from experiments). Let me describe the building as it now stands.

We are born, so the story goes (Claxton, 1984a), with natural abilities to register experience and to learn from it — that is, to distil it into useful and increasingly accurate generalizations about the world, and especially about how we can nudge the world, through our actions, in ways that we need or want it to go. To start with we are naïve, and all-of-a-piece. But as we grow in sophistication, so, through the comments and admonitions of others, we begin to develop an *identity*. Other people start to tell us who we are: 'boy'/'girl', 'clever'/'stupid', 'pretty'/'plain', 'good'/'bad'. Our natural learning ability goes on producing information about what *works* or *doesn't work* at the level of action, and what's *nice* and what's *nasty* at the level of experience. But overlaid on this, and somewhat out of true with it, we are led to construct another frame of reference, a set of *beliefs* about Who-I-Am and Who-I-Ought-To-Be. We learn to call 'good' things that don't feel right, and 'bad' some of those we enjoy. We develop our own characteristic set of responses and habits, but we learn to *see* ourselves in the mirror of other people's assumptions, values and judgments about us. Whatever my complexity, if I am called a 'boy', then I am expected to pour myself into the mould of their beliefs about what a boy is — and not just any boy, but a 'good boy', or a 'bright boy', a 'successful man', an 'attractive woman', a 'father', a 'forty-year-old', and, underlying all of these, an 'acceptable, valuable, worthwhile person' (Burrow, 1953).

We are then faced with a choice. Are we our experience? Or are we what they say we are ? Inevitably, but fatally — because 'they' are in a position to make us 'an offer we can't refuse' — we opt for the latter. We begin to see ourselves and present ourselves their way. And what happens to the awkward bits that won't go in the mould, the constant stream of intimations that we are 'really' both more and less than our image and our act? They have to be lopped off.

But here is a problem: we cannot 'really' get rid of who we really are any more than we can run away from our shadows. The best we can do is ignore them, pretend they're not there — that is, *withdraw our attention from them*: look the other way and busy ourselves with something else. Thus arises the unconscious, and other mechanisms of defensiveness. As we lose touch with the unacceptable face of our selves, so we come to see ourselves as a caricature, a crude cartoon, much of which is drawn not by our own hand but by others — parents, teachers, friends, 'society'. We begin to play our lives according to rules that we did not choose. And, where it is too uncomfortable to remember, we forget how much of this is counterfeit. We come to mistake the map for the land, the menu for the meal, the brochure for the holiday.

By doing so, we buy some peace and some acceptability, but at a price. The price is constant vigilance, like a John Le Carré 'mole', lest our true identity be uncovered and we stand exposed as aliens and imposters. The currency in which we pay, like the spy, is spontaneity, intimacy and vitality. Only with our loved ones, and perhaps not even then, can we dare to be just as weak, confused, inept or nasty as we are. Often we do not dare even with ourselves. You can feel the fear of knowing herself, and of being known, in Tricia's story. But you can feel the yearning, and the relief, as well.

Whatever we become identified with, whatever we write into the definition of ourselves, that we have to defend. And, when part of our identity is at odds with aspects of our own experience, that experience itself becomes a threat, a 'predator'. What are we to do in this situation? Three options are available. First, we can flee, either physically or, more usually, mentally. Second, we can fight, using effort and will to try to dominate our own dark side. These are the most common strategies. The third is to allow identity to be expanded to include the threatening experience so that its status is altered from 'alien' to 'family'. Nothing is changed except that my tears or rage or frailty lose power to threaten 'me' because I allow them to *become* 'me'. It is as simple as that — and as difficult, because in doing so we have to give up an aspect of what we thought we were. We have to 'die a little'. *This is experiential learning.* It is extending the boundary of identity so that previously denied experience gains access to consciousness again. Every time we do so, one more predator has its fangs pulled, and another bit of the terrain of ourselves becomes home ground.

People vary enormously in *what* they resist — the domains of experience that threaten them — and *how* they resist — their defensive strategies. But two kinds of experience that are very commonly viewed as threatening are being incompetent and being swept away by strong feelings, especially anger, fear, sexuality, loss and loneliness. To the extent that a person is identified with being competent and cool, failing and feeling are anathema. Thus while experiential learning is not necessarily about feelings and emotions, it turns out that, because it is areas of feeling that have often been disowned, it is these areas that often form experiential learning's subject matter. But threatening thoughts, images, memories, compulsions, obsessions and even body sensations can equally well be candidates for reincorporation. Though experiential learning has, in its wilder manifestations, been anti-intellectual (e.g., Kegan, 1975), and has certainly been attacked as such (Back, 1973), its most percipient theorists and exponents (e.g., Rogers, 1961; Gendlin, 1974) have always seen its focus as being that-which-threatens-a-person, whatever that experience may be.

How Is Experiential Learning Facilitated?

The facilitation of experiential learning occurs in two parts: the creation of a *context* and the use of *techniques*. Experiential learning can be pursued by an individual on his or her own. All that is required is the courage and the ability to look your demons in the eye. But it is difficult because it does take courage, and also because the defensive habits of avoidance, projection, denial, rationalization and the rest (Hamachek, 1978) are designed to prevent us ever meeting the demons. The points of the track on which the train of thought runs are fixed so that, in our daily lives, we simply do not have to travel by the charnel-house. So very often someone else is required who can (a) encourage us, by their presence and example, and (b) create situations in which that which we fear arises. With one hand they support, and with the other confront. First they help to generate a safe context, and then, with their techniques and skills, they help to conjure up some content to be looked at.

Rogers (1961, 1981) has focused heavily on the context. He has told us clearly what the background characteristics of the helping relationship are. He and Gendlin (1974) have rightly emphasized the importance of context over technique. If the safe atmosphere exists, techniques can accelerate learning. If it does not, then 'methods', however sophisticated, will not work and may even be harmful. Thus it follows that being a therapist, a counsellor or a humanistic teacher is relatively little to do with professional training, knowledge and expertise, and much more to do with a deeper quality or ability to let other people feel safe.

The personal qualities of an effective facilitator of experiential learning that Rogers identifies, and whose potency has been extensively demonstrated (e.g., Truax and Carkhuff, 1967) are *genuineness, acceptance* and *empathy*. People feel safe with other people who are 'being themselves', because you know where you stand with them, and they also provide a model of someone who is able to stay in touch with their own experience wherever it happens to flow. Second, people feel safe when they begin to see that the bits of themselves they reject are not condemned or judged by the other. They gradually come to see themselves as valued and cherished — and therefore as valuable and cherishable — in spite of (or even because of) all their own 'lousy failings', as Tricia put it. Third, people feel safe when they feel understood: the quality of being able to understand another's life, and to communicate that understanding, is what Rogers calls 'empathy', and he describes it thus (Rogers, 1981):

(Being empathic) means entering the private perceptual world of the other and becoming thoroughly at home in it. It involves being sensitive, moment to moment, to the changing felt meanings which flow in this other person, to the fear or rage or tenderness or confusion or whatever, that he/she is experiencing. It means temporarily living in his/her life, moving about in it delicately without making judgments, sensing meanings of which he/she is scarcely aware, but not trying to uncover feelings of which the person is totally unaware, since this would be too threatening. It includes communicating your sensings of his/her world as you look with fresh and unfrightened eyes at elements of which the individual is fearful. It means frequently checking with him/her as to the accuracy of your sensings, and being guided by the responses you receive. You are a confident companion to the person in his/her inner world. By pointing to the possible meanings in the flow of his/her experiencing you help the person to focus on this useful type of referent, to experience the meanings more fully, and to move forward in the experiencing.

To be with another in this way means that for the time being you lay aside the views and values you hold for yourself in order to enter another's world without prejudice.

What a teacher has to do in order to acquire these qualities is well caught by Jersild (1954):

In order to have insight into the child's strivings and the problems and issues he is coping with the teacher must strive to face the same issues within his own life. These issues are largely emotional in nature and the endeavour to understand oneself and others has a deep emotional meaning. It calls for more than intellectual cleverness and academic competence.

To appreciate another's feelings, one must seek to recognise and understand one's own. To be able to sympathise with the child who is hostile (and all children are, more or less) the teacher must face his own hostile tendencies and try to accept the implications of his anger as it occurs, say, in his annoyance with his pupils, his impatience with himself, his feuds with other teachers, his complaints against parents or school authorities or others on whom he fixes his ire.

Similarly, to realise the turmoil another is undergoing, a person must try to examine his own fears and anxieties. To do so may be more painful and threatening at the moment than to keep pretending they don't exist, but unless he can seek to fathom his fears as they appear in his phobias, squeamishness, fear of misfortune, timidity, uncertainties, fear of making mistakes, and fear of what others may think of him, his ability to perceive that others are frightened will be quite limited....

(For) a person's wisdom as he looks outward upon others can only be as deep as the wisdom he possesses as he looks inward upon himself. The farther a teacher goes in understanding himself and others, the more deeply he can realise the common humanity he shares with others, even with those whom he dislikes. The more genuinely he is involved in his own struggle to understand and to face the problems of life, the more he can realise this kinship with others, whether they be older or younger, or like him or unlike him in education, wealth, race, religion, social status or professional rank.

To be a teacher of this sort, therefore, one must be 'at home' with the areas of experience that others are finding anxiety-provoking. This may well require of the teacher a period of experiential learning that parallels, but precedes, the learner's.

Once the climate is established, techniques and 'games' become useful. There are many available — too many to do justice to here. Several compendia of techniques suitable for use in school are available and include those by Lewis and Streitfeld (1973) and Brandes and Phillips (1979). Each game is an invitation to the players to experience themselves in a way that is richer, or at least other, than the way they usually do. For example, instead of the normal chatter, forms of conversation between pairs of people might be suggested that encourage the participants to talk and to listen more openly than usual. Topics might include 'My simple pleasures', 'The things that upset me', 'How I feel about my body' or 'What we might talk about if I knew you better'. Often experiments in giving and receiving more fully are dressed up as drama or role-play. One exercise of Brandes and Phillips, for example, asks young people to imagine they are one of their parents at a party talking about their child — i.e., themselves. The children as a group then enact the party, going around telling each other essentially about their perceptions of their parents' perceptions of themselves. Through experience teachers have often found that to ask children to express such things directly is too threatening. But through the medium of the 'game', they are able to share something of their relationship with their parents, and the judgments, aspirations, disappointments and resentments that the relationship may contain. By so doing they may come closer to acknowledging such discomfitting feelings or conflicts, and thereby 'defuse' them somewhat; and through the communication with others, they may well come to see more clearly what is unique and (more usually) just how much is similar to their classmates.

Some experiential techniques are social, using interaction in groups or pairs, and some, like those we have just mentioned use words. But many of these methods are individual and/or non-verbal. It is difficult to convey on the page the involvement, insight and sense of release that even simple exercises frequently produce. For first-hand accounts of the successful use of these games with school-children, see Rogers (1969), Brown (1971, 1975) and Hunter (1972).

Experiential Education

Experiential learning and its facilitation are found most frequently in contexts that are called 'therapeutic' rather than 'educational': that is, it is undertaken by people whose defensive systems are unequal to the task of keeping anxiety, rage, deadness, strange thoughts or perceptions out of the eye of consciousness. They are unhappy, know it, and have chosen to seek relief. The situation in education is clearly quite different, and the use of experiential techniques there raises a number of ideological, ethical and practical issues. We might consider these under the headings *values, content, methods, teacher style, evaluation* and *problems*.

Although experiential learning is a branch of psychology, it is often incorporated into a set of *values* for education. It is seen not just as a kind of learning but as a desirable kind (Dennison, 1972; Brown, 1975; Lyon, 1971). A substantial part of the business of education, it is argued, is the expansion of awareness and the 'healing' of rifts and dissociations within the personality. Both Rogers (1961) and Maslow (1968) created descriptions of 'the fully functioning person' and 'self-actualizing man' and argued for an educational system that aimed at creating these ideal types. Because of our problems of mistaken identity we *all* fall short of these 'natural' or 'healthy' states, and experiential learning is therefore appropriate not just for the unhappy few, but for everyone, they say.

But experiential education is certainly not 'education' as we know it in our schools. It is concerned essentially and directly with the development of the whole person, with personality, whereas current schooling only nods rhetorically in that direction while pursuing its obsession with knowledge and skill (Hargreaves, 1982). School is about giving people *more* — more knowledge, more abilities, more certificates. Experiential education is about taking away from them illusions of threat, so that previously No-Go areas of experience become available again, and life becomes less guarded and so more lively, rich and joyful. In some areas of the curriculum such as tutorial lessons, drama or English, experiential learning may creep in, but it is very far from achieving the status of an idea that guides and motivates schooling as a whole.

The traditional question of what *content* to 'teach' in experiential education is pre-empted by the question whether it is appropriate to talk of content at all. Certainly we cannot identify a package of information that passes from teacher to pupil of anything like the same kind as 'The Tudors' or 'Transition Metal Chemistry'. The sole content of experiential learning is an individual's experience, especially that which happens to lie, in the moment, on the shifting margins of What-Is-Safe and What-Is-Me. Unfortunately the main, though still small, impact of experiential or humanistic ideas on school has been the appearance of curriculum packages on 'Personal Relationships', 'Anxieties of Living', 'Life Skills', 'Health Education', and the like. On the whole these are pernicious because they encroach on the one domain of a young person's experience that has up to now remained private and unschooled — their feelings and relationships — and transmute it into the traditional conceptual pedagogy of information and discussion. Even Sex' n' Drugs' n' Rock' n' Roll can be made boring and anaemic if they are rendered into information packs and questionnaires, because there is simply no question of a student's felt dilemmas, fears and confusions being welcomed. It requires a person rather than a pamphlet to make another person feel safe.

This brings us back to the heart of experiential learning as *method*. For its facilitation is, as we saw, a matter of personal quality first and clever technique a long way second. A child or anyone will only explore and admit unsafe experience in a safe context, and teachers are not trained in the requisite qualities, nor are schools as a rule congenial places for their expression. School is a major cultural transmitter of the mistaken beliefs that personal worth is related to success, on the one hand, and that one should have an ability to hide and control feelings, especially 'weak' ones, on the other. If it is important to be cool in school, then experiential learning is out. Indeed, if 'being wrong' is itself a threat, then *all* learning is jeopardized. John Holt, a phenomenological psychologist, though not acknowledged as such, has recorded in his classic *How Children Fail* (1969) the many ways in which children learn to evade and avoid learning when failure is a threat.

The methods of experiential education differ from those of the traditional school in many ways. The closest analogy might be to a practical science lesson in which the teacher issues instructions about how to do the experiment, and the students conduct it and make their own observations. But in the experiential learning 'laboratory', safety procedures are even more important; there will be no consensus expected or sought between the different sets of observations and conclusions; and the object being investigated is not a frog, or Substance A, but one's self.

Obviously *teacher style* must be quite different. The teacher has to give up being the custodian of the 'right answer'. She must be able to tolerate not-knowing, and to see herself as a learner. If her attitude is one of seeking to learn her students, the openness and receptivity required will help them to learn about themselves. In this delicate area she must be sensitive and responsive to a child's signals of threat or overload, and allow him to say 'No!' or 'Whoa!' when he wants, for the trick is to stay open to that which you would normally avoid, and once the threat becomes too much, and the defences are tripped, experiential learning shuts down.

It should be clear, by the way, that experiential education has much more precise aims and methods, and requires better defined qualities and skills of a teacher, than does 'child-centred' education. Experiential education *is* child-centred in that the concern is with the whole person, and the rate and extent of learning are under the learner's control, but it is not at all unstructured or laissez-faire.

Because experiential education aims not for greater competence (or not directly), but at greater wholeness, its *evaluation* is by no means straight-forward. The question: 'Is anything happening as a result of experiential education, and if so what?' can be tackled in a variety of ways. If we wish to know the learners' perceptions of the matter, we can ask them, and we may do so either informally, by getting them to write or talk freely, or more formally by devising a questionnaire. Not surprisingly, such anecdotal or self-report studies (e.g., Blume, 1981) tend to be favourable to experiential learning, although there is some suggestion that students' satisfaction with 'humanistic' methods depends on facets of their own personality (Ryback and Sanders, 1980).

The most extensive evaluation of experiential learning, in the form of 'encounter groups', with students was conducted by Lieberman *et al.* (1973). They examined the reported effects of a variety of styles of such groups both during their life and up to eight months after their completion. The most disturbing and widely publicized result of their survey was the high rate of so-called 'casualties': over 7 per cent of participants. However, detailed examination of these findings by Rowan (1975), Schutz (1975) and Smith (1975) has revealed serious flaws in the way such casualties are identified, and worse still in the way the groups themselves were constituted and conducted. A better estimate of those who rate their experience of experiential learning as 'negative' or even 'damaging' is 2–3 per cent.

If the biggest effect of the participant's personality on his/her satisfaction is his/her own willingness to take risks (Ryback and Sanders, 1980), the major 'external' factor, as revealed by the Lieberman *et al.* (1973) study is the personality of the leader, teacher or facilitator. In line with our earlier emphasis of context over method, bad experiences were correlated in the main not with the leader's technique but with their personal style. Following Jersild's (1954) description, we might characterize the potentially damaging facilitator as one who possesses enough experience, expertise or charisma to lead the learner *into* a threatening area of his/her experience, but who, because his own defensiveness is aroused there, is unable to lead the learner *through* the experience. Seeing or sensing the guide lose his nerve, the learner's belief in the 'realness' of a predator is not transcended but reinforced. For a facilitator to be of value, it is necessary that his limits be wider than those of his students, *and* that he knows and respects those limitations in himself. For further studies of experiential learning see Brown (1975), Keeton (1976), Roberts (1975) and Rubottom (1975).

Problems, Pitfalls and Criticisms

Experiential learning does happen, can be facilitated, and, according to many reports, is often seen in an overwhelmingly positive and liberating light. But there are problems, especially with the notion of experiential *education*, that need briefly reviewing. First, as we have seen, there is a small but non-negligible risk of experiential learning going awry. This risk is not avoided by demands for professional training and certification for the problem lies at a level deeper than expertise (Rogers *et al.*, 1967). The professional's jealousy of his reputation, or investment in his own competence, may make him as untrustworthy or manipulative as does the bigotry of the local priest or the naïvety of the lady next door.

Second, the standard of research in this area leaves much to be desired. Only recently has the liberal, value-laden fog of 'humanistic psychology' and the 'growth movement' begun to disperse and allow a clearer, more precise description of this process of experiential learning to be developed. This increased theoretical clarity and coherence is due in large measure to Wilber (1977, 1981). As yet, however, much of the empirical research remains characterized by exaggerated claims of either benefit or danger, depending, it seems, on the prior persuasions of the researchers. It is also, it must be said, an extremely difficult area to do good 'outcome research' in, as it is hard to specify objectively exactly what the crucial, observable outcomes might be.

Third, given that experiential education is possible, there are ethical questions about where and to what extent it is desirable. Do young people 'need' it? At what age are they 'ready' for it? Is it possible to have too much of this particular Good Thing? These are as much ideological as they are psychological issues, yet educators must face them.

Fourth, even if we grant the desirability of at least some experiential learning for young people, is it possible to offer it effectively within an institution — school — whose dominant value system is radically different, and in many ways antagonistic? Many of those who have tried it have met resistance not only from senior teachers, administrators and parents, but from the students themselves (Rogers, 1969; Hall, 1977). When others judge it to be either 'dangerous' or 'trivial', is it worthwhile, or even defensible, to pursue it? Does a teacher have the right to challenge, if only implicitly, the exam-oriented expectations of her students and her paymasters alike? Though what she is doing, and why she is doing it, may be clear to the experientially-minded teacher, it may be difficult to communicate to others.

My own feeling is that school may be too early and, as it stands, too unsympathetic a context into which to introduce very much in the way of experiential learning. By and large adolescents are too busy concocting a workable and acceptable identity (Coleman, 1980) to worry about how much of their own experience they are thereby excluding. Perhaps it is more appropriate to wait until they *feel* themselves constricted by the shell they have made before offering them a way out. It is often not until confronted with the limitations of their sense-ability and response-ability that people begin to feel cramped by their own beliefs, and it is at this point that experiential learning is required. In the light of this, it is not surprising that the most successful educational setting for experiential learning seems to be teacher training, for it is here, perhaps for the first time in their adult lives, that people are brought face to face with the buried threats of failure and rejection (Claxton, 1984b).

If you look back to the quotation with which this chapter started, I hope you will see that we have made some sense of how experiential learning happens; why people might choose to undertake it, yet be so fearful about doing so; what kinds of experience people struggle to deny and at the same time yearn to accept — for Tricia the feelings of neediness, of weakness and of caring; and what the successful outcome is — 'I feel more confident and run from difficult situations less often.' To conclude with another quotation from Tricia, there is at least one voice that is in no doubt about the relevance of experiential learning in education — for the teachers!

> 'The value of such real communication, real contact, in 'the system' must be obvious even to a blockhead. Any situation where one person is responsible for control or communication with groups of others, would benefit enormously. (At art school) the head of my faculty once advised me to 'take some tranquillizers'; he was 'sure I would feel much better as my wife takes them'. With such depth of sympathy at hand it was not hard to believe. . . .
>
> 'I feel my own personal problems and my acceptance of them has led me to a much deeper understanding of others. As a teacher I have a feeling of empathy towards the children. I don't have to pretend I understand, because I do. I have felt what they feel. Children can see straight through phoniness and are quite ready to tell you. Many times I have heard the children mimicking a particularly 'understanding' member of staff, because to them this wasn't real communication but merely 'Yes, dear, all right' (GO AWAY DON'T BOTHER ME), all said with a lipstick smile.
>
> 'I am sure many teachers do have a 'natural' attitude to children. Some people are fortunate enough to have grown up retaining the loving awareness and openness that I feel is a natural characteristic of any human being. However, for those who have been forced for defensive reasons to wear a 'mask' through which only a fraction of the real self shines, something ought to be available.
>
> 'What strikes me on re-reading my remarks is that it's all so simple and obvious really. Life is simple and easy if we allow ourselves to live it. It's the complicated, unnatural life style that's messing everything up. Consequently the remedies have to be complicated and unnatural.'

References

BACK, K.W. (1973) *Beyond Words*, Baltimore, Penguin.
BLUME, F. (1981) 'The role of personal growth groups at Johnston College', *Journal of Humanistic Psychology*, 21, 2, pp. 47–61.

BOWER, T.G.R. (1977) *A Primer of Infant Development*, San Francisco, Freeman.

BRANDES, D. and PHILLIPS, H. (1979) *Gamesters' Handbook*, London, Hutchinson.

BROWN, G.I. (1971) *Human Teaching for Human Learning*, New York, Viking.

BROWN, G.I. (1975) *The Live Classroom*, New York, Viking.

BURROW, T. (1953) *Science and Man's Behaviour*, New York, Philosophical Library.

CLAXTON, G.L. (1984a) *Live and Learn: An Introduction to the Psychology of Growth and Change in Everyday Life*, London, Harper and Row.

CLAXTON, G.L. (1984b) 'The psychology in teacher training: Inaccuracies and improvements', *Educational Psychology*, 4, 2, pp. 167–74.

COLEMAN, J. (1980) *The Nature of Adolescence*, London, Methuen.

DENNISON, G. (1972) *The Lives of Children*, Harmondsworth, Penguin.

GENDLIN, E. (1974) 'Client-centred and experiential psychotherapy', in WEXLER, D. and RICE, L. (Eds) *Innovations in Client-Centred Therapy*, New York, Wiley.

HALL, E. (1977) 'Human relations training in a comprehensive school', *British Journal of Guidance and Counselling*, 5, pp. 207–14.

HAMACHEK, D. (1978) *Encounters with the Self*, New York, Holt, Rinehart and Winston.

HARGREAVES, D. (1982) *The Challenge for the Comprehensive School*, London, Routledge and Kegan Paul.

HOLT, J. (1969) *How Children Fail*, Harmondsworth, Penguin.

HUNTER, E. (1972) *Encounter in the Classroom: New Ways of Teaching*, New York, Holt, Rinehart and Winston.

JERSILD, A. (1954) 'Understanding others through facing ourselves', *Childhood Education*, 30, 9, pp. 411–14.

KEETON, M.T. (1976) *Experiential Learning: Rationale, Characteristics and Assessment*, San Francisco, Jossey-Bass.

KEGAN, D. (1975) 'Paperback images of encounter', *Journal of Humanistic Psychology*, 15, 3, pp. 31–7.

LAING, R.D. (1971) *Self and Others*, Harmondsworth, Penguin.

LEWIS, H.R. and STREITFELD, H.S. (1973) *Growth Games*, London, Abacus.

LIEBERMAN, M. *et al.* (1973) *Encounter Groups: First Facts*, New York, Basic Books.

LYON, H.C. (1971) *Learning to Feel — Feeling to Learn*, Columbus, Ohio, Merrill.

MASLOW, A.H. (1968) *Toward a Psychology of Being*, 2nd ed., New York, Van Nostrand.

PERLS, F. (1972) *In and out the Garbage Pail*, New York, Bantam.

ROBERTS, T. (Ed.) (1975) *Four Psychologies Applied to Education*, Cambridge, Mass, Schenkman.

ROGERS, C.R. (1961) *On Becoming a Person*, Boston, Houghton Mifflin.

ROGERS, C.R. (1969) *Freedom to Learn*, Columbus, Ohio, Merrill.

ROGERS, C.R. (1971) *Carl Rogers on Encounter Groups*, New York, Harper and Row.

ROGERS, C.R. (1981) *A Way of Being*, Boston, Houghton Mifflin.

ROGERS, C.R. *et al.* (1967) *The Therapeutic Relationship and Its Impact: A Study of Psychotherapy with Schizophrenics*. Madison, University of Wisconsin Press.

ROWAN, J. (1975) 'Encounter group research: no joy?' *Journal of Humanistic Psychology*, 15, 2, pp. 19–28.

RUBOTTOM, A.E. (1975) 'Transcendental meditation and its potential uses for schools', in ROBERTS, T. (Ed.) *Four Psychologies Applied to Education*, Cambridge, Mass, Schenkman.

RYBACK, D. and SANDERS, J. (1980) 'Humanistic versus traditional teaching styles and student satisfaction', *Journal of Humanistic Psychology*, 20, 1, pp. 87–90.

SCHUTZ, W. (1975) 'Not encounter and certainly not facts', *Journal of Humanistic Psychology*, 15, 2, pp. 7–18.

SKINNER, B.F. (1974) *About Behaviourism*, London, Jonathan Cape.

SMITH, P.B. (1975) 'Are there adverse effects of sensitivity training?' *Journal of Humanistic Psychology*, 15, 2, pp. 29–47.

STORR, A. (1973) *Jung*, London, Fontana.

Guy Claxton

TRUAX, C.B. and CARKHUFF, R. (1967) *Towards Effective Counselling and Psychotherapy*, Chicago, Aldine.
WATTS, A.W. (1973) *Psychotherapy East and West*, Harmondsworth, Penguin.
WILBER, K. (1977) *The Spectrum of Consciousness*, Wheaton, Ill., Quest.
WILBER, K. (1981) *No Boundary*, London, Shambhala.
WOLLHEIM, R. (1971) *Freud*, London, Fontana.

Student Learning and Adult Education*

Noel Entwistle
University of Edinburgh

Research on Student Learning

Convincing descriptions of student learning have appeared surprisingly recently. Although a great deal was known prior to 1975 about students' entry qualifications, abilities, personalities, motivations and study habits in relation to degree performance, the *process* of learning had been largely ignored. Yet it is an examination of this process which proves most illuminating to teacher and student alike. The pioneering work of Marton (1975) and his colleagues in Gothenburg has encouraged a variety of attempts to understand learning from the student's own perspective (Entwistle, 1981, 1982). This research is based on a 'grounded-theory' approach: descriptive categories and analytic frameworks are derived directly from the participants' own experiences. They are *not* imposed in advance from pre-existing psychological or sociological theories.

The Swedish research, based on careful analyses of lengthy interviews, has been further developed in Britain. The resulting set of concepts enables us to identify distinctive *approaches to learning*, and to understand how these approaches are likely to be affected by students' reasons for studying — their *orientations to education*, and by the teaching and assessment procedures they encounter.

Orientations towards Higher Education

Hopper and Osborn (1975, p.123) define 'orientations' to education as 'the beliefs and attitudes people have about education as an object which they evaluate as their goal.' More recently Taylor (1983) has used the term to

* This is a shortened version of the article which appeared in Bourne R. (Ed.) (1983) *Part-Time First Degrees in Universities*, Goldsmiths' College, London.

denote a set of personal beliefs or expectations about studying and individual purposes in embarking on particular courses. She has identified four distinct orientations — *vocational, academic, personal* and *social* — existing in two forms — *extrinsic* and *intrinsic*. Extrinsic orientations involve looking towards the utility of the qualifications and experiences, while intrinsic orientations concern different forms of anticipated internalized reward. An outline description of these categories is shown in Table 1.

Subsequent interviews conducted by Taylor and her colleagues (1981, 1982) involved comparisons between students at the University of Surrey and adults enrolled with the Open University. Although the samples are small, it appears that school leavers are motivated predominantly by varying combinations of vocational, academic, and social concerns, while the Open University students seem to give personal development a higher priority in taking up studying again.

It may be interesting to gain something of the 'flavour' of this personal orientation. Mature students taking Open University courses said, for example (from Gibbs *et al.*, 1984):

> 'It's something I've always wanted to do. For personal reasons between me and my parents I didn't go to university when I should have done. I've had a hankering ever since to discover whether or not I could have done it.'

Table 1. Students' Orientations to Higher Education

Orientation	Interest	Aim	Concerns
Vocational	Extrinsic	Obtaining a qualification	Perceived worth of qualification
	Intrinsic	Being well trained	Relevance to future career
Academic	Extrinsic	Progression up educational ladder	Academic progress and performance
	Intrinsic	Pursuing subject for its own sake	Choosing stimulating courses or topics
Personal	Extrinsic	Compensation for past failures	Reassuring comments and pass marks
	Intrinsic	Broadening horizons	New insights and challenges
Social	Extrinsic	Having a good time	Facilities for sport and social activities

Source: Adapted from Gibbs *et al.*, (1984)

'I'm hoping I'll be able to see things from different points of view and not be too single minded about things. I hope at the end I'll be able to converse with people more easily without getting nervous.'

'I would like to think that it might make me more interesting really. I want to feel that I've had an exciting day and I've learnt something to-day or read something to-day — and so hopefully enrich me as a person.'

'The topics I like I will sit and read forever. If I think it will be useful to me, then I'll do more; but some things aren't that useful.'

'The reaction of people is terribly important — and it is not just seeing the reaction. I want to know the reason people react under various kinds of circumstances. So far, all I have is observations, you know — experiences. [The psychology course] is important because I hope it will help me to understand people more. But I'm not going to use the qualification at the end of the day, so that side of it is not important to me.'

Conceptions of Learning and Approaches to Studying

The difficulties that mature students have in coming back into formal education after years away from studying are well known, but it is essential to recognize that these difficulties are not just the result of 'being rusty' or lacking specific study skills or techniques. There is a much more fundamental problem, particularly for people who did not reach the sixth form.

Interviews with adults in Sweden have shown marked differences between people who have had extended education and those who left school early in the way they conceptualize 'learning' (Säjö, 1979,1981,1982). When they were asked 'What do you actually mean by "learning"?', the main distinction among their replies was between those who saw knowledge as always factual or learning 'taken for granted' as memorization, and others who discussed alternative meanings of learning under different conditions or circumstances.

The educationally inexperienced tended to equate learning with school, and school with rote memorization and the reproduction of factual details — and coming back to studying later on they expected the same demands to be made by teachers.

'I want questions which go straight to the point — "Who was Napoleon?" and "When was the French Revolution?" . . . because I think it is easier to learn and remember them.'

'A really important cornerstone of your studies is your memory, that you do remember things. That's just what makes it so depressing all the time, that one doesn't remember.' (Säljö, 1982, pp. 78, 82).

The more sophisticated learners recognized that there were different types of learning — rote and meaningful learning — and that each had to be used, but for different purposes.

'It all depends on what it is you are going to learn. In languages, if you are able to do the homework properly, then it is a matter of being able to reel off all the prepositions and such like . . . and then you sort of know it. But if it's something different, like in physics or something like that, you have to really know, then you sort of have to understand it.' (Säljö, 1982, p. 84).

These interviews were part of a series of studies in Gothenburg conducted by Ference Marton and his colleagues (Marton *et al.*, 1984) which have shown how students' perceptions of academic tasks affect their approaches to studying. If 'learning' is equated with 'memorization of facts', then academic articles are likely to be read with the intention of locating potential examination questions and learning those facts or ideas verbatim. This has been called a *surface approach* to studying. In contrast, other students approach an article with a more sophisticated conception of learning and with an intention to extract personal meaning: they adapt a *deep approach*.

'Whilst reading the article, I took great care in trying to understand what the author was getting at, looking out for arguments, and facts which backed up the arguments . . . I found myself continually relating the article to personal experience, and thus facilitated my understanding of it.' (Entwistle, 1981, p. 78).

The qualitative analysis of students' experiences of studying and reading articles have repeatedly shown a close relationship between the approach to learning and the level of understanding reached. This relationship is almost inevitable. Not only does a deep approach facilitate deeper understanding, it also aids factual recall, and is associated with better examination results (Marton and Säljö, 1976a; Svensson, 1977). Certainly the intention to rote learn rules out the possibility of developing personal understanding, although the intention to understand may, of course, not always be fulfilled.

Research conducted at Lancaster University (Entwistle and Ramsden, 1983; Ramsden, 1981) has shown the importance of previous knowledge in allowing a deep approach to be adopted, particularly in the sciences. The other crucial factors are interest or relevance, self-confidence as opposed to anxiety (Fransson, 1977), and the type of assessment procedure anticipated. Säljö (1975; Marton and Säljö, 1976b) has shown that when factual tests are anticipated, even the best students shift from a deep to a surface approach in their reading. As one Lancaster student said of termly tests:

'I hate to say it, but what you've got to do is have a list of the "facts": you write down ten important points and memorize those, then you'll do all right in the test. . . . If you can give a bit of factual information — so and so did that and concluded that — for two sides of writing, then you'll get a good mark.' (Ramsden, 1981).

The crucial effects of assessment procedures on studying have also been demonstrated in two well-known American studies. In *Making the Grade* (Becker *et al.*, 1968) students' activities were interpreted as being largely coping ploys designed to achieve the grades necessary to make progress through their degree courses. Subsequently Snyder (1971) explained such behaviour in terms of a distinction between the formal and the 'hidden' curriculum. The formal curriculum, as perceived by staff, demanded originality, problem-solving, independence of thought, and analytic skills. But what influenced students most was the hidden curriculum — their perceptions of what was most rewarded by the assessment procedures. Students believed that what mattered most was the correct reproduction of factual detail, and their study strategies were based on that belief.

So far, it is clear from interviews that students enter university with contrasting orientations and conceptions of learning which are likely to affect their initial approaches to studying. Through inadequate schooling, mature students may initially find it particularly difficult to adopt a deep approach. Yet many of them will have a predominantly personal orientation to higher education and will seek the satisfaction of developing personal meaning from a deep approach to learning. Inappropriate assessment procedures will be a barrier to this approach. But is there evidence about the types of teaching most likely to encourage meaningful learning?

The Effects of Teaching on Learning

The results of an SSRC research programme at Lancaster have extended our understanding of how teaching may affect students' approaches to studying. A questionnaire enabled estimates to be made of students' approaches to studying and of their perceptions of the departments in which they were mainly studying. These perceptions were described in terms of two main dimensions.

One of these — formal teaching methods, clear goals and standards, and vocational relevance — is chiefly descriptive of subject area differences. These characteristics of departments are perceived to be most often present in science and professional studies departments. The second main grouping is of scales which describe students' evaluations of the quality of the learning context in their department. Good teaching, freedom in learning, and staff openness to students are the defining characteristics of this evaluative dimension, with social climate and light workload playing lesser parts. (Ramsden, 1984; but see also Ramsden, 1981, and Ramsden and Entwistle, 1981).

It was found that, irrespective of subject area or discipline, departments differed considerably in terms of their students' evaluative judgments. Departments rated highly on good teaching and freedom in learning contained a higher proportion of students reporting deep approaches to learning. Surface approaches, in contrast, tended to predominate in departments rated as having a heavy workload and allowing little freedom in learning. It was clear that approaches to learning *were* associated with experiences of teaching — and comments in the interviews showed that the students themselves saw these as causal relationships. Students' attitudes to studying were also found to be related to their evaluations of the departments, but organized study methods seemed to be a characteristic of the students, relatively unaffected by their experiences of teaching.

Marton and Säljö (1976b) showed that surface approaches to learning were relatively easy to induce in students, while deep approaches were difficult to encourage. Just as we would expect from these findings, the survey analysis revealed that it was much easier to predict which departments would score highly on the (surface approach . . . than on the deep approach). In other words, it seems very likely indeed that some departments push students towards surface approaches; others appear to provide contexts which help students to develop an interest in the subject matter and permit them to use approaches aimed at understanding. The second type of departmental context does not, however, offer any guarantee that students will develop an orientation towards meaning. (Ramsden, 1984, p. 27).

It has already been noted that, particularly in the sciences, a deep approach depends on firmly established previous knowledge. The Gothenburg studies (Dahlgren, 1978) found that first-year students had particular difficulty in answering questions which demanded a thorough understanding of the basic concepts they had been taught. The educational psychologist, David Ausubel, puts particular emphasis on identifying the 'anchoring ideas' in a discipline, determining the students' current knowledge base, and on providing for students appropriate advance 'organizers' (ideational frameworks) into which subsequent information can be fitted. 'If I had to reduce all of educational psychology to just one principle, I would say this: the most important single factor influencing learning is what the learner already knows. Ascertain this and teach him accordingly' (Ausubel *et al.*,

1978, p. iv). Many mature students have had inadequate experiences of schooling. For them the importance of re-establishing the conceptual bases of the discipline will be fundamental to subsequent academic success.

The argument from this recent research into student learning is now complete. Mature students may be more likely to want to seek personal meaning in their studying, but they are also liable to be poorly equipped from previous education to carry it out. University departments are able to influence students' approaches to learning. They can certainly try to avoid the excessive workloads and restrictions in freedom in learning which will reinforce the limited, reproductive conception of learning. They can also try to provide the 'good teaching' which opens up opportunities to seek personal meaning. But what does 'good teaching' involve? From the students' perceptions it is clear that this will involve enthusiasm about the subject matter, explicit help with students' problems in studying, commitment to teaching, and the ability to pitch teaching at the right level. As we have seen, a deep approach is encouraged by interest and perceived relevance, while it becomes difficult if the necessary prerequisite knowledge is not available — or if assessment procedures overemphasize the importance of accurate reproduction of factual detail.

The Capabilities and Needs of Adult Students

Early psychological research on the intellectual capabilities of adults produced a rather depressing picture. It seemed that measured intelligence reached a peak towards the age of 20 and gradually declined thereafter. Cumulating evidence that abilities to reason logically diminished with age, that it became progressively more difficult to learn and remember facts, and that there was a steady increase of rigidity in both thinking and attitudes, served to create an impression of the adult learner as 'sans everything' necessary for advanced intellectual endeavour. This view is not shared by adult educators, and psychologists have now begun to present a more complex and differentiated picture of adults' intellectual capabilities (Lovell, 1980) and of their continuing personal development.

The Intellectual Capabilities of Adults

The use of intelligence tests to investigate changes in adult intelligence with age showed a steady decrease in scores beyond age 20 (Wechsler, 1958). But this research was cross-sectional and so ignored the restricted opportunities for schooling which had been available to the older age-groups: it also assumed that the types of questions found suitable to assess adolescent intelligence would be equally suitable for older people. Conclusions from the most recent longitudinal and cohort sequential studies show that although there is some decline in intellectual abilities, it does not become marked until old age. It is, however, clear that adults do less well on tests which involve the rapid solving of problems or assimilation of new information. They need longer to learn and, above all, a longer time to retrieve information from memory and to make appropriate responses (Thompson, 1982). Some adults also seem less able to reorganize incoming information to provide cues for subsequent recall.

> The general consensus then is that the actual storage of information is relatively unimpaired with age; the difficulty is bringing this information out of storage. [Moreover] as the amount of material to be remembered increases, older adults find it takes more time to search their memories for correct information. (Thompson, 1982, p. 80)

It might, then, be assumed that the educational achievements of adults will be below average. Of course this will be so, if adults' intellectual abilities are different — and if courses are geared to the particular strengths of younger students. The psychological evidence does suggest strongly, however, that this outcome is not inevitable (Thompson, 1982; Schaie and Parr, 1981; Foulds, 1981); if the intellectual demands are changed by using learning tasks more relevant to adults, by providing more advance structuring of information, and above all by allowing more time, the apparent decrement in learning capabilities with age largely disappears.

Intellectual and Personal Development during Adulthood

Ideas on intellectual decrements in adulthood derive mainly from research into logical and analytic skills which also treats knowledge as essentially quantitative. But the developmental tradition of research views intellectual performance on cognitive tests as an inadequate description of intellectual status. It emphasizes instead the qualitative growth in personal meaning, and assumes that higher education involves *transformation* of information and ideas, more than simply *accretion* of knowledge.

Ashby (1973) used Kohlberg's (1969) term 'post-conventional reasoning' to describe one of the main aims of university teaching. The student is expected to progress 'from the uncritical acceptance of orthodoxy to creative dissent over the values and standards of society ... [in universities] there must be opportunities for the intellect to be stretched to its capacity, the critical faculty sharpened to the point where it can change ideas' (pp. 147, 149).

In an influential investigation of the intellectual development of American 'Ivy League' students, Perry (1970) identified a progression from thinking which involved the simple dualism of 'right' or 'wrong', through a gradual recognition of relativism, to a commitment to an academic and personal 'world view' which was based on detailed knowledge, individual interpretation, and toleration of alternative positions. The more sophisticated students had developed disciplined, contextual relativistic reasoning which involved

> the capacity to examine thought, including one's own. Theories become not 'truth' but metaphors or 'models', approximating the order of observed data or experience. Comparison, involving systems of logic, assumptions and inferences, all relative to context, will show some interpretations to be 'better', others 'worse', many worthless. Yet even after extensive analyses there will remain areas of great concern in which reasonable people will reasonably disagree. It is in this sense that relativism is inescapable and forms the epistemological context of all further developments (Perry, 1981, p. 88).

In moving beyond relativism towards informed commitment, students had come to grips with the 'paradoxical necessity to be both wholehearted and tentative — attitudes that one cannot "compromise" but must hold together, with all their tensions' (p. 96). Perry describes emotional reactions of at least some students in coming to grips with ultimate uncertainty, and their anxieties in wrestling with conflicting ideas and interpretations to reach a personal understanding. He rejects the idea of education as the transmission of knowledge, arguing instead for 'the centrality of the individual learner as the maker of meaning.... We need to teach dialectically — that is, to introduce our students ... not only to the orderly certainties of our subject matter but to its unresolved dilemmas' (Perry, 1981, pp. 108, 109). Perry's evidence showed that intellectual development was not wholly a cognitive experience, and that few students, even at Harvard, reached the highest levels of his developmental 'scheme' while at college. Although the courses often encouraged development through confronting relativism, his research did not indicate whether similar development could be anticipated among young adults not at college by a reflective analysis of the contradictions and dilemmas of everyday life.

If such development does take place, perhaps some adults will have a developmental advantage in their modes of thinking to offset any diminution in rapid logical reasoning. Weathersby (1981) uses a similar developmental scheme (Loevinger, 1976) to demonstrate that adult students have progressed, in fact, further in their 'searching for coherent meanings in experience' (ego development) than most younger students. The equivalent of post-conventional thinking was detected in 81 per cent of students attending an external adult degree programme, compared with 68 per cent of 18-year-olds attending an Ivy League college, and 47 per cent in an urban university. Weathersby (1977) also found a wide variation among the adults in their conceptions of education, which she explained in terms of their differing developmental positions.

Nearly everyone says education is valuable; however, across stages the source of value shifts from concern with the practical benefit of getting a job, or a more desirable job, to a means of developing one's skills and capacities for advancement and personal growth, to help in coping with life and involvement in a lifelong learning process that has intrinsic value for self-fulfilment (Weathersby, 1981, p. 59).

Weathersby also found similar developmental changes in the reasons students gave for returning to studying. The most popular reason was that 'a degree was necessary for career goals' (22 per cent), but at the higher levels of development, additional more complex reasons were given:

(At the earlier stages) reorientation and redirection are the most salient ... (together with) getting a degree or finishing one's education, ... intellectual challenge and stimulation.... The importance of being able to study valued interests at depth becomes salient at post-conventional stages, as do personal growth and fulfilment. Responses at the lower ego levels are often flat and one-dimensional; (at higher levels) people give multifaceted reasons that reflect their personal goals and life experience. (p. 64)

What is striking in the extracts from interviews with the developmentally mature adults is that they see their university course as part of their own learning programme, and they resent formal institutional demands of fixed curricula which threaten to interfere with their long-term aims. It is perhaps not sufficiently realized that many adults are engaged in systematic attempts to develop knowledge and skills along their own lines. From surveys in several countries, Tough (1978) has estimated that:

About 90 per cent of all adults conduct at least one major learning effort each year. The average person conducts five distinct learning projects ... and 100 hours per learning effort in a year.... During the interviews, many unsolicited statements and actions conveying enthusiasm and commitment ... (indicated) the strong determination to succeed and the perseverance despite difficulties. (Tough, 1981, p. 297)

Advocates of continuing education often speak of the value of the adult's high level of motivation and experience of life. But that motivation may be narrowly focused on clearly defined personal objectives. Unless university courses for adult students are designed to utilize life experience, and allow students, to some extent, to follow their own idiosyncratic interests, their high level of motivation may all too easily turn into angry frustration. Yet the less mature, or more anxious, adult students may still prefer a tightly controlled curriculum and clear directions about what to study. Perhaps the most consistent message from the psychological literature is that we shall have to cope with an even wider range than usual of differences in ability, interests and levels of intellectual development. Attempts to distinguish in simple terms between the 'conventional' entrant and the 'adult student' are likely to be profoundly misleading.

Meeting the Needs of Adult Learners

The research on student learning showed the existence of contrasting orientations to education. It seemed that adult students might be more likely to have a 'personal' orientation than younger students. The work of Weathersby in the USA developed this idea further by showing how conceptions of education and reasons for studying changed not so much with chronological age as with developmental maturity. Nevertheless, people over 40 are more likely to have strong personal interests in studying than is true of the younger students who are predominantly interested in obtaining qualifications and training. Many adult students are, of course, still young and retain strong vocational motives. Among adult learners, many will have had discouraging previous experiences of formal education. They will have continued to learn experientially and may have developed considerable interest in specific subject areas. Such adults will come into higher education with strong, but narrowly focused, motivation. They will want to gain a personal understanding of the topics they are interested in, but may have an inappropriate conception of learning, and poorly developed study skills. The method of teaching will have to be carefully geared to provide strong initial support and guidance, together with the freedom to pursue individual interests as skills and confidence are developed.

As the possibility of following a 'deep approach' towards personal meaning demands both perceived relevance and prior knowledge, particular attention will have to be paid to locating and remedying incomplete understanding of the 'anchoring ideas' and basic interpretative or analytic skills of the discipline. New information and ideas can then be presented on a secure foundation. But it will also be important to provide 'ideational scaffolding' to help the students organize their developing knowledge effectively, and ensure that they are not overburdened initially either with unnecessary factual detail or with excessive workloads (particularly long reading lists without structure or guidance). In these early stages adult students have to be helped to learn how to learn and to gain self-confidence. It is probably in this initial stage, where the return to formal education may seem alien and threatening, that they are most likely to drop out.

References

ASHBY, E. (1973) 'The structure of higher education: A world view', *Higher Education*, 2, pp. 142–51

AUSUBEL, D.P. *et al.* (1978) *Educational Psychology: A Cognitive View*, New York, Holt, Rinehart, and Winston.

BECKER, A.S. *et al.* (1968) *Making the Grade: The Academic Side of College Life*, New York, Wiley.

CHICKERING, A.W. (Ed.) (1981) *The Modern American College*, San Francisco, Jossey Bass.

DAHLGREN, L.O. (1978) 'Qualitative differences in conceptions of basic principles in economics', paper read to the 4th International Conference on Higher Education at Lancaster, 29 August–1 September 1978.

ENTWISTLE, N.J. (1981) *Styles of Learning and Teaching*, London, Wiley.

ENTWISTLE, N.J. (1982) *Learning from the Student's Perspective*, Leicester, British Psychological Society.

ENTWISTLE, N.J. and RAMSDEN, P. (1983) *Understanding Student Learning*, London, Croom Helm.

FOULDS, A.M. (1981) *Age Differences in Aspects of Memory Performance*, University of Nottingham, Department of Adult Education.

FRANSSON, A. (1977) 'On qualitative differences in learning IV — Effects of motivation and test anxiety on process and outcome', *Br. J. Educ. Psychol.*, 47, pp. 244–57.

GIBBS, G. *et al.* (1984) 'The world of the learner', in MARTON, F. *et al.* (Eds) *The Experience of Learning*, Edinburgh, Scottish Academic Press.

HOPPER, E. and OSBORN, M. (1975) *Adult Students: Education, Selection and Social Control*, London, Frances Pinter.

KOHLBERG, L. (1969) 'Stage and sequence: The cognitive-developmental approach to socialization', in GOSLIN, D.A. (Ed.), *Handbook of Socialization Theory and Research*, Chicago, Rand McNally.

LOEVINGER, J. (1976) *Ego Development: Conceptions and Theories*, San Francisco, Jossey Bass.

LOVELL, R.B. (1980) *Adult Learning*, London, Croom Helm.

MARTON, F. (1975) 'What does it take to learn?' in ENTWISTLE, N.J. and HOUNSELL, D.J. (Eds), *How Students Learn*, University of Lancaster, Institute for Post-Compulsory Education.

MARTON, F. and SÄLJÖ, R. (1976a) 'On qualitative differences in learning I — Outcome and process', *Brit. J. Educ. Psychol.*, 46, pp. 4–11.

MARTON, F. and SÄLJÖ, R. (1976b) 'On qualitative differences in learning II — Outcome as a function of the learner's conception of the task', *Br. J. Educ. Psychol*, 46, pp. 115–27.

MARTON, F. *et al.* (1984) *The Experience of Learning*, Edinburgh, Scottish Academic Press.

MEDSKER, L. *et al.* (1975) *Extending Opportunities for a College Degree: Practices, Problems, and Potentials*, Berkeley, Center for Research and Development in Higher Education (ERIC Document ED 125 418).

PERRY, W.G. (1970) *Forms of Intellectual and Ethical Development in the College Years: A Scheme*, New York, Holt, Rinehart and Winston.

PERRY, W.G. (1981), 'Cognitive and ethical growth: The making of meaning', in CHICKERING, A.W. (Ed.), *The Modern American College*, San Francisco, Jossey Bass.

RAMSDEN, P. (1981) *A Study of the Relationship between Student Learning and Its Academic Context*, unpublished PhD thesis, University of Lancaster.

RAMSDEN, P. (1984) 'The context of learning', in MARTON, F. *et al.* (Eds) *The Experience of Learning*, Edinburgh, Scottish Academic Press.

RAMSDEN, P. and ENTWISTLE, N.J. (1981) 'Effects of academic departments on students' approaches to studying', *Br. J. Educ. Psychol.*, 51, pp. 368–83.

SÄLJÖ, R. (1975) *Qualitative Differences in Learning as a Function of the Learner's Conception of the Task*, Gothenburg, Acta Universitatis Gothoburgensis.

SÄLJÖ, R. (1979) 'Learning about learning', *Higher Education*, 8, pp. 443–51.

SÄLJÖ, R. (1981) 'Learning approach and outcome; some empirical observations', *Instructional Sci.*, 10, pp. 47–65.

SÄLJÖ, R. (1982) *Learning and Understanding*, Gothenburg, Acta Universitatis Gothoburgensis.

SANDERS, C. (1961) *Psychological and Educational Bases of Academic Performance*, Brisbane, Australian Council for Educational Research.

SCHAIE, K.W. and PARR, J. (1981) 'Intelligence', in CHICKERING, A.W. (Ed.) *The Modern American College*, San Francisco, Jossey Bass.

SNYDER, B. (1971) *The Hidden Curriculum*, Massachusetts Institute of Technology Press.

SVENSSON, L. (1977) 'On qualitative differences in learning III — Study skill and learning', *Br. J. Educ. Psychol.*, 47, pp. 233–43.

TAYLOR, E. (1983) Orientation to study: A longitudinal investigation of two degree courses in one university', unpublished PhD thesis, University of Surrey.

TAYLOR, E. *et al.* (1981) 'The orientations of Open University students to their studies', *Teaching at a Distance*, 20, pp. 3–12.

TAYLOR, E. *et al.* (1982) *Students' Perceptions of Gains from the Social Science Foundation Course*, Study Methods Group Report No. 11, Open University, Institute of Educational Technology.

THOMPSON, D. (1982) 'Adult development', in MITZEL, H.E. (Ed.), *Encyclopedia of Educational Research*, 5th ed., London, Collier Macmillan.

THOMPSON, J.B. (1981) 'An interview study of the attitudes, expectations, and motivations of 124 students in higher education', unpublished PhD thesis, University of Lancaster.

TOUGH, A. (1978) 'Major learning efforts: Recent research and future directions', *Adult Education*, 28, pp. 250–63.

TOUGH, A. (1981) 'Interests of adult learners', in CHICKERING, A.W. (Ed.), *The Modern American College*, San Francisco, Jossey Bass.

WEATHERSBY, R.P. (1977) 'A developmental perspective on adults' uses of formal education', unpublished doctoral dissertation, Graduate School of Education, Harvard University.

WEATHERSBY, R.P. (1981) 'Ego-development', in CHICKERING, A.W. (Ed.), *The Modern American College*, San Francisco, Jossey Bass.

WECHSLER, D. (1958) *The Measurement and Appraisal of Adult Intelligence*, 3rd ed., Baltimore, Williams and Williams.

Teaching Study Skills*

Graham Gibbs
Oxford Polytechnic

Students new to higher education, and even those new to sixth forms, are asked to tackle learning tasks which make demands on them different from any they have ever faced before. It is not simply the sheer quantity of material to be learned, or even the new responsibilities students have to take for the way they go about this learning, which makes the heaviest demands. The meaning of learning itself changes. Students have to become independent not only in their self-discipline and self-organization in order to cope with studying, but also, ultimately, in their epistemological stance.

While I passed A-level history at school by memorizing the eight causes of the French Revolution, history students at the institution where I now work are asked to evaluate alternative theoretical frameworks for making sense of such social changes as those associated with the French Revolution — and this in their first term, perhaps only four months after taking their A-levels! This sort of difference in the nature of learning tasks can be enormously difficult for students to recognize and adjust to. While teachers can help in the teaching methods they use and in making their teaching goals explicit and clear, this is often not enough. Students need time and space to examine not just the subject matter of their learning, its *content*, but also the *process* of their learning itself. Most teachers do not have a lot of experience of helping students to examine the process of their learning, and they not unnaturally turn to books on the subject for advice. However, until very recently there were simply *no* books written for teachers on this subject. There are over a hundred *How to Study* guides written for students, with advice on how to take notes, how to concentrate, and so on, but these are of very limited use to teachers. It is the ineffectiveness of simply giving advice to students that led to the development of student-centred workshops which

* This article comprises extracts from *Teaching Study Skills* (1981) Milton Keynes, Open University Press.

encourage students to share their previous experiences of learning, led by their own teachers or lecturers using specially prepared materials and group discussion methods.

Taking a Student-Centred Approach

I have been trying for a student-centred approach of some sort ever since the first didactic study skill courses I ran were a disaster. Students start off not as complete blanks, as *tabula rasa,* but with habitual ways of going about reading, writing and discussion, and they develop from and change these ways slowly and with difficulty. They do not adopt entire new approaches wholesale. Conceptions of what learning and studying involve are usually deep-rooted, often based in powerful experiences from school. It is these conceptions which form the framework for the way techniques are adopted and employed. Unless existing habits and conceptions are taken into account, little of significance will occur.

Also the students themselves are in the best position to judge the appropriateness and value of new techniques. Whether a technique suits an individual, whether it meets the demands of the learning tasks, and whether it can be used appropriately, given the present level of intellectual development of the individual can only be decided by the individual himself. Our job is to help the individual make the decision.

Giving Responsibility to the Student

Improvements in studying do not take place only during study skills courses and at no other time. They take place at any and all times during studying and when expert advice is not available. Developing as a learner is a continuous process, and unless the student takes responsibility for this process — for becoming aware of how he is learning and noticing what works and what does not — then change will be impeded. Instead of making students dependent on expert advice and evaluation, self-evaluation and self-awareness should be encouraged. Only when students can see for themselves what the advantages and disadvantages of different ways of going about a study task are is development likely.

There is a tendency to carefully explain to students exactly what is good and bad about some notes or an essay, when in fact they are perfectly capable of judging for themselves. Students are often surprised when they realize they already have plenty of criteria available to them to judge essays, and even more surprised when they discover that their criteria are very similar to their tutor's. In the past they have simply not been in the habit of applying these criteria to themselves, but have left all judgments to teachers. Helping students to judge their studying for themselves is a crucial aspect of helping them to develop as learners. This emphasis on personal responsibility is based in Carl Rogers' 'principles of learning':

> Learning is facilitated when the student participates responsibly in the learning process. When he chooses his own direction, helps to discover his own learning resources, formulates his own problems, decides his own course of action, lives with the consequences of each of these choices, then significant learning is maximised.
>
> Independence, creativity and self reliance are all facilitated when self-criticism and self-evaluation are basic.... (Rogers, 1969, pp. 162–3)

Making Change Safe

Studying, and especially assessment, can be very threatening to students. Flexible and effective ways of studying can involve risks. Fransson (1977) has demonstrated experimentally that students who were made highly anxious by a test approached their study in a 'surface processing' way and made ineffective, reproductive attempts to answer the test questions. He concluded: 'If deep level processing is valued, every effort must be made to avoid threatening conditions.... ' This is obviously not a new discovery. Dewey (1913) discussed this effect seventy years ago and the role of threat in inhibiting meaningful learning is a central theme in Carl Rogers' 'principles of learning' (1969), including his fifth principle: 'When threat to the self is low, experience can be perceived in differential fashion, and learning can proceed.' Similarly, analysis of the motivation of students to study suggests that limited, inflexible and surface processing approaches to learning are common among students motivated by a fear of failure (Entwistle and Wilson, 1977; Biggs, 1976).

Under threat we sometimes regress to cruder ways of seeing things which we have employed at an earlier stage in our understanding. Perry (1977, p. 123) has observed that: '... a student, as he loses confidence in himself, tends paradoxically to fall back on less and less productive methods of learning.' Similarly, Perry (1970) has described how students revert to earlier stages in their intellectual development when their ideas are under threat. It has always seemed to me that it is exactly those students who are most in need of a more flexible approach to their learning and who feel least secure in the efficiency of their existing approaches who are most deeply entrenched and least likely to change.

Any attempt to help students to develop must provide a safe context for students to examine their existing methods and try out new methods without personal risk. Evaluating students' study methods or their outcomes can obstruct their development.

Graham Gibbs

Emphasizing Purpose Rather Than Technique

This is simply what I argued for above. The emphasis should always be on what study methods are *for* rather than merely on the steps to take to use them. What they are *for* involves the student's overall orientation, conception of learning and stage of intellectual development, and these influence the perceived demands of learning tasks. Techniques should be seen as ways of meeting these demands.

Emphasizing Reconceptualization of Study Tasks

As I argued above, the most important changes which take place as students develop are changes in the way learning is conceptualized and in the epistemological stance taken. Working within a student's existing stage of development allows a certain limited scope for greater efficiency, but often only a broad reconceptualization of what a study task is about will provide scope for significant development. There is little point in teaching a student to go about essay writing in a thoroughly organized and efficient manner if, overall, the student takes a surface approach from an absolutist intention to reproduce the 'right' answer.

Emphasizing Students' Awareness

I have argued that students become more aware about learning in various ways. They become able to reflect on it, and to recognize and distinguish between various different demands made on them by learning tasks. Above everything else, it is the encouragement of students' active reflection about their studying which is the cornerstone to their development. Simply adopting a new technique will be to little avail if it is not accompanied by the student actively thinking about what he is trying to do with it when it is applied. Sophisticated and inept learners may be almost indistinguishable in terms of their observable study habits. Neither may appear organized. Their notes may look equally haphazard, their essay plans entirely missing. But the sophisticated student will be able to explain the process and purpose underlying his apparently hopeless study methods, while the inept student will be able to say practically nothing about his.

Awareness and reflection are not merely symptoms of developments in learners, they bring about the developments. It is through engaging students in reflecting upon the process and outcomes of their studying that progress is made. Passively following advice results in little such reflection, and so little improvement.

What the Lecturers Learned

One of the 'unexpected' outcomes of the workshops, which seems enormously beneficial, is that teachers can discover some of the consequences of their teaching and curricula and how they affect the way students study. If students are being given advice on how to study this does not happen. But if a student-centred exercise is used, teachers can discover that, for example, their students are spending a disproportionate amount of time on an activity not considered important by the teacher. Not all learning problems are the students' fault, and student-centred exercises can be dramatically effective in isolating other causes of ineffective learning. I should like to give a couple of examples here to illustrate this.

I was asked to come in to a language department at a university on one occasion, in order to improve the way their students learnt, which was considered by the lecturers to be inept. One of the students' ineptitudes was considered to be that they read extremely slowly, and I was asked to train them in speed reading techniques. Instead I asked the lecturers to select an example of the sort of reading material they felt students should be reading more of, and in an exercise asked both lecturers and students to start reading the particular book chosen. After a while I simply stopped everyone and asked them to describe to each other what they had been doing and why. Students eventually formed groups of four and then reported their conclusions, and the four lecturers did the same. It emerged that the students had been reading extremely carefully. The book was a parallel text of a classic novel in the particular language, with English on one page and the language on the other. Students had been trying to identify the author's characteristic style and a wide variety of devices of literature: irony, pathos and so on. They had been trying to memorize vocabulary they did not know, and work out grammatical forms with which they were unfamiliar. They were, without exception, reading extremely slowly. In contrast the lecturers had devoured half a chapter in the same time. It quickly emerged that the students had gained completely the wrong impression of what sort of task they had been set. The lecturers explained that they wanted students to get plenty of practice at reading the language, and had chosen the particular novel for its academic respectability, though motorbike magazines or thrillers would have done just as well. Their main concern was for sheer quantity of reading. The students had assumed that universities were concerned with more esoteric matters and were going about their reading for entirely different reasons. There was no study skill problem — only a problem of understanding the demands of a study task, and this was cleared up by making those demands more explicit.

As a second example I have chosen a situation where the diagnosed problem was identical, but the cause quite different. Again a university department, in this case a psychology department, was concerned about the study skills of its first-year students. In particular they seemed not to be reading enough. The scale of this problem quickly became apparent when, in an exercise on how students actually spent their time before and after the course started, it emerged that students had actually been reading *more* psychology *before* the course started! But the cause was not far away. Three-quarters of all their time outside class contact hours was spent writing up laboratory reports! This turned out to be because laboratory reports were marked severely and the students were worried about not passing the first year. In fact there was a pass-fail entry into the second year and a student would have had to commit murder to fail, but the students did not know this. Their lack of reading was a direct consequence of a fear of failure and the perceived demands of the assessment system. Again, apparent poor study skill was caused by teachers.

If teaching students to learn is undertaken by specialist counsellors or study skill experts — because it is seen as a very demanding teaching task — then these sorts of outcomes seldom get back to teachers and the root of the learning problem is never tackled. Only if an approach is adopted which is so easy that teachers can use it in the context of their own departments, even in their own classrooms, is it likely that they will be tackled. In every exercise I have ever run issues have arisen which were to do with *constraints* on students' learning over which the students had no control. To approach teaching students to learn in a way which does not bring out these issues is to ignore half the problem. Either giving advice, or using specialist agencies to undertake the task, is to ignore half the problem.

This brings me to a final point: that you can bring a horse to water, but you cannot make him drink. Occasions will inevitably arise, if you use this approach, where your own and your students' goals in education become clarified publicly, and they are found to be profoundly different: where what you want your students to be doing is different from what they are doing and what they say they want to be doing. I have had students tell me after a series of exercises that they could now see the way they *could* go about studying on their course, but that they were not going to because it was not necessary to do so in order to pass their examinations. All this approach can hope to do is to help students to be in a position where they can see and understand the learning options open to them, and where their awareness makes them free to make their own decisions as to what to do. It may take fundamental changes in the whole educational context within which students study for them to choose to study in the way you would like them to.

References

BIGGS, J.B. (1976) 'Dimensions of study behaviour: another look at a.t.i.' *Br. J. Educ. Psychol.*, 46, pp. 68–80.

DEWEY, J. (1913) *Interest and Effort in Education*, Boston: Houghton Mifflin.

ENTWISTLE, N.J. and WILSON, J.D. (1977), *Degrees of Excellence: the Academic Achievement Game*, London, Hodder and Stoughton.

FRANSSON, A. (1977) 'On qualitative differences in learning, IV — Effects of motivation and test anxiety on process and outcome', *Br. J. Educ. Psychol.*, 47, pp. 244–57.
PERRY, W.G. (1970) *Forms of Intellectual and Ethical Development in the College Years: A Scheme*, New York, Holt, Rinehart and Winston.
PERRY, W.G. (1977) 'Studying and the student', *Higher Education Bulletin*, 5, pp. 120–4.
ROGERS, C.R. (1969) *Freedom to Learn*, Columbus, Ohio, Merrill.

Understanding the Quality of Pupil Learning Experiences

Charles Desforges, University of East Anglia
Neville Bennett, Anne Cockburn and Betty Wilkinson,
University of Lancaster

Several recent studies have raised concern about the quality of the learning experiences provided for pupils in schools (Anderson, 1981; HMI, 1978, 1982). Specifically, it appears that many of the tasks given to pupils are not well matched to their attainments. In some areas of the curriculum HMI found that over two-thirds of the work given to children was not appropriate to fostering their learning. Anderson (1981) showed that for many children inappropriate tasks were an enduring fact of classroom life. In particular, tasks which were too difficult were assigned frequently to low-achieving children. Unfortunately it is one thing to recognize a problem and quite another to know what to do about it.

There is no shortage of advice on the matter. This advice is very familiar to teachers. In the recent Cockcroft report, for example, it was recognized that in specifying good mathematics teaching, '. . . we are aware that we are not saying anything which has not already been said many times and over many years' (Cockcroft, 1982, p. 72).

Psychologists especially have been more than forthcoming in offering teachers prescriptions on how to design ideal learning environments. It is now widely recognized that such advice has had very little impact on the practice of teaching (Atkinson, 1976; Ausubel and Robinson, 1969; Farnham-Diggory, 1976; Glaser *et al.*, 1977). There are no doubt many reasons for this lack of impact. Some arise out of the manner in which those who have studied teaching and learning have oversimplified the lives of classroom participants (Bronfenbrenner, 1976). Until recently, research on learning has ignored the processes of teaching, and research on teaching has neglected the processes of learning. Consequently some of the advice to teachers emanating from research was consistent only with theories of cognition and therefore did not attend to the constraints on the teacher.

The approach from theories of cognition has been adopted by Bruner (1964), Ausubel (1968) and Posner (1978), for example. It is also manifest in most of the attempts to generate pedagogic implications from Piaget's theory (Duckworth, 1979; Schwebel and Raph, 1974). Typically ignored here are the teacher's limited resources of materials and time and the attention she must pay to the social and emotional needs of her pupils. Typically overestimated is the teacher's autonomy of action in respect of the choice of aims, teaching materials, timetable organization and the selection of priorities. The impracticality of this approach has long been asserted (Sullivan, 1967, for example) and is now accepted as an issue to be taken seriously in the development of pedagogy (Biggs and Collis, 1982; Ginsburg, 1981; Kuhn, 1979). Conversely, some of the advice was consistent only with theories of teaching and set aside the problems and potential of the learner.

Advice generated from research on teaching is exemplified in the recent work of Denham and Lieberman (1980). These authors exhort teachers to make tasks clear, obtain and sustain pupil attention, assign appropriate reinforcement and feedback and to cover the material which will be on the end-of-session tests. That these processes are important has never been in contention. However, such research findings have barely caught up with common sense (Jackson, 1977; McNamara, 1981), contribute nothing to an understanding of why teachers behave otherwise in classrooms (Desforges, 1978; Doyle, 1980) and totally ignore the dangers and limitations of the model advocated (McNamara, 1981; NcNeil and Popham, 1973). These dangers include '... curtailment of the teacher's freedom, a disproportionate amount of time spent upon accounting activities and testing, an over concern with static educational objectives and a concentration on those parts of the curriculum which are being tested' (McNamara, 1981).

The Complexity of Classrooms as Learning Environments

It is becoming increasingly clear that classrooms are much more complex learning environments than has previously been admitted by researchers (and possibly by teachers) and that if efforts are to be made to improve the quality of learning experience provided for pupils, then attempts must first be made to understand the connections between the processes of teaching and learning as they operate, and interact, in real classrooms.

Some of the complexity of classroom teaching and learning is illustrated in the following account and analysis of a 7-year-old girl's efforts to work through a mathematics assignment allocated by her teacher. The girl, Helen, is of average ability for her top infant class and she is one of twenty-eight children being taught by a very experienced teacher of infants. The events were recorded as part of a routine observation of the classroom during a major research study on the quality of pupil learning experience in primary schools (Bennett and Desforges, 1983).

The teacher had placed a number of workcards in Helen's book. Helen collected her book and then the following took place:

9.25 a.m.   In Helen's book the teacher had written '1.4.81. money' under which Helen wrote:

    I have 9p

    I buy a box of crayons for _____.

    I have _____ change.

9.30 a.m.   Helen looked at a price list.

9.40 a.m.   The teacher asked Helen what she was looking for and concluded that Helen had mis-read 'crayons' and had been trying to locate the cost of chocolate instead.

9.42 a.m.   The teacher showed Helen the price list she should have been looking at. Helen studied it and eventually found the price of crayons.

9.44 a.m.   She began counting out amounts in half-pence pieces but did not have enough of them for her purposes. She then got a box of cardboard money and counted out 9p in half-pence pieces. After laying these out on her desk Helen counted out 11p in half-pence pieces. She counted all the half-pence and wrote 15p in the space for recording the change.

9.49 a.m.   Helen's next card was as follows:

    I have 19p

    I buy a car for _____

    I buy a rocket for _____

    I spend _____

    I have _____ change.

Having read the card, Helen searched the pictures on the price list for the cost of the items.

9.53 a.m.   She established that a car cost 10p but failed to find the cost of a rocket.

9.55 a.m.   Eventually Helen found that a rocket cost 7p. She began counting half-pence pieces and then announced, 'I've lost count now.'

9.57 a.m.   Helen had 19 pence worth of half-pence pieces on her desk.

9.59 a.m.   She collected 10p and put it on her desk. She then apparently went in search of more coins but changed her mind and returned to her desk without any. She counted out 17p in half-pence pieces.

10.02 a.m.   Helen counted all the half-pence pieces on her desk and wrote down 18½p.

10.03 a.m.   She returned all the coins to their box and went to the teacher's desk.

10.04 a.m.   The teacher marked Helen's work and asked her what 'change' meant.

The work in Helen's book looked like this:

    I have 9p

    I buy a box of crayons for 6½p

    I have 15p change

> I have 19p
> I buy a car for 10p
> I buy a rocket for 7p
> I spend 1½p
> I have 18½ change

On the basis of the above record it seems that this task is very much too difficult for Helen. She appears to be struggling with some of the reading necessary to the task. She does not appear to know when to subtract in respect of these money problems. She does not appear to know about the denomination value of coins and indulges in a strange preoccupation with half-penny pieces. This in turn leads her into performance difficulties. She fails to keep track of her counting behaviour in the face of the sheer quantity of half-pence coins. Finally, she does not appear to know what the word 'change' means.

Helen appears to be so far out of touch with this task that we are bound to ask why she was given it in the first place. Why was the teacher so late in discovering that Helen did not know what the word 'change' meant? How had the teacher failed to notice all of Helen's other problems?

Before observing Helen the research worker had asked the teacher why she had allocated this task to her. The teacher had said that she wanted to familiarize Helen with half-pence in simple shopping sums. All the children had been working with money for some time. The teacher pointed out that half-pence had been introduced two days earlier in accordance with the very detailed school mathematics scheme. In the light of this information the teacher's behaviour becomes much more comprehensible. That is not to say it was justifiable. However, it is at least clear that the teacher was moving Helen through the maths scheme.

When Helen had completed her work for the teacher, the research worker interviewed her in an attempt to understand her problems with the task. He first established that she could read the workcards and the price lists. The following then took place:

The fieldworker asked her to do this sum:
> I have 9p
> I buy a box of crayons for _____
> I have _____ change.

Helen wrote in that the crayons cost 6½p but, having collected a pile of half-pence coins, she appeared to give up and did not complete the sum. When the fieldworker asked what was missing she said '7p'. The conversation continued in the following manner:

Fieldworker: 'Helen if I have 9p and I spend 5p, how much would I have left?'

Helen: '4p.'

Fieldworker: 'If I buy a car for 10p and a kite for 15p, how much do I spend?'

Helen: [Having got out a 10p coin and fifteen 1p coins replied] '25p.'

Fieldworker: 'If I have 20p and I buy a doll, how much have I left?' [The card in front of Helen showed that a doll cost 10p.]

Helen: '10p.'

Fieldworker: 'Can you do this card for me?'

I have 13p. I buy tomatoes for 3p and carrots for 5p.

I spend ____

I have ____ change.

Helen completed the card writing that she spent 8p and had 2p change.

Fieldworker: 'If I have 5p and I spend 2½p, how much do I have left?'

Helen: '2p.'

Fieldworker: 'Can you do this sum for me please?'

I buy a box of crayons for 6½p and a pencil for 1½p. How much do I spend?

Helen wrote '8p'.

This interview forces us to reappraise radically our initial view of Helen's limitations. It appears that she can read the pertinent materials. She does know when to add and subtract on money sums. She does know the denomination value of at least some coins. There is still some doubt about whether she understands the word 'change'. She can add half-pence but, it appears, cannot subtract them.

The teacher's behaviour in assigning the task now becomes much more comprehensible. The task would not appear, on the basis of the above interview, to be well beyond Helen. Why, then, did she have such problems with it? Why did she make it so much more difficult than the teacher intended by attempting to do it in half-pence only? And why did the teacher not recognize her difficulties?

We have to infer answers to these questions. Helen had done money sums over the previous two days. Every sum had focused on half-pence and their conversion to pence. Every sum had been done using half-pence only. On the day of the shopping sums the teacher had given Helen no specific instructions. The nature of the task was assumed. Helen knew what to do when she found the cards in her book, that is, she assumed that they had to be worked in half-pence. The performance problems caused by handling such large quantities could have caused her to regress in the execution of familiar, simple skills. Such regression is well known (Jensen, 1974). On her own initiative Helen presumably got little but confusion out of this task.

The teacher's behaviour can be understood if it is recalled that Helen took her work to the teacher's desk. The teacher did not see Helen in action on these sums. She did not see the processes by which Helen got into a muddle. She saw only the product. Given that, the teacher's insight was impressive in identifying Helen's difficulty with the word 'change'. Nonetheless she was of no help to the child on this task. Clearly, even if the teacher had monitored Helen's on-task performance closely and had thereby dealt with her confusion as it emerged, it is likely that she would have missed another problem somewhere in the class. A teacher cannot be everywhere at once.

The above is an account of only one classroom event. A great deal of supplementary evidence was necessary even to begin to comprehend the actions of the participants. It is dangerous to make generalizations from a unique event. However, whilst this event was unique, it had many features in common with hundreds of other events observed in the course of the research project referred to earlier. It was selected for illustrative purposes because its features exemplify a pattern which is not at all unusual in the classrooms observed.

In this respect, two critical features must be stressed. First, the child does not merely receive the task given by the teacher. Children do not act as a tape recorder for the teacher's instructions. They interpret and frequently adapt the tasks assigned. Sometimes, as in the above case, the adaptation has negative consequences. Sometimes the consequences are more difficult to evaluate. In another classroom, for example, a teacher had required children to make up their own addition sums by rolling dice. They were expected to roll two dice three times to make up a three-element sum. The children observed simplified the task set by ignoring all large numbers produced by rolling. This adaptation made their lives easier but probably did not advance their mathematics learning. The general point to be emphasized here, however, is that children are inventive learners who adapt to and in part alter the demands made on them in classrooms.

The second common and critical feature is that teachers are rarely cognisant of the processes by which children adapt to and process tasks. They work with the products of children's efforts rather than the processes. This must not be interpreted as the consequences of lazy teaching habits. With limited resources at her disposal (especially the resource of time) and thirty children to work with, the teacher too must adapt to her classroom in a way which apparently gives her maximum return on effort. In terms of the actual quality of learning as experienced by pupils, the evidence suggests that this return on effort is significantly less than ideal.

Understanding the Quality of Learning Experience

If the above argument is accepted, it is clear that repeating the old familiar advice to teachers about good management, increasing time on task, developing carefully structured schemes and the like is going to have the effect it always had: that is, no effect at all. Helen was working in a well managed classroom; she spent a large amount of time on her task and she was moving through a detailed and respected number scheme. In order, for example, to improve the quality of Helen's learning experience, it seems essential first of all to lay bare the adaptive and inventive processes of classroom teaching and learning. Once these are comprehended there may be some prospect of manipulating them to the advantage of all concerned. In an effort to do this, some educational researchers have moved away from correlational studies of learning and teaching and adopted an ecological approach to understanding classroom life. Since this approach shows some promise, its essential features are outlined below.

Ecology is the study of how organisms shape and adapt to their environment. The essential characteristic of the ecological framework is that '. . . individuals and their environment are seen to be engaged in a process of progressive mutual accommodation' (Cohen, 1980). In order to understand these adaptations it is necessary to describe the main features of the environment and the resources of the inhabitants. The most detailed attempt to do this in respect of classrooms has been made by Walter Doyle (1979a, 1979b, 1980). Doyle characterizes classrooms as complex information systems with three important general properties. First, there is an abundance of information sources (books, exercises, verbal and non-verbal behaviour), any one or combination of which may assume instructional significance. Secondly, these sources are not consistently reliable as instructional cues. Thus, despite the amount of information available, that monitored for a given task may be inadequate. Finally, the classroom is considered to be a mass processing system. Many people take part and many interests and purposes are served. Many stimuli are generated at any given moment and the simultaneous occurrence of events leaves little time for participants to reflect. This confers an immediacy on experience and decisions. It also limits the degree to which the quality of information can match the needs of a particular pupil.

The complex information environment of the classroom is inhabited by teachers and pupils all of whom are considered to have severe limitations on their capacity to deal effectively with the abundance of information. They cannot attend to many things at once. Here Doyle has adopted a familiar model of human intellectual functioning. It is called the 'limited capacity information processing model'. The details of this can be found elsewhere (Norman and Rumelhart, 1975).

The limitations on attentional capacity are such that selections must be made from potentially available sources of information. Strategies must be developed to optimize these selections in order to increase the predictability of classroom life. To this end it is necessary to make many actions routine. The advantage of making actions automatic is that it reduces the load on information processing capacity or focal attention. This frees more attention for monitoring the environment. This process of automation may be compared with that of learning to drive a car. Initially basic controls demand almost all the driver's attention. Once the basics are made automatic, attention is available for the road. When reading the road becomes routinized or automated, attention is available for conversations with the passengers. Perhaps this example illustrates not only the advantages but the potentially serious disadvantages of making behaviours automatic.

In Doyle's view, the notion of the classroom as a complex and abundant information environment to which people with limited capacities for dealing with information must adapt, represents the context in which classroom learning must be understood. In this respect the crucial aspect of the environment which links teachers and pupils is considered to be the tasks which teachers present for pupils to process. Pupils endeavour to accomplish tasks in a process which Doyle describes as 'an exchange of performance for grades', that is, *the pupil tries to deliver what the teacher is predicted to reward*. In order to adapt to the environment the pupil must indulge in those activities which make clear to him which performances will deliver the good grades. It must be emphasized that in this model the learner is not the passive recipient of the teacher's instructions. On the contrary, pupils are seen as to some extent determining the level of demand which teachers make on them. In other words, they 'set the rate for the job' to some degree.

From the researcher's point of view, understanding learning entails discovering how the pupil influences, and subsequently interprets, the task structure and ultimately delivers the required performance in exchange for the expected rewards. From the pupil's adaptive point of view, the assessment structure operating in the classroom offers him the clearest specification of what he must do to be 'successful'. That is to say, those behaviours which the teacher rewards are the behaviours to strive for. Doyle suggests that, 'answers a teacher accepts and rewards define the real tasks in the classroom.' Thus if a teacher emphasized 'quality of organization' as a property to strive for in essay writing, but rewards essay *length*, then the adaptive response from pupils would be to deliver long essays in order to collect the predicted rewards.

The problem for the pupil in his struggle to adapt is to acquire 'interpretive competence', that is the capacity to discern what the teacher wants. This is not easy to attain because both tasks and rewards may be complexly and ambiguously defined in classrooms. For example, a teacher was recently observed to talk to a class of 6-year-old children for forty-five minutes about the countries of origin of the produce commonly found in fruit shops. This monologue was illustrated using a tiny map of the world and extensive reference was made to many foreign countries. She finished by asking the children to 'write me an exciting story about the fruit we eat'. The children had to decide what she meant by this! They were helped in part by the fact that they had heard the instruction before in respect of other contents. In fact the children wrote very little. They took great pains to copy the date from the board. (The teacher did not ask them to do this. It was presumably taken for granted as part of the task specification.) They formed their letters with great care and used rubbers copiously to correct any slips of presentation. Whilst this went on the teacher moved about the class commending 'neat work' and 'tidy work' and chiding children for 'dirty fingers' and 'messy work'. No further mention was made of 'exciting' content or of 'stories'. It seemed that the children knew perfectly well what the teacher meant when she asked for an 'exciting story about fruit' even though in this case the overt task definition (the teacher's instructions) stood in sharp contrast (although not necessarily in contradiction) to the reward structure.

Once they have discerned what teachers want there is some evidence that pupils offer resistance to curriculum change (Davis and McKnight, 1976). They show a marked lack of interest and an increase in disruptive behaviour when new demands are made on them. This is especially the case when the manner in which to fulfil the demands is difficult to discern (as is the case in problem-solving approaches to learning, for example). Doyle (1980) suggests that pupils learn how to respond to one form of task specification — an achievement which brings predictability to their classroom lives — and resist having to discover a new specification and how to fulfil it.

The ramifications of this model in terms of the problems teachers might have in providing appropriate explanations of task demands for a large group of individuals, and those that the pupil might have in identifying and/or controlling a teacher's task demands are provocative. It must be stressed, however, that Doyle's model is not an account of how classroom learning comes about, but an account of what, in ecological terms, pupils come to believe is expected to be learned. Thus, for example, the pupil who does manage to acquire the interpretive competence to learn that, overt remarks notwithstanding, his teacher reinforces long essays, still has to learn how to write a long essay. Doyle provides no account of how pupils might learn either 'interpretive competence' or the skills necessary to convey such competence into reward earning performances.

In order to account for school learning it seems clear that the processes of both task allocation and task working must be monitored in classrooms. However, this in itself would be insufficient. It seems additionally necessary to ascertain the cognitive demands which tasks place on children, the manner in which children meet, avoid or adapt these demands, and the impact that these experiences have on the child's cognitive progress.

Improving the Quality of Learning Experience

Attempts to improve the quality of learning experience must involve altering the learning environment and/or the capacities of the participants by, for example, providing new materials or new skills. These alterations would shift the ecological balance of the classroom. This in turn would produce corresponding changes in adaptation. The relationship between innovation and outcome at the level of classroom learning might, in this light, be expected to be complex. It might nonetheless be predictable in ecological terms.

Thus some apparently major shifts (for example, adopting a new scheme or giving the teacher more subject expertise) might be expected to have little or no effect, since they leave the classroom behaviours and reward structures relatively untouched. On the other hand, apparently minor alterations in teaching behaviour might be expected to demand major readaptations on the part of pupils. For example, if a teacher adopted a policy of occasional but detailed interviews with each child in which the child's capacity to reveal his thinking processes was rewarded (as opposed to his capacity to fill a page neatly), children might be expected to develop ways of meeting this new demand. It would not be possible, or necessary, to interview all children on all tasks: it would be sufficient that the child expected to get such an interview — and that occasionally he did.

Such an apparently minor change requires great skill and planning in its execution and interpretation. Done clumsily, the interview turns into an interrogation focusing on the child's weaknesses. Children might then adapt by staying away from school. But interviews based on developing specific competencies could help the teacher better to understand the pupil's difficulties and the child to learn that schooling rewards the development of personal understanding and not simply the reproduction of 'correct answers'.

These points are somewhat speculative. The major point to be emphasized is that an ecological approach to understanding classroom life can be used to design and predict the outcomes of innovations aimed at improving the quality of pupils' learning. It also provides a caution about the dangers of oversimple analysis and interpretation.

Acknowledgements

The authors wish to thank Anne Desforges and Noel Entwistle for their detailed and constructive comments on earlier drafts of this chapter.

The lessons used as illustrative materials in this chapter were observed as part of an SSRC-funded research project published as 'The Quality of Pupil Learning Experiences,' Lawrence Erlbaum, 1984.

References

ANDERSON, L.M. (1981) 'Student responses to seatwork: Implication for the study of students' cognitive processing', paper presented to AERA, Los Angeles.
ATKINSON, R.C. (1976) 'Adaptive instructional systems: Some attempts to optimise the

learning process', in KLAHR, D. (Ed.), *Cognition and Instruction*, Hillsdale, N.J., Lawrence Erlbaum Associates.

AUSUBEL, D.P. (1968) *Educational Psychology: A Cognitive View*, New York, Holt, Rinehart and Winston.

AUSUBEL, D.P. and ROBINSON, F.G. (1969) *School Learning: An Introduction to Educational Psychology*, New York, Holt, Rinehart and Winston.

BENNETT, S.N. and DESFORGES, C. (1983) *The Quality of Pupil Learning Experience*, report on an SSRC funded research project.

BIGGS, J.B. and COLLIS, K.F. (1982). *Evaluating the Quality of Learning*, New York, Academic Press.

BRONFENBRENNER, U. (1976) 'The experimental ecology of education', *Teachers College Record*, 78, 2, pp. 157–204.

BRUNER, J. (1964) 'The course of cognitive growth', *American Psychologist*, 19, pp. 1–15.

COCKCROFT (1982) *Mathematics Counts*: Report of the committee of inquiry into the teaching of mathematics in schools, London, HMSO.

COHEN, M. (1980) 'Policy implications of an ecological theory of teaching: Towards an understanding of outcomes', in BLUMENFELD, P.C. *et al*, (Eds), *Ecological Theory of Teaching*, Research report ETT 80–85, San Francisco, Calif., Far West Laboratory.

DAVIS, R.B. and MCKNIGHT, C. (1976) 'Conceptual, heuristic and algorithmic approaches in mathematics teaching', *Journal of Children's Mathematical Behaviour*, 1, pp. 271–86.

DENHAM, C. and LIEBERMAN, A. (1980) *Time to Learn*, Washington, National Institute of Education.

DESFORGES, C. (1978) 'Professional competence and craft performance in the reception class', paper presented to the British Psychological Society, Durham.

DOYLE, W. (1979a) 'Classroom tasks and student abilities', in PETERSON, P.L. and WALBERG, H.J. (Eds), *Research on Teaching: Concepts, Findings and Implications*, Berkeley, Calif., McCutchan.

DOYLE, W. (1979b) 'Making managerial decisions in classrooms', in DUKE, D.L. (Ed.), *Classroom Management*, Chicago, University of Chicago Press.

DOYLE, W. (1980) *Student Mediating Responses in Teacher Effectiveness*, Denton, Tex., North Texas State University.

DUCKWORTH, E. (1979) 'Either we're too early and they can't learn it or we're too late and they know it already: The dilemma of "applying Piaget"', *Harvard Educational Review*, 49, 3, pp. 297–312.

FARNHAM-DIGGORY, S. (1976) 'Toward a theory of instructional growth', in KLAHR, D. (Ed.), *Cognition and Instruciton*, Hillsdale, N.J., Lawrence Erlbaum Associates.

GINSBURG, H.P. (1981) 'Piaget and education: The contributions and limits of genetic epistemology'. in SIGEL, I.E. *et al*. (Eds), *New Directions in Piagetian Theory and Practice*, Hillsdale, N.J., Lawrence Erlbaum Associates.

GLASER, R. *et al*. (1977) 'Some directions for a cognitive psychology of instruction', in LESGOLD, A.M. *et al*. (Eds), *Cognitive Psychology and Instruction*, New York, Plenum Press.

HMI (1978) *Primary Education in England: A Survey by HM Inspectors of Schools*, London, HMSO.

HMI (1982) *The New Teacher in School*, HMI, Matters for Discussion No. 15, Department of Education and Science.

JACKSON, P.W. (1977) Comments on chapter 11 by Berliner and Rosenshine, in ANDERSON, R.C. *et al*. (Eds), *Schooling and the Acquisition of Knowledge*, Hillsdale, N.J., Lawrence Erlbaum Associates.

JENSEN, A.R. (1974) *Educational Differences*. London Methuen.

KUHN, D. (1979) 'The application of Piaget's theory of cognitive development to education', *Harvard Educational Review*, 49, 3, pp. 340–60.

MCNAMARA, D.R. (1981) 'Time on task and children's learning: Research or ideology?' *Journal of Education for Teaching* 7, 3.

MCNEIL, J.D. and POPHAM,W.J., (1973) 'The assessment of teacher competence', in TRAVERS, R.M. (Ed.), *Second Handbook of Research on Teaching*, Chicago, Rand McNally.

NORMAN, D.A. and RUMELHART, D.E. (1975) *Explorations in Cognition*, San Francisco, W.H. Freeman.

POSNER, G.J. (1978) 'Cognitive science: Implications for curriculum research and development', paper presented to the AERA, Toronto, March 1978.

SCHWEBEL, M. and RAPH, J. (1974) *Piaget in the Classroom*, London, Routledge and Kegan Paul.

SULLIVAN, E. (1967) 'Piaget and the school curriculum', *Bulletin of the Ontario Institute for Studies in Education*.

Problems and Strategies in Learning to Read

Hazel Francis
University of London Institute of Education

When children begin to learn to read the task usually facing them is to develop the art of communication with the written form of a language they can already use reasonably well in speech. My concern is with the ways they go about it. What is commonly thought is that a very firm link has been established between systems of sound and meaning and that the additional building of a link between sight and sound will establish a command of the written language. In general terms this is clearly reasonable, but in more specific terms what does it entail? And what of attempts to build a direct link between sight and meaning?

To ask these questions is to risk walking into a veritable hornet's nest of pedagogic argument. That I am not going to do, but from the complexity of flight-paths will extract a line or two which are pertinent to my main theme. To do so I will depict sight, sound and sense as three vertices of a triangle. Sound and sense are thought to be firmly linked for the normally speaking 5-year-old who is about to be subject to some method or other of teaching reading in school. Written language may already be weakly associated with spoken and with sense, but teachers see it as their task to promote firm links for both, thus completing the '3S' triangle. Where teachers are encouraged to differ is in the relative importance and timing of the links and in ways of going about promoting them.

Making a firm link between sight and meaning entails encouraging children to read words, phrases or sentences without any more link with sound than the introductory saying aloud by teacher and pupil of the words concerned. It is associated with very early steps in reading, with 'look and say' methods, and with 'sentence reading' approaches. It is criticized as being severely limited by the child's memory for seen words, as being no way to enable the child to break out of the restricted pool of words he has learned into the freedom of reading widely, and, in its narrowest form of word-learning, as not being a genuine link with meaning in language.

Making a link between sight and sound entails teaching the child ways of pronouncing from a written word so that he can recognize it as a word in his language, or, conversely, of helping him to spell out a word according to his own analysis of its sound. It is associated with 'phonics' methods, special alphabets, and usually with later stages in learning. It is criticized insofar as children do not always find it helpful, it may distract from reading for sense, and it meets problems with English spelling. Nevertheless, since it appears to be the only way of ensuring the breakthrough into free reading, the link is usually thought to be at least necessary as a part of teaching reading, and at most sufficient for such teaching. The extreme view would suggest that if the sight and sound link is made, then sight and sense automatically follows, whereas in no way can the converse hold. That silent reading is often accompanied by sub-vocalization, and that reasonably fluent readers can 'sound' both real words and nonsense syllables, tend to reinforce the view that some element of phonics is required in teaching reading.

From Teaching to Learning

This debate, however, is about teaching methods. What of the business of learning? I think the question is important because somehow the advocacy of teaching method, however logical, must meet the psychology of children's learning. Many experiments have been conducted to evaluate methods, but it is not sufficient to treat children as equivalent to some hypothetical average recipient of a teaching method in order to consider what might be best for them. Such treatment does not square with concern for individuals nor with our knowledge of children as learners. They are far from being passive recipients. As teachers well know, they set their own problems and construct their own knowledge in the face of teaching strategies, sometimes in most unexpected ways. In this paper, I want to consider children's learning strategies, asking how they set about forging links between the spoken and the written language and reading for meaning.

For those of us who read a great deal, take much for granted about literacy, and have little memory of a personal pre-literate condition, it can be a very salutory experience to observe and talk with primary school children and begin to perceive how they view matters. In my research in primary schools in the past decade I have had many conversations with children at various stages of learning to read. Most particularly I have talked with ten children I selected randomly from the intake of one school and who shared their experiences with me for their first two or three years in that school. One of the effects on me of my research has been to cause me to reconsider the links between sense, sound and sight in two important ways. I have come to appreciate the extent of the background assumptions that are often made about children's understanding of language on entering school, and to question their validity. The background to learning requires discussion. I have also found more than I had anticipated in exploring the links between sight and sense. I shall take these in turn.

Understanding Literacy

To speak of building links between sight, sound and sense without concern for children's understanding of what they are about cannot be sensible. The acts of talking and listening are used to good purpose by children, whether they are aware of it or not. The acts of writing and reading need also to be appreciated as meaningful activities, but how does such knowledge come to children? I found, as earlier studies by Vernon (1971), Reid (1966) and Downing (1970) had done, that lack of understanding was common, and that misunderstanding raised problems that could interfere with or hinder learning, and could affect the strategies children adopted. The following illustrations may be of interest.

John learned to read quickly and well during his first two years in school, but his writing was dreadful. It was untidily executed and sparse in amount, yet he could copy geometrical figures very accurately with clear lines; and his number work, which included short statements, was also neat. So what was he doing when he was writing? I think he did not at first understand much about it. Although he had learned to gain information from bus numbers, street names and such-like before he started school, and was able to talk about his parents' reading, he did not speak of writing, nor could he write his name. He continued to read for information, making use, for example, of newsprint to find out about television programmes, while his early experience with the Breakthrough to Literacy materials was of simple sentences of everyday information. Had he ever connected machine-produced print with the act of writing? Was he aware that behind the stories he was beginning to enjoy there was a human hand, writing for him and for other children? I think probably not, and his experience of learning to write did not help him. He was expected first to arrange his Breakthrough words, printed on cards, into short sentences and then to copy them; thus writing followed print, not vice versa. Writing carefully in number work made sense to him, because the truth of what was written mattered and there was no ready-made printed intermediary. He was the author. Inventive writing seemed not to make sense until it happened that his teacher explained that she wanted *him* to write a story for *her*. Once he felt such interest in what he wrote, as distinct from simply writing, it was as though he were freed from his incomprehension and he began to write more fully and neatly, writing for a reader.

Children are used to the idea of talking purposefully, and they expect that speaking and hearing go together, but they may not at first realize that reading and writing do so too. In a different school from John's, David told me that he didn't think his father could read. I was rather puzzled since I knew that the father was a university lecturer who had many books at home; but, before I could comment, David assured me that although his father couldn't read he was always writing! David enjoyed drawing and copying, but made little effort to read until he had been in school for a year or two. I believe that in seeing mostly one side of the coin he may well have delayed learning to read.

These children, however, were not unduly handicapped by whatever misapprehensions they may have had. Other children were, and lack of comprehension could be more fundamental. Much seemed to depend on experience prior to starting school, for some of the children I spoke with really had very little idea at 5 of the nature of reading or writing, and one or two could say nothing about either. For some the difference between being told stories and having them read to them was not clearly discriminated. Numbers and letters could not be distinguished, and even simple numbers below 5 could not be recognized by some of the children. Some seemed to find the idea of thinking about spoken language very strange, and most took some months to grasp the notion of a word as an identifiable element. For these children Vernon's comments about understanding the principle of representing spoken language in alphabetic print were apt. 'But a thorough grasp of this principle necessitates a fairly advanced stage of conceptual reasoning, since this type of organisation differs fundamentally from any previously encountered by children in their normal environment' (Vernon, 1971).

Closely allied to these conceptual difficulties were varied and sometimes unhelpful ideas about learning to read. Children sometimes thought that the ability to read would come upon them suddenly when they were a little older; some of them felt it didn't matter if they didn't learn because they could see no disadvantage to classmates nor even to older children and adults who couldn't read. Others thought reading was important in the infants' school but not thereafter, and many from less educationally advantaged homes had no idea of what they might read as they grew older. This contrasted with children who could speak of the fiction, poetry, history and science books they had seen in the hands of older siblings and adults. Overwhelmingly, however, whatever the school I visited, the children's main reason for wanting to learn to read was to please their parents and their teachers. Was this a measure of their slender understanding of what reading was about?

I tried with some of the children who seemed most lost to discover what strategies they adopted in the face of teachers' provision of pre-reading and reading activities. For those who had insufficient understanding that writing could be read for meaning and that spoken language could be an object of attention and analysis there was little they could do except watch, listen and try to do what they were told.

Learning was a slow business because much was by rote and was not retained long enough to contribute firmly to any developing skill. There were no organizing principles or intentions to link one activity with another. As educators we can see so readily the links between listening to stories, telling stories, writing information, learning to form letters accurately, learning to distinguish between written words, listening for alliteration and for rhyme and so on. Some children at 5 know that they are all to do with reading and writing, some are even astute enough to avoid certain activities because 'if we do that we'll have to write about it', but for others this integrating knowledge comes late. It emerges from the apparently disparate activities they are asked to perform, instead of informing these tasks. When I began to observe such children I knew some might not realize that the story in a book lay in the print, thinking that it was gleaned from the pictures, and I had met children cheerfully reading aloud an entirely different rendering from that in print because they were pretending they could read; but I had not till then met a child like Sara who, while connecting print with speech, did not realize that it was something more than a signal to say whatever came into her head. Print functioned like a traffic signal! Sara spent two years in school before she began to identify different sentences as occasions for saying what was unique and appropriate for each. During this time I once found her playing with word cards with two other children. They were taking turns to draw cards from a bag and to ask each other to read them. Her friends knew that it was possible to be wrong. Sara did not. Her understanding was that any spoken word would do for any written one. There was some small comfort to be found in the observation, however, since she had somehow managed to learn to confine herself to individual spoken words. (Perhaps I should add that although she was very shy and had a most unsettled home background Sara's general ability appeared to be within the normal range.)

This observation of a problem in relating sound to print is a suitable point for returning to my '3S' triangle. I have said enough to show that it must be sensible for teachers to consider what children understand of spoken language, how far the very acts of reading and writing are meaningful for them, and what sense they make of classroom activities. In some of the schools I have visited a number of children have taken up to two years to gain much sense of these matters and their learning to read has developed very slowly.

The Development of Reading

In my introduction I said that on entering school children are thought to have established a firm hold on spoken language. In many respects this is true of most children. They have a reasonably extensive vocabulary, command a basic range of syntax and use speech to good effect in everyday life. In these respects they are adequately equipped to begin reading. What seems more uncertain is the extent to which they are aware of language as an object of interest in its own right. And, if children can consider this abstraction, there is the further question of how far they are able to operate with it, to identify its elements, to make comparisons between them and to experiment with ways of putting them together. These questions are important if learning to read requires conscious analysis of speech. There is now an extensive research literature, usefully summarized by Downing and Leong (1982), which suggests that language awareness, and analytic competence as applied to language develop for many children during the process of learning to read rather than before it. This being so, I shall examine children's strategies of linking written language both with sense and with sound with some caution about the direct link between sound and sense.

Sight and Sense

I start with this side of the triangle because it is normally, though not invariably, both the beginning and the end of learning to read. Few children begin by linking sounds with letters before they are able to recognize any words, and most end by being able to read silently. It is therefore of interest to see how children set about the tasks of linking the symbols of written language with sense when they have come to some appreciation of the general point that making such links is itself sensible. This implies that they see that there is some conventionally established correspondence between written and spoken sense.

It is worth observing first that sense can be derived from single words, that it is not the province only of continuous speech or prose. Most children have such a strong sense of personal identity and property that the labelling function of written words can easily be appreciated. This is part of the everyday sense of names of houses, streets, bus routes, shops and so on, and it readily invades the classroom. It should be noted, however, that correspondence between written and spoken labelling is not exact. Written labels are attached to relevant objects, but speech labels require additional syntax or non-verbal indication of the objects. Picking up a box of crayons marked 'John', David can understand that it belongs to John; but if the label were not there, another person would have to say more than the single word 'John' to trigger the same understanding. Whether it is helpful to write full sentences such as 'This is John's box', as some teachers do, is debatable. On the one hand it displays a correspondence between writing and speech, if the child appreciates the point; but on the other it is an unconventional way of using language and not conducive to the notion that written language functions in its own right and its own way. The single word makes sense in its written form in some contexts, just as it does in the spoken in others. Acquiring a written vocabulary of individual words in what might be called a 'Look and Say' manner can be a sensible activity and the words themselves can make sense to the child.

But I would go further than this in allowing a direct link between single words and meaning. Although children use speech without awareness of its structure many are capable from the age of 4 or thereabouts of playing word-association games. In reply to the request to say the first thing they think in response to a single word, they can often supply complementary single words. Thus if one says 'car' they may well say 'driver' or 'garage' or 'bus', or 'red' or 'sports'. Such a 'game' is a well-recognized probe used by psychologists to explore the organization of words in memory. The patterns of response by children imply a mental organization which relates words according to their meanings in the language. For such children it is therefore reasonable to think that individual words do tap networks of meaning, and thus spoken versions of examples in print are far from being meaningless. Moreover, since memory is not passive but is actively constructed, new words are likely to be entered into the network according to the sense allotted to them.

But although written word identification may make sense to children, recognition is not always easily established. How do they remember the links they make?

My observations of children learning in school suggest that rote learning is not a strategy they are encouraged to use. Even when teachers used a look and say technique, they did not stress repetition to any criterion of learning, particularly for individual children. It was more like an introduction, 'Meet Mary', with the corresponding problem of remembering Mary's name at a future meeting. On the other hand, a relatively small number of words were used at first, thus giving a relatively high probability of coming across them often, when identification might or might not be made.

One strategy I noticed children using to try to recall a word was to remember the context of being introduced to it. In a class where the Breakthrough to Literacy materials were being used I saw children able to recognize a word on the big cards used in the teacher's display, but be unable to recognize it on the same cards held by me, or on their own smaller cards. I also found them able to recognize a word copied into their writing book from a Breakthrough card, but be unable to recognize it on the card. The writing book was a unique context, the card was like any other card. There was also a little girl who could identify 'house' on the wall display of Breakthrough words but not in any other context. In none of these cases could it be assumed that the children were using anything more about the word than its physical location. Recognition was like standing again in the room where Mary had been introduced and remembering her name was 'Mary', not because her appearance came to mind but because she was again standing near the telephone. How often do we experience some embarrassment because we fail to recognize a person in an unfamiliar context? So it seemed to be with beginning readers and their introduction to words.

Whatever the reason, some children found it relatively easy to improve their recognition and to begin to find sufficient familiarity with the appearance of a few words to identify them in different locations. For children with some experience of words in their pre-school years this generalizing seemed to come as second nature, but for those less advantaged it was something to be learned. This was not as simple as it might seem, for words written on classroom materials are not at all the same as those of the everyday environment. Outside school there is some evident organizing principle behind the word 'road' when the child walks home along Maple Road, Church Road, and Wood Road, for example, but what is there behind the word 'road' on free-floating cards, in mysterious arrangements of cards, on wall displays, and in writing-books?

In children who readily generalized I found interesting ways of making use of detail within words in order to aid recall. The literature on learning to read, as summarized, for example, in Gibson and Levin (1975), suggests that children may attend to the overall shape of a word or to individual letter detail. It also discusses whether they notice first letters, last letters, capital letters, and so on. It is easy to form the impression that research should come up with a single definitive answer about what is recognized, but this would surely be mistaken, at least with respect to the early stages of learning. My own observations suggested that not only did children notice different features, but that each child noticed different kinds of feature in different words. This was in part a very personal matter. When children could name and recognize a letter or two, often from their own names, they noticed these more readily than other features. They also noticed capital letters, their recognition errors showing use of this cue when they misread one word for another, both being words they had met with upper-case first letters. Sometimes double letters were salient for them. Thus, in personal and somewhat unpredictable ways they developed strategies of recognizing words from detail they had noticed, as well as from the contexts in which they had met them. Since these strategies were deployed within the framework of a common reading scheme and a common introduction to letter identification by the teacher they led to personal constructions of word recognition knowledge within and around a common core.

In the process of learning to recognize a relatively small number of words, both in isolation and in sentences, children began to notice similar-ities. Sometimes they commented on these, and quite often they misread one for another. They still showed signs of using context as well as appearance to identify a word, but context was being extended from general location to location in written language, location in a sentence and to sentence meaning. Children began to think of words as those they had met in written form. They did not readily refer to words in speech. They also showed some interesting restrictions in their understanding. For example, the repetition of simple sentence frames such as 'I like X' and 'I see X' led to expectations of finding 'I' at the beginning of a string of words. At an early stage with the Breakthrough materials I asked children if 'I am a boy' and 'am I a boy' were sentences. Most agreed that the first one was but that the second was not. Their reasons were either that the words were not in the correct order or that 'I' should come first. This was said even when the children could readily read both aloud. Moreover, the same sort of reply was given to other examples. Further, words which were read in sentences could not always be recognized in other sentences or in lists. For example, when Dave could read 'I see a dog' and 'I see a television' he could not recognize either 'dog' or 'television' in other contexts.

These observations led me to explore the children's strategies of reading words as they continued to build their mental visual dictionaries during their first year in school. Because some, having learned to use their Breakthrough materials to some extent, and having been introduced through them to the early vocabulary of the Gay Way reading scheme, had learned sufficient to attempt to read the first pages of the first book in that scheme, I used sentences and word lists derived from those pages for my explorations. I extended my observations to twenty-four children in each of two schools in order to avoid generalizing too readily from a small number of children. I have reported the study elsewhere (Francis, 1977) and will here content myself with something of a summary.

First, I found that it did not make a great deal of sense to think of children as knowing or not knowing a word. Rather, on any particular occasion they would be able to make some attempt, with a degree of success which might vary from zero to a quick and accurate performance. On a different occasion, or even in the same piece of text, the level of success might well be different. I gave the children a set of sentences constructed from the vocabulary and phrases of their reader, and I interspersed these with two short word lists covering the same vocabulary. The two lists had some words in common. I found that the words in common were not necessarily read similarly by the children, even though there was less than five minutes between the readings. Sometimes a word read correctly in the first was misread in the second, and vice versa. Further, I found that words were more likely to be read correctly in sentence contexts than in lists, and especially so if the sentence was one that had been read previously. Misreadings usually made sense in relation to what had gone before in a sentence, though when sense was lost a reading could degenerate into a 'list' performance. At this rather early stage of reading children did not self-correct, and it did not appear that they used the words after a point of uncertainty in a sentence in order to help their reading. They were, however, sometimes able to miss a word and carry on reading, picking up the sense again. Clearly, then, the children were using strategies which were yielding the best estimates of the moment in the light of cues from appearance and context sense.

There was still some evidence of 'location' sense, as, for example, when a child completed a sentence with the phrase he knew as the one following on in the reader, or even misread a sentence by producing the one which followed the previous 'test' sentence in the reader. These examples were a useful corrective to any false assumption that the child might be truly attempting each word as he came to it. For the most part, however, the moving finger and eye seemed to move and pause together, and individual word misreadings in the context of otherwise correct reading suggested serious attempts to tackle reading at both the sentence and the word level.

Since the words had been taken from text the children had read in their school work there was no attempt to explore how they might tackle new words, only how they tried to deal with those they could not recall. The absence of guesses derived from their wider vocabularies — all misreadings were words they had met in reading activities — suggested that the over-riding strategy was to try to recall words within their school reading experience. Reading was a well-defined activity based mostly on recall.

Since I gave this particular task to the children before they received any phonics instruction in school (other than naming some letters in a 'phonic' manner), it was not surprising that not one of them attempted to deal with an elusive memory by trying to sound a word. It was, however, useful to know that this strategy did not seem to be known from any other source, or, if it was, that it was not being applied in school. Observations of the children's attempts to read to the teacher, and to me, confirmed the absence of phonic attempts at this stage. Overall, then, they were relying on memory and using cues from location, sense and sight to arrive at estimated readings. As they told me in conversation, if they couldn't read a word they would think hard or ask someone.

As the children became more proficient during their second and third years in school, so for some this multiple strategy approach became more sophisticated and more complex. Children were doing more than using sight to arrive at sense, they were using both together to read. The sense of text was used more fully to make self-correction a possible and useful man-oeuvre. But so was the letter information contained in the words. This was used both to aid direct visual reading and for sounding words in order to arrive at a reading, but before coming to the latter I should like to say more about the visual approach.

Spelling, Sight and Sense

I noticed that a number of early misreadings resembled the target words, sometimes quite closely, and that such resemblance was also to be found in the errors of children who had learned to read quite well. It seemed to me that visual similarity suggested at least some recognition of the spelling of both the word to be read and the misreading, and that the degree of similarity could be used as an index of the children's knowledge of spelling. I was encouraged to consider investigating the development of such knowledge by reading the work of Biemiller (1970) and Weber (1970). Both reported increasing similarity between errors and target words as children's reading improved from the first grade. Weber found that even in the first year there was greater similarity in the errors of the better readers than of others, while Biemiller commented particularly on the development of first letter similarity as children added more attention to visual detail to their reading for sense. Soderbergh (1971), reporting the development of reading skill in a very young child, also found that errors became increasingly like correct words, particularly if they were attempted readings of new words in isolation rather than in text. She also found a predominance of first-letter similarity. Barr (1972) disputed Biemiller's claim that such development would occur whatever teaching method might be employed, considering instead that the development of spelling similarity between target and error was a response to phonics instruction. Later, however (Barr, 1978), she also allowed that graphic resemblance would also be influenced by the extent to which the child could use context to determine a reading. Words in isolation, or in text when sense was lost, would be more likely to yield graphically similar misreadings than words largely read by sense. She also noted that reading influenced by phonic instruction also included errors which were non-words.

Since my own data for first year children did not include non-word errors, this increased my confidence that phonic-type strategies were not being used and that whatever spelling similarity was developing between errors and correct readings was due to increased knowledge of word spelling. So did my data look anything like Biemiller's and Weber's? The simple answer is that they did. A full answer can be found elsewhere (Francis, 1982, 1984), but it is sufficient for this argument to say that increased reading ability, both within and across chronological age, correlated with increased graphic similarity between error and target. Much similarity rested with the initial letter but there could be as many as two or three letters in common in words averaging three or four letters in length. Some similarity was due to plural and past tense suffixes, not surprisingly if it is remembered that context influenced error.

In summary, then, the children's reading errors showed a development of graphic similarity much like that reported elsewhere in the literature together with an appreciation of the sense of what was being read. For the most part the errors were words met previously by the children when reading in school, but as time went on they were not only responses to target words already met but also to new words. The sense of text and the spelling of the word continued to evoke estimates from recall, but was it enough to lead to suggestions of words not previously read? Was children's increasing familiarity with word spelling of assistance in new reading?

Sound and Sight

Before considering this question further, the impact of phonics instruction must be considered. Doubt has been cast on Barr's claim that error graphic similarity is a response to phonics — it may be, but it is not necessarily so — but some response must surely occur to phonics. How did the children in my own study respond?

They were introduced to sounding as an accompaniment to sentence building and word identification from the end of their first year. Although the Gay Way readers are based on a vocabulary which is devised to accord with a phonics approach, this is not true of the Breakthrough vocabulary. The children were therefore not led into a heavily emphasized phonic approach to reading. They knew at an early stage that simple phonics did not always 'work' as an aid either to recall or to reading new words. But equally they were encouraged to give it a try.

I noticed when listening to children reading that although they were able to take part intelligently in simple phonics instruction they did not necessarily generalize it to their reading. Some did, and they would typically read out a word with a sound corresponding to each letter known to them. They did not at first know how to sound some of the letters, but if they were really trying to sound a whole word they would ask when they didn't know. They met two main difficulties, one being the relatively high frequency of bigrams and of vowel variability, and the other that of combining separate sounds to form whole words. These problems led them to prefer to rely on sense and sight and on correction by themselves or by the listener. Production of non-words as described by Barr was thus a rare occurrence. Several children were very impatient if asked to sound a word, since it slowed them down and detracted from the sense of their reading. They did have some success, however, in sounding the first letter or so of a word and using this to cue them into a reading. Such an attempt usually accorded with the sense of the reading though it was not always correct. In this respect it was also a graphic similarity error, the difference being whether or not any letter was 'sounded' as a prompt to the reading.

This strategy in no way detracted from, or entirely explained, the increase in knowledge about spelling shown in the graphic similarity errors. Some similar patterns did not entail phonic similarity. Consider, for example, the 't' in 'the' and 'top'; the 's' in 'she' and 'sat'; the 'w' in 'we' and 'who'; the 'o' in 'of' and 'over'; and the 'i' in 'like' and 'live'. Other examples of such pairs of error and correct word could be cited. A further suggestion that graphic similarity was not always related to phonic strategies could be found in the fact that regularly spelled words, which should have yielded readily to phonic coding, were as likely to be misread as irregular. It was also the case that similarities such as plural and tense suffixes, 'silent e's' and letter groups like 'thr' and 'own' were hard to explain on the basis of simple sound mediation.

I was led to conclude, therefore, that there was considerable correspondence between spelling and sense which was not dependent on that between sight and sound. To put it another way, although there was some learning of letter-sound correspondences, this by no means accounted for the development of reading skill, nor did it account for the increasing knowledge of spelling displayed in graphic similarity errors.

From Recall to New Reading

The critical importance of phonics, if seen as the sight-sound link in my triangle of sense, sound and sight, rested on the argument that reading must entail decoding of new words, for it cannot rest on recognition alone. Decoding has been seen as the conscious translation of a written form into its spoken counterpart. I now pose again the question whether it is possible to move from recognition-bound to free reading without such decoding. Is increasing knowledge of spelling sufficient assistance?

It must first be noted that some children do learn to read without formal phonics instruction. But are such children, and are those who use both graphic and phonic strategies, not somehow using covert phonics when moving into free reading? I think that they may be, but that if or when they do, their ability rests on prior familiarity with letter identity and word spelling, and crucially on the reading aloud of the words they encounter. In the pedagogic arguments about 'look and say' methods versus 'phonics', too little attention has been given to the 'say' as the basis for phonic analysis. If, with increasing experience of seeing and hearing words, children gain a firmer knowledge of individual word spellings and begin to respond to general features of spelling in English, such as letter order and position as well as significant patterns such as suffixes, and if they also begin to sense something of syllabic structure as they find single-syllable spellings appearing in more complex words, then the repetition of pronouncing and hearing some of the words with spelling similarities (particularly initial letter) may establish the first spelling-sound correspondences without the child necessarily being aware of the fact. There may also be correspondence at the syllabic level. This learning is probabilistic, though it is mediated through generalization and analogy, and, because language is rule-governed, generally conforms with linguistic regularity. The combined use of context sense and spelling information enables children to hazard very reasonable estimates of new words, spelling sometimes allowing pronunciation of at least part of the word by similarity or analogy. If children have become aware of spelling-sound correspondences, either through discovery or instruction, this partial or complete effort may be an overt sounding strategy. It should be noted, however, that such appreciation of spelling-sound correspondences from one word to another, as in being helped to read 'sharp' by familiarity with 'shoe', may be more useful than attempting to thoroughly decode each word. Thus by using multiple strategies and hazarding reasonable guesses children can move from recall-bound to free reading.

Two major features underlie the above account. The first is the way children use a variety of cues from a very early stage in the growth of automaticity or swift smoothness in making a reading. Their strategies are like those of fluent readers. Where text is familiar, and ability matched to it, then much of the reading process is automatic, but unfamiliar or difficult text brings out the slower processes of searching for sense and of reading aloud or sub-vocalizing. I think, therefore, that it is worth considering as applicable during learning both the automatic information processing theory which Laberge and Samuels (1976) developed regarding the performance of fluent readers, and the theory of interaction between reading from the print and from the sense which was proposed by Rumelhart (1977). The second is the probabilistic nature and the complexity of word recognition. Here I think the theory of letter and word perception put forward by McClelland and Rumelhart (1981, 1982) should find application to, and be testable against data on, the skills and knowledge of beginning readers. Theories which have hitherto depended on experimental work with fluent readers and on the difficulties of those with reading disabilities should in principle show coherence with theories and data concerning the development of reading ability.

It should now be evident why my observations of children's reading altered my view of the sense-sight-sound triangle. I came to appreciate that the visual processing entailed in learning to read was not a simple letter-by-letter matter, but a complex system of letter-pattern recognition and prediction. It usually functioned below the level of awareness, and as it developed it gained in smoothness and automaticity, so that if due consideration were given to its nature then some review of the relationship between sight and sound was required. I came to wonder whether it was correct to apply the linguistic logic of the relationships between speech and writing to learning to read, and to regard phonic decoding as necessary for 'free' reading. Instead I inclined to the view that the phonic route from sight to sense is made possible through learning to read rather than being a necessary condition for such learning.

This is not to dismiss phonics from reading instruction, but rather to suggest that it be looked at carefully. On the one hand, more thought might be usefully paid to devising practices which promote direct knowledge of the visual appearance of spelling in the language (remembering that the relevant information processing is a complex, coherent, and largely unconscious activity). On the other hand, more attention might be given to considering under what conditions and for which children some forms of phonics instruction appears to be needed. Reliance on different kinds of cue in what is a multiple-strategy activity of a probabilistic and inferential kind depends on the nature of the text and the abilities and knowledge of the readers, whether they be expert or novice.

References

BARR, R. (1972) 'The influence of instructional conditions on word recognition errors', *Reading Research Quarterly*, 7, pp. 509–29.

BARR, R. (1978) 'Influence of instruction on early reading', in CHAPMAN, L.J. and CZERNIEWSKA, P. (Eds), *Reading: From Process to Practice*, London, Routledge and Kegan Paul.

BIEMILLER, A. (1970) 'The development of the use of graphic and contextual information as children learn to read', *Reading Research Quarterly*, 6, pp. 75–96.

DOWNING, J. (1970) 'Children's concepts of language in learning to read', *Educational Research*, 12, pp. 106–12.

DOWNING, J. and LEONG, C.K. (1982) *Psychology of Reading*, New York, Macmillan.

FRANCIS, H. (1977) 'Children's strategies in learning to read', *British Journal of Educational Psychology*, 47, pp.117–25.

FRANCIS, H. (1982) *Learning to Read*, London, Allen and Unwin.

FRANCIS, H. (1984, forthcoming) 'Children's knowledge of orthography in learning to read', *British Journal of Educational Psychology*.

GIBSON, E.J. and LEVIN, H. (1975) *The Psychology of Reading*, Cambridge, Mass., MIT Press.

LABERGE, D. and SAMUELS, S.J. (1976) 'Towards a theory of automatic information processing in reading', in SINGER, H. and RUDDELL, B. (Eds), *Theoretical Models and Processes of Reading*, Newark, N.J., International Reading Association.

McCLELLAND, J.L. and RUMELHART, D.E. (1981) 'An interactive activation model of context effects in letter perception: Part 1. An account of basic findings', *Psychological Review*, 88, pp. 375–407.

REID, J. (1966) 'Learning to think about reading', *Educational Research*, 9, pp. 56–62.

RUMELHART, D.E. (1977) 'Toward an interactive model of reading', in DORNIC, S. (Ed.) *Attention and Performance VI*, Hillsdale, N.J.: Lawrence Erlbaum.

RUMELHART, D.E., and McCLELLAND, J.L. (1982) 'An interactive activation model of context effects in letter perception: 11. The contextual enhancement effect and some tests and extensions of the model', *Psychological Review*, 89, pp. 60–94.

SODERBERGH, R. (1971) *Reading in Early Childhood*, Stockholm, Almqvist and Wiksell.

VERNON, M.D. (1971) *Reading and its Difficulties*, London, Cambridge University Press.

WEBER, R. (1970) 'A linquistic analysis of first-grade reading errors', *Reading Research Quarterly*, 5, pp. 427–51.

Motives and Motivational Styles in Education*

Béla Kozéki
Institute of Psychology, Budapest

If teachers are asked to explain the differing levels of attainment of their pupils, the explanations will usually fall into three main categories — home background/parental attitudes, ability/aptitudes, and conscientiousness/ motivation. Each of these areas has been examined by educational psycho-logists, and to some extent they have confirmed the importance of these 'commonsense' explanations. Certainly teachers generally recognize not only that a child's motivation is important, but that the way they teach will also affect that motivation. When we look at the research on school motivation, however, it is difficult to see, at first, how the findings might help teachers.

Early work tended to be part of the wide-ranging attempts to *predict* levels of school attainment. Once the limitations of intelligence tests were recognized, improved prediction was sought through the use of personality tests (Eysenck and Cookson, 1969; Cattell and Butcher, 1968), and also through scales of academic (achievement) motivation (Finger and Schlesser, 1965; Buxton, 1966). Some limited improvement in prediction came from the use of such inventories (Lavin, 1965; Entwistle *et al.*, 1974). But it is of little use to the teacher to be able to predict which children are likely to do badly, if the reasons are not fully understood, and so appropriate remedial action remains unclear.

Ball (1977) reviewed some of the many theories which have been used to try to understand motivation in education. He found that each theorist introduced one or two main explanatory constructs of his own, and these covered only parts of the area covered by 'school motivation'. He argued that there was a need for a general theoretical integration of these separate descriptions of motivation, and suggested that at least five distinct aspects of school motivation could be identified, namely a positive orientation towards school learning, a need for social recognition, the motive to avoid failure, curiosity, and conformity. Besides describing the different facets of the

* Part of one section of this article was published previously in *British Journal of Educational Studies*, 1983.

concept of motivation, it would also be necessary to identify the characteristic combinations of the main motives commonly found among pupils. Ball argued that 'for any given child, there seems to be a preferred motivational style. We coin this term to indicate that each child has more or less of each of the long listings of motives. Assessing this internal integration of motives, this motivational style, is perhaps the key to further understandings in this area' (Ball, 1977, p. 189).

This article summarizes the results of an extensive series of studies, carried out mainly in Hungary and Central Europe (Kozéki, 1975, 1980), which found nine main motives in three broad areas or domains. It has also been possible to identify characteristic motivational styles and to suggest how these originate in the interactions between the child's underlying personality and experiences at home and in the school. From this integrated framework, appropriate remedial action becomes clearer for both parent and teacher.

Personal Relationships and the Development of Motives

One of the limitations of previous research into motivation in education has been a preoccupation with exclusively cognitive explanations of academic performance. Even the attempts to show personality correlates of learning have rarely included any consideration of the role of personal relationships in the establishment of the stable motivational styles which affect school learning. The Hungarian research was based on the initial assumption, later amply justified, that children's motivational styles are firmly rooted in their relationships with 'significant others' — particularly with their parents, teachers and close friends.

This work began with a thorough review of the literature on motivation and an extensive series of interviews with both parents and children, pupils from the earliest to the latest stages of the Hungarian school system (ages 6 to 18). To date some 1000 interviews have been conducted and recorded, and from repeated listening certain recurring comments became salient in relation to previous theories of motivation. Analysis of these comments led to the identification of nine separable motives (see Table 1) within three main motivational areas or domains.

The first domain describes emotional and social forms of reinforcement. At the simplest level it is clear that motivation depends on reinforcement, on a pleasurable consequence to action, which leads to the repetition of that behaviour. In the early stages of child-rearing the relationship with the parents establishes one strong and continuing motivation — pleasing parents provides its reward in the expression of *warmth*, of caring, loving sentiments. *Identification* with parents, and later with teachers, becomes for the child one sure way of ensuring adult approval — and so is a strong secondary form of motivation. As the child's social network extends,

Table 1.   *Nine Motives in Three Domains*

Main source of reinforcement	Affective	Cognitive	Moral
Relationships with Parents	Warmth (M1)	Independence (M4)	Self-Esteem and Trust (M7)
Teachers	Identification (M2)	Competence (M5)	Compliance (M8)
Peers	Sociability (M3)	Interest (M6)	Responsibility (M9)

approval from peers becomes increasingly important — with rewards from acceptance by friends or *sociability*. These first three forms of motivation were clearly recognizable in the interviews at all ages, and represent the affective domain not commonly found in descriptions of school motivation — yet of fundamental importance both in understanding pupils' behaviour and in planning effective methods of education.

Reinforcement within the second domain of motivation comes from cognitive and practical accomplishments. As children develop, the strong bond with the parents is challenged by an increasing demand for autonomy and *independence*. The sense of freedom, of achieving something in their own way, becomes increasingly important for adolescents — but was also identified in younger children. The importance of *competence* motivation has been established previously by White (1959). Children seek to extend their mastery over the environment through acquiring knowledge and skills — the feeling of competence has its own strong reinforcing quality. *Interest*, and the rewards of self-expression, represent the final cognitive dimension which could be clearly delineated from the interview data.

The first two domains of motivation can be seen as mapping out the external sources of reinforcement regularly available to pupils. Finally, there are rewards deriving from personal and social responsiveness — the moral domain. It describes the attempts to integrate and control the various sources of pleasure and pain, and to reach personal decisions on what types of action are right or wrong, or potentially rewarding or punishing, according to both personal and social values. Living up to the trust of others develops *self-esteem* and can be seen as a form of control internalized in the conscience from the previous actions of parents, teachers and friends. The next motive, *conformity*, reflects the controlling influence of accepted social norms, higher-order moral values, or religious beliefs, acceptance of which can also be satisfying. Finally, pupils develop, and enjoy, personal *responsibility*, judging their behaviour in terms of their own internalized standards of what is acceptable.

The repeated analyses of pupils' interviews, together with discussions with parents and teachers, gradually established that these nine motives within three domains represented a parsimonious, but full, description of the motives most closely related to school behaviour.

Characteristic Motivational Styles

Although this set of nine motives provides the type of integrated framework sought by Ball, it still lacks two important characteristics. It fails to draw attention to the dynamic nature of motivational development, and it does not make clear how the motives interact within the individual to form relatively stable motivational styles. The differing strengths of these motives, and the balance between them, can be explained in terms of complex interactions between individual maturation and the differing types of reward and punishment experienced in the home, at school, and from the peer group.

Crucial to the development of distinctive motivational styles is the establishment of recognized links between the strivings and actions of children on the one hand and their consequences on the other. Children need to have consistent rewards or punishments associated with their actions, and to have these presented within the domains of human relations, cognitive activity, or responsibility, in ways which strengthen the child's developing motivational pattern. Children are not born with negative, say, aggressive, 'instincts'; these develop by imitation and through reinforcement in social learning (Bandura, 1978). It is thus possible systematically to strengthen the more positive behaviour patterns by recognizing the way in which motivational styles are formed.

The origin of distinct motivational styles can be traced to children's early experiences in the home, and later at school. Psychologists readily acknowledge that every event in life leaves a cognitive residue — a memory trace. But many events also involve important emotional responses — experiences of happiness or misery, of success or failure. They leave behind strong memories in which events or actions are associated with positive or negative feeling tones. Although nine different sources of satisfaction have been identified, different child-rearing and educational practices will make each more or less accessible to individual children, who will also respond differently to the varying types of reinforcement which are available. Gradually, out of the interaction between their basic temperament and their experiences at home and school, they begin to react more strongly to one or other form of reward or punishment. Some children find the approbation and emotional support of parents, friends or teachers most rewarding. Others seek satisfaction more from intellectual mastery or developing skills, while another group of children finds greater reinforcement from living up to trust or meeting standards set by family, school, or society at large.

When a child enters school, education provides additional opportunities for shaping the developing motivational style. A child's response to school, his school motivation, is a part of the complete motivational structure — the growing dominance of certain motives and their integration into identifiable patterns.

The existence of distinctive motivational styles was demonstrated by using a test to assess the main motivational dimensions. Statistical analyses (Kozéki, 1980) showed that the nine motives, in relation to *school motivation*, could be condensed into six factors, equally divided between the affective, cognitive, and moral domains as follows: emotional warmth (A1), sociability (A2), competence (B1), independence (B2), dependability (C1), compliance (C2). Similar factors have recently been identified in Britain (Kozéki and Entwistle, 1984). Each pair of factors can be seen as a stronger and a weaker expression of the same underlying motivational domain. Looking then at the test scores for individual children it was possible to identify the dominant patterns in terms of the three domains. Using a simple division into high (+), medium (○), and low (−) scores in each domain, twenty-seven possible combinations are theoretically possible. In fact, however, scores were found to be quite strongly intercorrelated, meaning that combinations of + and − were rare. It was also uncommon to find all the motivational virtues or vices in a single child. The most common motivational patterns thus proved to be combinations of positive or negative with neutral categories. Figure 1 summarizes the patterns and indicates their percentage occurrence in Central European samples. Each pair of columns in the diagram represents the more, and the less, positive forms of each main motivational style.

In considering these characteristic motivational patterns, the balance between dominant and other motives, it is important to recognize that these patterns are dynamic. Over time, and under parental and educational influences, the child may move upwards, downwards and, to some extent, sideways within Figure 1. These movements represent a continuing structuring and balancing of the motives, which helps to explain both the preponderance of positive intercorrelations between motives, and the simplification in motivational structure found in school motivation (six factors rather than nine motives). The styles in Figure 1 are described in terms of the relative scores (+, ○, −) in the affective, cognitive and moral domains, with the dominant domain indicated by a '★'. There are three clearly distinctive styles, which contain subsidiary forms. Each of these main styles represents an equally effective, although characteristically different, way of relating to the world and to other people.

★ ○ +   For this type of pupil it is most important to establish a warm reciprocal relationship with others, to earn respect, liking and praise. For this reason he is diligent, very reliable, but his basic motivation is 'fear of failure'. The pupil is likely to be rather dependent, a passive follower who is likely to be seen as a conformist. If the strong affiliative motive is not supported by responsibility (+○○ or +− −), the pupil may want to solve everything by relying on personal relationships and so become anxious, overdependent, even hypocritical and insincere.

+ ★ ○   This pupil works very effectively and may well be creative, but the lack of any strong moral dimension indicates a tendency towards selfishness and non-conformity. He is strongly motivated towards competence, but the

Béla Kozéki

Figure 1.   Characteristic Motirational Styles

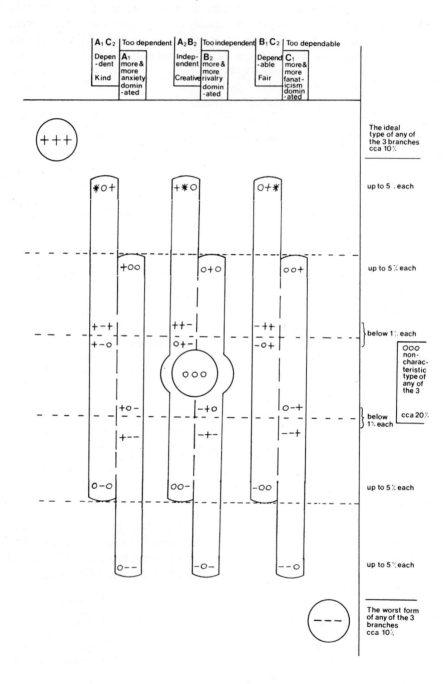

supporting strength of affiliation indicates the need for applause. This combination implies a 'me first' attitude, a belief that 'the end justifies the means'. The pupil is sociable, but not warm: the need is to be popular rather than friendly. If the affiliative needs diminish ($\circ + \circ$ or $-+-$), there is likely to be an accompanying increase in ruthlessness or aggression.

$\circ + \star$ This type of pupil is again achievement-oriented, but not success-orientated. He is emotionally independent of others. The strong moral motives imply not only interest in academic work but also in doing it well,

Figure 2. *Relationships between Motives, Factors, Domains and Styles*

Main motives or needs of children	Factors within school motivation	Motivational domains of reinforcement	Motivational styles of children
(M1) *Warmth* Need for nurturance and emotional closeness	(A1) *Warmth* Good emotional relationships and intimate friendships	Emotional and social ties	$\star \circ +$ (A1 with C2) Warm, compliant, anxious to please parents and teachers, making efforts to avoid failure
(M2) *Identification* Need for acceptance by adults, particularly teachers	(A2) *Sociability* Acceptance and standing among adults and peers		
(M3) *Sociability* Need for belonging, mainly to peer group			
(M4) *Independence* Need to find own way in life	(B1) *Competence* Gaining knowledge and developing skills	Cognitive and practical accomplishments	$+ \star \circ$ (B2 with A2) Interested, sociable, seeking challenge and competition, but following own interests
(M5) *Competence* Need for new experiences and gaining knowledge	(B2) *Interest* Adventurousness, play, and achievements		
(M6) *Interest* Need for enjoyable activities shared with others			
(M7) *Self-Esteem and Trust* Need for the esteem of self and others	(C2) *Compliance* Acceptance of school norms and reward-structure	Personal and social responsiveness; morality	$\circ + \star$ (C1 with B1) Concerned with self-improvement, fulfilling expectations, and 'playing' according to the rules
(M8) *Compliance* Need for order	(C1) *Responsibility* Acceptance of responsibility, self-esteem, and conscientiousness		
(M9) *Responsibility* Need for self-integrity, being a moral person			

living up to what is expected. The pupil is likely to be independent-minded, responsible rather than compliant, and probably an unconventional radical. Where the moral strength loses cognitive support ($\circ\circ+$ or $--+$), the person may be seen as having iron self-discipline and may become over-demanding on self or others. In the extreme ($--+$) this motivational style includes the fanatic, single-minded and unreasonably demanding.

In describing children's motivation, it has proved necessary to use the terms 'motive', 'factor', 'domain' and 'style'. Figure 2 is an attempt to show how these represent variations on a single theme, with the emphasis shifting from the identification of separate motives or (in school) factors, to the general domains, and from there to the integration of dominant motives within the individual child.

Implications for Child-Rearing and Education

The sources of school motivation will be found in the relationships between parent and child. The child-rearing practices adopted both mould, and interact with, the developing personality of the child. Perhaps the crucial point to be recognized from the description of the three most successful motivational styles ($\star\circ+$, $+\star\circ$, $\circ+\star$) is that, in each case, the dominant motivational domain is balanced by strength in a complementary area. Thus child-rearing and teaching practices must reflect a similar balance. Parents and teachers may, however, utilize rewards and punishments predominantly from only one of the domains. They may, for example, be unconditionally supportive or coldly demanding; they may guide and encourage involvement or leave the child to his own devices; finally, they may show trust and consistent control or demand unthinking obedience. Although in each case one extreme may be seen as positive and the other negative, it was clear from our interviews that even the positive characteristics, without complementary strengths from other domains, led to the weaker and less successful motivational styles shown in Figure 1. Thus parents and teachers who showed unconditional love and support were likely to develop in the children an overdependence on personal relationships, leaving them anxious and uncertain of their own capabilities. Strong reliance on reward or punishment in the cognitive domain seemed to produce excessive competitiveness and rivalry, while overemphasis on the moral domain might lead to apathetic compliance in some cases or in others a form of fanaticism (believing absolutely in a particular code of conduct and trying to impose it on others).

The implications for child-rearing and teaching practice thus involve first identifying the child's predominant motive and ensuring that adequate support for that motive is provided. Using emotional rewards with an unresponsive child who is seeking competence will not work; neither will a cool compliment on correct behaviour reinforce an emotionally dependent child. Having identified the dominant motive, the next step must involve providing a strong and appropriate balancing motive. Thus if a child is emotionally dependent, it would make sense to encourage responsibility through encouraging greater autonomy in, for example, taking decisions.

While the parent may achieve such sensitivity in dealing with the individual child, the task is much more difficult for teachers. In classrooms all that may be possible is to set up a climate within which all three main forms of reinforcement are used consistently, and to ensure that the teacher's own style of teaching (reflecting, as it will, her own personality and motivational preferences) is not unbalanced. For example, the 'unconditional regard' advocated by Rogers (1969) might lead to irresponsibility among the pupils: it seems essential that children are given clear indications of the behavioural limits beyond which disapproval or punishment would be the justifiable outcome. Teaching should, of course, be made interesting, but children should not come to expect all learning to be play. Application and hard work should be accepted as being necessary to achieve competence. Overemphasis on control and punishment, or excessive formality in teaching, in contrast, could be expected to encourage excessive passivity, unresponsiveness and a failure to develop personal responsibility. Finally, many schools have so strongly rewarded the acquisition of mental skills and knowledge that children's emotional and moral needs have gone unrecognized.

Figure 3 presents a simplified model of the three motivational domains indicating the observed links between the behaviour of parents or teachers and children's motivational styles. What this simple static model again fails to incorporate is the dynamic nature of motivation, the ways in which the balance between motives may change gradually with experience. Motivational styles are fairly stable by early adolescence, but there is still scope for educative intervention. The balance achieved in a stable style will, from time to time, become diffuse. The child will feel the need of something, without being clear what it is. At that point an aim is required and appropriate action. Restlessness in children can be seen either as something to be suppressed, or as an opportunity to provide an aim, and to encourage determination towards successful completion. Each rewarded (or punished) activity reminds the child of the consequences of actions. Through careful control of this mechanism of reinforcement a stronger and more balanced motivational style can be facilitated by parent or teacher.

In everyday life, and often at home, the relation between action and consequence may be neither clear nor consistent. Consequences may seem to be a matter of chance. But within education it is possible, repeatedly and systematically, to draw the attention of the child to the emotional outcomes of different types of behaviour, to emphasize the value of being kind to others, of being open to experiences, and of being responsible for your own actions. The teacher can show that feelings of happiness come from being friendly, active and responsible, while unhappiness is associated with being aggressive, passive or uncontrolled. In this way some motives are streng-

Béla Kozéki

Figure 3. A Model Relating Sources of Motives to Motivational Styles

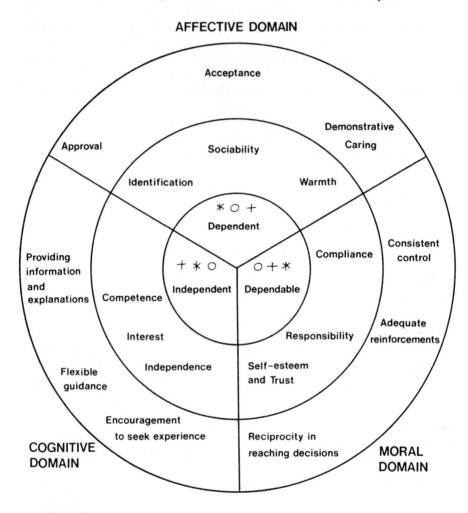

AFFECTIVE DOMAIN

Key:

Outer circle: behaviour of parents or teachers;

Inner circle: motives;

Centre: most successful motivational styles.

thened: the child becomes more ready to act in ways which are, for example, kind, curious, or compliant. Later on, these motives become more consciously recognized as intentions to be friendly, decisive, or socially responsible because such actions bring with them feelings of satisfaction and a strengthening of self-esteem.

Conclusion

It is argued that the description of motivation which has emerged from the combination of interviews and testing provides both an integrative framework incorporating a wide range of educational aims, and a set of explanations which will help parents and teachers to see how to encourage in their children the development of a balanced motivational style which will be satisfying to the child and useful to society.

References

BALL, S. (1977) *Motivation in Education*, New York, Academic Press.

BUXTON, C.E. (1966) 'Evaluations of forced-choice and Likert-type tests of motivation to academic achievement', *Br. J. Educ. Psychol.*, 36, pp. 192–201.

CATTELL, R.B. and BUTCHER, H.J. (1968) *The Prediction of Achievement and Creativity*, New York, Bobbs-Merrill.

ENTWISTLE, N.J. *et al.*, (1974) 'Motivation and study habits', *Higher Education*, 3, pp. 379–96.

EYSENCK, H.J. and COOKSON, D. (1969) 'Personality in primary school children: I — Ability and achievement', *Br. J. Educ. Psychol.*, 39, pp. 109–22.

FINGER, J.A. and SCHLESSER, G.E. (1965) 'Non-intellective predictors of academic success in school and college', *School Review*, 73, pp. 14–29.

KOZEKI, B. (1975) *Motiválás es Motiváció* (Motivating and Motivation), Budapest, Tankönyukiadó.

KOZEKI, B. (1980) *A Motiválás és Motiváció*, Budapest, Akadémiai Kiadó.

KOZEKI, B. and ENTWISTLE, N.J. (1984, in press) 'Identifying dimensions of school motivation in Britain and Hungary', *Br. J. Educ. Psychol.*, 54, (in press).

LAVIN, D.E. (1965) *The Prediction of Academic Success*, New York, Russell Sage Foundation.

ROGERS, C.R. (1969) *Freedom to Learn*, Columbus, Ohio, Merrill.

WHITE, R.W. (1959) 'Motivation reconsidered: The concept of competence', *Psychol. Rev.*, 66, pp. 297–333.

4
Psychology in Teaching and Assessment

Introduction

This section illustrates new directions in applying psychology to teaching and assessment. The selection of articles tries to achieve a balance both in the age-ranges involved, and in the theoretical underpinnings to the approaches described.

The starting point is where Béla Kozéki left off — the role of parents in their children's education. Studies by Jenny Hewison and William Schofield, supervised by the late Jack Tizard, investigated the effects of parental coaching on children's reading. This article was selected both for its importance in highlighting ways in which parents and teachers can work in partnership, and as an illustration of how psychological research progresses through a series of steps, investigating one aspect of a problem at a time and trying to establish the most salient influences on educational attainment. The alternation between survey and experiment is also typical of such research.

The second article was again chosen for two reasons. First it provided a summary of an influential research study by Michael Rutter which sought to identify differences between schools in their educational effects on pupils. This represents a developing research area. But this article is unusual, as it takes the form of a discussion between researchers. Studies which are concerned with current educational issues generally attract publicity. That publicity not only oversimplifies the findings, it also ensures that they are given intense scrutiny by other researchers. And the difficulties in measuring 'school effects' and 'school ethos' allow scope for considerable disagreement. Research moves forward by debates over research methods and the interpretation of findings. Thus this article illustrates another aspect of the research process which is not often visible beyond the 'invisible college' of interested research workers.

Schools have recently been forced to ensure that boys and girls are given equal opportunities. It is easy enough to provide woodwork for girls and cooking for boys, but it is much more difficult to make science and technology subjects attractive to girls, and to deal with the blockage that some girls find with mathematics. Elizabeth Badger asked, 'Why aren't girls better at maths?' Her careful review of the research findings shows how it is possible to piece together a wide range of studies in ways which at least avoid the tendency to jump to easy conclusions. An important function of educational research is to analyze everyday classroom problems in ways which, while highlighting their complexity, also indicate ways of resolving them.

Skinner's ideas on behaviourism continue to influence education, although no longer in the specific ways suggested by Skinner himself. Kevin Wheldall argues the case for an 'applied behavioural analysis' approach to education and provides illustrations of its value in considering problems in classroom management, such as whether children learn better when sitting at tables or in rows. The results challenge the conventional wisdom — or at least current practice in primary schools. But such findings should not be accepted as having general applicability: the results might be quite different in other classrooms, or for children of other ages or ability levels. The research does however challenge the teacher to try simple experiments of this kind, rather than accept too readily current fashions in education.

The articles by Neville Bennett and James Block represent other extensions of a different form of behavioural analysis applied to the processes of teaching. Bennett develops a model of teaching-learning processes in primary schools which draws attention above all to the fact that it takes time to learn. Dennis Child introduced the general principles of mastery learning in Section 1, and time is at the heart of Block's discussion of how these ideas can be applied in practice. Instead of explaining lack of academic success in terms of intellectual deficiencies in the pupil, he argues that it is possible to arrange instructional procedures to ensure, given time and appropriate resources, that all pupils will experience the motivating experiences of success and developing competence.

Another way of using educational psychology in analyzing teaching and learning will be found in the next two articles which focus on difficulties in learning at 16+ as pupils face up to important external examinations in Britain. The examples chosen are both Scottish, as imminent changes in the examination system have generated a substantial research and development programme there. Mary Simpson and Brian Arnold conclude that the sources of pupil difficulty they have identified apply to a wide range of school subjects, and are readily interpretable in terms of the ideas of Ausubel and Piaget (see Section 2). The article by Noel Entwistle and Carolyn Hutchinson looks at the difficulties pupils experience in answering examination questions. Question wording is seen as a powerful influence, not just on the level of difficulty, but also on the quality of answer that the pupil is able to give. Moreover, the quality of answer can be described in terms of an extension to Piaget's ideas developed by John Biggs and related to the ideas of Ference Marton which were discussed in Section 3.

The final two articles bring us face to face with the new technology of computers applied to education. Alastair Pollitt describes the contribution which computer-based item banks can make to school assessment. The computer could provide for the teacher tailor-made tests designed for a specific syllabus and ability level, and also a diagnostic assessment of the strengths and weaknesses of individual pupils. Roger Hartley evaluates the current impact, and the future potential, of microcomputers in the classroom. At present a majority of the programs available to teachers are based on Skinner's oversimple principles of learning. There are, however, different types of learning which can be stimulated by more imaginative uses of even the current generation of microcomputers.

It now seems possible that advances in computer design, supported by the growth of information technology, could bring about a revolution in teaching methods. Even then it would still be important to recognize the computer as no more than a sophisticated teaching aid, under the control of the teacher. It would not be appropriate to draw parallels with industry, where car production has been taken over by robots. Computers provide a tool to facilitate thinking and learning; they can also provide communication aids for the handicapped. But as we found in Section 3, it is crucial to recognize schools as being far more than knowledge factories. One of their crucial functions is to facilitate broad individual and social development, and for this function teachers and parents will retain their paramount influence and importance.

Parental Involvement and Reading Attainment

I — The Survey*
Jenny Hewison, University of Durham
and
Jack Tizard, University of London

The research reported here is concerned with the influence of parental help on the reading attainments of 7- and 8-year-old children. The work reported in the first part of this article forms part of a more wide-ranging investigation by Hewison (1979) into relationships between the child's home background and his success in school. It is well established that scores obtained by children on tests of academic attainment are strongly associated with demographic characteristics, as measured by social class, material circumstances and size of family — also that attitudinal factors such as parents' newspaper reading habits and the number of books in the home are related to children's educational success (Douglas, 1964; Davie *et al.*, 1972). The aim of Hewison's (1979) study was to investigate whether differences in school achievement *within* a working-class population could be related to differences in the home backgrounds of the children; demographic, cultural and attitudinal variables were to be taken into account, but the main concern was to be with characterizing parental *behaviour* and day-to-day child-rearing activities.

Children aged 7–8 years were chosen for study, because that is the age of transfer from infant to junior school and because social class differences in achievement are already well established by that age. Reading attainment was chosen as the measure of school achievement in the studies because at 7–8 years of age it is not only the best index of how well a child is currently doing in school but also the best single predictor of subsequent school achievement.

* This section is a shortened version of an article which appeared in the *British Journal of Educational Psychology*, 50, 1980, pp. 209–15.

The Pilot Study

Method

The pilot study was carried out in two infant schools. An attempt was made to interview the mothers of all children in final-year classes at the two schools. Introductory letters were sent to the homes, then an interviewer (J.H.) called at each house and asked the mother if she would agree to be interviewed. Eighty-one homes were contacted in this way. Three mothers did not wish to participate in the study, and seven repeatedly broke interview appointments. Incomplete information was obtained from six homes, where the interviewee was not the full-time guardian of the child. Thus the size of the final interview sample was sixty-five.

In the pilot study structured open interviews were used to obtain the home background information. Topics covered included attitudes to children's play and discipline, the sharing of activities and conversation, reading to the child and hearing him read, a series of questions about how the child spent his leisure time and another on attitudes to school. The time taken to carry out the pilot interview ranged from thirty minutes to two and a half hours.

The reading attainment of the children was assessed using the Southgate Reading Test I. Reading test scores were not obtained on two children who were repeatedly absent from school, so the final sample size for the pilot study was sixty-three. The study took place towards the end of the school summer term, i.e., in June and July when the age range of the children in the sample was 6:11 to 7:09.

Results

In general, Bernstein's (Bernstein and Brandis, 1970; Brandis, 1974) and others' findings of modest correlations between aspects of the child's behaviour and circumstances at home and his level of attainment were confirmed. There was, however, one question to which replies correlated strongly with the children's reading attainments. This was whether or not the mother regularly heard the child read. Most of the other significant findings between reading ability and parental practices could be accounted for statistically by the fact that parents who displayed attitudes and behaviour which appeared to favour the development of reading ability in their children were also more likely to have the habit of hearing the child read ('coaching'). Analysis by partial correlation showed that, for example, the association between 'attitudinal' factors and reading attainments came about because the 'attitudes' were correlated with 'coaching' — children whose parents had good 'attitudes' but who did not receive 'coaching' were not advanced in their reading.

The Survey

Method

The results of the pilot inquiry were both striking and unexpected. In the second study of the series, the ideas generated in the pilot were put to the test on new data.

The names of thirty children were randomly drawn from the first-year roll in each of four junior schools. As in the pilot study, introductory letters were sent to the parents of the selected children before an interviewer (J.H.) visited them at home. Once contacted, no mother refused to be interviewed, and none persistently broke appointments: interviewing was terminated when a minimum of twenty-five successful interviews had been carried out in each school area, 107 interviews being carried out in all.

A closed interview schedule, based on the framework of response coding developed in the pilot study, was used to obtain the home background information. Topics covered in the interviews again included attitudes to school and parental help with reading at home. Aspects of the mother's language behaviour were assessed using two scales devised and employed by members of Bernstein's research team (Brandis, 1970; Henderson, 1973; Brandis, 1974). The first of these scales was designed to assess a mother's willingness to chat to her child in a number of different physical circumstances, and the second her willingness to answer a variety of different 'awkward' questions. The time taken to carry out each interview ranged from thirty minutes to one hour. Scores on a standardized reading test (the NFER Test 'A') and on the WISC were obtained for the sample children. The IQ tests were administered by trainee educational psychologists from the London Institute of Education. The testers were not informed about the purpose of the main investigation and since their work was carried out under the supervision of their course tutor, the results are probably as valid, and the testing as reliable, as is normally the case.

One child was absent from the reading testing, and six from the IQ testing. The final sample size, for whom full reading, IQ and home environment information was available, was therefore 100. The study took place in the autumn term, when the age range of the sample children was 7:02 to 8:02.

Results

Significant correlations were again obtained between a number of different aspects of the home environment and reading performance. As in the pilot study, the factor which was found to be most strongly associated with reading success was whether or not the mother regularly heard the child read — not whether she read to the child but whether she heard the child read.

Taking this factor into account substantially reduced the correlations of the other home environment variables (including whether or not the mother read to the child) with reading performance.

Analysis of variance calculations revealed no significant differences in reading performance among the four schools in the study, nor between boys and girls. No significant school or sex differences were found in the proportions of mothers who heard their children read, and no interactions were found between these variables and the 'coaching' factor in the determination of reading performance, i.e., the 'coaching' effect was observable in all four schools, and for both boys and girls.

Table 1 shows, first, that the effect of being coached is observable at all levels of IQ; and second, that the higher the IQ band, the higher the proportion of children receiving this form of help with their reading.

Table 1. The Relationships between Coaching and Reading Performance in Groups of Children Banded for IQ

IQ band (Mean IQ = 102.4)		'Poor Readers' Test Score ≤ 94	'Good Readers' Test Score ≥ 95	Total
87 or less	Not coached	10	0	10
	Coached	1	1	2
88–102	Not coached	21	5	26
	Coached	6	10	16
103–117	Not coached	9	3	12
	Coached	2	14	16
118 or above	Not coached	4	1	5
	Coached	2	11	13
(Total N)		(55)	(45)	(100)

A Replication Study

Method

A weakness of the studies so far was that no assessment was attempted as to the amount of coaching children were receiving at the time or had received in the past. To get an idea of this, a further sample of children and their parents was studied. Unfortunately it was not possible this time to assess the children's IQs. The study was a quick one designed simply to find out whether the amount of coaching was related to reading attainment score.

The procedure followed in the main study for obtaining a sample was again adopted. The names of thirty children were randomly drawn from the first-year rolls of the same four junior schools (the study took place twelve months after the previous one) and the contacting and interviewing of parents carried out as before. One hundred and six mothers were contacted, and 105 agreed to be interviewed. One child missed the reading testing, so the final sample size for the study was 104.

Detailed questioning of parents, using a closed interview schedule, made it possible to classify the amount of help their children had received into one of the following five categories: *regular*, or *occasional*, help in the juniors; *regular*, or *occasional*, help in the infants only; *no help* at any time.

Results

Table 2 gives the mean reading scores of children in the five 'coached' categories.

Table 2. Mean Reading Scores of Children in Five 'Coached' Categories

Help received	Mean Reading Score	SD	N
Regular help in juniors	104.9	10.9	39
Occasional help in juniors	98.3	8.8	23
Regular help in infants only	91.2	9.3	19
Occasional help in infants only	86.7	9.0	11
No help at any time	81.1	10.3	12
Total sample	96.3	12.8	104

An analysis of variance carried out on the data revealed that the relationship between amount of help given and reading performance was highly significant statistically ($F = 18.5$, df = 4.99, $P < 0.0001$).

The results are very consistent indeed. They fully confirm the earlier findings, and suggest in addition that reading attainment scores vary in stepwise fashion with the amount of coaching in reading which the children have received.

II — The Experiment[*]
J. Tizard, University of London
W.N. Schofield, University of Cambridge
and Jenny Hewison, University of Durham

The 1980 survey left a number of questions unanswered. Parents who listened to their children read were a self-selected group, and possibly the

[*] This section is a shortened version of an article which appeared in the *British Journal of Educational Psychology*, 52, 1982, pp. 1–15. Further details of the study have been reported by Schofield (1979a, 1979b).

improvement was mainly due to the interest which they took in their children's schooling, of which help at home was only one powerful indicator, rather than to the help itself. Attitudinal data collected at the time went against this hypothesis; but questioning by parental interview may not be a very effective method of finding out about differences in parental style of upbringing. Further, it might have been the case that only the best readers at school were allowed, or wanted, to take their reading books home.

More importantly, survey findings obtained from self-selected groups throw no light on the question of how far parental attitudes and practice are subject to change: can one, in other words, persuade all, or nearly all, parents to help their children at home — in this case, by hearing them read? Is it feasible for class teachers to try to ensure that *all* children will take their books home? Will they return books if they do? How many books will get lost or destroyed? How many parents will argue that it is the school's job not theirs to teach the three Rs? How many parents will 'help' in such a punitive or unsatisfactory way that children will be put off, rather than turned on, by reading practice at home? Can non-English speaking or illiterate parents be involved? And finally, will active parental help of the kind suggested actually lead to a measurable improvement in children's reading performance?

Questions such as these can only be answered by experiment, and we were fortunate in being able to carry out such an experiment, in partnership with the primary advisers and heads and class teachers in six infant and junior schools in the London borough of Haringey.

The overall purpose of the project was to find out if there was a causal relationship between active parental help and reading performance. To this end the main task of the project team was to establish an arrangement whereby all children in certain experimental classes were heard to read at home. The effectiveness of this treatment was to be measured against control children both within the schools where the intervention was to take place and in different schools, and also against a separate control in which children were given extra reading tuition by a qualified teacher in school, rather than by parents at home. The purpose of this control procedure was to gain some understanding of process factors: parental help, it was argued, might aid reading performance simply because it represented extra time spent on the learning task; alternatively, the improvement might follow primarily from the increased motivation of children whose parents became involved in their learning. By providing some children with extra practice given in school, it was planned to obtain some idea of the relative importance of these two factors as mediators of any established causal relationship between parental help and reading performance. As the schools sampled were multiracial, problems of organizing extra reading practice in homes where English was not spoken and in homes where neither parent could read English were also to be examined.

Method

The main sampling frame was an opportunity sample and included all children in the middle infant, top infant, first-year junior and second-year junior classes at six schools in a disadvantaged working-class area of the London borough of Haringey.

The field work for the interventions took place over a two-year period (1976–78) with a cohort of children studied first in the final year of their infant schooling (i.e., when the children were 6 to 7 years old), then in the first year of their junior schooling (7 to 8 years old). At the end of the 1975/76 school year baseline reading tests were given to all children in the four year-bands at the six project schools. The schools were assigned at random to three groups: parent involvement, extra teacher help, and control. One top infant class at each of the two parent involvement schools (schools 1 and 2) was chosen at random to receive the research intervention, and the remaining classes at each school formed the within-school control group for that school. Similarly intervention and control groups were randomly chosen at the two schools (schools 3 and 4) where the extra teacher help was to be given at school. It had been established previously from the summer reading data that the year group concerned had not been streamed, and that there were no significant differences in reading performance between those classes which would be receiving the interventions and those which would not. There were no interventions at schools 5 and 6 other than annual testing of reading attainment.

An experienced and qualified teacher was appointed to implement the intervention at schools 3 and 4. She worked four half-days each week at each school for the two years of the intervention. Her work was planned, in consultation with the class teacher, and involved not only hearing the children read but all aspects of the teaching of reading, since it was felt by the LEA advisers and the staff concerned that a teacher could not merely hear the children read as was intended for the parents. A second difference from the parent intervention was that the children were seen in small groups rather than individually, although of course reading was heard individually within those groups, each child reading to the teacher on average once or twice a week. These were professional decisions made by the staff concerned who felt that they were an advantage for the children receiving the extra practice in a school context.

The intervention began at schools 1 and 2 with a visit by a member of the project team (W.S. at school 1 and J.H. at school 2) to the home collaboration class assigned to his or her care: this division of responsibility was maintained for the two years of the intervention, and although the two researchers were in frequent contact with each other they advised and monitored exclusively in one school and with one home collaboration class. Thus an element of replication was built into the design.

Parents, almost without exception, said that they welcomed the project and agreed to hear their child read at home as requested and to complete a record card showing what had been read. All parents also agreed to allow the researcher to visit them at home two or three times each term to hear the child reading to them; the first of these visits was made to each home immediately after half-term and the intended monitoring was maintained for the two years of the intervention. At both schools advice and demonstrations were given to the very small minority of parents — no more than one or two in each group — who adopted strategies which the researcher judged to be potentially counter-productive. It was noted that parents responded to these demonstrations, and were in general eager for advice and suggestions. This level of interest and cooperation was maintained, with only two or three exceptions, over the full two years of the project.

The school side of the home reading was organized at each school by the headteacher, the class teacher and the researcher. Teachers kept their usual records and in addition special records for the project including a reading card for parents to complete at home. The nature and frequency of reading material sent home varied between the two schools and between the infant and junior years of the intervention, in accordance with the wishes and customary practice of the teacher involved, but the common objective of reading practice at home was maintained. Mostly books were sent home on a minimum of three or four nights per week at school 1 and two or three nights per week at school 2.

As has been mentioned reading tests were given to all middle infants and top infants, and to all first and second year juniors at the conclusion of the 1975/76 school year immediately before the interventions began. This pattern of testing all four school year groups was repeated in July, 1977, on conclusion of the infant year of the intervention; again in July, 1978, on conclusion of the junior year; and finally, once again, in July, 1979, twelve months after the researchers had left the schools. (Not all of these tests were used in extracts reprinted here.)

Results

Table 3 presents the mean reading scores of pupils who experienced additional help. In both home collaboration schools a clear divergence of reading performance between experimental and control groups can be observed. At both schools the differences were highly significant (for school 1, $F = 19.60$; df $= 1, 70$; $P < 0.0001$: for school 2, $F = 7.02$; df $= 1, 63$; $P < 0.01$). The pattern of results was less clear at the schools where the intervention had taken the form of extra teacher help. Although the mean score for children who received the extra teacher help at school 4 was higher than for the controls the difference was not significant ($F = 1.79$; df $= 1, 44$). At school 3 the children who received the extra teacher help had a lower mean score than the control subjects, but again the difference was not

Table 3. Middle Infant Reading Scores on Southgate Test at Beginning of Intervention Period (July 1976) and First Year Junior Scores on NFER Test A at the End of the Two-Year Intervention Period (July, 1978)

School	Group	Southgate Raw Score 1976 Mean	SD	NFER A Standardized Score 1978 Mean	SD	N
1	Home collaboration	16.7	6.34	107.0	8.35	23
	Control	16.1	6.90	95.6	10.94	49
2	Home collaboration	18.1	7.21	101.9	12.74	28
	Control	18.5	6.79	94.1	11.06	37
3	Extra teacher help	11.6	7.82	93.2	17.51	20
	Control	12.9	7.02	97.9	13.80	45
4	Extra teacher help	16.2	7.32	104.3	15.86	25
	Control	16.3	7.31	98.5	13.34	21

Table 4. Proportion of Children Falling into Four Reading Bands for the 1978 Results

Schools	Group	NFER Test A score band 84 or less	85–99	100–114	115 plus	N
1 and 2	Home collaboration	5.9	27.5	49.0	17.6	51
	Control	17.4	53.5	22.1	7.0	86
		($\chi^2 = 18.77$, df = 3, P < 0.0003)				
3 and 4	Extra teacher help	26.7	22.2	33.3	17.8	45
	Control	18.2	37.9	31.8	12.1	66
		($\chi^2 = 3.58$, df = 3, not significant)				
(Standardization sample		15.1	33.6	34.6	16.7	7249)*

* *Source*: National Foundation for Educational Research (1973).

significant ($F = 1.37$; df = 1, 63). An analysis of mean scores for the Spooncer test produced exactly the same pattern of results.

As mean scores provide only limited information, more extreme groups on the reading scale were examined. Since the number of children falling in the separate bands was small the data for schools 1 and 2 were pooled to give a combined parental help group and a combined control group. A similar pooling of groups was made for schools 3 and 4. Table 4 compares the proportions — expressed as percentages — of experimental and control children falling into four reading bands for the pooled data. Chi-squared tests revealed that the distribution of the children across categories was significantly different for the experimental and control children from the two parent involvement schools ($\chi^2 = 18.77$, df = 3, P < 0.0003), but not for the groups from the extra teacher help schools ($\chi^2 = 3.58$, df = 3). From Table 4 it can be seen that parental help both reduced the proportion of failing readers (scores of 84 or less) and increased the proportion of able readers (scores of 115 or above). The lack of significant effect for the extra teacher help children appears most evident in the lowest attainment band. (The advantage shown for the home collaboration group was, however, attributable mainly to school 1; school 2 was no better than school 4, when tested on other occasions.)

Discussion

There is an increasing awareness of the need for cooperation between the home and the school. Also, the significant part that a child's home environment plays in determining his educational progress has been well documented in, for example, the two longitudinal studies carried out by Douglas (1964) and the National Children's Bureau (Davie *et al.*, 1972). Both the Plowden Report (1967) and the Bullock Report (DES, 1975) discussed cooperation between parents and teachers and made constructive suggestions as to how this could be improved.

In general, these recommendations have been concerned with ways of changing the attitudes of teachers and parents. What matters most, according to the Plowden Report, is 'whether there is a genuine mutual respect, whether parents understand what the schools are doing for their individual children and teachers realise how dependent they are on parental support.'

There has been much less discussion of parental involvement in children's actual school work. The Plowden and Bullock Reports both made some reference to parents helping their children with work at home, but neither report made explicit its views as to the desirability or otherwise of this practice.

The Bullock Report was primarily concerned with the teaching of reading and other language skills in a school setting. Discussion of parental involvement was restricted to general remarks about the role of parents in extending children's language development, and fostering positive attitudes to books and reading. Talking to children and reading to them were considered the most appropriate activities for parents to engage in, and specific warnings were issued against the use by parents of more formal techniques, such as helping their children work through the books in a reading scheme.

The experimental findings reported here provide evidence for a causal relationship between parents hearing their children read and reading attainment. Although further research would be required if the variables underlying the relationship are to be understood, this lack of understanding may not be important for most practical purposes. Of much greater practical significance is the fact that teachers and parents working in collaboration did improve the academic performance of the children without the parents being given any special training in the techniques of tutoring, other than advice and brief demonstrations during the monitoring of home reading or at meetings with the class teacher. A number of studies have examined the effect of non-professional tuition on reading performance, but in all cases the parents or other helpers were first given detailed instructions in the techniques of prompting and reward-giving favoured by the researcher directing the project (Ellson *et al.*, 1968; Ryback and Staats, 1970; Staats *et al.*, 1970; Wallach and Wallach, 1976; Glynn *et al.*, 1979; Morgan and Lyon, 1979). Adopting a very different approach to reading failure, Lawrence (1972) concentrated on the motivational and emotional needs of poor readers; he reported performance gains by children who had received non-professional counselling to improve their self-esteem, but no direct help with reading. Since these projects looked at children of different ages, and with varying degrees of reading difficulty, it is unfortunately not possible to compare the gains made by children given different types of help, and so increase understanding of the relative contributions made by practice and motivational factors to the reading progress observed.

The project involved not only the organization and monitoring of the intervention and the testing of attainment but also the collection of qualitative, descriptive information on what was happening in the homes and schools relevant to each child's progress. Drawing on both sources a number of general conclusions follow with implications for future research and practice in schools. Firstly, in inner-city, multiracial schools it is both feasible and practicable to involve nearly all parents in formal educational activities with infant and first-year junior school children, even if the parents are non-literate or largely non-English speaking. Secondly, children who receive parental help are significantly better in reading attainment than comparable children who do not. Thirdly, most parents express great satisfaction in being involved in this way by the schools, and teachers report that the children show an increased keenness for learning at school and are better behaved. Fourthly, the teachers involved in the home collaboration also reported that they found the work with parents worthwhile and they continued to involve parents with subsequent classes after the experiment was concluded, as did teachers who had taught parallel control classes during the intervention years. Fifthly, small-group instruction in reading, given by a highly competent specialist teacher, did not produce improvements in attainment comparable in magnitude with those obtained from the collaboration with parents. Sixthly, the collaboration between teachers and parents was effective for children of all initial levels of performance, including those who at the beginning of the study were failing to learn to read. Finally, the fact that some children read to parents who could not themselves read English, or in a few cases could not read at all, did not prevent improvement in the reading skills of those children, or detract from the willingness of the parent to collaborate with the school.

Current developments in educational thinking and practice underlie the potential importance of these findings. The Taylor Report (1977) and the ongoing discussion about parental involvement in education suggest a need for further studies of ways in which parents, and the wider community, can be brought into closer partnership with schools and teachers. The fluctuations in pupil numbers and in the supply of teachers that are a feature of industrial societies today, coupled with the need for economy in resource allocation, raise profound issues concerning the training of teachers and the ways in which they can use their time most effectively. From a different perspective, the Warnock Report (1978) laid emphasis on the special needs of the large minority of pupils in ordinary schools who continue to present chronic educational problems. The findings of the present study suggest that staffing resources at present allocated by LEAs for remedial work in primary schools might be better employed, at least in part, in organizing contact and collaboration between class teachers and parents — all parents, before failure is manifest for some children — on specific, practical teaching matters, and that this might prevent many children from falling behind with their reading in the first place.

Acknowledgements

The first part of this paper is based on a doctoral thesis submitted by J. Hewison in partial fulfilment of the requirements for the degree of PhD at the University of London. The empirical work was supported by an MRC postgraduate scholarship, and carried out under the direction of the late Professor J. Tizard.

The second study was supported by a grant from the Department of Education and Science to the late Professor Jack Tizard who directed the research and to William Schofield for the preparation of the final report.

The research team, which included Mrs Ena Abrahams and Mr A.C. Everton of the Haringey Education Service, were grateful to the Director of Education, London Borough of Haringey and his staff, and to headteachers, teachers, ancillary staff, parents and children; and to many others who helped with organization, testing, scoring, data management, computing, or other aspects of the project.

References

BERNSTEIN, B. and BRANDIS, W. (1970) 'Social class differences in communication and control', in BRANDIS, W. and HENDERSON, D. (Eds), *Social Class, Language and Communication*, London, Routledge and Kegan Paul.

BRANDIS, W. (1970) 'Appendix II: A measure of the mother's orientation towards communication and control', in BRANDIS, W. and HENDERSON, D. (Eds), *Social Class, Language and Communication*, London, Routledge and Kegan Paul.

BRANDIS, W. (1974), Personal communication.

DAVIE, R. *et al.* (1972) *From Birth to Seven: A Report of the National Child Development Study*, London, Longman.

DEPARTMENT OF EDUCATION AND SCIENCE (1975) *A Language for Life* (The Bullock Report), London, HMSO.

DOUGLAS, J.W.B. (1964) *The Home and the School*, London, MacGibbon and Kee.

ELLSON, D.G. *et al.* (1968) 'A field test of programmed and directed tutoring', *Reading Res. Q.*, 3, pp. 307–67.

GLYNN, E.L. *et al.* (1979) *Remedial Reading at Home: Helping You to Help Your Child*, Wellington, New Zealand Council for Educational Research.

HENDERSON, D. (1973) 'Contextual specificity, discretion and cognitive socialization: With special reference to language', in BERNSTEIN, B. (Ed.), (1973), *Class, Codes and Control: Volume 2*. London, Routledge and Kegan Paul.

HEWISON, J. (1979) 'Home environment and reading attainment: A study of children in a working class community', unpublished PhD thesis, University of London.

LAWRENCE, D. (1972) 'Counselling of retarded readers by non-professionals', *Educ. Res.*, 15, pp. 48–51.

MORGAN, R. and LYON, E. (1979) 'Paired reading — a preliminary report on a technique for parental tuition of reading-retarded children', *J. Child Psychol. Psychiat.*, 20, pp. 151–60.

PLOWDEN REPORT (1967) *Children and Their Primary Schools*, Report of the Central Advisory Council for Education, London, HMSO.

RYBACK, D. and STAATS, A.W. (1970) 'Parents as behavior therapy technicians in treating reading deficits (dyslexia)', *J. Behav. Therapy Exper. Psychiat.*, 1, pp. 109–19.

SCHOFIELD, W.N. (1979a) 'The Haringey Reading Project: An experiment designed to test the effect of a collaboration between teachers and parents in organizing home reading practice for children', Paper presented at the Scientific Programme of the Association of Child Psychology and Psychiatry, at the Institute of Child Health, London, 5 December 1979.

SCHOFIELD, W.N. (1979b), 'The Haringey Reading Project: Collaboration between teachers and parents in assisting children's reading', Final Report to the Department of Education and Science. (Copies are available from W.N. Schofield, Department of Experimental Psychology, University of Cambridge, Downing Street, Cambridge CB2 3EB.)

STAATS, A.W. *et al.* (1970) 'Learning and cognitive development: Representative samples, cumulative-hierarchical learning, and experimental-longitudinal methods', *Monograph of the Society for Research in Child Development*, 35.

STAATS, A.W. *et al.* (1970) 'A token-reinforcer remedial reading programme administered by black therapy-technicians to problem black children', *Behav. Ther.* 1, pp. 331–53.

TAYLOR REPORT (1977) *Report of the Committee of Enquiry into Management and Government of Schools*, London, HMSO.

WALLACH, N.A. and WALLACH, L. (1976) *Teaching all Children to Read*, Chicago, University of Chicago Press.

WARNOCK REPORT (1978) *Report of the Committee of Enquiry into the Education of Handicapped Children and Young People*, London, HMSO.

Secondary Schools and Their Effects on Children: A Review Dialogue*

Neville Bennett, University of Lancaster and Michael Rutter, University of London

The point has been made elsewhere that the impact and treatment of research findings depends crucially on the contemporary educational climate (Cronbach, 1975; Bennett and Shipman, 1979). At the level of the academic review this climate can interact with prejudice or ideology to produce a critique which is less than constructive or objective. The comments of active fieldworkers and armchair snipers can usually be distinguished, the former recognizing that in the real research world as opposed to the 'whiter than white research handbook' human behaviour is often unpredictable and can have a marked impact on research design. Philosophers of the research endeavour are also beginning to take an interest in this area. Fenstermacher (1978), for example, argues that research criticism comes in three varieties. The first is useless because it is uninformed and unintelligible. The second is useful because it is pertinent to the research effort and directed to reparable defects. The third kind, although apparently significant, cannot be heeded because the remedy is unknown or because its implications are that 'the shop be closed and a new calling found'.

The acknowledgement of the foregoing, together with the recognition that each research project meets unexpected, sometimes idiosyncratic, problems requiring inevitable compromises would strongly argue for a dialogue between reviewer and reviewed. The aim would not only be for a more balanced comment, but that it be educative as well as evaluative.

Initially this dialogue was conceived as a face-to-face interview with Michael Rutter but he was on sabbatical leave in the United States at the time. Thus the criticisms and responses were relayed by letter. Following an overview of the study (Rutter *et al.*, 1979), each criticism is presented together with the authors' response (*italic*).

* This article appeared in the *British Educational Research Journal*, 6, 1, 1980, pp. 97–102.

Neville Bennett and Michael Rutter

Overview

This is clearly an important contribution to the emerging body of research on schooling and teaching. Findings from a sample of twelve inner-London comprehensive schools are presented which indicate quite clearly the power of the individual school to affect their pupils' achievement, attendance and behaviour even when such factors as pupil ability at entry, social and home background are taken into account. Furthermore the authors suggest that the pattern of relationships between these outcomes and school process variables is a causal one. The important school variables are not physical and administrative characteristics but what teachers and pupils do in school and their mutual expectations. Thus pupils made better progress both academically and behaviourally in schools which placed an emphasis on academic matters, an emphasis reflected in a well-planned curriculum, high teacher expectations, the setting of homework, good coordination between teachers, a high proportion of teaching time spent on the subject, sound preparation as seen in reduced administration and class management time, and lessons that run their full length. Marked variation between schools was found on all these variables. The authors rightly argue that such findings are in line with previous research, much of which has been carried out at primary school level.

But there were one or two surprises. Although the balance of the intake emerged as important, differences in sex composition did not. Another to feed the prejudices is that the greater the emphasis on pastoral care the worse the pupil behaviour.

How valid or generalizable are these findings? It is a research cliché that no study is perfect and this is no exception. Three aspects of the methodology require comment — sampling, the measurement of differences in intake and the observational study.

Twelve schools were chosen which the authors claim are representative: 'there is every reason to believe that the associations we found and the conclusions we derived from our findings are still applicable to schools as a whole.' However, the data they themselves provide would seem to argue against such a view. All the schools were within a few miles of inner-London, an area which shows marked family adversity. One-quarter of the children in this area have fathers who are unskilled, over one-third come from families with four or more children, over one-half live in overcrowded conditions and over one-quarter had a mother who had some handicapping psychiatric disorder. From data on O-level success it was shown that in the twelve schools studied less than one-third of the children gained more than one O-level compared to over 40 per cent nationally. In addition, there was at the time high teacher turnover, some part-time schooling and school reorganization. On those bases it would appear that a more cautious interpretation concerning representativeness is necessary.

Although we argued that the findings might have general application, I don't think that we claimed that the twelve schools themselves were 'representative' of all schools. In particular, it seems very probable that there will be major differences between these schools, and those serving either rural areas or much less disadvantaged families. The poorer examination results of our twelve schools are, however, partly due to the fact that more than half of the most able children at the primary schools transferred to either selective or independent schools rather than to the twenty comprehensive schools which served the area.

Although further studies of entirely different sorts of areas are undoubtedly required, there is reason to suppose that the associations are likely to apply, for the most part, to other schools and to other areas. Obviously we cannot derive that conclusion from our own data. Rather, we have to rely on comparisons with other studies in different areas — none of which, of course, has used quite the same measures or quite the same research design. However, insofar as there are other studies, they produce findings which seem to us to be broadly in keeping with our own. There are, in addition to those studies quoted in the book, a variety of American investigations in utterly different sorts of areas which also come up with very comparable findings. It is that replicability which gives us some confidence that many (but doubtless not all) of the conclusions have some general validity.

The question of the schools' emphasis on pastoral care is an interesting one. The scale used here was attitudinal in content and was constructed from interviews with the headteacher at each of the schools. Almost certainly the finding reflects the fact that the more successful schools had fewer pastoral and discipline problems with which to cope. The actual pastoral care provided was probably very good in that it seemed to have prevented too many problems from developing. These schools did not have to emphasize pastoral care because they had already achieved some success in this area (as indicated, for example, by the findings on pupil reports of their willingness to consult teachers about personal difficulties).

My major concern relating to the validity of the findings is on the way in which differences in intake were controlled. These differences were based on the responses of primary school teachers on a behavioural questionnaire when the pupils were 10 years of age, and of secondary teachers when they were 14. The authors note that 'different teachers tend to rate the same children in a fairly comparable fashion' and that 'questionnaire scores generally agree with more detailed diagnostic assessments' but in neither case is a reliability coefficient provided. In addition it was admitted that 'associations with the child's behaviour in later years are only modest.'

To examine differences between schools after differences in intake were controlled first required a determination of the relationship between the primary and secondary teachers' ratings before constructing a standardization formula. Even accepting the utility of this approach there are several sources of unreliability, and thus validity, in the final scores. These include the unreliabilities of both individual primary and secondary teachers, the unreliability associated with differences in perception across primary and secondary school teachers, together with the unreliability of the difference between primary and secondary school teachers in relation to individual pupils.

In short, I feel less confident than the authors when they state, for example, that variations between schools in child behaviour and the delinquency rates could *not* (their emphasis) be explained in terms of questionnaire scores at primary level.

In this instance, perhaps, you may have been somewhat less than fair in that your arguments seem to suggest that that is the only measure of control of intake which we used. In fact, of course, it is not, and we did not use behaviour at all as a control variable for the measures of outcome obtained when the cohort were in their final year of compulsory schooling. What we did in each case was precisely as you suggested we should have done. That is to say, we empirically determined which was the best predictor, or which combinations of variables were the best predictors, of the outcomes we were interested in. And having empirically determined that, we used the findings as basis of our choice of intake measures.

I would of course accept the limitations which apply to any attempts to control intake. Inevitably we are limited (as everybody else has been) by the measures of intake which are available. By statistically controlling for intake, all we can legitimately conclude is that the observed variations are not explicable in terms of the intake measures which we examined. Obviously, that does not mean that the variations could not have been explained by other intake measures which we have not been able to take into account. So far as this point is concerned, it seems to me that we are exactly in the same position as anyone else. I would claim that our measures of intake were as good (if not better) than those available in previous studies of schooling. But I would be the first to admit that they are limited in scope.

Now to come to your specific points: I feel that in your final paragraph you have been inadvertently misleading. Surely you must accept that the variations between schools could not be explained in terms of questionnaire scores at primary level. This is not an inference; it is simply a statistical statement. What you are querying, I think, is whether our measures of behaviour were adequate to conclude that the children's outcome in secondary school was not a function of their behaviour in primary school, in terms of behaviours not covered by our questionnaire. That is a reasonable point, but I would respond to it like this. There is quite an extensive body of data on the questionnaire used and the empirical research findings show that the questionnaire is as reliable and valid as any other questionnaire which is currently available. We know a good deal about its re-lationship with much more detailed measures of behaviour, and we know a good deal about the extent to which children's behaviour is consistent or inconsistent over time. In brief, what the results show is that there is a satisfactory degree of inter-rater reliability when two different teachers are compared in relation to their ratings of the same child; but equally, that even within primary school there is a considerable degree of change in children's behaviour from year to year. That conclusion about change, incidentally, applies not only to the questionnaire but to much more detailed measures of children's behaviour. I think it would be seriously mistaken to assume that the changes are an artifact of unreliability in the measuring instrument (although obviously that enters into it). . . . Rather, at least in part, the changes over time reflect real alterations in children's behaviour from situation to situation and from time to time. The basis of our argument would be that one (but only one) of the elements involved in this change is the influence of school.

In short, we would accept many of the limitations you outline with respect to our attempts to control for differences in intake, but argue that we could not have done any better with the range of intake measures available to us.

Given that school processes turned out to be the major variable in relation to outcomes it is unfortunate, in retrospect, that so little emphasis was placed on the observation of teaching. That was limited to one week per school on average ability third-year pupils only. The subject area was not controlled which is a major weakness given the evidence, albeit mostly at primary level, that teaching and interaction patterns differ markedly in different subject areas. The effect of this in this study could have been to distort the between-school differences. Also the inter-observer reliability data are strangely reported in significance levels leaving the reader devoid of information regarding inter-observer agreement. That some of the significance levels are reported at the 0.05 level gives a little cause for concern here. Neither was I completely happy with the manner of combining self-report and observational data to form the criterion for pupil behaviour.

I think you are a little hard on us here in terms of our classroom observations. It is all very well to say that we only had one week per school for third-year pupils, but in fact that meant making detailed observations second by second for more than 500 lessons. Of course I am bound to agree that that is a limited data base; but it is very considerably more than has been available in previous studies. Incidentally, it is not true that we only had it on third-year pupils; as you recall, we also had more limited observations on first-year pupils. The subject area of the lesson observations was, in fact, controlled to the extent that we observed a complete week in each school. These third-year pupils had very similar time-tables in all the schools, so that the balance in terms of time spent in different subjects was essentially comparable. Where we did find major differences in teaching styles and patterns of interaction was between lessons in art, craft and PE, and in the more 'academic' subjects, all the analyses presented in the book in fact focus only on this latter group of lessons.

On the question of inter-observer agreement, we would of course be happy to provide further details for any readers who are interested. We used a correlational approach which would have necessitated reporting a series of correlations for each individual measure. Instead, we chose simply to report significance levels to indicate how likely we would have been to gain these results by chance. As a general guide, correlations significant at the 0.05 level would have been 0.8 or greater.

Finally, a short comment on interpretation. When studied carefully the results do not always appear to be as consistent as the text indicates. In the table relating schools and outcomes, for example, the best school on achievement is also the best on attendance and behaviour, but the second-best school on achievement and attendance is the worst for behaviour. Similarly, the third-best school for attendance and behaviour is among the worst for achievement, and so on. It would be a mistake therefore to claim that good schools tend to be good on all criteria as the report suggests. On the same theme it would have been useful to have numbered the schools throughout the presentation of tables to allow the reader to check across the four outcome measures.

I hope we have not claimed that good schools tend to be good on all criteria. As you point out, the best school on academic achievement is also the best on attendance and behaviour, but the second-best on achievement and attendance is fourth on behaviour and the third school on attendance and behaviour is average (sixth out of twelve) on attainment. What we have said is that there is a general tendency for the outcomes to go in the same direction. However, the correlations are well short of unity and, as you indicate, there are some schools which are, as it were, out of step. The very fact that this happens does, of course, raise some very important questions for further research.

Conclusion

Research directors constantly struggle to maintain a good research design whilst operating within the constraints of time, finance, staffing and the level of technology and methodology currently available. For example, Rutter admits that there were limitations with respect to the measures of behaviour and intake but reasonably asks, 'do you know of any better?' He agrees that the observational data base was limited but points to the time involved and the paucity of such data in previous research. Constraints and compromises are integral elements in all research studies such that all findings are better to be regarded as suggestive rather than definitive. A more realistic aim for researchers who operate in natural settings might therefore be to seek improvement in the light of others' experience in the same field rather than try to meet the idealistic criteria found in 'whiter than white research handbooks'. It is hoped that review dialogues might play a small part in this.

References

BENNETT, S.N. and SHIPMAN, M. (1979) 'Educational research and the media', *Res. Intell.*, August, 1979, pp. 5–13.

CRONBACH, L.J. (1975) 'Five decades of controversy over mental testing', *Amer. Psychol.*, 30, pp. 1–14.

FENSTERMACHER, G.D. (1978) 'A philosophical consideration of recent research on teacher effectiveness', in SHULMAN, L. (Ed) *Review of Research in Education 6.* Peacock, Hasea, Illinois

RUTTER, M. *et al.* (1979) *Fifteen Thousand Hours: Secondary Schools and their Effects on Children*, London, Open Books.

Why Aren't Girls Better at Maths?*

Elizabeth Badger
National Foundation for Educational Research

Introduction

The developmental aspect of sex differences in mathematics performance has intrigued both educators and psychologists. Up until adolescence, girls and boys show no more difference in mathematics achievement than they show in general intelligence. Basically, their scores are comparable. However, in their early teens girls' performance begins to decline in relation to boys' until, by the end of compulsory schooling, there is a dramatic difference between the sexes in their mathematical competence as well as in their training and qualifications. Girls not only fail to continue their study, but their rate of success in all mathematical work is generally lower than that of boys. For example, while approximately equal numbers of boys and girls are entered for the CSE arithmetic and mathematics examinations, a disproportionately small number of girls are entered for the GCE O-level mathematics examination. Furthermore, girls perform less well than boys in whatever mathematics examination they are entered for.

It appears that girls and boys in this country follow the same pattern of development that has been found in the United States. There, the National Assessment of Educational Progress (NAEP) reported that among 13-year-old pupils, girls performed significantly better than boys in computation, whereas boys surpassed girls in number applications. Among the 17-year-old pupils, boys had increased their advantage in number applications; were scoring significantly higher than girls in probability and statistics, geometry and measurement; and were performing as well as girls in computation (Armstrong, 1980).

That this phenomenon is not confined to England and the United States is evident from data collected by the International Association for the

---

* This is a substantially shortened version of an article which appeared in *Educational Research*, 24, 1981, pp. 11–23.

Evaluation of Educational Achievement (IEA). Surveying mathematical attainment in twelve countries in 1964, the Association reported that within each country boys performed at a higher level than girls on both computation and verbal problems. Furthermore, as with other studies, the sex differential in performance was greater at pre-university level than at the 13-year-old level (Keeves, 1973).

Until recently this situation has not been questioned. That boys do well at mathematics has been an accepted truism. However, an examination of the data suggests that such easy generalizations obscure the complexities of the situation. A number of statistical studies have been made recently that bear on the problem of sex differences in mathematical performance. These studies revolve around the questions of whether there are some specific innate sex-related aptitudes that account for these differences or whether they are determined by sociological and psychological factors. Because of the diversity of the findings, as well as their inconsistent relevance to the classroom situation, it seems worthwhile to bring together some of the results for critical examination.

Is the Truism True and Universal?

Generalizations regarding boys' superior performance in mathematics seem to rest upon the assumption that performance in mathematics is contingent upon some unitary trait or aptitude. There is, however, abundant evidence that this is not the case.

Although girls generally score less well than boys on tests that aggregate results over a variety of mathematical topics, their relatively poor performance is not unconditional. For example, girls generally perform at equal or superior levels to boys in arithmetic or algebraic-type work and in some of the more modern mathematical topics such as matrices (Armstrong, 1980; Preece, 1979). The major discrepancies in performance arise in two general areas. One involves spatial ability and judgment. The other involves the recall, combination and application of relevant knowledge to a problem, and is often termed 'problem-solving'. Within these two broad areas there are specific topics, such as geometry, measurement and proportionality, which appear to present consistent difficulty to girls. However, in most cases difficulties can be discussed in terms of the broader areas of problem-solving and visual problems.

Aside from these content areas, there are certain behavioural patterns that characterize girls' approach to mathematics. One is their tendency to keep to specific methods that have been approved by their teachers. Another is their apparent 'blindness to the real world significance of some of the problems'. For example, not only do girls show a poor grasp of such practical features as relative size and scale, but they are 'less alert to thoroughly implausible solutions' (Wood, 1976). Finally, there is girls' consistent failure to follow a problem through to its conclusion. That is, when problems involve a number of steps for their solution, girls are more likely to stop at the first stage (Armstrong, 1980; Wood, 1976). All these types of behaviour have relevance to number application or problem solving and may offer some explanation for girls' poorer performance.

In addition, more specific factors have been suggested. On the one hand, it has been proposed that the masculine content of most mathematical problems affects the motivation of girls, who see these problems as irrelevant to their interests (Carey, 1958; Milton, 1959). On the other hand, it has been argued that a lack of spatial ability forces girls to rely upon an inappropriate verbal strategy in attempting to solve certain problems (Werdelin, 1958). Others have suggested that a debilitating anxiety prompts them to grasp at a problem solution before a thorough consideration of alternatives (Tobias, 1978). Each of these explanations is supported by research which will be discussed in the following sections.

A Possible Sex-Linked Cognitive Factor: The Influence of Spatial Ability on Mathematics Performance

It has been argued that girls' marked decline in mathematics achievement at adolescence is causally linked to deficiencies in spatial ability. As in the case of mathematics, girls and boys show little difference in performance on spatial tasks during childhood. However, at approximately 13–14 years old, boys begin to perform at a higher level than girls and they tend to increase this advantage throughout their adolescent period (Maccoby and Jacklin, 1974). Since spatial tasks are considered more of a measure of innate ability than of achievement, it has been argued that girls' lower performance in mathematics can be accounted for by their comparative lack of spatial ability, and that the extent of the discrepancy in performance between the sexes may be contingent upon the degree to which mathematics is dependent upon this ability.

Sex-Related Factors

Attempts to account for the developmental aspect of spatial ability have linked behaviour to changes in the levels of sex hormones during the adolescent period (Broverman *et al.*, 1968). It has been hypothesized that the physiological effects of different levels of androgen and estrogen between the sexes may cause some of the observed differences in spatial ability. However, the evidence is not easy to interpret in that the effects of these hormones are complex and their influence can only be inferred from correlational evidence.

Other theorists have attempted to explain spatial differences by referring to the differential rate of brain lateralization between the sexes. It is generally acknowledged that cerebral functions relevant to spatial perception are localized in the right hemisphere of the brain. One group of theorists (Levi-Agresti and Sperry, 1968) has maintained that men's superior spatial performance is the result of a stronger lateralization of brain functions. In contrast, women's cerebral hemispheres are less specialized, and this lack of specialization interferes with their perceptual abilities. Another group of theorists (Buffery and Gray, 1972) has argued the opposite ground. They have maintained that men's superior spatial ability stems from a *lesser* degree of specialization, and that girls' early verbal development results in a stronger localization of verbal functions in the left hemisphere and spatial in the right.

Two recent studies in the United States and Australia have helped to delineate the areas of potential sex differences in spatial ability (Connor and Serbin, 1980; Wattanawaha, 1977). Both gave a variety of spatial tasks to large groups of adolescent boys and girls, and both studies reported similar findings: (1) not all spatial tests or items on spatial tests show significant differences between the sexes, but those differences that do occur are in favour of males; (2) the tests or items that most consistently differentiate between the sexes are those that demand both three-dimensional thinking and kinetic manipulation of imagery. Furthermore, Wattanawaha found that context appears to exert an important influence on performance. Almost invariably boys performed better than girls on items which pictured piles of blocks in contrast to items involving paper folding. This result is in general concurrence with the Connor-Serbin study which reported that sex differences occurred on the Space Relations sub-test, requiring the matching of a two-dimensional net with a three-dimensional solid, while no difference occurred on the Paper Folding Test, a presumably less sex-biased task.

Environmental Influences

Fennema and Sherman (1977) have argued that, although sex-related differences in spatial ability may be due to biological factors, they are strongly influenced by learning and environmental influences. This conclusion is supported by the results of a study of almost 3,000 pupils from grades 6 to 12 (ages 11 to 17, approximately). Also using the Space Relations Test as a measure of visualization, they found significant differences attributable to school district and age but not to sex in their sample of pupils in grades 6 to 8. Among the older pupils boys scored significantly higher than girls in two of the four schools sampled. However, in both these schools boys also took a significantly greater number of space related courses. When this factor was controlled for sex, differences in spatial visualization scores were eliminated. Furthermore, in a follow-up study of the younger sample three years later (Sherman, 1980), female scores on spatial measures continued to remain comparable to males.

On a broader scale, cross-cultural studies have noted that sex differences on certain spatial tests (e.g., the Embedded Figures Test) appear only in highly stratified cultures in which males exercise strong authoritarian control over females. Less structured societies show little difference (Fairweather, 1976).

Furthermore, those studies that have used training methods to improve results on spatial scores generally report that the discrepancy between the sexes is diminished after training. Logically, spatial visualization would appear to be related to geometry. However in addition to its apparent relationship with the visually-based aspects of mathematics, spatial ability may exert an indirect influence on other areas such as problem solving. For example, it has been argued that boys' greater success at problem solving is due to their greater ability to visualize, which allows them greater flexibility in the solution of problems.

In his examination of a variety of cognitive measures, Werdelin (1958) found a spatial visualization factor positively related to a factor of mathematical reasoning but negatively related to a number or computational factor. This suggested that an emphasis on computation or number skills could interfere with the development of spatial visualization ability to the detriment of mathematical reasoning. As a result, girls' superior performance on the more 'executive' tasks such as computation may be achieved at the cost of lower performance in problem solving. Because of their early verbal advantage, girls may tend to rely upon a symbolic approach to a greater degree than boys.

In summary, the importance of spatial ability on mathematics performance is probably dependent upon the measure used. Certain types of spatial ability, particularly visual imagery, may account for some of the sex-related differences in performance. Not only is it directly relevant to the solution of visual problems, but the possession of spatial skills may permit greater latitude in dealing with a range of problems, in that an excessive reliance on verbal strategy may hinder girls' flexibility in their mathematical work. On the other hand, the aetiology of sex differences in spatial ability is unclear, and although there is evidence of a genetic basis in favour of males, it is also evident that whatever potential does exist is affected by training and experience.

The Influence of Attitudes on Mathematics Performance

Probably the most comprehensive investigation of the influence of attitudes on mathematical performance was conducted by Fennema and Sherman among nearly 3000 pupils from grades 6 to 12 (Fennema and Sherman, 1977, 1978; Sherman and Fennema, 1977; Sherman, 1980). Unlike earlier studies, which tended to use one scale as a measure of general attitude toward mathematics, these researchers developed a series of short scales focusing on specific components of attitude which they believed to be related to performance. For example, pupils were asked, not only about their perception of mathematics as useful, but about the extent to which they saw their parents as supportive of their mathematics learning and the extent to which they believed that mathematics was a male domain. In all, eight scales were used, and these were correlated with various cognitive measures.

The most pervasive of the Fennema-Sherman findings were those pertaining to self-confidence. From grades 8 to 11 (approximately 13 to 16 years old), boys showed a consistently greater degree of self-confidence in their ability to learn mathematics than did girls. Furthermore, among the older pupils, the scale which measured confidence in mathematics correlated almost as highly with mathematics performance (0.41) as did measures of spatial visualization and vocabulary. Finally, scores on this scale were found to predict later mathematics performance for girls although not for boys. The fact that girls were significantly less self-confident in their mathematical ability before they showed any signs of poorer performance tends to confirm the influence of this variable on performance.

A further longitudinal study of the 13-year-old group found that from ages 13 to 15 girls showed more and deeper declines in their attitudes toward mathematics than boys (Sherman, 1980). In eighth grade, the only significant sex-related difference in attitude was girls' stronger denial that maths was a male domain. By eleventh grade, boys and girls differed significantly in many areas; boys were significantly more confident of themselves as learners of maths, they regarded maths as more useful, and they continued to regard maths as more of a male domain. By grade 11, boys were also performing significantly better than girls in tests of problem solving and mathematical concepts.

The only comparably large study in England was conducted by Preece and Sturgeon (1980), who assessed attitudes toward mathematics among approximately 2500 boys and girls aged 10 to 15. Their questionnaire consisted of three scales measuring liking of school, liking of maths, and maths as a male subject. No achievement measures were reported, so the results dealt only with differences in attitudes in relation to age and sex. They indicated that, in general, many of the same patterns of attitude that have been reported in the United States can be found in England. For example, whereas in the last year of junior school significantly more girls reported favourable feelings toward maths, by fourth year secondary school their attitudes had become significantly less favourable. Whereas positive attitudes toward mathematics generally declined among all pupils throughout the five years, the drop was more dramatic in the case of girls.

From these and similar studies (Stallings, 1979; Brush, 1979) it appears that the most significant factor that distinguishes between girls' and boys' attitudes toward mathematics is girls' lower estimation of their own ability. Secondly, there is some indication that a girl's relative success in mathematics is related to her refusal to regard mathematics as part of a masculine intellectual domain. Linked to this is the extent to which girls perceive mathematics as useful in their lives. It is obvious that the relationship among these facets of attitude is complex. Furthermore, by the nature of their research design, attitude investigations can only suggest relationships; they cannot explain the causes for such relationships. In an attempt to explain the psychological mechanisms that may account for them, areas of social psychology have been examined for evidence of broader, sex-related differences.

The Influence of Cultural Factors on Mathematical Performance

The Sexual Stereotyping of Tasks

That girls and boys begin to show the greatest differentiation of intellectual functioning at adolescence suggests that the phenomenon is caused by developmental changes at this time in life. Biological sources, particularly in reference to visual-spatial ability, have been proposed but, as discussed previously, correlational evidence in their support has been weak and inconsistent. Social theorists have suggested that these changes are primarily the result of boys' and girls' initiation into the adult roles which are dictated by society. In a society which differentiates role in terms of gender, it follows that individual behaviour will be influenced by what is considered to be sexually appropriate. Since the expenditure of time and energy on any task is contingent upon the value which has been assigned to it, tasks which are considered to be not useful or sexually inappropriate will be ignored in favour of more appropriate or useful tasks. If society deems that science, mathematics and mechanical activities are the province of males, whereas literature, languages and social studies are the province of females, these judgments will be reflected in the amount of effort expended by girls and boys on these subjects. It is not surprising, therefore, that adolescent boys pursue mathematical studies to a far greater extent than do girls and are more successful.

As Nash (1979) has pointed out, such theories are more complex than is commonly presented. The salience of the feminine or masculine role varies with individuals so that the value of any task reflects not only society's judgment of sexual appropriateness but the value that appropriateness holds for the individual. However, there is evidence that the ratings of tasks as sexually appropriate or not are most extreme at adolescence, suggesting the strong influence of the concept at this stage of development. Furthermore, such theory forms a useful framework in which to examine girls' increasingly negative attitude towards mathematics at this time.

In a study of children from grades 2 to 12, Dwyer (1974) reported that the extent to which interests and activities were labelled as masculine or feminine contributed significant variance to reading and arithmetic scores of both sexes, but the effect was stronger for boys. The actual perception of areas as sex-appropriate or inappropriate contributed more variance to those scores than the child's biological sex, individual preference for masculine or feminine sex role, or liking or disliking of the subject. She also found that there was more agreement between the sexes as to what constituted girls' activities than there was to what constituted boys', with boys more likely to label topics and activities as exclusively male.

These findings, although indicating the influence of labelling on pupils' performance, are relevant to mathematics performance only if it can be shown that girls do perceive mathematics to be a sexually inappropriate activity. Here there is much less direct support. Although it has been found that pupils consistently view social-verbal and artistic skills as feminine and spatial, mechanical and athletic skills as masculine, arithmetic is less readily classified (Stein and Smithells, 1969). For example, although second-grade boys and girls both thought that arithmetic was more appropriate for their own sex, by twelfth grade it was considered as masculine by both sexes. Nevertheless, although pupils' perception of arithmetic as a masculine subject increased with age, it was not seen to be as strongly a masculine domain as were athletics or spatial and mechanical tasks. It should be noted, however, that the focal subject in these studies was designated as 'arithmetic' not 'mathematics'. It has been widely observed that girls' relatively poorer attainment tends to be limited to the higher-level mathematical processes and has not been observed in reference to the more arithmetical skills. Consequently, this lack of sex-type differences in reaction to arithmetic may not necessarily generalize to mathematics. Furthermore, Ormerod (1981) has argued that, on the basis of subject preference, maths is clearly regarded as a male subject among English secondary school pupils.

Sex-related differences have been found in problem-solving performance, and attempts have been made to relate such differences to theories of sex appropriateness. For example, it has been hypothesized that the masculine content of most problems deters girls from achieving their potential. Contending that sex-related differences in problem-solving are partly due to culturally defined behaviour, Milton (1959) demonstrated that simply rephrasing logical-mathematical problems in feminine terms improved performance of college women. However, although male superiority was reduced, it was not eliminated. Men solved more problems than women, irrespective of content. Furthermore, the results were not replicated in other studies in which mathematics ability was held constant (Hoffman and Maier, 1966). As a general rule, the inferences drawn from various studies should be regarded with some caution. Theories dealing with sexual stereotyping are complex, based on prior assumptions that are not always made explicit.

The Relevance of Attribution Theory to Performance

The perception of a task as sex-appropriate may also affect pupils' expectations for success. Investigators in achievement motivation have increasingly turned their attention to the ways in which individuals explain success or failure on a variety of tasks. They have classified such explanations with reference to the stability of the cause to which performance is attributed. For example, stable causes include attributions by reference to ability and task difficulty; unstable causes include attributions in terms of effort and luck. It has been found that both expectations and attributions for success (and failure) show differences between boys and girls. Girls show a persistent tendency to underestimate their performance, while boys tend to overestimate theirs. This applies regardless of actual performance levels and is particularly evident when the tasks have been labelled as 'masculine' (Deaux, 1976). Faced with such tasks, girls have been found to attribute success to 'luck', and failure to 'lack of ability'. Indeed, girls' tendency to attribute failure to poor ability appears to be a general phenomenon. Nicholls (1979) found that it was evident even in cases in which girls' attainment was rated significantly higher than boys' by both girls themselves and their teachers. The obvious corollary to such findings is that girls will lack persistence on tasks where there is no rational basis for continuing to expend effort. On such tasks, luck can hardly be relied upon for continued success and a lack of ability is not conducive to continued effort. It is not surprising, therefore, that the attribution of success or failure to such factors is often associated with deterioration of performance.

Girls' lack of confidence in their intellectual competency has been discussed further by Dweck and Bush (1976), who suggest an explanatory theory of 'learned helplessness'. These authors cite numerous studies that have shown primary school teachers' tendency toward negative evaluation of boys' behaviour in the classroom. Since much of this criticism is directed toward general behaviour and is irrelevant to the quality of their academic work, Dweck and Bush suggest that boys tend to discount such criticism as a valid reflection of their intellectual capability. Furthermore, teachers' attributions of boys' failure to lack of motivation allows boys to explain their failures in terms of lack of effort rather than ability. The classroom interaction yields the opposite effect for girls. Since teachers are largely positive in attitude toward girls and, furthermore, since girls are generally hardworking and conscientious in their academic work, girls cannot explain negative feedback in terms of general behaviour. They must accept it as a valid and objective assessment of abilities. As a consequence, failure will more often be attributed to lack of ability rather than to lack of effort on the part of girls.

That girls show a consistent tendency to attribute failure to lack of ability in a variety of situations does lend strong support to this argument. Nevertheless, the generality of the findings makes the theory less useful in explaining girls' performance in relation to one particular subject (e.g., mathematics). The argument has been made that the importance of the theory is not as a direct explanation of why girls perform less well than boys, but as an explanation of why girls do not persist either in their mathematical education or in the solution of specific mathematical problems.

The Influence of School Factors on Performance

It is a common finding in any large-scale study of mathematical achievement that the occurrence of sex differences varies from school to school (Fennema and Sherman, 1977; Wood, 1976; Preece and Sturgeon, 1980). Fennema and Sherman reported that sex differences in performance are linked to sex-related differences in attitude. However, no investigation has been reported which has focused on the ethos of schools that appear to be conducive to equality in performance on the part of both sexes.

On the other hand, the sexual balance of schools has been considered. In a review of large-scale surveys of attainment in coeducational and single-sex schools, Dale (1974) reported that mathematics was the one subject in which girls in coeducational schools performed better than their peers in single-sex schools. Although their performance was still generally inferior to that of boys, the discrepancy was less than in the case of similar comparisons between single-sex schools. The advantages of coeducation to girls' performance in mathematics is not clear. Dale suggests that, although girls may benefit from the presence of boys in the same class, their relatively superior performance may be due to the higher qualificational level of mathematics teachers in coeducational schools.

The more intimate and possibly more influential academic unit is the classroom. In an attempt to isolate features that may affect girls' perform-ance, some studies have used recording schedules to quantify the interaction between teachers and students within secondary school mathematics classes in the United States (Stallings, 1979; Becker, 1981). Although each focused on a different constellation of behaviour, both concurred that the large amount of teacher-initiated interaction in mathematics classes was directed toward boys. For instance, Becker noted that although girls initiated all types of teacher contact to a greater extent than boys, teachers initiated a significantly larger number of their contacts with boys. This, she suggests, is indicative of the teachers' greater encouragement of boys in their academic abilities and pursuits. During the period of observation boys received 70 per cent of positive contacts while girls received 83 per cent of non-encouraging or discouraging comments. Teachers also showed more persistence with male pupils, gave a greater amount of individual help, and initiated more non-academic contacts with them. On the other hand, when asked for self-report, teachers seldom express or show consciousness of sex bias in the perception of pupils (Stallings, 1979). Nor is there evidence that girls perceive teachers to be any less positive (Fennema and Sherman, 1977).

The actual effect of teachers' behaviour on pupils is unclear. Whereas Stallings (1979) found that, among high-achieving females, pupils' course taking was more determined by the usefulness of the course than by positive feelings toward the teacher, other researchers have reported a strong influence of the teacher in encouraging pupils to continue their study (Fox *et al.*, 1979; Casserly, 1980).

Conclusions

The search for factors which can account for sex differences in mathematics performance has covered many areas of research, from physiology to social psychology to educational practice. In the end, few definite conclusions can be drawn. It is not possible to single out one factor as the prime cause for such differences. Instead, there seems to be a constellation of factors which influence performance in varying degrees.

It does seem clear that those differences which exist in spatial ability do favour boys. Therefore, to the extent to which mathematical performance depends upon spatial ability, genetic factors may play some role. However, this dependence is not clearly established. Although spatial visualization has been found to correlate highly with performance, this does not imply a causal relationship. Undoubtedly, the influence is a mutual one, for practice and experience in space-related activities have been found to increase both mathematics and spatial scores. Yet girls, on the whole, do not participate in these activities, and their performance suffers as a result.

More apparent than any genetic factors is the vulnerability of girls' performance to affective influences. Girls' relative lack of self-confidence in their mathematical ability is a consistent finding in the literature, as is their withdrawal from mathematical activities. This may be explained by the extreme sexual stereotyping of tasks which takes place at adolescence. Although girls generally tend to underestimate their performance, this tendency is particularly apparent in regard to 'male' activities, which includes mathematics. In actual terms, girls' relative success in the subject is related to their denial of mathematics as a male domain.

Finally, although teachers report no sex bias, the two published studies which observed mathematics classes in the United States reported significantly more teacher-initiated contacts with boys. Teachers were also reported as having a major influence on girls' persistence in mathematics study.

The body of research seems to indicate that girls' relatively poorer performance in mathematics is linked to broader social attitudes that are particularly powerful at adolescence. Although many of the research findings have emanated from the United States where socialization processes as well as educational structure differ from those in this country, they should be weighed carefully for their relevance to this society.

References

ARMSTRONG, J. (1980) *Achievement and Participation of Women in Mathematics: An Overview*, Education Commission of the States, Denver, Colo., National Assessment of Educational Progress.

BECKER, J. (1981) 'Differential treatment of females and males in mathematics classes', *Journal for Research in Mathematics Education*, 12, 1, pp. 40–53.

BROVERMAN, D. *et al.* (1968). 'Roles of activation and inhibition in sex differences in cognitive abilities', *Psychological Review*, 75, pp. 23–50.

BRUSH, L. (1979) *Encouraging Girls in Mathematics: The Problem and Solution.* Cambridge, Mass., Abt Associates Press.

BUFFERY, A. and GRAY, J. (1972) 'Sex differences in the development of spatial and linguistic skills', in OUNSTED, C. and TAYLOR, D.C. (Eds) *Gender Differences: Their Ontogeny and Significance*, Baltimore, Williams and Wilkins.

CAREY, G. (1958) 'Sex differences in problem solving performance as a function of attitude differences', *Journal of Abnormal and Social Psychology*, 56, pp. 256–60.

CASSERLY, P. (1980) 'Factors affecting female participation in Advanced Placement programs in mathematics, chemistry and physics', in FOX, L., *et al.* (Eds) *Women and the Mathematical Mystique*, Baltimore, Johns Hopkins University Press.

CONNOR, J. and SERBIN, L. (1980) *Mathematics, Visual-Spatial Ability and Sex-Roles*, Report to the US National Institute of Education.

DALE, R. (1974) *Mixed or Single-Sex Schools?* Vol. III, London, Routledge and Kegan Paul.

DEAUX, K. (1976) 'Sex: A perspective on the attribution process', in HARVEY, J.H. *et al.* (Eds) *New Directions in Attribution Theory Research*, Vol. 1, Hillsdale, N.J., Erlbaum.

DWECK, C. and BUSH, E. (1976) 'Sex differences in learned helplessness. (1) Differential debilitation with peer and adult evaluators', *Developmental Psychology*, 12, pp. 147–56.

DWYER, C. (1974) 'Influencing children's sex-role standards in reading and arithmetic achievement', *Journal of Educational Psychology*, 66, 6, pp. 811–16.

FAIRWEATHER, H. (1976) 'Sex differences in cognition', *Cognition*, 4, pp. 231–80.

FENNEMA, E. and SHERMAN, J. (1977) 'Sex related differences in mathematics achievement, spatial visualisation and affective factors', *American Educational Research Journal*, 14, 1, pp. 51–71.

FENNEMA, E. and SHERMAN, J. (1978) 'Sex-related differences in mathematics achievement and related factors: A further study', *Journal for Research in Mathematics Education*, 9, 3, pp. 189–203.

FOX, L. *et al.* (1979). 'Sex role socialization and achievement in mathematics', in WITTIG, M.A. and PETERSEN, A.C. (Eds) *Sex Related Differences in Cognitive Functioning: Developmental Issues*, New York, Academic Press.

HOFFMAN, L. and MAIER, N. (1966) 'Social factors influencing problem solving in women', *Journal of Personality and Social Psychology*, 4, p. 382.

KEEVES, J. (1973) 'Differences between the sexes in mathematics and science courses', *International Review of Education*, 19, 1, pp. 47–63.

LEVI-AGRESTI, J. and SPERRY, R. (1968) 'Differential perceptual capacities in the major and minor hemispheres', *Proceedings of the National Academy of Science*, 61.

MACCOBY, E. and JACKLIN, C. (1974) *The Psychology of Sex Differences*, Stanford, Calif., Stanford University Press.

MILTON, G.A. (1959) 'Sex differences in problem solving as a function of role appropriateness of the problem content', *Psychological Reports* 5, pp. 705–8.

NASH, S. (1978) 'Sex role as a mediator of intellectual functioning', in WITTIG, M.A. and PETERSEN, A.C. (Eds) *Sex Related Differences in Cognitive Functioning: Developmental Issues*, New York, Academic Press.

NICHOLLS, J. (1979) 'Development of perception of own attainment and causal attributions for success and failure in reading', *Journal of Educational Psychology*, 71, 1, pp. 94–9.

ORMEROD, M. (1981) 'Factors differentially affecting the science subject preferences, choices and attitudes of girls and boys', in KELLY, A. (Ed.) *The Missing Half: Girls and Science Education*, Manchester, Manchester University Press.

PREECE, M. (1979) 'Mathematics: The unpredictability of girls', *Mathematics Teaching*, 87, pp. 27–9.

PREECE, M. and STURGEON, S. (1980) *Investigation into the Attitudes toward Mathematics of Some Sheffield School Children*, paper presented to the British Education Research Association.

SHERMAN, J. (1980) 'Mathematics, spatial visualization and related factors: Changes in girls and boys, grades 8–11', *Journal of Educational Psychology*, 72, 4, pp. 476–82.

SHERMAN, J. and FENNEMA, E. (1977) 'The study of mathematics by high school girls and boys: Related variables', *American Educational Research Journal*, 14, 2, pp. 159–68.

STALLINGS, J. (1979) *Factors Influencing Women's Decisions to Enroll in Advanced Mathematics Courses*, Report to the US National Institute of Education.

STEIN, A. and SMITHELLS, J. (1969) 'Age and sex differences in children's sex-role standards about achievement', *Developmental Psychology*, 1. 3, pp. 252–9.

TOBIAS, S. (1978) *Overcoming Math Anxiety*, New York, Norton.

WATTANAWAHA, N. (1977) 'Spatial ability and sex differences in performance on spatial tasks', MEd thesis, Monash University.

WERDELIN, I. (1958) *The Mathematical Ability*, Copenhagen, Lund.

WOOD, R. (1976) 'Sex differences in mathematics attainment at GCE Ordinary Level', *Educational Studies*, 2, 2.

The Use of Behavioural Ecology in Classroom Management*

Kevin Wheldall
University of Birmingham

Behaviour modification is still largely unheard of, or at best misconceived, by most British teachers (Wheldall and Congreve, 1980). Behaviour modification in general has been slow to take off in Great Britain but nowhere more slowly than in the sphere of education. For the past seven or eight years I have been attempting to proselytize among teachers, seeking to convert them with a near-evangelical zeal to what we might call 'behavioural pedagogy' — the behavioural science of teaching and learning. Indeed, I have sometimes been accused, only half-jokingly, of presenting radical behaviourism as a religious creed! I still do believe that radical behaviourism as a guiding philosophy and applied behavioural analysis as a technology of behaviour management offer the greatest hope for solving social problems, especially in education, and in inspiring a better future for mankind in general (Wheldall, 1975). But none of this is meant to deny that I have doubts about, and criticisms of, some aspects of current behavioural practice in education.

The Dangers of 'Behavioural Overkill'

It may seem rather ironic, after campaigning vigorously for the acceptance of behaviour modification in teaching, that I am now sounding a note of caution and urging restraint but, as I hope to show, my criticisms and fears stem from *within* applied behaviour analysis. In other words I am not criticizing applied behaviour analysis (ABA) per se but rather a bastardized

* This paper was presented to a one-day conference of the Association for Behaviour Modification with Children on 'Behaviour Modification in Educational Settings: Current Perspectives in Theory and Practice', University of Exeter, 18 October 1980. An abbreviated version was originally published in the conference proceedings, GURNEY, P. (Ed.), *Behaviour Modification in Education*, Perspectives No. 5, School of Education, University of Exeter.

version which has come to be identified by the term 'behaviour mod' and which in some respects represents a crude parody of what ABA is all about. Where behavioural approaches are being applied in schools they are often at the crudest level of contingency management. Unnecessarily powerful procedures are used in interventions; sledgehammers are frequently employed to crack peanuts. An extreme example might be when a teacher sets up a full-scale token economy to stop one child picking his nose! The token economy, in fact, is probably the most abused 'heavy' behavioural procedure. (I also have doubts about 'time out' and 'overcorrection' enthusiasts and suspect that these procedures prove particularly appealing to former straightforward advocates of punishment, who find in these procedures a sophisticated justification for the use of aversive techniques.) If a distinction can be drawn between ABA and 'behaviour mod', as I believe it can, then the former is barely in evidence in current educational practice. Few, for example, appreciate the importance of A in the ABC, three-term analysis of behaviour, a point to which we shall return shortly. Neglect of setting events and overemphasizing, often artificial, contingency management approaches can lead to what I have termed 'behavioural overkill' (Wheldall, 1980). This may be defined as the employment of unnecessarily 'heavy' behavioural technology to control behaviour, with concomitant, predictable 'by products' including poor generalization to the control of more naturally occurring reinforcers.

We will not dwell further here on criticisms of current practice in the use of behaviour modification in schools except to say that several other behaviourally-oriented psychologists are currently expressing concern. In a recent *Bulletin of the British Psychological Society*, Berger (1979) has warned of the 'dangers of a mindless technology', Harrop (1980) has argued that it is a 'time for caution', whilst Owens and Walter (1980) have criticized the 'naive behaviourism' sometimes displayed by those applying behaviour modification procedures. A more extreme position has been taken by Ryan (1979) who has argued that not only are behaviour modification techniques unnecessary with normal children but that such procedures can be dangerous when, for example, extrinsic reinforcers are used with children already under the control of intrinsic reinforcers, leading to the problems associated with 'overjustification' (Lepper and Greene, 1978).

In summary then, we advocate an applied behaviour analysis approach to education rather than an approach based on an oversimplified model of 'behaviour modification'. Behaviour modification constitutes in fact a subset of applied behaviour analysis and it has tended to become associated, rightly or wrongly, almost exclusively with consequence management, in British educational contexts, virtually ignoring the importance (and power) of the antecedent conditions or setting events for behaviour. Since behaviour is influenced by the contextual events preceding it as well as by its consequences, more appropriate behaviours may be increased by manipulating these variables instead of, or possibly as well as, consequences. We will return to this shortly. Similarly, consequence management strategies, where necessary, should be approached with care, with a view as to how the behaviour will be generalized to other contexts and transferred to the control of more naturally occurring reinforcers. Hence, contrived consequence management systems dependent upon 'unnatural' reinforcers (i.e., reinforcers which are unlikely, or seldom likely, to educe such behaviour in the real world) should only be viewed as a means to the end of transferring control of the behaviour to naturally occurring reinforcers. (Tokens, if used, for example, should give way to fullsome praise which gives way to occasional praise and finally to 'job satisfaction' and other intrinsic reinforcers.)

Behavioural Ecology

We will all have noticed how the behaviour of a certain class varies depending on who is teaching them or even depending on where they are being taught. In other words, the behaviour of classes of children comes under stimulus control whereby different stimulus conditions are followed by different forms of behaviour. Being in Softy Simpson's room may become the setting event for unruly behaviour, whilst few would dare even to breathe too loudly in Biffer Barnes' class. Similarly, academic lessons, held by necessity in the art and craft room by the same teacher, may lead to more off-task or disruptive behaviour than when held in a regular classroom. Being in the art and craft room has become a setting event for a different form of behaviour, involving movement around the room perhaps. I referred earlier to the need to consider such variables in the context of the ABC model of behaviour which it might be helpful to review here.

It is not sufficient to attempt merely to analyze behaviour in terms of responses and reinforcers. As well as considering what occurs after a behavioural response is emitted (the consequence) we must also consider what happened *before* the response occurred. We must examine both stimuli which preceded and stimuli which followed behaviour. This is often referred to as the three-term analysis of behaviour or the ABC model:

A refers to the antecedent stimuli or conditions:
B refers to the behaviour or response itself; and
C refers to the consequences following the behaviour.

For example, the teacher asks a child a question in class (A or antecedent stimulus), the child gives a silly answer (B, the behaviour), and his classmates laugh (C, the consequences). Thus we might expect the child to produce silly answers upon subsequent occasions since his classmates reinforced him by laughing. He would probably be less likely to do so, however, when his classmates were not around to reinforce him. Thus, presence or absence of peers may be a powerful variable influencing this child's behaviour. Peer presence may become a setting event for this particular form of behaviour. Vargas (1977), similarly, cites the example of how the same child may cry when he grazes his knee when playing near the teacher (who usually offers sympathy) but not when playing with the big boys, who might be less sympathetic. These crude examples give some of the idea behind the need to consider the context in which behaviours occur. It is the relationship between A, B and C, the antecedent conditions, the behaviours and the consequences which constitute what are known as the contingencies of reinforcement.

Thus we should concern ourselves with the A in the ABC model as well as, or even instead of, the C. We must concern ourselves with the setting events for behaviours and examine *ecological* variables, leading to an area of study which Risley (1977: Krantz and Risley, 1977) refers to as 'behavioural ecology'. Ecological variables take many forms. Russell and Bernal (1977), for example, have shown how temporal and climatic variables appear to influence rates of desirable and undesirable behaviours in 5–7-year-old boys. Manipulation of classroom temperature would be an obvious extrapolation of these findings to determine the optimal level for increased on task behaviour, for example.

Moore (1981) has shown how location, where children sit in class, dramatically affects the number of questions they are asked. Similarly, Krantz and Risley (*op. cit.*), in two beautifully designed studies, have shown how manipulation of two ecological variables influenced task behaviour in black kindergarten children. First, they showed that during story sessions and demonstrations on-task behaviour was higher when the children were placed so as to allow space between each child and his neighbours than when they clustered around their teacher. On-task behaviour was also higher if the session was preceded by a rest period rather than by a session of vigorous activity, giving the lie to the commonsense view of children being quieter after having got 'their energy out of their systems'. Moreover, these two manipulations were equally as powerful as consequence management strategies in producing appropriate behaviour change, for less effort.

Behavioural ecology thus appears to offer alternatives to contingency management procedures and is a potential means of avoiding behavioural overkill. We have employed such alternatives in several recent studies, the first of which incorporates a manipulation of a setting event, in this case the amount of work set.

Light Behavioural Technology in the Secondary School

We have recently completed a study as a result of a challenge from one of my undergraduate students, Bob Austin, to demonstrate the effectiveness of behavioural approaches to classroom management in the secondary school. He pointed out that few of the mass of reported studies referred to secondary schools, a view recently endorsed by McNamara and Harrop (1979), and was sceptical of success in such settings, believing that at best it would necessitate a token economy. Consequently this study evolved to demonstrate that control could be achieved in a secondary classroom using only 'light' behavioural procedures.

We selected a large comprehensive in a deprived, urban area and located a difficult class of twenty-five 14–15-year-olds from the lowest three of ten 'streams'. Since all teachers involved with this class admitted difficulties privately, but were reluctant to admit this publicly by volunteering, the headmaster, who taught the class remedial maths for five lessons per week, volunteered. Our observations of him and the class revealed that he was an impressive teacher who rarely shouted and who, relatively speaking, used a lot of praise. The class appeared to like and respect him but our eleven days of baseline observation showed that they were on-task only 55 per cent of the time. Many of the students were often off-task because they had finished the set work (usually a set of 'sums' put up on the board) and did not know what to do next, or had not finished but were being disturbed by those who had. Consequently, I suggested that a few more problems be put up on the board for the quicker ones to get on with while the slower ones caught up (i.e., a manipulation of a setting event for on-task behaviour). Bob Austin was initially unsure of this ('that's not behaviour modification!'), but agreed to try it. The head also agreed and the observations for the next seven lessons showed improved on-task behaviour by nearly 15 per cent, to an average of around 70 per cent. We decided that this could be improved still further, and a compromise was reached between my preferred 'light' strategy of using a simple 'rules, praise and ignore' procedure and Bob's 'heavier' alternative of a watered down token system, whereby points could be earned which gained free time. This resulted in a multi-element or alternating conditions design in which simple contingent praise alternated daily with the strategy whereby, on a group contingency basis, the class could earn one minute's free time each time they were all on-task when a timer sounded (variable interval two minutes), as judged by the head. Free time was taken during the Friday afternoon lesson; twenty-five points won the whole forty-minute lesson off.

The head agreed to these procedures and the results were dramatic. The multi-element design clearly showed further improvement in on-task behaviour to over 80 per cent produced by the rules, praise and ignoring strategy and to over 90 per cent during timer game sessions. The two strategies finally merged at around 95 per cent 'on-task'. The study thus provided: (1) a clear demonstration of successful behavioural approaches in a secondary school; and (2) proof of the power of simple procedures such as contingent praise and manipulations of setting events ('more sums' in this case). Both the head and Bob Austin were persuaded of the power of behavioural procedures by this study which is reported in more detail in Wheldall and Austin (1980).

Kevin Wheldall

Class Seating Arrangements: Rows or Tables?

We have also recently carried out studies comparing the effects of different seating arrangements in classrooms. This work was inspired by Axlerod *et al.* (1979) who observed classes for amount of on-task behaviour and rate of pupil disruptions when seated in rows and when seated around tables. Our research effectively replicated and extended the findings of Axlerod and his co-workers (Wheldall *et al.*, 1981). My students, Marian Morris and Pamela Vaughan, and I have recently carried out two parallel studies comparing 'tables' and 'rows' seating arrangements in classes in two state junior schools.

In both schools a fourth-year class of 10–11-year-old children was chosen. In the first study the class consisted of twenty-eight mixed sex and ability children attending a school in an urban residential area whereas the second study involved a similar class of twenty-five children from a school on a council housing estate. The design, procedure and, indeed, results of the two studies were very similar.

In both classes the children normally sat around tables in groups of four, five or six, except for end-of-term tests when they sat in rows. Seating around tables has become the norm in the post-Plowden days following the mid-sixties, apparently because it was believed that this facilitates learning by discovery, project work, etc. To my knowledge no empirical evidence was produced to justify this change but then education generally is like this: strong on theory and speculation, weak on evidence and objective data.

In both classes the children were initially observed for two weeks (ten days) in their normal seating arrangements around tables. An observation schedule using a time sampling procedure was employed to obtain estimates of on-task behaviour. This was defined as doing what the teacher instructed, i.e., looking at and listening to her when she was talking to them, looking at their books or work cards when they were required to complete set work, only being out of seats with the teacher's permission, etc. In the second study observations were carried out at different times including all lessons except PE, art and music, whereas in the first study observations were made only during purely academic lessons when the children had been given specific work to complete. Calling out, talking to neighbours, interrupting, etc. were, of course, regarded as off-task in both studies.

The observation schedule required each child to be observed twice per lesson in random order for thirty seconds. This was broken down into six, five-second periods. If the child was on-task for the whole five seconds he scored one point; if off-task for any of the five seconds he did not score. Hence, this yielded a score out of six for each thirty-second period and a score out of twelve for the two observation periods per lesson combined, which was subsequently converted to a percentage. This gave us an estimate of percentage on-task behaviour for each child for each lesson which, when averaged, gave an estimate of on-task behaviour for the whole class.

After collecting two weeks of baseline data, the desks/tables were moved into rows without comment from the teacher and the children were observed for a further two weeks (eight days in the first study, ten days in the second study) using the same procedure. Finally, the desks were moved back to their original positions again without comment for a further two weeks of observation (seven days in the first study; ten days in the second study). This time there were a few complaints from the children since they *preferred* sitting in rows. Reliability data were collected in each phase and was found to be acceptable at around 90 per cent. In short, on-task behaviour rose by roughly 15 per cent when the children were placed in rows and fell by nearly as much when returned to tables. Table 1 shows how similar the general picture is for the two classes.

Table 1. Average Percentage On-Task Behaviour in Each Phase

	Tables	Rows	Tables
Study 1	72	88	69
Study 2	67	84	72

As far as individual children were concerned, the vast majority showed marked improvement in on task behaviour in rows except for those whose on task behaviour was already very high, where, as is to be expected, the effect was lessened. One or two children in each study showed higher on task behaviour in groups; especially one child in the second study, the noisy ringleader of an anti-school group, who spent most of his time in rows trying to regain contact with his group!

We have also carried out a more detailed study in a special school for ESN (M) children with behaviour problems. This was carried out with one of my masters students, Josephine Ng, and examined other dependent variables, adding disruptive behaviour and teacher behaviour to our observations of on task behaviour. This study was very detailed and a huge amount of data was collected of which only a brief report can be presented here.

Three classes were observed for four phases of ten observations spread over approximately two week intervals. Again, seating was normally arranged around tables and in the first phase observation was carried out in the usual conditions, to establish baseline, followed by phase 2 when the class was moved into rows. Phase 3 was a return to the tables seating arrangement (return to baseline) and finally phase 4, in which seating was again arranged in rows. All lessons took place in the same room and were maths lessons given by the same teacher to all three classes: 2U — a class of eleven 14–15 year old children; 3U — a class of eleven 13–14 year old children; and 4U — a class of twelve 12–13 year old children.

The observation schedule was adapted from C.T.P.1 originally devised by Frank Merrett (Merrett, 1980; Merrett and Wheldall, 1980) which includes 3 sets of observations to be carried out in a different order for each lesson. These were:—

1   *Teacher behaviours.* The teacher was observed for three periods of three minutes per lesson and the number of approving and disapproving remarks and non-verbal signals made was recorded to both social and academic behaviours of the children separately.

2   *Disruptions.* The number of disruptions by children in the class in three, three minute observation periods per lesson was recorded (including calling out; out of seat; etc.).

3   *On-task behaviour.* This was recorded in two ways: (a) using Merrett's technique in which the class is divided into groups of children who are observed for five seconds each. The number on-task out of the total number in the group is recorded. This was repeated three times per lesson for the whole class; (b) by observing each child in random order for thirty seconds and using a stopwatch to record at each five-second interval whether the child was on- or off-task. This procedure was repeated giving scores out of twelve which were subsequently percentaged.

For the last two phases of the study the same classes of children were also observed during their English lesson where no manipulations of seating arrangements took place. This served as a control condition.

Table 2.   *Average Percentage On-Task Behaviour in Each Phase*

	Tables 1	Rows 1	Tables 2	Rows 2
Class 2U	27	72	32	68
Class 3U	34	72	37	71
Class 4U	37	73	36	69

Table 3.   *Average Number of Disruptions in Each Phase*

	Tables 1	Rows 1	Tables 2	Rows 2
Class 2U	49	10	28	9
Class 3U	25	9	24	7
Class 4U	18	6	19	8

The results confirmed and extended our previous findings as Table 2 and 3, show, even more dramatically this time. For *every* class on-task behaviour *doubled* during rows and fell during tables conditions. Similarly, rate of disruptions trebled during tables and fell during rows.

We also observed changes in teacher behaviour. Positive comments consistently went up during rows conditions whilst negative comments decreased. Thus the teacher found it easier to praise and refrain from disapproval when the children were seated in rows. In the control condition no differences were found between phases for on-task behaviour, disruptions or teacher behaviours.

I must immediately emphasize that I am *not* advocating a return to rows for all work — only for academic work which requires the child to concentrate on the specific academic task in hand without disruption. Rows would be totally inappropriate, for example, for small group discussions or group topic work, where table arrangements might prove more effective. Similarly the lessons to be learned from social psychology inform us that a horse-shoe arrangement around the room facing inwards might well facilitate our class discussion sessions. These are empirical questions which we hope to tackle in our future research. Similarly, we also need to prove that increased on-task behaviour is accompanied by increased *quantity* and *quality* of academic work accomplished. We hope to begin research on this shortly. We would also like to look more closely at the effect on teacher behaviours.

These are but a few of the lessons to be learned from behavioural ecology when applied to behavioural pedagogy. Certainly they should cause us to doubt our current preoccupation with fixed classroom seating arrangements and to encourage us to experiment with seating so as to optimize the appropriate behaviour for the task in hand and to discourage unwanted behaviours.

Concluding Comments

In the 1 April issue of *The Guardian* an amusing spoof on behaviour modification techniques was published, purporting to report pioneering work on 'terminal disciplinary techniques'. (Subjects were strapped into metal chairs and 'a charge of approximately 25,000 volts passed through the body'; subsequent intensive observations of subjects revealed that 'no signs of anti-social behaviour were manifested, indeed there were no signs of any behaviour at all'!) We might argue that this constitutes extreme behavioural overkill!

More seriously, it is significant that behavioural procedures are now becoming sufficiently well known to warrant satire in the pages of *The Guardian*. If the eye of the press is beginning to fall on what I have called 'behavioural pedagogy', then we must be increasingly vigilant about the dangers of behavioural overkill and attempt to curb the wilder excesses in terms of the utilization of unnecessarily heavy behavioural technology in schools.

I still believe that 'the behaviourist in the classroom is the teacher of tomorrow' (Wheldall, 1981) but (s)he must be a far more subtle behaviourist with a good grounding in behavioural psychology. We must replace the notion of a peanut pushing, smartie smothering, token trafficking, behaviour mod 'enthusiast' with the concept of a skilled behaviour analyst. In order to avoid the dangers of behavioural overkill, as outlined, we must ensure that only the lightest behavioural technology necessary to do the job is employed. More specifically, we must emphasize the lessons to be learned from behavioural ecology and remember that A should always come before C.

References

AXELROD, S., HALL, R.V. and TAMS, A. (1979), 'Comparison of Two Common Classroom Seating Arrangements'. *Academic Therapy*, 15, 29–36.

BERGER, M. (1979), 'Behaviour Modification in Education and Professional Practice: The Dangers of a Mindless Technology'. *Bulletin of the British Psychological Society*, 32, 418–419.

HARROP, L.A. (1980), 'Behaviour Modification in Schools: A Time for Caution'. *Bulletin of the British Psychological Society*, 33, 158–160.

KRANTZ, P.J. and RISLEY, T.R. (1977), 'Behavioural Ecology in the Classroom'. In O'LEARY, K.D. and O'LEARY, S.F. (Eds.), *Classroom Management: The Successful Use of Behaviour Modification*, Pergamon, Oxford.

LEPPER, M.R. and GREENE, D. (Eds.) (1978), *The Hidden Costs of Reward: New Perspectives on the Psychology of Human Motivation*, Lawrence Erlbaum Associates, Hillsdale, N.J.

McNAMARA, E. and HARROP, L.A. (1979), 'Behaviour Modification in the Secondary School: A Cautionary Tale'. *Occasional Papers of the Division of Educational and Child Psychology of the British Psychological Society*, 3, 38–41.

MERRETT, F.E. (1980), 'The Application of Behaviour Modification in the Primary School Classroom'. *Collected Original Resources in Education*, 4, 11 fiches.

MERRETT, F.E. and WHELDALL, K. (1980), 'Natural rates of teacher approval and disapproval in middle and primary school classrooms'. Paper presented to the Third Annual Conference of the Association for Behaviour Modification with Children, Coventry, May 1980.

MOORE, D. (1981), 'Location as a Causal Factor in the Unequal Distribution of Teacher Questions: An Experimental Analysis', in HOME, D.J. DEL. and McMURRAY, N.E. (1981) Behaviour Therapy in Australia; Proceedings of the Third Australian Conference on Behaviour Modification. Australian Behaviour Modification Society, Melbourne.

OWENS, R.G.and WALTER, A.J. (1980), 'Naive Behaviourism and Behaviour Modification', *Bulletin of the British Psychological Society*, 33, 312–314.

RISLEY, T.R. (1977), 'The Ecology of Applied Behavioural Analysis' in ROGERS-WARREN, A. and ROGERS-WARREN, S.F. (Eds.), *Ecological Perspectives in Behaviour Analysis*, Baltimore, University Park Press.

RUSSELL, M.B. and BERNAL, M.E. (1977), 'Temporal and Climatic Variables in Naturalistic Observation'. *Journal of Applied Behaviour Analysis*, 10, 399–405.

RYAN, B.A. (1979), 'A Case Against Behaviour Modification in the Normal Classroom'. *Journal of School Psychology*, 17, pp. 131–136.

VARGAS, J. (1977), *Behavioural Psychology for Teachers*, Harper and Row, New York.

WHELDALL, K. (1975) *Social Behaviour: Key Problems and Social Relevance*, Methuen, London.

WHELDALL, K. (1980), 'Applied Behavioural Analysis in British Educational Contexts (with Particular Reference to the Work of the 'Birmingham Group')', British Psychological Society, Education Section Review, 5, 17–25.

WHELDALL, K. (Ed.) (1981), '*The Behaviourist in the Classroom: Aspects of Applied Behavioural Analysis in British Educational Contexts*', Educational Review Publications, Birmingham.

WHELDALL, K. and AUSTIN, R. (1980), 'Successful Behaviour Modification in the Secondary School: A Reply to McNamara and Harrop' in *Occasional Papers of the Division of Educational and Child Psychology of the British Psychological Society*, *4*, 3–9.

WHELDALL, K. and CONGREVE, S. (1980), 'The Attitude of British Teachers Towards Behaviour Modification'. *Educational Review* 32, 53–65.

WHELDALL, K., MORRIS, M., VAUGHAN, P. and NG, Y.Y. (1981). 'Rows versus tables: an example of the use of behavioural ecology in two classes of eleven year old children,' *Educational Psychology*, *1*, 171–184.

Time to Teach: Teaching-Learning Processes in Primary Schools

Neville Bennett
University of Lancaster

The path of educational progress more closely resembles the flight of a butterfly than the flight of a bullet (Jackson, 1968). In the specific context of classroom teaching this has been due in part to the differing conceptions and definitions of 'good' teaching. In the earlier part of this century it was generally felt that teaching was an art, the belief being that 'a little learning and a way with children sufficed for the teacher' (Bennett, 1917). Good teachers were born not made, or had been lucky enough to stumble on its secrets by chance. This conception was later strongly contested by proponents of the view that teaching was a science. They poured scorn on the analogy of teachers with artists and musicians and argued that the content of teacher training resembled the treasured store of traditions passed on by one witch doctor to another, and that the best corrective to such shallow speculation and sentimentality was the development of a body of scientific knowledge relating to children's learning and effective teacher behaviour.

Contemporary thought eschews both these stances. Teaching is now seen to embody both artistic and scientific components. The teacher uses judgment, insight and sensitivity within a framework provided by the rules and concepts of scientific knowledge. A favoured analogy is with engineering where, in solving problems, artistry is used in balancing the claims of competing considerations within the context of a strong scientific foundation. Neither engineering nor teaching is a true science; both use science to achieve useful, practical ends.

This acceptance of a scientific basis for the art of teaching requires the dual development of, first, advances towards a science of teaching, and secondly, the design of relevant training in the practical art of teaching. This duality was recognized a long time ago. William James, writing in 1899, wrote 'knowing science is . . . no guarantee of good teaching. To advance to that result we must have an additional endowment altogether, a happy tact and ingenuity to tell us what definite things to say and do when the pupil is before us. That ingenuity in meeting and pursuing the pupil, that tact for the concrete situation, though they are the alpha and omega of the teacher's art, are things to which psychology cannot help us in the least.'

It is, in fact, to psychology that educators have turned for theories of learning and child development. But despite the discipline having a central role in the curriculum of teacher training, and books on educational psychology continue to proliferate, it would appear that it has had little impact on teachers' classroom activities. Teachers appear to be sceptical of the value of learning theories and reasons are not hard to find. Typically these theories have been developed from highly controlled laboratory experiments on the acquisition of relatively simple skills among college students and the white rat, whereas teaching and learning takes place in contexts quite unlike this. Teaching is an opportunistic process which takes place in a setting marked by multidimensionality, simultaneity and thus unpredictability (Doyle, 1977). In restricting themselves to laboratory settings psychologists have seriously neglected the social character of learning.

Many educators now consider that the only road to a scientific basis for teaching is to the classroom. 'Traditional psychological theory cannot be of any significant value until the investigators of classroom behaviour have themselves produced significant theoretical explanations of classroom events. The need is not for further adaptation and stretching of old theory but for the creation of new theory which arises directly from the natural grain and details of the behaviour it is intended to explain' (Nuthall, 1968). In short, the demand is for the identification, description and understanding of the varied behavioural dimensions of the classroom and how these behaviours relate to pupil achievement. A small, but growing band of educational researchers has accepted this challenge over the past decade, concentrating in particular on mathematics and language in the primary school. The task now is to develop models or theories which allow a meaningful ordering of the findings of these research efforts in order to ascertain the possibility of generalizations, implications and further hypotheses. What follows is the presentation of a model of teaching-learning processes which attempts to fulfil this task.

The Model

'No matter how constructed and arrived at every model serves to bring order of some kind to nature, or rather our understanding of her' (London, 1949). This particular model is based on recent empirical research on teaching and learning undertaken in classrooms; following a brief overview of the model as a whole, each element of the model will be considered separately prior to an assessment of its implications for teaching practice.

The perspective adopted conceives that the pupil's behaviours and activities are central to his learning, and that the total amount of time actively engaged on a particular topic is the most important determinant of achievement on that topic. It is recognized that the amount of time different pupils need to achieve the same level of achievement on the same topic will vary enormously. The teacher, on the other hand, is seen as the manager of the attention and time of pupils in relation to the educational ends of the classroom (cf. Westbury, 1977). In other words, the teacher manages the scarce resources of attention and time. The model is shown in Figure 1.

Figure 1.   A Model of Teaching-Learning Processes

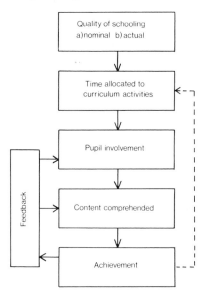

Overview

Quantity of schooling is the total amount of time that the school is open for its stated purpose and is defined by the length of school day and school year. The nominal amount may not be the actual amount since the school may be closed for a number of reasons — extra holidays, teacher strikes, or building alterations. The actual amount will also be reduced for a particular pupil by his absences. This time is allocated to various curricular activities, curricular used here in its broadest sense to include administration and transition time between activities as well as time devoted to content. The curriculum emphasis or balance achieved varies from school to school and class to class. This element is termed 'curriculum allocation'. The amount of time allocated to a given curriculum activity is, however, unlikely to match the actual amount of time a pupil will spend on it. Disruptions, distractions, lack of interest in the task or poor persistence are all factors likely to reduce the use a pupil makes of the opportunity to study a given content. The next element termed 'pupil involvement' acknowledges this. The underlying assumption here is that only the active portion of the time assigned to a task is effective for learning that task. But whether this active portion is achievement relevant will depend upon a number of other variables subsumed under 'comprehension'. According to this model, achievement relevant time is mediated by a number of factors including the aptitude and prior achievement of the pupil, clarity of instructions, task difficulty and pacing. Thus only that portion of time during which a pupil is actually comprehending the task is effective for its acquisition and thus has a direct link to achievement on that task. The remaining element is feedback since this is assumed to influence both involvement and comprehension and thereby achievement.

Quantity of Schooling

The exposure of pupils to schooling depends in the first instance on the nominal quantity of schooling defined by length of school day and school year. The length of the school year in Britain is fixed at 190 days but more flexibility is possible in the length of the school day. The regulations lay down a minimum of three hours per day for infants and four hours for juniors, although in practice primary schools work for longer hours than these regulations require. The evidence available indicates marked variations across schools. A study in Surrey (Hilsum and Cane, 1971), recently replicated in Lancashire (Lane, 1979), found that the amount of time the schools were open varied from twenty-two to twenty-seven hours per week. When lunch times, breaks, assemblies and administration are deducted, the amount of time remaining for teaching varied from a little over nineteen to twenty-four hours per week. At the extremes, therefore, some children are exposed to schooling for five hours per week more than others, effectively a gain of one day per week. Over the school year this difference amounts to six school weeks.

These nominal amounts of time are likely to be differentially decreased by such events as teacher or caretaker strikes, structural repairs, use of schools as polling stations and so on. The actual amount of schooling for any individual pupil will also depend on his absences from school. These differences are important. A number of studies have now related the length of school day to pupil achievement and have found positive and significant relationships (Stallings, 1975; Wiley and Harnischfeger, 1974). Further, studies which have related pupil absence to achievement have typically reported negative relationships (cf. Bennett, 1978). The latest large-scale study of the effect of pupil absence examined the relationship between school attendance at ages 7 and 15 and reading and mathematics achievement at age 16. The conclusion was that 'children with high attendance levels obtain on average higher scores on tests of reading, comprehension and mathematics' (Fogelman, 1978). There was also a low but positive link between attendance at age 7 and later achievement at age 16 which could suggest that the effect of early absence persists into secondary school.

Curriculum Allocation

Within the constraints of the actual amount of schooling available, the primary teacher subdivides the time by curriculum area and plans and implements corresponding allocations of pupil time either in class, group or individual activities. The curriculum emphasis in primary classrooms is often determined by the class teacher, mediated by school policy, attitudes and aims based on perceptions of the needs of the children and their levels of achievement. The lack of central control of curriculum in Britain is reflected in the large variations found in curriculum emphasis.

A number of recent studies have investigated this and despite differences in methodology and definitions the results are surprisingly consistent (Bennett, 1976; Ashton *et al.*, 1975; Bassey, 1977; Lane, 1979; Bennett *et al*; 1980). Although the average times spent on say mathematics (five hours) and language (seven hours) are consistent, variations between teachers are large. For example, in mathematics some teachers stated that they spend less than one hour per week whereas others devote eight hours to this subject. An identical variation is true of thematic studies, here defined as covering what is conventionally known as environmental studies — an integration of history, geography, nature study and science. The discrepancies in the opportunity to study language are greatest, varying from less than one hour per week to ten hours. Other findings of interest from this body of research are that the number of subjects comprising the primary curriculum varies from more than eight to five or less, and that the pattern of time allocation across days of the week differed across classrooms. Some teachers felt that mathematics, for example, should be taught daily, others four days per week, whilst a minority group felt that no regular commitment was necessary but was demanded as and when necessary.

What is clear is that children are receiving quite different educational diets dependent on the school they happen to go to, and as in other areas of human functioning diet relates to growth. The limited number of studies which have investigated this link have shown positive relationships. The largest study concluded 'time allocated to instruction in a content area is positively associated with learning in that content area' (Fisher *et al.*, 1978). This was consistent at both infant and junior levels and in both mathematics and reading. Thus the pattern of time allocation to various subject areas is an important consideration when planning and implementing instruction (cf. Brookover *et al.*, 1978).

Pupil Involvement

If we conceive curriculum allocation as the opportunity that teachers provide pupils to study a given curriculum content, then pupil involvement can be conceived as the use that pupils make of that opportunity. Here too there is evidence of wide variation. The problem here is that the answer gained crucially depends on the question asked. Some researchers have computed a proportion of the time that pupils are actively engaged on the task set in relation to the length of the school day. The question posed in this instance is, 'What proportion of the school day is the pupil involved'?, and this inevitably includes administration and transition time which serves to depress the size of the proportion gained. Other researchers have posed the question, 'What proportion of an identifiable lesson is the pupil involved'?, and this obviates the inclusion of transition time.

In an open plan study we computed both. Here the average proportion of the school day spent was 66 per cent for juniors and 61 per cent for infants but these averages mask marked divergences across schools. Some schools managed to average over 80, others only 50 per cent. And if the individual pupil is taken as the unit of analysis, the variation was from approximately 20 to nearly 90 per cent. In other words, some teachers were able to keep their pupils involved for nineteen hours per week, others only thirteen hours. If transition time is removed the proportions increase substantially to over 75 per cent, and when these data were further broken down it became evident that involvement was lowest in mathematics and language. That which is allocated most time apparently generates least involvement.

The variable here labelled pupil involvement has numerous synonyms — attention, task persistence, active learning time and engagement, but irrespective of nomenclature the central question is whether this variable relates to achievement. Was William James correct when he argued in 1902 'whether the attention comes by grace of genius or by dint of will, the longer one does attend to a topic the more mastery of it one has'? The short answer is 'yes'. There is clear support for such a view from investigations at all levels of schooling. At nursery and reception level it has been reported that the effect of harnessing and focusing the children's attention is dramatic (Tyler *et al.*, 1979), and that interest and task orientation in kindergarten are the best predictors of achievement in infant school (Perry *et al.*, 1979). Studies of the attention-achievement link among 6 (Samuels and Turnure, 1974), 7 (Fisher *et al.*, 1978), 8 (McKinney *et al.*, 1975), 11 (Cobb, 1972; Fisher *et al*, 1978) and 12-year-old children (Laharderne, 1968) have all demonstrated positive and significant relationships. In the secondary field an analysis of several international evaluation studies on achievement delineated time and opportunity to learn as the most important factors to emanate from these studies (Postlethwaite, 1975).

The evidence would indicate that the involvement-achievement link is valid for all ages of schooling. Indeed, researchers have been criticized in a recent review for not showing more concern with this area: 'our contention is not that time is the complete explanation of all observed test differences ... it is simply being maintained that in the absence of clear evidence that different procedures are in fact associated with different treatments, time differences potentially and parsimoniously account for much of the observed data' (Faw and Waller, 1976).

Comprehension

But time is not the complete explanation of test differences. It has in fact been called an 'empty box' (Gage, 1978) which requires filling with comprehensible and worthwhile content. Comprehension and feedback are considered separately in the model as it stands but could be joined to provide a more general element relating to structuring the conditions for learning. The cluster of variables of concern here includes the manner of presentation of task, the sequence, level and pacing of content and the teacher's levels of expectations of pupils as judged by the tasks and activities provided. Unfortunately, classroom researchers have tended to neglect this area to date. There are one or two reports of positive relationships between the teacher's clarity of instructions and pupil achievement but no classroom-based research on sequencing content.

Despite this, sequencing has continued to be regarded as central by instructional theorists and some experimental studies have reported that content structure can make a difference in terms of performance and the rate of concept acquisition (Tennyson and Tennyson, 1977). But a recent review of this area contended that despite long debates on the issue no satisfactory answer has been developed and no adequate prescription should be expected in the near future. The conclusion was that 'we have very little information based on hard data regarding the consequences of alternative content sequences and will need a good deal more research effort before we are able to satisfactorily report how the content should be sequenced' (Posner and Strike, 1976).

Of current concern is the nature of the match between the demands of the task or activity set and the pupils' capacities to undertake it. This is variously referred to as the match or level of difficulty, and was highlighted in the recent survey of primary education undertaken by Her Majesty's Inspectorate. It was their judgment that the top third of pupils in any class were doing work that was insufficiently challenging. Teachers were underestimating these pupils' capacities. Evidence of poor matching is also available from the United States where, for example, it is claimed that the failure to adjust the material and the instruction to the range of reading capabilities found within the classroom is probably the most important single cause of reading disability (Bond and Tinker, 1973).

These assertions about the effect on achievement of poor matching gain limited support from recent classroom-based studies. Support from the HMI survey itself was indirect. They found that exploratory or progressive teaching practices were related to poorer achievement in maths and reading and that matching was least satisfactory there. Direct support is only available from American studies at this stage. One approached the problem by rating the number of errors children made in their work and found that the proportion of time spent on tasks where they have low error rates is positively associated with learning (Fisher *et al.*, 1978). More significant perhaps, in terms of its implications, is the finding of an interaction effect with pupil ability. The evidence would indicate that the lower ability pupils learn more by having less taught to them, and by having it taught redundantly to the point of overlearning, proceeding in small steps that they can master without undue cognitive strain. In contrast, higher ability children can cover the same material more quickly and furthermore will learn optimally by being challenged with slightly more difficult questions and assignments (Brophy and Evertson, 1976).

The extent to which children are challenged by the teacher appears to be important. There is research to indicate that increasing the demands made on pupils increases involvement and performance (Block and Burns, 1976). This notion of the more you demand, the more you are likely to get is supported by other studies. One investigated teachers who consistently gained higher achievement in maths and compared them with those who tended to gain low achievement. They found that the high achieving teachers typically pushed pupils through textbooks at a much faster rate, covering on average ninety pages of text in eighty days compared to fifty-six pages of the low achieving teachers. Incidentally, attitudes to maths were also higher in the faster paced classes (Good *et al.*, 1978). A similar conclusion was reached in a large-scale comparative study of the mathematics achievement of British and Californian children. The much better performance of British children was interpreted in terms of differing requirements or expectations. 'In California much less was expected of pupils in arithmetic, more limited objectives were formulated for children of primary school age and less emphasis was placed on rapid progress in mechanical arithmetic than was customary in England and Wales' (Pidgeon, 1970). Classroom-based research on the variables included within the comprehension category is fairly limited. Nevertheless, it appears to be consistent in indicating that these factors do have an effect on learning outcomes and that interactions can be expected with pupil ability and attitude.

Feedback

'Feedback confirms correct responses, telling the student how well the content is being understood and it identifies and corrects errors, or allows the learner to correct them. This correction function is probably the most important aspect of feedback, and, if one were given the choice, feedback following wrong responses probably has the greatest positive effect' (Kulhavy, 1977). The effectiveness of the correction function can be shown in recent classroom research. Opportunities for immediate practice of skills, together with opportunity for immediate corrective feedback, have been found to be important, particularly with the lower ability pupil. One report concluded: 'the most successful teachers, in terms of pupil gains conducted group lessons by giving initial demonstrations and then quickly moving around having each student try out what has been demonstrated and providing feedback on an individual basis' (Brophy and Evertson, 1976).

An aspect of feedback which has attracted considerable research has been the relative utility of verbal praise and criticism. Until the early seventies it was thought that praise was preferable, but research since that date has tended to modify this. The focus or topic of feedback has been shown to be more important than type of feedback (Stallings and Kaskowitz, 1973), and interactions with pupil ability have also been found. These would indicate that the most successful teachers of low ability children motivate primarily through gentle and positive encouragement and praise, while the most successful teachers of high ability children motivated through challenge and a critical demandingness which involved communicating high expectations and criticizing their pupils for failing to meet them (Brophy and Evertson, 1976).

Symbolic as well as verbal feedback would seem to be effective. It has been found that the use of symbolic rewards such as gold stars and 'smiling faces' placed upon papers to be taken home and shown to the parents, or placed on charts in a room, showed consistent positive association with learning gains' (Brophy and Evertson, 1976). Classroom-based experiments on material incentives support their efficacy (cf. Benowitz and Busse, 1976).

Conclusion

A model of teaching-learning processes has been presented and its implications assessed. Although clothed in complexity, some of the underlying ideas are unremarkable — that what is taught is reflected in what is learned, that the pupil's performance on a topic is likely to improve the more time he spends on it, and so on. Indeed, one may even dismiss such findings as no more than common sense. But it would be dangerous to do so, as the authors of a recent influential study on secondary schools pointed out. Their findings were that children benefit from attending schools which set good standards, where the teachers provide good models of behaviour, where they are praised and given responsibility, where the general conditions are good and where the lessons are well conducted. The authors concluded: 'Indeed this is obvious but, of course, it might have been equally obvious if we had found that the most important factors were attending a small school in modern purpose-built premises on one site, with a particularly favourable teacher-child ratio, a year-based system of pastoral care, continuity of individual teachers, and firm discipline in which unacceptable behaviours were severely punished' (Rutter *et al.*, 1979). In fact *none* of the items was significantly associated with outcomes however measured. We must also recognize that common sense is not always common practice and is culture bound. What is regarded as common sense in one era or cultural milieu is dismissed as irrelevant in another. A prime example is the concept of pupil involvement. In the earlier part of this century much research effort was expended on this topic but interest in it died for almost forty years until taken up again recently. As one commentator writing in the late 1960s argued:

> In education courses and in the professional literature involvement and its opposite, some form of detachment, are largely ignored. Yet, from a logical point of view, few topics would seem to have greater relevance for the teacher's work. Certainly no educational goals are more immediate than those that concern the establishment and maintenance of the students' absorption in the task at hand. Almost all other objectives are dependent for their accomplishment upon the attainment of this basic condition. Yet this fact seems to have been more appreciated in the past than it is today. (Jackson, 1968)

He explained the disappearance of interest as a sign of the times. In the progressive era which followed the Second World War when classrooms were billed as democratic settings, pupil involvement was regarded as an authoritarian issue and dismissed.

There is a tide in the affairs of issues reflecting changes in the economic, cultural and social ethos. Hearings given to social evidence and attention paid to concepts thus depend on the times. No doubt the cycles of fashion evident in educational practice reflect this as does the educator's penchant for rediscovering the wheel. This can also be illustrated by the following quotation which might be felt to adequately summarize the argument so far.

> The art of teaching ... comprehends all of the means by which the teacher sustains the attention of his class. By attention, we do not mean the mere absence of noise and trifling; not that inert passive state in which the class, with eye fixed on the teacher, it may be, gives no symptom of mental life; not that intermittent and almost unconscious attention bestowed on some casual topic which strikes their fancy; not the partial attention given by a few who may be in the immediate neighbourhood of the pupil addressed. The only satisfactory attention is that which is given voluntarily and steadily by all during the entire instruction, and in which the mental attitude of the class is actively engaged along with the teacher in working out their own instruction.

But that was written by Currie in 1884.

References

ASHTON, P. *et al.* (1975) *The Aims of Primary Education: A Study of Teacher Opinions*, London, Macmillan.

BASSEY, M. (1977) *Nine Hundred Primary School Teachers*, Nottingham, Nottinghamshire Primary Schools Research Project, Trent Polytechnic.

BENNETT, H.E. (1917) *School Efficiency: A Manual of Modern School Management*, Boston, Ginn and Co.

BENNETT, S.N. (1976) *Teaching Styles and Pupil Progress*, London, Open Books.

BENNETT, S.N. (1978) 'Recent research on teaching: A dream, a belief and a model', *Brit. J. Educ. Psych.*, 48, pp. 127–47.

BENNETT, S.N. *et al.* (1980) *Open Plan Schools: Teaching, Curriculum and Design*, Slough, NFER.

BENOWITZ, M.L. and BUSSE, T.V. (1976) 'Effects of material incentives and the classroom learning of middle and lower class children', *Psychol. in the School*, 10, pp. 79–83.

BLOCK, J.H. and BURNS, R.B. (1976) 'Mastery learning', in SHULMAN, L.S. (Ed.) *Review of Research in Education 4*, Itasca, F.E. Peacock.

BOND, G. and TINKER, M. (1973) *Reading Difficulties: Their Diagnosis and Correction*, New York, Appleton Century Crofts.

BROOKOVER, W.B. *et al.* (1978) 'Elementary school social climate and school achievement', *Amer. Educ. Res. J.*, 15, pp. 301–18.

BROPHY, J.E. and EVERTSON, C.M. (1976) *Learning from Teaching*, Boston, Allyn and Bacon.

COBB, J.A. (1972) 'Relationship of discrete classroom behaviours to fourth grade academic achievement', *J. Educ. Psych.*, 63, pp. 74–80.

CURRIE, J. (1884) *The Principles and Practice of Common School Education*, Cincinatti, R. Clarke (quoted in WESTBURY, 1977).

DOYLE, W. (1977) 'Learning the classroom environment: An ecological analysis of induction into teaching', paper presented at AERA Annual Conference, New York.

FAW, H.W. and WALLER, T.G. (1976) 'Mathemagenic behaviours and efficiency in learning from prose materials: Review, critique and recommendations', *Rev. Educ. Res.*, 46, pp. 691–720.

FISHER, C.W. *et al.* (1978) *Teaching Behaviours, Academic Learning Time and Student Achievement: Final Report of Phase IIIB, Beginning Teacher Evaluation Study*, San Francisco, Far West Lab.

FOGELMAN, K. (1978) 'School attendance, attainment and behaviour', *Br. J. Educ. Psych.*, 48, pp. 148–58.

GAGE, N.L. (1978) *The Scientific Basis of the Art of Teaching*, Teachers College Press, University of Columbia, New York.

GOOD, T. *et al.* (1978) 'Curriculum pacing: Some empirical data in mathematics', *J. Curric. Stud.*, 10, pp. 75–81.

HILSUM, S. and CANE, B. (1971) *The Teacher's Day*, Slough, NFER.

JACKSON, P.W. (1968) *Life in Classrooms*, New York, Holt, Rinehart and Winston.

JAMES, W. (1899) *Talks to Teachers*, London, Longman Green.

KULHAVY, R.W. (1977) 'Feedback in written instruction', *Rev. Educ. Res.*, 47, pp. 211–32.

LAHADERNE, H.M. (1968) 'Attitudinal and intellectual correlates of attention: A study of four sixth grade classrooms', *J. Educ. Psych.*, 59, pp. 320–4.

LANE, R. (1979) 'The Teacher's Week: An Appraisal', unpublished MA dissertation, Department of Educational Research, University of Lancaster.

LONDON, I.D. (1949) 'The role of the model in explanation', *J. Genet. Psych.*, 74, pp. 165–76.

MCKINNEY, J.D. *et al.* (1975) Relationships between behaviours and academic achievement, *J. Educ. Psychol.*, 67, pp. 198–203.

NUTHALL, G. (1968) 'Studies of teaching: Types of research on teaching', *New Zealand Journal of Educational Studies*, 3, pp. 125–47.

PERRY, J.D. *et al.* (1979) 'Kindergarten competencies as predictors of third grade classroom behaviour and achievement', *J. Educ. Psych.*, 71, pp. 443–50.

PIDGEON, D.A. (1970) *Expectation and Pupil Performance*, Slough, NFER.

POSNER, G.H. and STRIKE, K.A. (1976) 'A categorisation scheme for principles of sequencing content', *Rev. Educ. Res.*, 46, pp. 665–90.

POSTLETHWAITE, T.N. (1975) 'The surveys of the International Association for the Evaluation of Educational Achievement (IEA): Implications of the IEA surveys of achievement', in PURVIS, A.C. and LEVINE D.V. (Eds), *Educational Policy and International Assessment*, Berkeley, McCutchen.

RUTTER, M. *et al.* (1979) *Fifteen Thousand Hours*, London, Open Books.

SAMUELS, B.J. and TURNURE, J.E. (1974) 'Attention and reading achievement in first grade boys and girls', *J. Educ. Psych.*, 66, pp. 29–32.

STALLINGS, J.A. (1975) 'Relationships between classroom instructional practices and child development', paper presented at AERA Annual Conference, Washington DC.

STALLINGS, J.A. and KASKOWITZ, D.H. (1974) *Follow through Classroom Observation Evaluation*, Menlo Park, Calif., Stanford Research Institute.

TENNYSON, R.D. and TENNYSON, C.L. (1977) 'Content structure as a design strategy variable in concept acquisition', paper presented at AERA Annual Conference, New York.

TYLER, S. *et al.* (1979) 'Attention and activity in the young child', *Br. J. Educ. Psych.*, 49, pp. 194–97.

WESTBURY, I. (1977) 'The curriculum and the frames of the classroom', paper presented at AERA Annual Conference, New York.

WILEY, D.E. and HARNISCHFEGER, A. (1974) 'Explosion of a myth: Quantity of schooling and exposure to instruction, major educational vehicles', *Studies of Educative Processes*, Rep. No. 8, University of Chicago.

Promoting Excellence through Mastery Learning[*]

James H. Block,
University of California, Santa Barbara

Introduction

Mastery learning is first and foremost an optimistic theory about teaching and learning. Essentially this theory asserts that any teacher can help virtually *all* students to learn excellently. In practice, mastery learning is an effective set of individualized instructional practices that consistently help *most* students to learn excellently, whether the approach is group-based and teacher-paced (which fits more readily into current school arrangements) (see Block and Anderson, 1975) or individually-based and student-paced as in Keller's *Personalized System of Instruction* (*PSI*) (see Keller and Sherman, 1974). The initial assumption in either form of mastery learning is that virtually all students can master a great deal of what they are taught in school if the '... instruction is approached systematically, if students are helped when and where they have learning difficulties, if they are given sufficient time to achieve mastery, and if there is some clear criterion of what constitutes mastery' (Bloom, 1974, p. 6; see also Bloom, 1976).

How Does It Work?

How do mastery learning strategies work? Let us describe the group-based teacher-paced 'Learning for Mastery' strategy. This strategy reflects all the basic mastery learning concepts and ideas. Moreover, it has proven to be one of the easiest mastery learning strategies to implement. We shall begin by describing the various steps in implementing the strategy. Then we shall examine the basic mastery learning concepts and techniques that underpin these steps.

[*] An edited and substantially shortened version of an article which appeared in *Theory into Practice*, 1980, 66–74.

The 'Learning for Mastery' strategy is designed for use in instructional situations where the calendar time allowed for learning is relatively fixed and where students must be taught largely in groups. This strategy attempts to minimize the time a group of students need to learn excellently so that it is within the fixed amount of calendar time available for instruction. This is accomplished through two distinct sets of steps. One set — the Preconditions — occurs outside the classroom and prior to the instruction; the second set — the Operating Procedures — takes place inside the classroom and during the instruction.

Preconditions for Mastery Learning

Defining Mastery.   The teacher who wishes to use a 'Learning for Mastery' approach begins by formulating what is meant by 'mastery' of the subject. Ideally, the teacher would first define what material all students will be expected to learn. This entails the formulation of course objectives. Next, the teacher would prepare a final or summative examination (Bloom, Hastings and Madaus, 1971) over all these objectives for administration at the course's close. Lastly, the teacher would set a summative examination score indicative of mastery performance. Students who perform better than this predetermined standard would be graded 'masters'; those who do not would be graded 'non-masters'.

In actual practice, though, teachers have found it useful to use their old course achievement tests as working definitions of the material that each student will be expected to master. They have also found it convenient to administer one or more of these tests throughout the course for grading purposes. Finally, rather than grade the student's performance on a mastery/ nonmastery basis, the teachers have found it useful to fix an absolute grading scale wherein mastery corresponds to a grade of A and nonmastery corresponds to a grade of B, C, D, or F. The teacher forms this scale by determining the level of performance that students traditionally had to exhibit on the course examinations in order to earn an A, B, C, D, or F. All students who achieve to a particular level using mastery learning methods then receive the grade that corresponds to this level.

Planning for Mastery   Now the teacher breaks the course to be taught for mastery into a sequence of smaller learning units, each of which typically covers about two weeks' worth of material. In practice, these units correspond roughly to chapters in the course textbook or to a set of topics.

Next, the teacher sequences these units. After all, the teacher has broken the whole course into pieces, she must now recast the pieces into a whole. Teachers of mathematics and sciences have tended to sequence their units linearly so that the material in each unit transfers directly to the next unit. Teachers of arts, humanities and social sciences, however, have tended to sequence their units hierarchically so that the material in each unit transfers, but not necessarily to the next unit. It may transfer to a subsequent unit.

Then, for each unit the teacher develops perhaps the single most important component of the mastery learning strategy: the unit feedback correction procedures. These procedures will serve to monitor the effectiveness of the group-based instruction and to supplement it where necessary to better suit the learning requirements of certain students.

First, the teacher constructs a brief, ungraded diagnostic progress test or 'formative' evaluation instrument (Bloom, Hastings and Madaus, 1971) for each unit. These tests are explicitly designed to be an integral part of each unit's instruction and to provide specific information or feedback to both the teacher and the student about how the student is changing as a result of the group-based instruction.

Next, the teacher specifies a score or performance standard on each formative test which, when met, will be indicative of unit mastery. Usually a score of 80 to 90 per cent correct on a formative test indicates that the student is not having learning problems.

Finally, the teacher develops a set of alternative instructional materials and procedures or 'correctives' keyed to each item on each unit's formative test. Typically these correctives have consisted of cooperative small group study sessions, individual tutoring by classmates, or alternative learning aids such as different textbooks, workbooks, audiovisual materials, academic games puzzles, and affective exercises.

Each corrective is designed to reteach the material tested by certain items on the unit formative test, but to do so in ways that will differ from the unit's initial group-based instruction. The correctives may present the material in a different sensory mode or modes or in a different form of the same mode than the group-based instruction. They may involve the student in a different way and/or provide not only different types of encouragements for learning but also different amounts of each type. Hence, should a student encounter difficulty in learning certain material from the group-based instruction unit, he can then use the correctives to explore alternative ways of learning the unmastered material, select those correctives best suited to his particular learning requirements, and overcome his learning problems before they impair subsequent learning.

Operating Procedures for Mastery Learning

Orienting for Mastery   The teacher is now ready to teach. Since students are not accustomed to learning for mastery or to the notion that they all might earn A's, the teacher usually must spend some time at the course's outset orienting them to the procedures to be used — what they are expected to learn, how they are generally expected to learn it, and to what level they are expected to learn. My experience has been that this orientation period —

combined with continual encouragement, support, and positive evidence of learning success — is crucial in developing in most students the belief that they can learn and the motivation to learn.

Teaching for Mastery Following this orientation period, the teacher teaches the first learning unit, using his/her customary group-based teaching methods. When this instruction has been completed, and before moving to the next unit, the teacher then administers the unit's formative test to the entire class. Next, each student usually corrects his/her own test. Finally, using a show of hands to discover the test results, the teacher certifies those students who have achieved the unit mastery standard and identifies those who have not. The former students are free to engage in enrichment activities and/or to serve as tutors for their 'slower' classmates; the latter are asked to use the appropriate correctives to complete their unit learning.

The teacher then announces when the group-based instruction for the next unit will commence, and both sets of students are given responsibility for making use of the opportunities provided. If the teacher desires to postpone the start of the next unit, the students are given in-class as well as out-of-class time to discharge their respective responsibilities. If the teacher does not desire to postpone the start of the next unit, then the students must use out-of-class time.

The teacher repeats this cycle of initial instruction, diagnostic progress-testing, and certification or individual correction, unit by unit, until all units have been taught. The cycle is paced so that the teacher covers just as much material as would ordinarily be covered. Two pacing options are possible. If all the student enrichment tutoring or correction responsibilities are to be discharged outside of class, then the teacher may pace each unit's instruction as in the past. However, if some or all responsibilities are to be discharged in class, the teacher can adjust the pace of the instruction, allowing more time for the early units and less time for the later ones. Essentially, the teacher borrows time that would ordinarily be spent on later units and spends this time on the earlier units. The assumption is that this borrowed time will not be needed later if students learn for mastery earlier.

The management of learning is executed in three basic stages by mastery practitioners. In the orientation stage, they indicate in a concrete fashion how and toward what ends students will be taught. Obviously, no instructional technique can succeed if the ground in which it is sown is not properly prepared.

In the teaching stage, they then vary, as necessary, how and how long each student is taught by using their pre-planned instructional units. The original instruction for each unit gives all students a chance to learn excellently from one method of instruction over one period of time. The feedback instrument and mastery standard indicates those students for whom the original instruction and the initial learning time was sufficient and for whom it was not. The unit's correctives provide these latter students with the opportunity to master the material not mastered from the original instruction using additional methods of instruction and additional learning time as necessary.

In the grading stage, the practitioner evaluates students on a more personal basis. Students are graded for what they actually have learned. In short, they are graded for mastery. Such mastery grading is designed to engage what White (1959) has called 'competence motivation,' *i.e.*, the intrinsic desire to compete against oneself and the material to be learned, and to disengage what I (Block, 1977) have alluded to as 'competition motivation,' *i.e.*, the extrinsic desire to compete against others. From the standpoint of developing the talent of all students, rather than a few, the engagement of the former motivation makes much more sense than the engagement of the latter.

How Well Does It Work?

How well, then, does mastery learning work? As numerous practitioners have discovered, mastery learning represents a particular commitment about education, *i.e.*, an innovative philosophy and set of practices for its improvement (Dunkin and Biddle, 1974). But is this commitment, like so many others, 'attractively argued but unsupported by data' (Dunkin and Biddle, 1974, p. 51) or supported by data that indicates it works 51 per cent of the time and fails 49 per cent of the other? The answer is 'No' Mastery learning strategies may not work quite as well as their advocates propose, but they do work very well indeed.

Consider, for example, a recent review by Block and Burns (1976) of some forty rigorous studies of student outcomes under mastery and non-mastery approaches to instruction. This review's findings echoed the general findings of earlier and later reviews. Block and Burns (1976) reported the following:

Learning Effectiveness Mastery-taught students typically learned more effectively than their non-mastery-taught counterparts. Whether learning was measured in terms of student achievement or in terms of student retention, they almost always learned more, and usually significantly more, and they learned more like one another.

Learning Efficiency Mastery-taught students also typically learned more efficiently than their non-mastery-taught counterparts. Whereas in the non-mastery-taught classrooms some students learned several times as fast as other students, in the mastery-taught classrooms individual differences in learning rate were substantially less. In fact, in these latter classrooms individual differences in learning rate seemed headed toward a vanishing point in which even the 'slowest' students would learn roughly as fast as the 'fastest' students.

Learner Affect Lastly, mastery-taught students liked their learning, their teaching and themselves better than their non-mastery-taught counterparts. They virtually always responded more positively than their counter-parts, for example, on measures of interest in and attitudes toward the subject matter learned, of self-concept (academic as well as general), of academic self-confidence, of attitudes toward cooperative learning, and of attitudes toward the instruction. Whether their more favorable affective responses were just momentary expressions of enthusiasm or more perma-nent ones that would carry over into their subsequent work was, however, indeterminable.

Conclusion

Much that we have learned about mastery learning theory, practice and research will, of course, seem 'old hat' to some educators. After all, an optimistic faith in all students' capacity for excellent learning, an approach to instruction that is systematic, proactive and learning oriented, and an approach that consistently promotes student cognitive and affective growth have long been the trademarks of the *paragons* of the teaching profession. What should be 'new hat,' however, is the message that mastery learning theory, practice and research now offers these trademarks of our best teachers to *all* our teachers. Surely, at a time when public confidence in the teaching profession is low, such a message cannot be ignored.

* * * *

Further details about the procedures and strategies of mastery learning will be found in the following references: Anderson and Block (1976); Block (1971, 1974, 1979 and the full version of this article); Carroll (1971); Okey (1975); Okey and Ciesla (1975); Spady (1978); and Torshen (1977).

References

ANDERSON, L.W. and BLOCK, J.H. (1976) 'Mastery learning', in TREFFINGER, D., DAVIS, J. and RIPPLE, R. (Eds), *Handbook on Educational Psychology: Instructional Practice and Research*, New York: Academic Press.
BLOCK, J.H. (Ed.) (1971) *Mastery Learning: Theory and Practice*, New York: Holt, Rinehart and Winston.
BLOCK, J.H. (Ed.) (1974) *Schools, Society, and Mastery Learning*, New York: Holt, Rinehart and Winston.
BLOCK, J.H. (1977) 'Motivation, evaluation, and mastery learning', *UCLA Educator*, Winter, vol. 19, no. 2, pp. 31–6.
BLOCK, J.H. (1979) 'Mastery learning: the current state of the craft', *Educational Leadership*, vol. 37, no. 2, November, pp. 114–7.
BLOCK, J.H. and ANDERSON, L.W. (1975) *Mastery Learning in Classroom Instruction*, New York: Macmillan.
BLOCK, J.H. and BURNS, R.B. (1976) 'Mastery learning', in SHULMAN, L. (Ed.), *Review of Research in Education*, vol. 4, Itasca, Ill: F.E. Peacock.

BLOOM, B.S. (1974) 'An introduction to mastery learning theory', in BLOCK, J.H. (Ed.), *Schools, Society, and Mastery Learning*, New York: Holt, Rinehart and Winston.

BLOOM, B.S. (1976) *Human Characteristics and School Learning*, New York: McGraw-Hill.

BLOOM, B.S., HASTINGS, J.T. and MADAUS, G.F. (1971) *Handbook on Formative And Summative Evaluation of Student Learning*, New York: McGraw-Hill.

CARROLL, J.B. (1971) 'Problems of measurement related to the concept of learning for mastery', in BLOCK, J.H. (Ed.), *Mastery Learning: Theory and Practice*, New York: Holt, Rinehart and Winston.

DUNKIN, M.J. and BIDDLE, B.J. (1974) *The Study of Teaching*, New York: Holt, Rinehart and Winston.

KELLER, F.S. and SHERMAN, J.G. (1974) *The Keller Plan Handbook*, Menlo Park, California: W.A. Benjamin.

OKEY, J.R. (1975) 'Development of mastery teaching materials' (Final Evaluation Rep., USOE G-74-2990), Bloomington: Indiana University, August.

OKEY, J. and CIESLA, J. (1975) *Mastery Teaching*, Bloomington: National Center for the Development of Training Materials in Teacher Education, Indiana University.

SPADY, W.G. (1978) 'The concept and implications of competency-based education', *Educational Leadership*, vol. 36, pp. 16–22.

TORSHEN, K.P. (1977) *The Mastery Approach in Competency-based Education*, New York: Academic Press.

WHITE, R.W. (1959) 'Motivation reconsidered: the concept of competence', *Psychological Review*, vol. 66, pp. 297–333.

Educational Psychology and the Teaching of Specialist Subjects*

Mary Simpson and Brian Arnold
Aberdeen College of Education

Much of the psychological research into learning and its associated problems at levels equivalent to O-grade and beyond has been largely theoretical in nature and has been carried out to test the application of particular learning theories, e.g., Barnes and Clawson (1975), Bender and Milakofsky (1982), Okey and Gagné (1970). Few of the results of such research have been commonly perceived by teachers as being of immediate relevance to their classroom teaching perhaps because learning theories which are expressed in general terms are not readily regarded as having a useful application to the particularity of teaching a specialist subject. The studies which are welcomed and accepted as being relevant are those which are directed to the development of improved techniques for teaching specialized topics, e.g., Gill (1980) and Jones (1982). Such studies seldom have any appreciable psychological component. It is probable that underlying this lack of recognition by teachers of the possible contribution of psychological learning theories to secondary education is the assumption that pupils who are selected for O- and H- grade courses generally have no intrinsic learning difficulties. Any problems which arise tend to be attributed to a lack of ability or application.

Reflecting these assumptions, the statistics of O-grade marks are seen as a result of the operation of an effective sorting system, distinguishing pupils according to their abilities and application. This has significant effects on curriculum development. Consistently low test scores associated with a particular topic tend to be attributed axiomatically to its inherent level of difficulty, causing pupil failure to be inevitable. Consequently, such scores are seen as being cues for the exclusion of that topic from the syllabus, regardless of educational requirements. Thus, for example, the fact that H-grade pupils were demonstrably having difficulty in understanding water

* This article appeared in *Scottish Educational Review*, 14, 2, 1982, pp. 109–117.

potential, a concept which many biologists considered essential to comprehension of osmosis, failed to prompt the commissioning of any study of the origins of those difficulties, but resulted instead in its exclusion from the examination syllabus.

Two research projects on which we have been engaged had their origins in the puzzlement of one of us, a principal examiner, that so many able and apparently well motivated pupils failed to gain any genuine understanding of the processes of photosynthesis and osmosis as taught at O- and H-grade. Since a superficial analysis of the content of these topics did not suggest that their understanding demanded so high a level of reasoning as to make failure for most pupils inevitable, it seemed likely to us that other factors were inhibiting or actively blocking effective learning. The aims of our research were to uncover the origins of these pupil difficulties and to produce teaching and diagnostic aids for classroom use. Full details of our studies have been published elsewhere (Arnold and Simpson, 1980, 1982). The purpose of the present paper is to review the findings of those and related studies and to discuss them in the wider context of the relevance of psychological theories to secondary science education.

Methods

Each of our studies had three stages: a critical examination of what was taught and how; the determination and analysis of the discrepancies between what was taught, what was expected of pupils and what actually learned; and the production of learning aids for classroom use. The last of these will not be discussed in this paper.

In the first stage, information on the content matter and mode of presentation was obtained by examination of the worksheets and commonly used texts and by questionnaire responses from Scottish biology teachers, especially those in Grampian and Highland Regions. The topic was then analyzed in terms of behavioural objectives (Bloom *et al.*, 1956) and of concept structure and development according to a modification of Klausmeier's scheme (Klausmeier, 1976). Since it was important to know what information the pupils already possessed, the teaching content of relevant previous courses was also examined and compared with what had actually been retained. This was assessed by individual semi-structured interviews and by short written tests administered to pupils in years S1 to S4. In our first study, the interviews were extended to P7 pupils in order to trace back the origins, and to assess the incidence, of certain ideas and misconceptions.

This stage completed, it was possible to predict the nature of some of the difficulties and confusions which pupils were likely to encounter in learning the topics of photosynthesis and osmosis in their O-grade courses, to anticipate the types of wrong information they were likely to acquire and to design objective tests to examine these predictions. These tests, which were piloted with a sample of secondary pupils and student teachers, were administered to certificate biology pupils (approximately 600 per study) towards the end of their course. The tests were supplemented by further semi-structured interviews with smaller samples of pupils; these were designed to assist and validate the interpretation of the objective test responses. A sample of teachers whose pupils were involved in the study also sat the tests and submitted anonymous returns and comments. The tests and interviews were compiled to discover not whether pupils had learned most of the presented material, but more precisely what information they had learned and understood. Some of the questions were straightforwardly assessing mastery, some were designed to determine whether the pupil could discriminate between examples and non-examples of the processes and between criterial and non-criterial attributes, while others tested whether the pupil had specific misconceptions. Similar questions were posed in different contexts in order to discover how readily pupils would abandon a correct answer under pressure or temptation and whether information 'known' in one situation would be used in another.

Results and Discussion

The results of our separate studies of photosynthesis and osmosis suggest that similar factors were responsible, though in different degrees, for pupil difficulties in learning these topics. The similarities give us some confidence in the more general applicability of our comments. The factors fall into three groups, the first being deficiencies in the prerequisite knowledge of the pupils, the second comprising the prior possession by pupils both of incorrect knowledge, misconceptions and alternative frameworks, which actively block learning, and of correct knowledge, which because it is not adequately distinguished from newly taught information, causes interference. The third group comprises deficiencies in the teaching material and its presentation.

Deficiencies Which Impede Learning

The major theories of cognitive learning and development, those of Ausubel, Gagné and Piaget, acknowledge, although in different ways, that the learning of new tasks is critically dependent on the learner's possession of appropriate knowledge or skills. The results of our objective tests and interviews indicated that one of the most potent sources of pupil difficulty was the lack of mastery of basic concepts. Of the hundreds of pupils tested, only a minority was judged (Arnold and Simpson, 1982; Simpson and Arnold, 1982) to have gained the knowledge prerequisite to an understanding of the more complex topics. Thus, the 50 per cent of pupils who did not know that all molecules of a given substance are exactly the same size would inevitably fail to gain an unambiguous understanding of the key prerequisite information for osmosis given in texts that 'the small water molecules pass readily through a semi-permeable membrane while the large sugar molecules do not.' Similarly, one in three of the pupils who were required to understand the gas exchange processes of photosynthesis described a gas and its properties in words and images identical to those used by primary pupils. We found serious inadequacies too in their concepts of living things, food and energy. These observations prompt two questions: why did the earlier courses fail to impart the knowledge which was prerequisite to a comprehension of the new material, and why were the new courses started without any test of the pupils' possession of that prerequisite knowledge?

In response to the first of these questions, it must be remarked that the early science courses (S1–S4) show signs of having been developed without any regard for well-established psychological theories of concept development, despite the expressed intention of the curriculum planners and course designers (Curriculum Paper No 7, 1969; Heinemann Teachers Guide, 1977) that whenever possible, concepts rather than facts should be taught. Much of the instructional material from which it is expected that pupils will develop concepts fits the description given by Markle (1975) as consisting of 'so-called concept presentations' in which learners are confronted with 'a definition that does not define very well, if at all, accompanied in most cases by an example or two that in no sense exemplifies....' Thus, in relation to the present studies, the understanding of diffusion and osmosis requires a well developed concept of the particulate nature of matter. Notwithstanding this, in none of the texts and worksheets purporting to teach this idea was there any attempt to aid development of the concept of matter by contrasting it with non-matter. It is hardly surprising that when one teacher, prompted by discussions with us, asked his biology class for examples of non-matter he received the reply 'living things, they are made of cells, not atoms and molecules.'

The thinking which appears to underlie most science courses up to and including O-grade, is that if a pupil engages in laboratory activities which are programmed to lead him to make a 'discovery', he will thereby gain a concept which will be more meaningful and stable than one gained by direct instruction. More meaningful and stable it may be, but not necessarily accurate and comprehensive. This kind of concept acquisition is perhaps more appropriately designated 'concept formation by experience' — a process recognized by psychologists to be slow and far from orderly and accurate (Bruner *et al.*, 1956; Ausubel *et al.*, 1978). Irrespective of the instructional method, the complex concepts of modern science will only be acquired with any speed and in an organized and accurate form if the structure of the concept is made explicit, e.g., its salient and non-salient critierical attributes are clearly emphasized and if possible interference from salient non-critierical attributes is specifically dealt with. We found many examples of confusions experienced by pupils in discriminating between osmosis and diffusion, and of errors in recognizing distinguishing character-istics, e.g., 'diffusion occurs only in gases', which we regard as attributable to a lack of formal concept instructional material to back up discovery learning.

In response to the second question, it seems that, despite their experience of pupils' performance on norm-referenced tests, teachers are content to proceed, or are forced to do so by the shortage of time, on the assumption that pupils know most of what they have been previously taught, and that, at most, only a brief period of revision is necessary. 'But they should have known that!' was the exasperated response of many teachers to the results of our tests which showed critical gaps in the pupils' knowledge. Moreover, although they may have abandoned the study of chemistry and/or physics, O-grade biology pupils need sound concepts, e.g., of liquids, solutions and pressure, from those subject areas. Teachers clearly thought it inappropriate that they spend time in the certificate biology course to advance their pupils' concepts to the necessary level of maturity. Appropriate or not, such an advancement is necessary if topics such as osmosis are to be understood.

The Presence of Knowledge Which Impedes Learning

The second group of sources of pupil difficulties in understanding photo-synthesis and osmosis is attributable to the pupils' possession of particular forms of erroneous ideas which blocked the learning of prescribed material, and to their correct and previously acquired knowledge, which, because it is not adequately distinguished from newly taught and different information, causes interference. The first of these derives from the fact, self-evident but seemingly surprising to many educators, that pupils do not know only what they are taught. 'But I didn't teach them that!' was a comment often voiced by teachers.

From both of our studies it became evident that teachers were unaware of many of the serious misconceptions of their pupils: none seemed to know that a large minority of certificate pupils (S3, 44 per cent; S4, 28 per cent) considered that carbon and carbohydrates were gases. This is probably because most classroom tests, whether norm or criterion-referenced, are not designed to detect whether pupils hold wrong information but to assess only assimilation of classroom presented material. The former can be detected only by detailed investigation or, considerably less expensively, by sensitive listening and response to pupils' discussions.

Some of the erroneous ideas of the pupils are to be classed as alternative frameworks (Driver and Easley, 1978), theories concerning the nature of events and processes which have been derived from the pupils' life experiences, observation and thought, and which are contrary to the taught scientific explanations. Teachers in our first study rated the concept that 'plants make their own food' as the most important idea to be taught in photosynthesis and as relatively easy for pupils to understand. We found that, on the contrary, despite having experienced two courses dealing with the topic of photosynthesis, one-third of fourth year certificate biology pupils retained the belief, held by most primary pupils, that plants obtain their food from the soil. In the second study, none of the certificate biology pupils interviewed spontaneously mentioned osmosis as the mechanism for water entering the plant root; the most commonly offered 'explanations' were naturalistic — e.g., 'plants suck up water because they need it.' Viennot (1979), Deadman and Kelly (1978) and Brumby (1979) similarly report that 'intuitive' schemes in physics and biology are commonly retained into college years and are frequently used in preference to the prescribed knowledge.

Further, equally complex erroneous ideas result from the incorporation of correctly learned material into the pupils' alternative frameworks. Thus, for example, 48 per cent of the S1 and S2 pupils had correctly learned that plants use a gas to make food, but had incorporated this into their belief as to the source of the plant's food and concluded that plants absorb that gas through their roots. Ausubel's theory of subsumption (Ausubel *et al.*, 1978) accounts for this process. The stability of these alternative frameworks is almost certainly due to the fact, noted by Ausubel, that the explanatory schemes worked out by the learner tend to be more meaningful to the individual than received explanations. Doubtless too, it reflects the fact that the presented explanations are abstract and demand formal levels of reasoning (Shayer, 1974), whereas the alternative frameworks are at a concrete level and are attractive in that they relate to analogies with the pupils' knowledge of themselves.

Other erroneous ideas arise as the result of the pupils' faulty association of correctly learned information and are to be regarded as the outcome of the active cognitive efforts of pupils to forge meaningful links between concepts. Thus, for example, pupils who had correctly learned that the body obtains its energy from food and that food is broken down by the process of digestion had linked these two ideas parsimoniously, but incorrectly, to attribute the release of energy from food to the process of digestion (S2, 47 per cent; S4, 32 per cent).

Little information is available on teaching strategies for the replacement of these kinds of erroneous ideas by the prescribed theories, but the first requirement is clearly that their existence be recognized. This may be effected by the adoption of a listening strategy in teaching, as already discussed, or by the use of specifically designed diagnostic tests such as those produced as a part of our study of the teaching of osmosis (Arnold and Simpson, 1981). Nussbaum and Novick (1981) have suggested that after a detailed exploration of their existing beliefs, and after being forced to consider the evidence which conflicts with those specific beliefs, pupils should be encouraged to 're-invent' more appropriate theories. We regard this as an application of the theory of conflict learning (Ginsberg and Opper, 1979) derived from Piaget's work.

Other confusions which we encountered are attributable to interference — the interaction of two separate but similar pieces of information (Hilgard *et al.*, 1979). Thus pupils were commonly found to confuse photosynthesis with respiration, both being energy conversion processes involving identical but opposite gas exchange. Interference could have been reduced if the pupils had been helped to separate information on the two processes, possibly by providing a mnemonic to aid coding. The quite distinct processes of digestion and osmosis also tended to be confused, doubtless because the same experimental apparatus had been used to demonstrate the salient features of both. In this case interference could have been prevented had the experimental model been used for only one of the two processes until the pupils had gained sufficient information on both to avoid confusion.

Deficiencies in the Teaching Material

In the study of pupil difficulties in learning osmosis we noted unfortunate aspects of the way in which it was taught at O-grade. Many criticisms of the way in which intrinsically difficult topics are taught may be traced, ultimately, to a lack of agreement on the reasons for the inclusion of those topics in the curriculum and on the exact teaching aims. If it is regarded as essential that pupils understand precisely *how* osmosis occurs, an explanatory model is necessary. Johnstone and Mahmoud (1980) are undoubtedly correct in asserting that the topic should not be taught and indeed is not understandable at an explanatory level without reference to concepts, e.g., that of intermolecular forces, which are notably absent from the biology model. In practical support of this, they have produced teaching aids which include animated film, to assist the teaching of the essential details of this dynamic process. The assessment of Shayer (1974), however, indicates that an explanatory model of osmosis in terms of molecular movement requires for its comprehension a level of formal reasoning unlikely to have been fully attained by more than a minority of 16-year-old pupils (Shayer and Wylam, 1977). If, in view of these claims, it is regarded as more appropriate that pupils at this stage merely become aware of the phenomenon of water movement and learn to derive and to apply empirical rules for it, a purely descriptive model of the process is adequate. It seems to us that in adopting an objective mid-way between these two positions, biology teachers have been forced to use simplifications, conceptual fictionalizations such as the ideas that solute molecules dissolve by fitting into the spaces between water molecules and that sugar molecules do not cross a semi-permeable membrane (MacKean, 1978). It should be recognized that the formulation of such simplifications demands of teachers a great deal more care and precision of thought in lesson presentation than is required for instruction in material which is more in accord with the teachers' own more mature concepts. Our study revealed abundant evidence of a lack of this necessary care and precision in the teaching of osmosis. The texts and worksheets contained inconsistencies and ambiguities, 'facts' which, given the restrictions of the chosen simplified model, were logically absurd, and showed evidence of commuting between alternative and mutually incompatible models. Simplification by omission is a legitimate, even an essential teaching strategy. Fictionalizations are of much more doubtful validity and there is, moreover, little evidence to suggest that concrete 'props' used for an extended period to facilitate understanding at an early age can readily be abandoned when the pupil is required to advance to more accurate and abstract concepts. Their use is a response to the requirements of teaching this topic at a stage in the curriculum which we consider to be premature. Criticisms have also been made of the premature teaching of difficult topics in chemistry and physics (Dow *et al.*, 1978; Physics Teacher, 1980). Bruner's dictum that 'any subject can be taught effectively in some intellectually honest form to any child at any stage of development' (Bruner, 1966) ought to be regarded as a dangerous precept of classroom teaching until appropriate simplifications have been developed and the process of their necessary later replacement by complex concepts investigated.

Conclusions

The two research projects reviewed in this paper were funded by the Scottish Education Department and had the defined aims of investigating the origins of learning difficulties and of providing teaching aids and diagnostic procedures in two particular areas of school biology, osmosis and photosynthesis, which were manifestly difficult for O-grade pupils. Since the sources of pupil difficulty which we uncovered can in no way be described as peculiar to these topics or to pupils at O-grade, we believe that our finding should be regarded as relevant to all teaching areas and to pupils of all levels of ability. There is indeed nothing new in our observations as far as cognitive psychology is concerned. Much is known about the necessity of linking new knowledge to old if meaningful rather than rote learning is to take place (Ausubel *et al.*, 1978), about the way in which concepts develop and are structured (Bruner *et al.*, 1956; Klausmeier, 1976), about the development of reasoning skills in children (Inhelder and Piaget, 1958) and the need to match these with the level of reasoning demanded by particular learning tasks (Shayer and Adey, 1981). What is new is the practical demonstration that when these important principles of learning are disregarded by specialist teachers in the selection of the material for teaching or in its presentation, widespread learning difficulties will occur even among able and selected pupils.

In the seminars in which we have presented our findings, the response of biology teachers has been positive and attentive, as if we were offering entirely new insights. Yet the same teachers, in the compulsory psychology course which was part of their professional training, had been instructed in the principles we were advancing, though undoubtedly at a general level and not extensively in their particular subject area. Perhaps in college education as in school, the general should be exemplified by the specific and made relevant in practice.

The need for a closer examination of the expression of psychological principles in subject content areas is being increasingly recognized both by educationalists and reseach workers (Head, 1982; Stewart *et al.*, 1982). The guidelines produced by the Advisory Committee on the proposed Diploma in Learning Difficulties and approved by the Joint Committee of the Colleges of Education in Scotland (JCC, 1981) acknowledge that the scope of learning difficulties is much wider than has been hitherto recognized and that many difficulties may arise because of the way in which the curriculum is designed and presented. It is envisaged (SED, 1978) that in their consultative role, holders of this diploma should be in a position to alert subject teachers to the full range of different causes of learning difficulties and advise in the diagnostic process. We believe that if they are to be effective in this role they will need to recognize that pupil difficulties are not infrequently attributable to the subject content and its presentation and that their prevention requires the practical expression of cognitive learning theories in the classroom. It is hoped that the studies of the teaching of topics in physics by Mr W. Dow of Dundee College of Education, in chemistry by Dr A. Johnstone and his collaborators at Glasgow University, and in biology by ourselves in Aberdeen will contribute to that recognition process and may help to form the much needed bridge between psychology and science teaching in secondary schools.

References

ARNOLD, B. and SIMPSON, M. (1980) *An Investigation of the Development of the Concept of Photosynthesis to SCE 'O' Grade*, Aberdeen, Aberdeen College of Education.

ARNOLD, B. and SIMPSON, M. (1981) *Diagnostic Testing for Pupil Difficulties in Osmosis: A Teachers' Handbook*, Aberdeen College of Education.

ARNOLD, B. and SIMPSON, M. (1982) *Concept Development and Diagnostic Testing — Osmosis in 'O' Grade Biology*, Aberdeen College of Education.

AUSUBEL, D.P. *et al.* (1978) *Educational Psychology: A Cognitive View*, 2nd ed., Holt, Rinehart and Winston.

BARNES, B.R. and CLAWSON, E.U. (1975) 'Do advance organisers facilitate learning? Recommendations for further research based on an analysis of 32 studies', *Review of Educational Research*, 45, 4, pp. 637–59.

Mary Simpson and Brian Arnold

BENDER, S. and MILAKOFSKY, L. (1982) 'College chemistry and Piaget: The relationship of aptitude and achievement measures', *Journal of Research in Science Teaching*, 19, 3, pp. 205–16.

BLOOM, B.S. *et al.* (1956) *Taxonomy of Educational Objectives*, New York, David McKay Co.

BRUMBY, M. (1979) 'Problems in learning the concept of natural selection', *Journal of Biological Education*, 13, 2, pp. 119–22.

BRUNER, J.S. (1966) *The Process of Education*, Cambridge Mass., Harvard University Press.

BRUNER, J.S. *et al.* (1956) *A Study of Thinking*, London, Wiley.

DEADMAN, J.A. and KELLY, P.J. (1978). 'What do secondary school boys understand about evolution and heredity before they are taught the topics?' *Journal of Biological Education*, 12, 1, pp. 7–15.

DOW, W.M. *et al* (1978) *Pupils' Concepts of Gases, Liquids and Solids*, Dundee, Dundee College of Education.

DRIVER, R. and EASLEY, J. (1978) 'Pupils and paradigms: A review of literature related to concept development in adolescent science students', *Studies in Science Education*, 5, pp. 61–84.

GILL, J. (1980) 'A simplified experimental scheme for the study of mitosis', *Journal of Biological Education*, 14, 3, pp. 219–22.

GINSBURG, H. and OPPER, S. (1979) *Piaget's Theory of Intellectual Development* 2nd ed., Prentice Hall.

HEAD, J. (1982) 'What can psychology contribute to science education?' *School Science Review*, 63, 225, pp. 631–41.

HEINEMANN, SCOTTISH INTEGRATED SCIENCE (1977) *Teachers Guide*, London, Heinemann Educational Books.

HILGARD, E.R. *et al.* (1979) *Introduction to Psychology*, 7th ed., New York, Harcourt Brace Jovanovich.

INHELDER, B. and PIAGET, J. (1958) *The Growth of Logical Thinking from Childhood to Adolescence*, New York, Basic Books.

JOHNSTONE, A.H. and MAHMOUD, N.A. (1980) 'Isolating topics of high perceived difficulty in school biology', *Journal of Biological Education*, 14, 2, pp. 163–6.

JOINT COMMITTEE OF COLLEGES OF EDUCATION IN SCOTLAND (1981) *Proposed Diploma in Learning Difficulties*, submission by the Advisory Committee to the Committee of Principals, mimeo.

JONES, G.A. (1982) 'The mechanics of osmosis — an alternative theory with working model', *The School Science Review*, 63, 224, pp. 479–83.

KLAUSMEIER, H.J. (1976) 'Conceptual development during the school years', in LEVIN, J.R. and ALLAN, V.L. (Eds) *Cognitive Learning in Children: Theories and Strategies*, Academic Press.

MACKEAN, D.G. (1978) *Introduction to Biology*, colour ed., London, John Murray.

MARKLE, S.M. (1975) 'They teach concepts don't they?', *Educational Researcher*, 4, pp. 3–9.

NUSSBAUM, J. and NOVICK, S. (1981) 'Brainstorming in the classroom to invent a model: A case study', *School Science Review*, 62, 221, pp. 771–8.

OKEY, J.R. and GAGNÉ, R.M. (1970) 'Revision of a science topic using evidence of performance on subordinate skills', *Journal of Research in Science Teaching*, 7, 4, pp. 321–5.

PHYSICS TEACHER (1980) 'Too much, too fast, too soon', *Physics Teacher*, 18, Editorial.

SCOTTISH EDUCATON DEPARTMENT (1969) *Curriculum Paper No. 7. Science for General Education: For the First Two Years and the Early School Leaver*, Edinburgh, HMSO.

SCOTTISH EDUCATION DEPARTMENT (1978) *Progress Report on the Education of Pupils with Learning Difficulties*, Edinburgh, HMSO.

SHAYER, M. (1974) 'Conceptual demands in the Nuffield "O" Level Biology Course', *School Science Review*, 56, pp. 381–8.

SHAYER, M. and ADEY, P. (1981) *Towards a Science of Science Teaching: Cognitive Development and Curriculum Demand*, London, Heinemann.

SHAYER, M. and WYLAM, H. (1977) 'Development in thinking of middle and secondary school pupils', *School Science Review*, 59, 207, pp. 377–8.

SIMPSON, M. and ARNOLD, B. (1982) 'Availability of prerequisite concepts for learning biology at certificate level', *Journal of Biological Education*, 16, 1, pp. 65–72.

STEWART, J. *et al.* (1982) 'Science content as an important consideration in science education research', *Journal of Research in Science Teaching*, 19, 5.

VIENNOT, L. (1979) 'Spontaneous reasoning in elementary dynamics', *European Journal of Science Education*, 6, 2, pp. 205–21.

Question Difficulty and the Concept of Attainment*

Noel Entwistle and Carolyn Hutchinson
University of Edinburgh

In Scotland at present a new system of examination at 16+ is being planned. Previously pupils took an O-grade examination. Over the next few years a new system will be introduced which involves three levels (Foundation, General and Credit). A recent research study has been looking at differences in the difficulty levels of O-grade questions in an attempt to provide guidance to subject panels in setting papers at the highest of these three levels (Credit). This involved, to begin with, an attempt to clarify the concept of 'attainment' as it might be used by the examiners, and to describe the different levels of attainment that might be recognized in pupils' answers.

The Concept of Attainment

The concept of attainment is rarely discussed explicitly. It has to be inferred from the syllabus laid down, from the topics commonly included in the examinations, and from the types of questions asked. The questions may make very different intellectual demands on candidates. Indeed the form of the question may have been specifically chosen to make particular demands, perhaps using the familiar Bloom taxonomy with its classification into 'knowledge', 'comprehension', 'analysis', 'synthesis' and 'evaluation'.

In considering the concept of attainment appropriate to the proposed Credit Level, examiners are faced with an even more tenuous definition than is implicit in previous examination syllabuses and papers. The Dunning Report (1977) indicated only that the pupils taking Credit Level would be those who would be expected to sit 'Higher' the following year. The target

* This article comprises edited extracts from *Attainment at Different Ability Levels: An Analysis of 'O' Grade Questions and Answers*, Final Report to the Scottish Education Department, submitted by the Godfrey Thomson Unit, University of Edinburgh, 1983. A revised version was subsequently been published by Scottish Academic Press (1984) under the title *What Makes Exam Questions Difficult?*

population could thus be envisaged as involving up to the top 20 per cent of pupils in any school subject. Our task in identifying difficult questions among the O-grade papers could be seen as helping to clarify the concept of Credit Level attainment by providing a set of potentially appropriate questions. But without defined syllabuses for Credit Level we would necessarily have to rely more on question type than on content in outlining the likely meaning of a Credit Level pass.

Inevitably the description of Credit Level as being taken by the top fifth of the age group, and the experience that pupils going on to Highers are likely to get consistently high grades in the 16+ examination, suggests that questions at Credit Level should be designed for pupils of high intelligence. The problem in translating this idea into appropriate examination questions is that 'intelligence' has traditionally been defined in terms of intellectual skills which are intended to be 'content free'. A typical 'intelligence' test will demand from the pupil the ability to undertake logical analysis at speed, to grasp relationships quickly, to spot absurdities, illogicalities or non-sequiturs, to make valid generalizations, and to think effectively in terms of abstract concepts when necessary. Questions which explicitly demand these skills would not be accepted as valid indicators of 'attainment' which is necessarily content-bound, at least to some extent. The alternative reliance on Bloom's categories is also unsatisfactory as these provide too little indication of the thought processes or specific skills involved in the different subject areas.

Research on Levels of Children's Thinking

One way forward towards defining attainment at different levels is through Piaget's ideas on the development of the intellect through a series of distinctive stages. Children's thinking follows a sequence during the school years from what is termed *pre-operational*, where the child is dominated by immediate visual impressions, first to *concrete operations* and a recognition of relationships between the properties of concrete concepts or material objects, and gradually to *formal operations* during which the hypothetico-deductive thinking characteristic of the scientist begins to emerge. Only in the adolescent years do children become capable of consistently dealing with relationships between abstract concepts, and of thinking systematically about complex abstract problems. Even then not all children seem to reach these levels of thinking. The recent work of Shayer (Shayer *et al.*, 1976; Shayer and Adey, 1981) has indicated that only some 20 per cent of 14-year-olds in a large national sample could be classified as using formal operational thinking on Piagetian tasks.

Piaget's theory was developed out of simple scientific experiments, yet implications were extended to education across the whole curriculum. These simple extrapolations were largely unjustified and misleading. It was left to

Peel and several generations of students working with him at Birmingham to explore systematically the types of thinking exhibited by pupils in a variety of content areas. Peel (1971) asked adolescents to read a short passage or consider a problem, and then to answer a question designed to test understanding. Pupils' responses could usually be categorized into one of three main types:

Mentioning — tautological, partial, or inconsistent responses

Describing — a mainly correct listing of aspects of the passage

Explaining — responses which used additional related ideas to interpret the meaning of the passage.

A more developed form of explanation was found in the responses to some of the passages which Peel characterized as 'a capacity to combine more than one piece of evidence with outside ideas and to evoke cause and effect' (p. 25).

An example may make the meaning of Peel's categories clearer. In geography pupils were provided 'with demographic charts setting out the problem facing crofter farmers in the Isle of Lewis. No text was used but maps were provided showing the essential geographical features of the island and bringing out the generally poor quality of the land. Charts were also provided, showing the proportion and nature of crops as against pasture and the number of sheep and cattle. Rainfall and temperature charts were also included' (Peel, 1971, p. 90). The pupils were asked, 'Are the crofters making the best use of their land by growing crops only over such a small area?' Peel comments that satisfactory answers depend on the pupil resolving 'the conflict between the land apparently available and unused and its quality, and he needs to consider the grazing habits of the animals.' Typical answers were reported as follows:

i Personal, tautological answers: 'Yes, because they've got the beauty of the deer in the forest', 'They're making good use of their land.'

ii Seizure of *one* piece of visual evidence: 'If they didn't have so many animals, they could have more crops.'

iii The beginning of taking account of more than one factor: 'Yes, because he does not need too many crops. The more pasture he has the better his sheep and cattle are fed.'

iv A detailed, systematic appraisal of the difficulties presented to the crofters by their restricted environment:

The crofters are sensible in growing only a few crops over a little area because the ground is mainly mountains and very rough. It would be hard to get the necessary amount of crops needed to feed the crofters, the only crops which they have cultivated with a little success are the hardier, tougher crops, oats and potatoes. The land can be made of better use by rough grazing with sheep on the hills and mountains.

I think they are using their land to full extent because what they can't grow, they can get by selling the fish that they catch, to other places far inland who cannot fish for their own fish. Also on the rough ground they can graze their cattle and sheep from which they can obtain milk and also meat. From the milk they can make their own butter and cheese. What cereals and vegetables cannot be grown, can be imported from nearby Scotland. (Peel, 1971, pp. 90–1)

A more fully developed category system has been described by Sutherland (1982) who had carried out similar analyses of responses to biological questions. She used eight categories:

0   completely naive (unaware)
1   pre-describer (grossly inaccurate or irrelevant)
2   elementary describer (very simple and limited description)
3   describer (some grasp of underlying concepts)
4   extended describer (use of abstract concepts but not as explanations)
5   transitional (occasional flashes of explanation)
6   explainer (full explanations in conceptual rather than perceptual terms)
7   theoretical (or extended) explainer (explanation in terms of theory and deduction from evidence).

Peel and his students describe these different categories in terms of a series of developmental stages in adolescent thinking — and, in part, this interpretation is justified. The quality of answers is related to both chronological and mental age. Thus the four categories of response to the question about farming in Lewis are linked to average (chronological plus mental) ages of 10.8, 12.2, 13.7, and 15.6 respectively (Peel, 1971, p. 92). But Peel recognized that the range of categories identified and the distribution of responses were also affected by the nature of the passage or subject area, and by the specific form of the questions asked. Providing more information or guidance in the passage, or using more directive questions ('Why do you think so?'), produced a higher proportion of explanations among the answers. It is thus possible to see Peel's work either as an extension of Piaget's work on stages in intellectual development or as the first step towards a systematic classification of the responses to fairly open questions.

Qualitative Differences in Answers

In a recent theoretical paper Marton (1981) argues persuasively that we should distinguish the utility of recognizing different *categories* of thinking in relation to a particular task from the much less tenable assumption that we can classify children or adults within that same classification system. Karplus (1981), arguing in terms of reasoning patterns observed in school, has reached a similar conclusion. 'We propose classifying the application of a reasoning pattern, rather than the developmental level of an individual' (p. 289). It makes sense, then, to describe the quality of the thinking underlying pupils' responses to particular questions in terms of categories, as long as we do not move on to the assumption that a similar level would necessarily be found in the answers to other topics or to other subjects. Marton and Karplus are both challenging not only the use of the term stage, but also implicitly the concept of general intelligence. They imply that performance levels should be *expected* to vary across different tasks and contrasting subject areas.

In his empirical studies, Marton investigated how students approached the task of reading an academic article, and examined the range of understanding exhibited in students' answers to questions presented immediately afterwards (Marton and Säljö, 1976). He classified the approaches as deep (actively seeking understanding through personal rein-terpretation of the author's argument, evidence and meaning) and surface (concentration on the text itself, allied to attempts to memorize facts or isolated ideas, subsequently to be reproduced verbatim). He also introduced the idea of describing the range of answers emerging in terms of an *outcome space*. Once it is accepted that, for understanding, it is necessary to reinterpret incoming information in relation to a person's unique cognitive store of knowledge, experience, interest and attitudes, it becomes inevitable to accept that attempts to communicate that understanding would show wide *qualitative* differences. There would, of course, be differences in levels of understanding representing more or less adequate coverage of the author's intended argument and meaning — but at any one level there should also be expected to be wide differences in the types of answer presented. For certain purposes it may make sense to assess knowledge quantitatively in terms of the number of 'bits' of knowledge reproduced on demand. But it would never, within the Martonian framework, make sense to describe *understanding* in such terms. Understanding, with its personal reinterpretation and integration, cannot be adequately described in terms of the accretion of component parts. It can, however, still be conceptualized in terms of a two-, three-, or even multi-dimensional outcome space. In one two-dimensional form it is possible to envisage answers varying horizontally in terms of the personal linkages used to exhibit a particular level of understanding, and vertically to represent different degrees of adequacy *in relation to the question asked.*

The ideas of 'outcome space' and 'levels of understanding' can be readily applied to Peel's work. Mentioning, describing and explaining — each represents a qualitatively different response to questions about a prose passage or problem. They also provide the beginnings of a conceptual framework against which to compare the characteristics of questions at O-grade which pupils find difficult. A further refinement and extension of Peel's research became available half-way through our study and influenced the interpretation of our findings. Biggs and Collis (1982) have developed a set of categories, called SOLO (Structure of Observed Learning Outcomes), specifically designed to indicate qualitative differences in the responses to questions set. Their approach was based on ideas on human information processing applied to an analysis of students' essays (Schroder *et al.*, 1967). Their classification system has been built around four main categories relating to 'the way an individual receives, stores, processes and transmits information'. At the *uni-structural* level there is little recognition of a problem: an immediate, oversimple and usually erroneous answer is provided after little or no reflection, almost as a reflex response to a stimulus. When two or more aspects are recognized (*multi-structural*), these are presented without recognition or acknowledgement of possible links or contradictions between them and so lead to incomplete, conflicting, or inconsistent judgments. *Relational* responses point out and attempt to resolve conflicts, and show how similar ideas are related. They fall short, however, of the most sophisticated category of responses, *extended abstract*, which provide explanations and develop into generalized statements drawing on a wide range of relevant information and theoretical ideas. These four categories parallel closely the categories described independently by both Peel and Marton, and again can be understood better through a particular example.

Biggs and Collis (1982) report responses to the following historical passage (pp. 41–3). The responses come from pupils and students differing widely in both age and ability.

The Norman Conquest of England

In 1066 William of Normandy defeated the Anglo-Saxons at the Battle of Hastings. A Norman soldier wrote: 'It would have been just as if wolves and vultures had devoured the flesh of these English....' But such a fate seemed cruel to the duke and he allowed all who wished to do so to collect the bodies for burial.

The Normans soon conquered the rest of England but in 1069 the English in the North obtained help from the Danes: The Danes sailed up the Humber with 240 ships. York was captured and its Norman garrison killed. The Danes then returned to Denmark so William was able to reconquer the North of England. He carried out a terrible revenge upon the English. Many houses and cottages were burnt; the animals were killed or driven away; most of the people, perhaps the more fortunate, were killed; some fled to other parts of England but of those that remained the greater part died of famine. A man who lived at that time wrote: 'Men, women, and children died of hunger: They laid them down and died in the roads and fields, and there was no man to bury them. . . .' Between York and Durham every town stood empty, and in their streets lurked only robbers and wild beasts.

Question: Do you think William was cruel?

Besides the four categories mentioned above, Biggs and Collis here had to use a 'pre-structural' category to cover the lowest level of response.

Pre-structural: Pupil fails to see the problem; shows no felt need for consistency; is bound by specifics: 'Yes, he shouldn't have killed them', 'Yes, you shouldn't be cruel.'

Uni-structural: Only one relevant datum is used; shows no felt need for consistency; jumps to conclusions; can 'generalize' only in terms of only one aspect: 'I think William was cruel because it says that men, women, and children died everywhere'; 'I think William was cruel because it said that he carried out a terrible revenge'; 'No, he wasn't cruel really because he did let them bury the dead people.'

Multi-structural: Uses isolated pieces of relevant data; shows some consistency but 'closes' too soon; generalizes in terms of a few independent aspects: 'Yes, I think William was cruel because it says he carried out a terrible revenge, burning the houses and killing the people and the animals'; 'Most of them were only innocent people and there was no need to burn everything.'

Relational: Shows evidence of induction; is consistent within the information provided but makes no reference to data not explicitly relevant; generalizes within these data effectively to reach a single 'closed' conclusion: 'William was cruel because he destroyed the land and caused a famine but the English and the Danes had destroyed his garrison. He also allowed the people to collect the bodies of the people they wanted to bury.' [What does this prove then?] 'He could be cruel in winning a battle but after the battle was over he could allow the people a little more scope.'

Extended Abstract: Uses induction and deduction as appropriate; inconsistencies fully resolved; uses additional data peripheral but relevant to defined context to reach appropriate generalizations; reaches open conclusions which recognize alternative interpretations:

It depends on what you call cruel. If the definition of *cruel* is to kill and ravage and burn for any purpose whatever, William was cruel. On the other hand, if one is prepared to accept political necessity, William's cruelty was justified. Compared with many other feudal lords he was essentially a kind man. They ravaged generally for their own advantage and without care for the common folk or their land. Duke William, if the common people went with him, seems to have been prepared to protect the common people from ravages. If, however, they went against him he seems to have treated it as a deliberate breaking of faith and acted accordingly. So, by the standards of his own day, for we cannot really judge him by our standards, he was probably not a cruel man.

The work of Peel, Marton, and Biggs and Collis, is important to our own concerns in two main ways. It shows that it is possible to characterize qualitatively different levels of response to questions which demand explanation. One distinction between Credit and General may well involve more evidence of understanding and less reliance in mark schemes on just factual accuracy or 'coverage'. The research also provides a way of conceptualizing attainment which takes account both of the way the pupil constructs the answer out of the information available and of the intellectual skills utilized in reaching conclusions.

There are, however, limitations in applying these research findings to examination questions. These categorizations of outcome were based mainly on open questions, while examination questions tend to be mainly closed; they ask for answers which are more tightly limited by the question set. The previous research has paid little attention to the effects of question wording on the pupils' responses. Peel noted in a general way that there were identifiable effects. Biggs and Collis recognized that 'the wording of an item can exert an effect on the response' (1982, p. 177), but saw this only as a warning against 'poor wording'. In our work we have necessarily given equal weight to both question type and the range and variety of pupils' answers. As a result it has become clear how the content and form of an examination question can control the extent and nature of the outcome space made available to the pupil.

Question Difficulty and Question Characteristics

The analyses of pupils' responses to O-grade questions in English, French, geography, physics and mathematics enabled us to identify three main facets of difficulty and, within each of these, specific characteristics of the question which would affect its level of difficulty.

The three facets were described as follows:

1 *Subject or concept difficulty*, where one particular concept may be more difficult than another for an O-grade candidate to cope with;
2 *Process difficulty*, where a particular operation or sequence of operations demands manipulation of data at a level beyond the straightforward recall of specific learned items;
3 *Question-wording or stimulus difficulty*, where the guidance given to

candidates in directing their attention to a particular response, or the support given in terms of additional information or data, is either minimal or non-specific.

Within these three general categories, it is possible to suggest several more specific sources of difficulty in the questions set.

Subject or Concept Difficulty

(a) *Degree of familiarity.* The first source of difficulty may seem self-evident, that is, that the less familiar a word or concept to candidates, the more difficult it is likely to prove for them to use in answers. Less familiar items are likely to be those which are not central to the syllabus taught, and are therefore covered either only briefly, or only in a very specific context. Such items may include particular words or phrases in a language, which the candidate is unlikely to have used or encountered in a wide variety of written or spoken contexts and whose meaning is not easily guessed by comparison with more familiar language, or particular concepts in mathematics or properties in chemistry which again are not used repeatedly in a number of different operations or experiments and not easily derived from the familiar core of the subject. Such words and concepts could therefore be described as peripheral to the central core of the curriculum, in that the candidate's frame of reference for them will be somewhat limited.

(b) *Abstractness of mode.* The second difficulty, closely related to the first, derives from the degree to which a particular idea is expressed in terms which have to be translated by the candidate into a form with which he can operate effectively. In mathematics this may involve decoding abstract notation until he can 'see' in his mind's eye the operation which he has to perform; in language, it may involve translating a metaphor into literal terms, or understanding how the encoding of an idea in idiomatic French may be expressed in English. In that these 'encodings' are a degree removed from the pupil's experience, this could also be seen as a problem of familiarity, since greater experience of such encoding may ultimately make it possible for the pupil to operate at the encoded level without the need to 'translate' for himself. Perhaps such a competence could even be said to represent a level of achievement in a particular subject.

(c) *Abstractness of idea.* The third difficulty concerns the abstractness of the idea or concept involved in the question. In chemistry, the question may require the candidate to create for himself a picture of something he has never seen, and probably will never see; in language papers, it may require an understanding of an abstract noun or phrase, the shade of whose meaning is affected by the context of the passage.

Process Difficulty

The second facet of difficulty is concerned not with the ideas under examination in a question, but with the operations a candidate is being asked to perform with those ideas, with the nature of the information-processing tasks he is being set. Our analyses suggested the following sources of process difficulty:

(a) *Explaining.* The need to explain a phenomenon in the terms of a particular subject seemed to be more difficult to candidates than simply describing it, as Peel has suggested. In chemistry, or geography, this might involve explanation in scientific terms of the reason for a particular reaction or phenomenon, rather than a straightforward description of an experiment or geographical situation; in English, it might involve explaining the effect of a particular word or phrase in critical terms, rather than just demonstrating understanding of it. Such tasks also have a strong productive element and can be linked with the difficulties of composing an answer, discussed below.

(b) *Generalizing from data.* In this process, bits of information must be grouped logically; in geography it may involve identifying the common element between a number of facts or locations, which may be quite diverse in terms of logical or areal breadth. In mathematics, a generalization may be required to link a new example to a learned one; the practice item will be insufficient for the solution. A similar process seemed to be at work where questions in chemistry focused on classes of substances rather than specific chemicals, and candidates were required to identify the distinguishing features which constituted the 'class' and were therefore held in common. In English, the process might rather involve the identification of overall meaning or effect from a number of examples, say of description or dialogue, or finding a common adjective to describe a number of different things.

(c) *Selection of data relevant to general theme.* Linked to (b), and perhaps even the reverse side of the same coin, is the process of recognizing the relevance of a particular piece of data to the question as set, so that learned examples in any subject can be aptly used as illustrations in the particular circumstances outlined in the question; or new data can be judged as matching learned data and therefore presumed to have similar properties. This process may operate both where the learned data are stored in the candidate's memory and must be recalled for comparison, for example, in searching for the solution to a mathematical problem, or it may apply where a number of statements in a passage of language could be relevant to a particular argument, and need to be matched to the stated argument for relevance.

(d) *Identifying a principle from data.* One step beyond the generalizing process described in (b) above is the process of recognizing a general learned principle from one or more specific instances. In geography, for example, this may take the form of identifying a general geographical principle from a number of locations; while in English, it may be a question of making a judgment about a writer's style or intention from the evidence of a passage. Closely linked to this process is its corollary, (e).

(e) *Applying a principle to new data.* This process involves the use of a learned principle in the consideration or manipulation of a new set of data, where the principle is not given. Thus the solution to an unfamiliar mathematical problem may be found by applying a learned principle; in chemistry, the identification of an unknown substance or the prediction of unknown properties of an unfamiliar substance will involve the application of general chemical principles; similarly the application of learned principles will be involved if children are asked to predict the consequences of certain possible changes to a given geographical system. In English, learned conventions of style, structure and syntax must be applied to a particular piece of writing in order to make an informed judgment about meaning or effect; in translation from a foreign language, learned grammatical conventions will have to be applied to unfamiliar phrases or complex pieces of syntax in order to derive their meaning accurately.

(f) *Forming a strategy.* Whatever the cognitive processes involved in answering an exam question, the task seems to be made more difficult for candidates if they must devise for themselves a strategy for answering, from their own resources. This may involve a number of the processes already discussed, as they select an appropriate route to travel along, from identifying the task to writing the answer. In mathematics, it may be a series of calculation steps or transformations, while in chemistry it may be the design of an experiment to prove a particular point. In English, it may involve expressing an original personal point of view using illustrations from a passage, and communicating it effectively to the reader through the logical structuring of the response. A similar process also seems to be demanded where candidates in French are required to write in French to express ideas which have only a tenuous link with those of the passage, and must therefore be highly selective about their use of the language in the passage as a resource for their response.

(g) *Composing an answer.* Closely linked to (f), and an extension of it, is the difficulty presented to a candidate where the language or information in the question and/or text or diagram cannot be used as a resource, and he must therefore compose an answer using his own appropriate words, expressions and diagrams in an acceptably structured way. This process seemed to apply to all our subjects with the exception of mathematics, and should be regarded as a general linguistic skill rather than a subject-specific problem. It should also be said that clumsy expression in geography or chemistry may not demonstrate lack of attainment in that subject, but rather quite specific difficulties of a productive nature which the examiner had not necessarily intended to test.

(h) *Cumulative difficulty.* In all our subjects, difficulty was affected by the number of steps required to arrive at an adequate response, since each step represented a point of potential error. This was true both where the discrete steps to be performed were made explicit to the candidate, and where he had to design his own answer strategy; the steps are likely in such cases to involve a variety of different processes of varying difficulty, each dependent to an extent on the previous one.

(i) *Need for monitoring, logical consistency.* In some cases, the cumulative difficulty described above had the added effect of diverting candidates' attention from the overall logic suggested by the question or the data. Thus a mathematical slip in a series of steps might lead to an answer which should be seen to be inconsistent with a reasonable outcome, but the complexity of the preceding task leads the candidate to 'close' too soon in Biggs' and Collis' terms, and fail to perform the final step of monitoring the logical consistency of his answer. A similar problem might arise in chemistry in remembering to report the result of a calculation in the appropriate units for example, and in both English and French language papers, where an error in interpretation or translation of an extended piece of language should be seen to be unreasonable in the light of overall meaning and context, or indeed just commonsense.

Question-Wording or Stimulus Difficulty

One of the weaknesses in the taxonomies mentioned, when they are applied to assessment, is that they tend not to take into account the wording of the question and the extent to which it directs candidates' attention to a particular approach or particular bits of information: in Marton's terms, this could be described as the extent to which question wording delimits 'outcome space' for the candidate. It was in this dimension that we found the most easily identifiable correspondence across subjects, perhaps because certain styles and traditions in the wording of questions tend to be applied whatever the subject matter.

The relationship between the question wording and the processes required of the candidates is of course extremely close, but it is by no means as simple as may be at first thought. In some cases a question may appear to demand of candidates the ability to apply their understanding of principles in a new context, but unintended cues or clues may obviate that need. In others, an apparently simple request for description may be marked in such a way that literary skills become more important than knowledge of the subject.

(a) *Open/closed response.* In all subjects, the greater the possibilities open to the candidate, the more difficult the question, since the candidate is then left to design for himself an appropriate strategy for answering, to select data and to construct a response; there will not be a 'right' answer, and responses are marked for qualities beyond the level of basic information. For example, there may be several acceptable ways to demonstrate the chemical properties of a substance; marks will be awarded on the basis not only of strategy, but also on the 'scientificness' of the approach and its logical consistency. In English, a candidate may be asked for his own reaction to a piece of writing; his answer will be marked for the way in which he supports his opinion in a critically acceptable mode.

(b) *Leaders, cues, clues.* Most of the questions which our sample found relatively 'easy' gave considerable support in that their wording directed candidates to particular data, or gave additional information of some sort. Supports might take the form of 'leaders', which actually told the candidate something new about a problem or set of data; 'key' words might refer him to a precise piece of data or word in the text or diagram; subdivision of the question into small bits might suggest an answer structure or a pattern of discrete steps towards a solution. Often such supports include specific instructions about what to include or exclude from an answer.

'Difficult' questions, on the other hand, tended not to give such support. The syntax of the question wording might superficially suggest a single task where in fact two or more were required; and the candidate might need to decode the question before even attempting a response, where the vocabulary is technical or subject-specific. This type of question is likely to pose problems particularly where the mark-scheme demands a 'closed' response, a correct answer, to the question.

(c) *Tailoring of resources.* In all our subjects, a considerable amount of information was provided for candidates in one form or another. In geography, this might take the form of diagrams, maps or numerical data in charts and tables; the same type of information might appear in mathematics and chemistry. In language papers, the passages were the principle source of data, along with the questions themselves, which by their chronological and logical arrangement might be extremely helpful. This particularly applied in French, where questions in English provided a skeleton translation of interpretation passages.

However, it was not necessarily the case that the more data provided, the easier the question, since the provision of 'untailored' data meant that the candidate had to select only what was relevant, or make reasoned judgments about its significance. In the language papers, this might mean sorting out for himself the chronological sequence of events, or searching across a whole passage for the answer to a particular question.

(d) *Provision of answer structure.* Closely corresponding to (g) above, *Composing an answer*, is the extent to which the structuring of a question suggests the structure of an answer. This may simply be the separation of discrete tasks into easily distinguished and separate sentences or phrases in the question; or it may be their labelling as (a), (b), (c), etc. Such features suggest, for example, paragraphing and physical layout for an answer. Where, on the other hand, the syntax of the question is relatively complex and unstructured, candidates are required to provide their own logical structure. As has already been suggested, examiners should perhaps be aware of this extra burden on candidates, and consider carefully whether or not they wish to assess such a skill in the context of 16+ examinations.

Illegitimate Difficulty

As a general rule, any of the features described above could be regarded as illegitimate if it was not both intended by the question setter, and marked accordingly. For example, a question which seeks to test a candidate's ability to explain something, but unintentionally tests strategy, may be regarded as only partly valid.

Several more specific problems were identified during the course of the research:

1 An apparently 'open' question was marked for specific details, and the mark scheme was therefore over-explicit about the anticipated response. This happened, for example, in one or two chemistry and geography questions where the question appeared to allow a candidate freedom to devise his own strategy, but in practice no such freedom was allowed.

2 Closely related to the above was the problem of an apparent mismatch between number of marks allocated and mark scheme, in that either candidates apparently misinterpreted the amount of information or the number of points required, or markers did not use the full range of marks available to them.

3 Apparently unintended cues or clues were given to candidates, so that what appeared to be a difficult task was in fact by-passed by candidates, a sort of illegitimate ease. The reverse happened when the answer to a question depended partly on non-subject specific knowledge, for example, in one French interpretation passage where candidates did not know that a bus could be started by pressing a button rather than turning a key.

4 Questions were marked for style and fluency or communicative ability where the intention was apparently to test knowledge or understanding of a concept, or understanding of words and phrases.

5 The question depended on knowledge of a word, concept, instance, experiment or experience likely to be unfamiliar to some candidates, but familiar to others; that is, dependent on the particular experiences given to pupils by their particular teacher. If the answer could be derived from knowledge or principles in the core of the syllabus, then the difficulty could be considered valid.

Controlling Question Difficulty

The stated aim of this research was to identify the features that determine the difficulty of 'O' grade questions to help subject panels set effective questions at Credit Level. However, the research may also prove useful in other examinations since the identification of the 'difficult' features of questions has increasingly emphasized for us the principle that the setting of good examination questions depends on gaining control of the processes involved in answering the questions set; controlling the 'outcome space' and the way that candidates come to define it for themselves; and ensuring a match between this and the examiner's own intended outcome space as explicit in the mark scheme. This control depends partly on an intimate knowledge of the subject to be examined as it is taught, but also on an understanding of the crucial effects of the wording and structuring of question papers on candidates' performance.

Figure 1 sets out the points at which the difficulty of a question may be affected by its various characteristics. Once the question setter has identified the particular concept, operation, phrase or piece of information he wishes to test, he has a number of options open to him:

1   The wording of his question will determine the 'outcome space' expected of the candidate. This may be 'closed' in that only one answer is deemed correct and it will be marked on a 1/0 basis; or it may be open, and marked accordingly for the appropriateness and quality of the response. Some questions may involve intermediates, or parts of both types. Two points should be emphasized:
    a   Question wording does not need to be complex even where the task involves a number of operations. The nature of the task should be made absolutely clear to candidates, to avoid misinterpretation of the task.
    b   It is essential to match the mark scheme to the question and to avoid assessing an open question as though it demanded a closed response.
2   The nature of the processes involved in answering will determine the basic difficulty of the question; but question setters can provide considerable support to candidates in the wording of the question, its logical and syntactic structure and extra information it presents. It may be possible to test a difficult process in such a way as to make it accessible to a very large proportion of candidates.
3   The question setter has at his disposal any number of potential pieces of additional information in the form of diagrams, tables, maps, charts, quotations, etc. Their inclusion as a resource for candidates may either prove supportive, where they are carefully tailored to suit the question; or they may add difficulty in that they are untailored and require processing before they can be used.

Figure 1: A Model of Question Construction

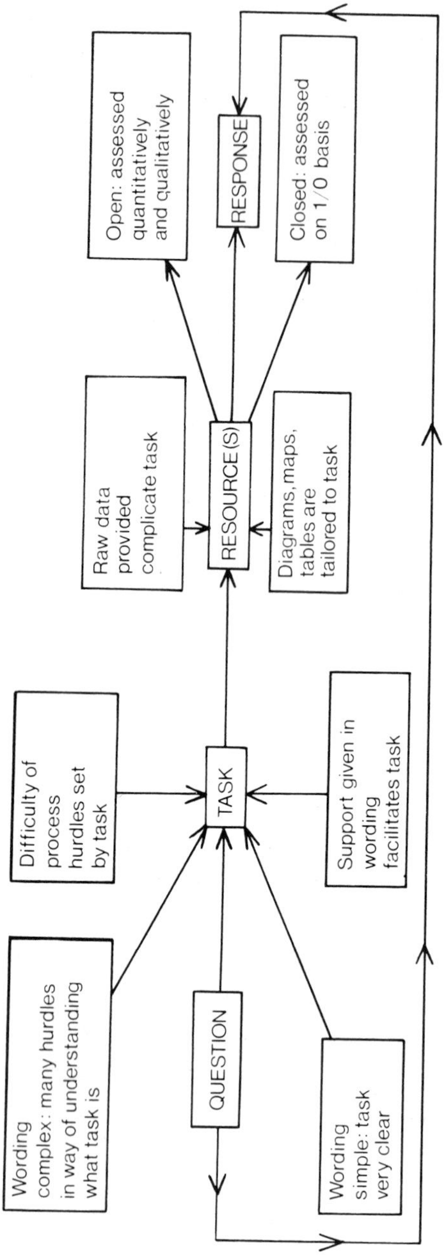

Again, the provision of tailored resources could potentially make a difficult process more accessible.

As these aspects of constructing questions become better understood, it may be possible to avoid distorting the original purpose of the question by providing too much or too little help to candidates. As question setters gain greater control of the questions they write, so the greater validity of the examination can be ensured.

Grade-Related Criteria

As has been suggested above, the question setter's greater control of the questions he sets may allow him to test a particular concept at a number of different levels, by adjusting the support given to candidates. If control of this type should prove in further studies to be feasible and reliable, then this would suggest that grade-related criteria could be linked not so much to the amount of ground covered by the syllabus, but more to the types of operations and levels of support given to candidates as they approach a particular concept. The differentiation would be qualitative rather than quantitative. Such an approach would also have implications for syllabus design, in that it would allow a relatively limited, largely common syllabus to be used across the ability range, with differentiation between levels made in terms of the level of pupil performance on particular tasks.

References

Biggs, J.B. and Collis, K.F. (1982) *Evaluating the Quality of Learning: The SOLO Taxonomy*, New York and London, Academic Press.

Bloom, B.S. *et al.* (1956) *Taxonomy of Educational Objectives: The Cognitive Domain*, New York, McKay.

Karplus, R. (1981) 'Education and formal thought: A modes proposal', in Sigel, I.E. *et al.* (Eds), *New Directions in Piagetian Theory and Practice*, New Jersey, Lawrence Erlbaum.

Marton, F. (1981) 'Phenomenography — describing conceptions of the world around us', *Instructional Science*, 10, pp. 177–200.

Marton, F. and Säljö, R. (1976) 'On qualitative differences in learning: 1 — Outcome and process', *Br. J. Educ. Psychol.*, 46, pp. 4–11.

Peel, E.A. (1971) *The Nature of Adolescent Judgement*, London, Staples Press.

Schroder, H.M. *et al.* (1967) *Human Information Processing*, New York, Holt, Rinehart and Winston.

SED (1977) *Assessment for All*, Report of the Committee to Review Assessment in the Third and Fourth Years of Secondary Education in Scotland (The Dunning Report), Edinburgh, HMSO.

Shayer, M. and Adey, P. (1981) *Toward a Science of Science Teaching*, London, Heinemann.

SHAYER, M. *et al.* (1976) 'The distribution of Piagetian stages of thinking in British middle and secondary school children', *Br. J. Educ. Psychol.*, 46, pp. 164–73.

SUTHERLAND, P.A.A. (1982) 'An expansion of Peel's describer-explainer stage theory', *Educational Rev.*, 34, pp. 69–76.

Item Banking and School Assessment

Alastair Pollitt
University of Edinburgh

Psychometrics and Standardized Testing

Through the principles and techniques of psychometrics, educational psychologists have in the past played a major role in educational assessment. Intelligence testing, for screening and guidance purposes, led the way in developing both the theory and the procedure for large-scale test production, epitomized in the standardized norm-referenced test.

The procedure for producing such a test involves:

1 Specification — choosing suitable content and question types to measure the ability in question;
2 Construction — several cycles of question writing and empirical trials, using statistical analysis to ensure the efficiency of the questions;
3 Formalization — final 'dress rehearsal' trials with the completed test to establish a standard procedure for administration;
4 Calibration — collection of results from a large representative sample of children to enable age-related norms to be produced;
5 Validation — collection of further data to establish that the test really does measure the ability in question.

This procedure enabled remarkably accurate measurements to be made of some mental traits. But it also tended to restrict the role of psychometrics in education to measuring general abilities or attainment over broad areas of subject matter, since the effort and expense involved could not be justified for the assessment of the content and objectives of a single unit of study which might be only a small part of a whole course. Standardized tests might be appropriate for *summative* assessment, that is, the testing of overall achievement at the end of a course (though even then only if there was a general consensus on the objectives of the course) but rarely for *formative* assessment, which is the frequent, small-scale testing of topics that have just been taught, for 'diagnostic' purposes. (See Popham (1978) for a fuller discussion of these limitations.) In the main, then, a teacher was left to her own resources in testing her pupils' achievement.

Experience has shown that many teachers are not good at test construction, as question-writing is a skill, or gift, only partly correlated with teaching ability. It is necessary to understand thoroughly both the subject matter and the thinking processes of the pupils being tested, but even then many good teachers find question-writing a very troublesome task. Experience has also shown that, however carefully questions are prepared, empirical evidence is necessary to ensure that unexpected problems do not invalidate a question as a measuring device.

Item banking was initially designed to circumvent these limitations to the utility of psychometric techniques in test or examination construction; but the possibilities opened up by surmounting them are such that item banks are evolving into much more than mere collections of questions.

What Is an Item Bank?

Item banking began, in an informal way, after the introduction of objective testing procedures into examinations. The multiple-choice format usually adopted in these is much less tolerant of ambiguities or unintended clues and hurdles in the question wording than any other format, and relatively simple statistical techniques can be used to monitor such questions when they are used. The difficulties of question-writing became obvious with these tests. These difficulties, combined with the expense of producing multiple-choice questions, or items, made it imperative to create a store or bank of such items which could then be used for a variety of purposes. Examination boards and groups of teachers began to develop collections of items which they had tested out, and which could be relied upon as 'good' items, that is, items which tested important points in the syllabus and which were free of unintended or irrelevant features.

But good items do not necessarily make good tests. Given a large collection of questions it is necessary to choose a suitable set of them for any particular test. Two indicators are usually attached to each item to help in selection, one describing the content or objective which it tests, and the other recording how difficult the item proved to be in use. The recommended procedure is that the teacher should plan the test carefully on a two-dimensional grid, specifying how many questions are required at each difficulty level and in each content category, and then searching the item bank to find suitable questions to fill out this specification. Such a procedure can work very well, but bank users do not always follow it. The temptation to go straight to the questions is often too great, and the bank is scanned for items that seem suitable or attractive, without the preliminary production of a rigorous specification. Experience has shown that such 'appealing' tests are often unbalanced and nearly always more difficult than was intended. If an item bank is really to save teachers work, and at the same time to produce good tests, then a fairly automatic selection system needs to be provided to choose the questions while the teacher concentrates on the design of the test.

Finally, if the maximum benefit is to be gained from an item bank, there is one further need. A test is a means for collecting information for some purpose, and its value is limited by the framework provided to interpret the results. A way must be found to give meaning to every possible score and, for an item bank, this interpretation must be available before the new test has ever been used. The traditional post-hoc techniques of standardizing a test on results from a representative sample of students are too cumbersome for the enormous variety of tests a single bank can generate, and a method based on the known statistics of individual items must be used. Some solutions to this problem will be discussed later. In summary, an effective item bank can be represented as in Figure 1. A standard test specification is prepared, as input to the selection system. This searches amongst the content labels and difficulty measures to choose the best test, technically speaking, that the item pool can supply for the specified purpose. Interpretative aids are then produced, based on the items chosen and the stated purpose of the test. In practice, a few extra features may be added. Items may also be classified as 'multiple-choice' or 'free response', or as requiring equipment, such as rulers or protractors. A human 'check' is probably needed, even in the most automated system, to ensure that the initial selection is acceptable. Finally, an item bank should never be seen as complete, but must evolve, growing in size and adapting to cope with changes in teaching and syllabus. A separate 'maintenance system' is needed both to introduce new items and to monitor the performance of old ones, continuously updating the item records and, occasionally, rejecting items that no longer seem to function properly.

Figure 1. An Item Bank

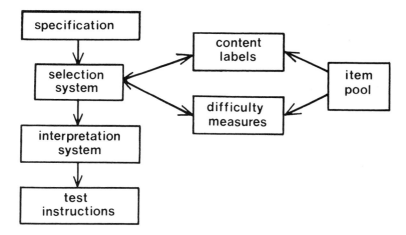

The Advantages of Item Banking

1 *The Item Pool*

The most obvious advantages of item banking arise from the existence of an adequate item pool. The teacher wishing to construct a test is assured of a ready supply of proven items, and saved the considerable, and difficult, task of writing her own. Testing children becomes less of a chore, and may be more easily integrated into teaching. It becomes easier to abandon the traditional and rather sterile practice of testing only at the end of each year or term (summative testing) in favour of a less formal and more frequent programme of assessment. Formative, or diagnostic, testing to check students' learning of a topic shortly after it has been taught, so as to catch misunderstandings quickly enough to allow easy remediation, has long been advocated as part of effective teaching, but is difficult to carry out successfully without an adequate item bank to provide the items. Indeed, the desire for formative testing has been the stimulus behind the development of many banks.

The item pool can serve another function. If the items have been vetted by curriculum specialists, they will represent a practical, or behavioural, definition of the objectives of the course. These are the tasks a child should be able to cope with by the end of a topic or course, and any test will represent a sample of the required tasks. As a means of communication of objectives between syllabus designers, teachers and students, an item bank may be more effective than any textbook. But there is, of course, a danger: that only the objectives that lend themselves to easy testing will be included. Banks, and especially those that are limited to objective test items, must guard against this danger.

A final advantage stemming from the item pool is the possibility for every teacher to obtain a locally ideal test. No published test is ever quite right; since they must be suitable for a wide market in order to be commercially viable, they are never perfectly suitable for any particular teacher. The balance of content is not what she would have chosen, or the style or format of some questions is not the way she would have presented it. But an item bank allows her to specify her own balance, and to reject any unsuitable item. Indeed, many bank systems will allow her to add a few items of her own, gratefully accepting them for inclusion in the bank if they pass statistical and expert scrutinies.

2 *The Interpretation Scheme*

The most frequently criticized aspect of many teachers' use of tests is the habit of noting only a child's total score on the test and judging his performance only on the basis of his rank order, or position in class. This practice is often called norm-referencing, but incorrectly, since there is no reference to any norms outside the class itself. Rank ordering is, in fact, used for want of anything better; children's performances are judged against their classmates' because there is no basis for comparing them to any external standard. It is this lack of reference that leads to rank ordering.

Item banks offer a variety of methods for interpreting performances against external standards. The most rigorous of these use 'latent trait' models of test performance. These assume that there exists a single scale on which all the items can be placed, ordered according to their difficulty, and that this order is fixed for all persons attempting the items. Furthermore, all the candidates can be placed on this scale, ordered according to their ability, and this order is independent of the actual items attempted. There is thus a single scale (measuring the latent trait) which measures (is) both difficulty and ability simultaneously. An analogy may be drawn with weighing people using a balance or see-saw: certain standard objects may be ordered according to their weights (difficulty of being lifted) and people may be tried against them, and ordered according to their weights (abilities to raise the objects). Both orders will be unique — whether the weighing is done on earth or on the moon.

An attempt to utilize this principle in relation to item banks led to the Rasch scale (Rasch, 1960; Wright, 1977) being introduced. It allows a pupil's ability to be described in terms of the defined difficulty of the items correctly answered. Latent trait banks attempt to apply the principles of measurement of the physical world to mental traits; a Rasch scale is thus a close analogy to the absolute scale of temperature measurement.

There is disagreement about the applicability of a single bank scale to the complex of abilities involved in many school subjects. Goldstein and Blinkhorn (1982) argue that this 'unidimensional' assumption is sometimes implausible and that the Rasch model could be expected to fit well in 'rather few interesting situations'. Wright and Mead (1979), on the other hand, find that the same model works quite adequately in practice, even in cases where the number of 'conceptual dimensions', or the range of skills involved, seems quite large.

The conflict may be resolved if the total freedom to combine any items from various parts of the bank can be abandoned, and each test be drawn instead from a specified domain within the bank. Effectively, then, there is a collection of little item banks, one for each domain, and each may be calibrated with its own domain scale. But more often a simpler approach is considered adequate. If the domains are made small enough, then each can correspond to a single syllabus topic or objective and be the subject of a single week's work. Then questions can be chosen to represent each objective at an appropriate standard for that objective. Each item is then assumed to be equivalent to each other within its domain and mastery of a sample of them (a test) indicates a child's mastery of the whole domain. This approach, called domain-referenced testing, has been adopted by many banks, especially those developed to serve a particular teaching scheme.

Whichever calibration method is adopted, item banks encourage the teacher to interpret a child's score on one test or topic with reference to his own scores on other topics, as well as to criteria or norms for that topic itself. By creating a 'profile' of these results for each child across the whole subject, or throughout the period of a course, and looking for any uncharacteristically low result, a topic that has been misunderstood or a skill which is relatively weak can be detected for remediation before too much damage has been done to the child's learning or motivation. Such an approach to classroom testing is often called diagnostic assessment. Profiles may, of course, show up surprisingly good performances as well as learning failures, with important implications for pupil guidance rather than for remediation.

Given so many possible interpretative schemes, no teacher using an item bank should be driven back to within-class rank ordering in an attempt to impose meaning on test results.

3   The Specification

Potentially the most significant change brought about by item banking lies in the shift of the teacher's task from writing questions to designing the test. The first step in responsible assessment is to express clearly the purpose or purposes which a test is intended to serve. This unambiguous statement can then be used to create the specification so that the bank will generate a test ideally suited to that purpose. By freeing her from the drudgery of question-writing, item banking encourages the teacher to spend her time, as a professional should, in designing her test; she becomes less a labourer and more an architect.

How should a teacher go about this process of design? The statement of purpose will first establish the type of questions that can be used, objective or short answer or essay; at present most banks contain only objective items, but this need not always be so, as any question can be banked if the instructions for marking are sufficiently precise. As already described, most banks require a test to be specified in terms of content labels and difficulty indices. The content labels may involve simple *pigeon-holes*, using a number of mutually exclusive categories set up in advance so that each item can be assigned to one and only one of them, in the way that letters are sorted in a postal sorting office. This system can be used in, for example, a bank set up solely for domain-referenced testing of a course, where each domain corresponds to a pigeon-hole.

A more flexible approach is a *hierarchy* in which a subject is broken down in stages into finer and finer subdivisions which are indicated by successive codes. Consider this mathematics question:

A cassette tape lasts for 45 minutes. How long will 7 tapes last for?
(hours)

This might be coded 2322, the separate numbers signifying

2   Time
−3   Units and conversion
−−2   Calculation of times
−−−2   Word problems of time

This approach is familiar as that used to classify non-fiction books in most libraries. But a teacher might object that this item is really about multiplication (7×45) or multiplication and division $\left(\dfrac{7 \times 45}{60}\right)$ and not time at all, while a third might protest that it's really about fractions $\left(\dfrac{45}{60}\right)$ or multiplication of fractions $\left(7 \times \dfrac{3}{4}\right)$. Each of these would lead to a completely different classification code for the item, and each would be just as appropriate as the others.

This problem, which defeats both pigeon-holes and hierarchies equally, has led many banks to adopt a third approach, the *thesaurus*. In this method each item is described by a small number of 'key-words'; the previous example might be tagged with:

Time, Calculation, Word Problem
(and perhaps Multiplication, Division and Fractions).

Unlike hierarchies, each key-word has equal status; no decision need be made as to whether the example is mainly testing time or calculation. Unlike pigeon-holes, the item can be retrieved by using any of its associated key-words; the example might appear in a test on time, or a calculation test or a test of word problems. Key-words may be combined, using 'and', 'or' or 'not', to give more precise specifications, such as

Length *and* Word Problem *not* Millimetres *and* (Addition *or* Subtraction).

Perhaps the crucial advantage of the thesaurus for school item banks is the naturalness of compound key-word statements like this. For a fuller discussion of these issues, see Hiscox and Brzezinski (1980).

There are two kinds of difficulty indices commonly in use. *Sample-based* indices may be descriptors like 'Very Easy', 'Fairly Easy', or a numerical four- or five-point scale, or more precise 'percentage correct' measures of difficulty. These report the results of one particular sample of children, but are simple to understand and use, and appropriate if the questions are intended for fairly specific uses with well-defined courses and at specified stages during these courses. *Sample-free* indices are used with latent trait calibrated banks and are measures of difficulty on the bank's fixed scale. They are considered to be fixed, and not to depend on whether the particular children who tried the questions were relatively high or low in ability. This constancy means that these indices are more flexible than sample-based ones, but they require the teacher to become familiar with the scale, in much the same way as if she was asked to indicate a suitable range of temperatures for mid-afternoons in April — in centigrade, not fahrenheit.

Whatever content and difficulty indicators are used, the teacher's problem is to translate her *purpose* for the test into a specification. For some purposes, such as monitoring performance or careers guidance, a wide range of content, sampling a whole course, is required, while for others, such as testing mastery of a topic, a narrow content range is indicated. A similar decision, wide or narrow, applies in specifying the range of difficulty required. A test containing easy, moderate and hard questions will provide a reasonably accurate measure of each child's current ability, where their abilities range widely, and may be needed where, for example, children are to be streamed into several ability bands or where the ability level of newly arrived children is not known. But if the purpose of the test is to divide the class into two groups — pass and fail, masters and non-masters, adequate and in need of remedial help — a more efficient procedure is to choose items all of more or less the same difficulty. Thus a screening test should only contain easy items, so that only those who cannot handle the easy tasks are identified for remedial help.

Test design, then, involves translating the statement or purpose into two decisions, wide or narrow content and wide or narrow difficulty, and then specifying more precisely the list and balance of content and the level or levels of difficulty required. A carefully designed test will be efficient for its purpose, minimizing the errors of measurement wherever important decisions are to be made.

Some Item Banks in Use

Item banks are finding applications throughout the education system, from primary school to university. In this section some examples are given of banks which have been or are being constructed for the following applications: examinations; monitoring; classroom assessment; and diagnosis.

Examinations. Many university and college departments are building up their own item banks, but there are also interesting experiments in making them available to several examining bodies at once. The Scottish universities, for example, share a bank of questions for examining in the first two years of chemistry courses. A potential benefit is the chance to compare standards between different boards or colleges before the examination is taken, thus doing away with the need for any post-hoc comparability study.

The Royal College of Physicians has since 1969 drawn from a bank of 8000 items for the first (and only written) paper in the Part II examination, thus ensuring equivalence between the College's three institutions. But a well calibrated bank would allow different institutions to construct different tests, yet still award equivalent grades. The Biology Item Bank (Duckworth and Hoste, 1976) can be seen as a first step towards an item bank system designed to facilitate internal assessment as part of school certificate examining. The developments resulting from the Dunning Report in Scotland (SED, 1977), and in particular the introduction of an internal component to 16+ certification, have stimulated the development of item banks linked to examination syllabuses. Here, each school, or each teacher, would use the bank to provide locally ideal tests fitting their own particular teaching, and the bank's interpretative scheme would play the role of moderator in ensuring comparability of standards across schools.

Monitoring. Banks such as these fulfil a monitoring role by maintaining the standard required in the examination, but item banks may be used to monitor performance more directly.

The Assessment of Performance Unit of the DES in England (APU) began its monitoring programme in autumn 1978 with a survey of mathematical achievement in schools in England and Wales. An earlier DES sponsored project, Tests of Attainment in Mathematics in Schools (Sumner, 1975, 1977), had developed two item banks, for 11- and 15-year-olds, and these were used to produce the original written monitoring tests. Item banking techniques allow a very large number of questions (647 in the first APU written mathematics survey) to be administered, and so a more detailed survey to be carried out than is otherwise feasible. Results of APU surveys have been published, by HMSO, in primary and secondary mathematics and primary language development, but seem to have had little impact on teaching (see, for example, Bond, 1982).

In the United States, the National Assessment of Educational Progress (NAEP) has been monitoring standards in ten learning areas every five years since 1969. Changes in performance over each period are analyzed with respect to various background variables such as sex, socio-economic status and racial and language background. All the items and data collected are made available to other researchers and to school systems who can thereby create their own monitoring materials to suit their own courses, and compare the results with those of similar districts or courses throughout the country.

Classroom assessment. Books of test questions or 'revision exercises' have always been popular with teachers, but have always been criticized, both as teaching aids and tests, for their possible influence on teaching practice and because they offer no interpretative framework or psychometric reference. Recent enthusiasm for 'criterion-referenced' tests has encouraged some publishers to produce books of items grouped under teaching objectives, and thereby, with no indication even of the difficulty levels of the items, to claim to be providing a reference system.

Clearly there is a need for good (pedagogically and psychometrically) test material for teachers which allows them to monitor: (a) the effectiveness of their teaching; and (b) the efficiency of each pupil's learning. Such material needs to be appropriate to the syllabus and style of each and every teacher, and simultaneously to refer scores to some measurement frame. Item banks seem best able to offer such flexibility.

Most work so far has been done in Australia, New Zealand or the USA. Tasmania (Palmer, 1974) has a Primary Social Sciences bank designed to provide the teacher with feedback on class achievement. The tests are constructed by the teacher, but marked and interpreted centrally. The New Zealand Item Bank: Mathematics, which ranges over six years of primary and early secondary school, and the Australian Item Banks in Mathematics, Science and Social Science, mainly aimed at 'Year 10' (ACER, 1978), are wholly school-based. Each of these banks consists of a published book (or books) containing all of the items on detachable pages. The teacher is required to choose items, photocopy the pages, cut out the items, and paste up and duplicate the test. Item difficulty is indicated on a four- or five-point scale, allowing rough control over test difficulty, but having no reference to normative or other data.

One fully operational item bank system for school use has been designed to reduce the amount of work required of the teachers. The Portland Public School system in Oregon, USA, has produced Rasch-calibrated item banks in mathematics, reading and language arts (Forster and Doherty, 1978). Teachers request tests for various purposes by specifying the required test characteristics and receive the test, either a master copy or multiple copies, within a week, together with reference and semi-diagnostic information.

A fully computerized item bank system is being developed in Scotland, capable of generating a large number of different tests each day, of providing both Rasch-based and domain-referenced interpretations and of building up these interpretations into a record of a child's performance. The test production system (Osman, 1984) enables a teacher to order a test by describing the required range of difficulty and the desired content in terms of a list of key-words which may be linked by 'and', 'not', 'or' to give, for example: 'LENGTH and AREA' or 'LENGTH and TIME and not SPEED'. The text of the items is stored on the computer, including diagrams if necessary, and a rough version of the test is produced for the teacher to approve. After any 'offending' items have been replaced, a final high-quality version is paged and printed for duplicating. If a Rasch-calibrated bank is being used, then interpretation tables are computed and printed to convert test scores into measures on the standard bank scale.

If the test is composed of subtests, groups of items on different topics, then further analysis is possible. Children may be asked to answer multiple-choice questions on special cards, or teachers can mark by hand and transfer 'right' or 'wrong' codes to the cards, and these cards may then be used as input to the marking system called SCRIBE (Mitchell, 1982). This system produces a report for each child showing his performance on each topic. Criterion levels may be set for each topic, and SCRIBE will then highlight areas of weakness, to indicate to teacher and child where remedial action may be needed. In addition, summaries of the class performance are produced to enable the teacher to evaluate her teaching on each topic.

The third system, SCOPE (Mitchell *et al.*, 1984) accumulates the kinds of data used by SCRIBE, building up a profile over the months or years of a course to show a child's performances in various aspects of the course. The analysis may be in terms of syllabus sections, or of attributes or functions such as 'knowledge', 'solving problems' or 'practical work'. The report may quote actual marks on tests or exercises, or use pre-defined grades or written comments, so that it may be sent immediately to parents or, perhaps, become part of the child's school leaving certificate. Together, these three systems show how much of the tedium may be taken out of assessment by automated item banks.

Item Banks in the Future

The Scottish projects described above show what can be done with item banks, but they also highlight some of the problems. The full potential of item banks to reduce the drudgery and increase the professionalism of school assessment is still limited by the state of computer technology. It is very expensive, in terms of equipment and time and storage, to maintain the text and diagrams of questions on a computer, and the sort of high-quality printer required to produce tests is also expensive. Although computing power is now quite cheap, the peripheral devices are not. But if these costs decline, so that manual assembly of tests is no longer necessary, and the rather awkward use of special card readers is also circumvented, what then becomes possible?

One immediate effect would be to bring the technology closer to the teacher. If a school has direct access to a bank and can generate its own tests, then item banking may become an everyday resource like textbooks, without the high technology mystique which still attaches to it. We may then expect demands for more than just test items to be banked. There is no reason why other teaching resources should not be provided too, such as worksheets for practical work. The Viewdata systems of the television companies (PRESTEL) could become the medium for dissemination of such banks.

Already some banks are being constructed of standardized exercises, which are far from the current objective test model. These may carry a bank of remedial suggestions to reinforce the exercises. From this it is a small step to a wholly individualized conception of the curriculum in which the banking system, under the supervision of the teacher, guides each child through his own unique version of the syllabus, allowing him to progress at whatever pace suits him, and in whatever direction he and his teacher decide he should follow. The distinctions between 'comprehensive' and 'selective' education would then disappear as each child pursued a course uniquely tailored to his 'age, ability and aptitudes'.

With such a differentiated curriculum, held together by the common assessment system provided by the item banks, it would be possible to do away with, or at least substantially reduce the influence on teaching of, the external common examination system. The professionalizing of assessment implies that teachers may take on the whole responsibility for designing not only their own formative assessment policies, but also the certification of pupils for future careers. The kind of negotiated targets of education advocated by Burgess and Adams (1980) become attainable, with pupils themselves taking a substantial responsibility for deciding what they will learn, how and when they will be assessed.

Who knows, item banking may even make assessment popular!

References

ACER (1978) *Mathematics Item Bank. Books 1 and 2 and Teachers Handbook; Science Item Bank, Books 1, 2 and 3; Science Item Bank Handbook; Social Science Item Bank (and Item Bank Handbook)*, Hawthorn, Vic., Australian Council for Educational Research.

BOND, G. (1982) 'Great potential, but careless application', *The Guardian*, 16 November 1982.

BURGESS, T. and ADAMS, E. (1980) *Outcomes of Education*, London, Macmillan.

DUCKWORTH, D. and HOSTE, H.R. (1976) *Question Banking: Approach through Biology*, Schools Council Examinations Bulletin 35, Evans/Methuen.

FORSTER, F. and DOHERTY, V. (1978) 'Using the Rasch approach to measurement to solve practical school testing problems', paper presented at the American Educational Research Association Annual Conference, Toronto.

GOLDSTEIN, H. and BLINKHORN, S. (1982) 'The Rasch model still does not fit', *Br. Educ. Res. J.*, 8, pp. 167–70.

HISCOX, M.D. and BRZEZINSKI, E.J. (1980) *A Guide to Item Banking in Education: Part 4*, Portland, Oregon, Northwest Regional Educational Laboratory.

MITCHELL, A. (1982) 'Using microcomputers to help teachers to develop their assessment procedures', *Prog. Learning and Ed. Tech.*, 19, pp. 251–6.

MITCHELL, A. *et al.* (1984, in press) 'Computer record keeping and reporting of assessment in technical education courses', *Scottish Curriculum Development Service (Dundee Centre) Journal*.

OSMAN, C. (1984) *Item Banking Facility: User's Manual*, Godfrey Thomson Unit, University of Edinburgh.

PALMER, D.G. (1974) *A Computerised Self-Moderation Procedure in Banks of Items for Primary Social Sciences*, Curriculum Centre, Education Department of Tasmania.

POPHAM, W.J. (1978) *Criterion-Referenced Measurement*, Englewood Cliffs, N.J., Prentice-Hall.

RASCH, G. (1960) *Probabilistic Models for Some Intelligence and Attainment Tests*, Copenhagen, Danish Institute for Educational Research; republished (1980), Chicago, University of Chicago Press.

SCOTTISH EDUCATION DEPARTMENT (1977) *Assessment for All* (Dunning Report), Edinburgh, HMSO.

SUMNER, R. (1975) *Tests of Attainment in Mathematics in School: Monitoring Feasibility Study*, Windsor, NFER.

SUMNER, R. (1977) *Tests of Attainment in Mathematics in School: Continuation of Monitoring Feasibility Study*, Windsor, NFER.

WRIGHT, B.D. (1977) 'Solving measurement problems with the Rasch model', *J. Educ. Meas.*, 14, pp. 97–116.

WRIGHT, B.D. and MEAD, R.J. (1979) *The Rasch Model: Unidimensionality and Item Bank Construction*, University of Chicago.

Using the Computer for Learning and Teaching

Roger Hartley
University of Leeds

It is not a new idea to use the computer for aiding learning and teaching. In fact the first significant steps were taken almost twenty years ago, but these were by a minority of funded research workers and practitioners who could be connected to a suitable mainframe. Technological advances have now brought the microcomputer within the purse of individual schools and departments, and there has been a corresponding initiative for funding from the Department of Industry. This, coupled with the teacher-training, curriculum developments and dissemination arising from the National Microelectronics Education Programme (MEP) and the Scottish Microelectronics Development Programme (SMDP) invite, even require, the classroom teacher to consider carefully the educational potential and value of these innovations.

Articles (for example, in *Educational Computing*) and publications from the fourteen MEP regions which cover England, Wales and Northern Ireland, summarize activities and generally take an optimistic stance. But there are cautionary notes (e.g., Hartley and Bostrom, 1982) and practising teachers, looking at available programs and reflecting on their possible uses, will see difficulties and have some questions.

First, there is likely to be disappointment at the small range and uneven quality of many of the materials. It is unfair to be scathing in these judgments. Programs are difficult to design and expensive to produce, and a significant number of current materials will represent a teacher's early attempts at development. Further, standards are continually rising and the quality of program presentation and supporting documentation from the publishing houses is often commendable. But what are the guarantees that the programs will develop learning, or could the instruction have been accomplished by other, cheaper means? What makes an effective program? Are there principles, perhaps evolving from educational or instructional psychology, which should underpin their designs?

A second difficulty is how to integrate these materials with conventional classroom teaching. The problem is more fundamental than a lack of hardware or the children's unfamiliarity in using the equipment — though these hindrances are real enough. Note that the microcomputer can calculate quickly, and in simulation programs adapt to the student's own ideas and decisions; it can also store individual responses and in tutorial programs select feedback and tasks to suit a learner's competence. In short, the computer operates most effectively when its users behave differently and develop in their own ways. In contrast, the teacher in order to manage a whole class of students has to limit and control the variance in their learning. So how are these opposing tensions to be resolved? At present there is a lack of evaluative case studies examining computer-assisted teaching styles and the types of learning benefits they produce.

A third issue concerns software tools for teachers. Having gained some experience with Computer-Assisted Learning (CAL), they may wish to amend programs or help in their design of programs so that they can suit particular aims and circumstances. How easily can this be done? Must the teacher either wait and select from published programs, or make a substantial commitment of time and learn a computer programming language such as BASIC? Even then, will the labour-intensive process of designing, implementing, testing and documenting a CAL program be economically viable? Recently there have been interesting developments in providing teachers with a wider range of software tools on microcomputers (for example, educational data base languages, special types of authoring systems, spread-sheet systems for simulation projects, and software learning environments such as LOGO). These enable teachers to prepare materials without first acquiring conventional computer programming expertise. However, they do require the user to be thoughtful and clear in educational aim and in learning design.

Finally, what will be the future role and direction of CAL? The history of other educational innovations, such as programmed learning or educational television, warns against overstatement. But Computer-Assisted Learning is linked to a strong, continuing computer technology and to significant lines of research. Cognitive psychologists are using the computer and computational metaphors to study and explain processes of cognition, decision-making and problem-solving. Workers in artificial intelligence are addressing such issues as knowledge representation, and developing techniques and software tools for manipulating and using knowledge structures. Thus there are many working groups and disciplines exploiting the computer across educational curricula, and it is important that teachers become more knowledgeable and experienced so that they can provide a greater weight of comment and guidance. Otherwise developments might take insufficient account of school education, leaving it with equipment and techniques that become progressively outmoded.

Task-Based Learning under Program Control

Some of the original influences on CAL were suggestions from programmed learning for the design and management of tutorial programs presented by machine. The underlying psychology was most clearly and forcibly argued by Skinner (1954, 1968) who considered learning to be a process of bringing responses under the control of stimulus material (for example, writing 17 to the task $9 + 8 = ?$). The method of achieving this control, (i.e., strengthening the association between stimulus and response) is to present a reinforcing stimulus — loosely, a 'reward' — immediately after the appropriate response has been given. (Typically, 'rewards' would be knowledge of results and/or approving comments.) Inappropriate answers are ignored and the stimulus re-cast. In order to ensure reinforcement, the materials have to be designed so that the probability of a correct response is extremely high. Hence learning steps are small. More complex behaviours are built up by 'shaping' (giving reinforcement initially for approximate responses or sets of responses, but then only for more accurate attempts) and by chaining and coagulating response sequences. Thus the important features for learning were that active and observable responses were made, that the process was reward-based, and that the presentation of material was carefully ordered to synthesize more complex response patterns. Skinner went on to demonstrate how, by following these principles, learning programs could be designed and elementary machines constructed to present them.

The resulting research interest provided a considerable number of experiments testing the effects of these factors in learning. Their results were surprising and worrying. For example, in Grundin's survey (Grundin, 1969) out of thirteen studies concerned specifically with feedback, not one showed significant differences in favour of providing reinforcement, i.e., knowledge of results. Anderson *et al.* (1971) provided some explanations when they used computers to present the materials under a variety of feedback conditions. Results showed that reinforcement aspects of feedback (i.e., giving knowledge of correct response only when right (KCR-R), as Skinner recommended) gave somewhat poorer results than KCR-W (providing feedback only when the learner was wrong). In short, students learn from their mistakes. Feedback may give reinforcement, but its main function in human learning is to locate errors and provide information for them to be corrected. Guthrie (1971) showed similar results.

In Anderson's experiments, all feedback treatments were superior to no feedback, but even this condition gave better performances than programs where students were made to 'cheat' and shown the answer before they typed a response. (This result may explain the relatively poor performances of programmed texts where such short-circuiting of the instruction can easily occur.) The benefits of having learners actively consider their mistakes for a few seconds before receiving knowledge of results were also demonstrated. Kulhavy *et al.* (1976) went further and collected more detailed on-line information by having students indicate, before receiving feedback, their confidence in the correctness of their answers. The computer also recorded the time spent studying knowledge of results, and comparisons were made between feedback and no-feedback groups. Not surprisingly, for confident and right answers, only a couple of seconds were spent on feedback, but nearly half-a-minute when the confident answer turned out to be wrong. However, for low-confidence answers there was little difference between these times. On post-tests, the informational benefits of feedback to the confident but wrong answers were clearly marked; in contrast, there was little difference to the low-confidence answers whether or not feedback was given. Kulhavy interpreted confidence of answer as a function of the student's understanding, and concluded that for those with a fair measure of competence in the topic, informational feedback was studied and was beneficial. For those less competent the feedback itself was not assimilated. Tait *et al.* (1973) had previously shown a complementary result with younger children studying arithmetic by computer. They distinguished between 'passive' printed feedback, and 'active' explanatory question-and-answer feedback in which the information had to be used by the learner to derive the correct answer. For the more competent, the two types of feedback were equivalent, but with the less able it was the active form which gave significant benefits.

The experimental evidence reinterprets the views of Skinner and they are less comfortable for the program designer. The quality of feedback depends upon the quality of information it conveys to the learner. This depends on how readily particular types of errors are diagnosed by the program, and upon its content enabling the learner to correct his mistakes. Its administration (active or passive) and the type and difficulty of task (which controls the frequency of feedback) should be adjusted to the learner's particular error patterns and to his competence. Programs which merely inform the correct answer and base decisions only on the correctness of the last response will perform poorly and appear little better than crude mechanical drills or machine presented programmed texts. In contrast, the best and most successful programs, for example Suppes and Morningstar (1972) and Tait (1974) — which could also compose remedial tasks on-line from a pupil's errors — have proved motivating and have shown significant learning gains in the classroom.

At present, perhaps because of the small number of microcomputers available for use in a school, adaptive tutorial and practice programs are not prominent in published materials. But they have a place, perhaps with remedial or other special groups, and they can provide the teachers with much useful diagnostic information.

The methods of designing tutorial programs usually include setting out a topic outline, stipulating the summary objectives in specific terms and analyzing these tasks to reveal the working procedures and related knowledge they entail. Perhaps a Gagné-like scheme might be followed (Gagné,

1974) where the learning outcomes are arranged hierarchically. This would suggest a sequence for the material, and competence criteria for the controlling decision rules. Within this framework anticipated errors, feedback material and student performance data-structures can be developed.

Almost all tutorial programs use pre-stored teaching material written in natural language, but containing the embedded commands and special identifying symbols of a chosen author language. These language conventions deal with the presentation of textual material at the terminal, the matching of student responses (to detect errors), the keeping and updating of student records, and the application of decision rules. Some versions of author languages are made so they need little experience to use, but their facilities are limited. Writing programs which properly discriminate and adapt to the individual learner, and attractively present and build up task sequences on the display screen, will prove difficult, even impossible with such simple languages. However, a way of providing the teacher with software tools which exploit the capabilities of the computer and are economical to use has been implemented and described by Tait (in press). It involves setting up a library of pre-programmed formats, which deal with presentation and feedback control. The teacher can select an appropriate format (i.e., an elementary teaching strategy) or a sequence of formats, and type in the teaching content. Computer programs then translate this material into the complex base author language, and prepare an efficient run-time version for student use. Through experience with different users, the library of formats increases, which adds variety and allows the preparation time for programs to be even further reduced.

Knowledge Structures Developed under Learner Control

The behaviourist traditions, which initiated tutorial programs concentrated on the observed and registered responses of the learner, deliberately ignored the mental processes which produced them. However, analysis of the ways information is perceived, organized, stored and applied, has developed rapidly within psychology, and information-processing is now a dominant theme. These studies must relate to human memory, and there have been significant advances since Hebb first proposed his two-stage model of short-term and long-term stores. From discussing the characteristics of these stores, research such as that of Wickens (1970), but particularly of Craik and Lockhart (1972), through the notions of 'depth' and 'spread' of processing, has moved the emphasis on to the mental activity needed to develop long-term semantic knowledge structures. The terms 'depth' and 'spread' proposed by Craik and Lockhart are somewhat ambiguous (see Eysenck, 1978, for a critical discussion), but they relate to the semantic organization mentally undertaken by the learner. Rating the pronouncability of sentences which make up a text is relatively shallow; paraphrasing text or answering an example question based on its propositions, is deeper; so is 'spreading' the processing to include previous knowledge, e.g., constructing a new example of the rule. Craik and Lockhart and other workers (e.g., Anderson and Biddle, 1975) demonstrated the superior recall and comprehension of deep over shallow processing. However Morris *et al.* (1977) showed that the demands of the post-test (shallow or deep) interacted with the demands during acquisition. Mayer and Greeno (1972) had come to a similar conclusion. They took equivalent content and developed two sets of teaching materials. One used the internal structure of the subject matter (applied statistics) for organization and stressed formulae; the other was structured round themes taken from everyday experience. On post-tests which featured calculations, the former treatment group was better, but on creating examples or explaining 'impossible' problems (where probabilities summed to more than 1.0), the second group was superior. Mayer and Greeno's interpretation was that the type of processing interacts with the type of material and so the learner initiates and develops qualitatively different knowledge structures.

A further question of interest is how such processing is controlled. Shiffrin and Atkinson (1969), in their computer simulation model, pointed out some necessary requirements, and there have been other developments in the notions of working memory and its relation to automatic and controlled processing (Shiffrin and Schneider, 1977). Short-term store is now seen as that activated subset of long-term memory in which the semantic 'node-network' of new and old knowledge components is being connected and pruned. This requires controlled processing, and Frederickson (1975) has shown, in his studies of comprehension, how learners adapt to the limited processing capacity of memory. For example, they forget conditional phrases which are part of the sentences (overgeneralizing), and use previous knowledge to substitute and elaborate material given in the text. Further, these characteristics are not reduced on successive reading-recall sequences. Gentner (1976) demonstrated that, initially, the best predictor of recall of material was if adjoining sentences had been recalled, but, following further readings of the text, it was the semantic neighbours that gave the better indications. Both these studies show that knowledge structures are progressively developed from the remembered/comprehended propositions retained in memory. Comprehension is a process of construction rather than replication. Bonnie Meyer devised methods for analyzing the ideational propositions contained in a text and for showing their dependencies. Her experiments (Meyer *et al*, 1980) suggested that those ideas which are high in the hierarchy are better remembered, and form an organizing framework.

It might be thought that this emphasis on cognitive processing and its control through previous knowledge and semantic organization is analogous to the concerns of the behavioural psychologists. After all, they underlined the need for active responses and the sequencing of material to build up more complex behaviours. But there are important differences in their conclusions, as well as in their aims and methods. For example, the pre-knowledge of the learner (i.e., his response repertoire) is used by the behaviourist to determine the starting point from which more complex, specified behaviour can be conditioned by the learning program. For the cognitivist, previous knowledge is used as a base from which the learner can develop his own cognitive structures. Indeed, for Ausubel (1968), the degree of meaningful, as opposed to rote, learning of new material requires its interaction with previous knowledge. To aid this process, Ausubel suggests that prior to instruction, organizing material of greater generality should be studied by the learner.

Such a process of development requires the student to assume a greater responsibility for managing his own learning, and Pask and Scott (1972) have shown that there may be individually preferred styles. Some (labelled 'serialists') gather together and relate material through a series of relatively simple, conceptual linkages. Others (labelled 'holists') tend to build more complex associations and are more wide-ranging in the material they bring together within their mental frameworks. Merrill (1980) has argued that only by allowing students to make choices, to justify them and to see their effects will they become self-evaluative and learn how to learn. Clearly there are difficulties in allowing student control when learners have inaccurate views of their competence and effective learning styles. Also, the consequences of adopting unwise learning goals or strategies may not be immediately apparent. Such feedback can be hard to gather and be difficult to interpret. However, cognitivists would argue that such guidance should be a matter of advice and discussion, not a process of conditioning and imposed control.

Representing a topic as a knowledge structure, which students learn to develop and control, has resulted in different styles of CAL. One of the large-scale examples has been that of TICCIT (Time-shared, Interactive, Computer-Controlled Instructional Television). In this system the course material is arranged in connected topics and subtopics, and, within this, into rules, explanatory examples and test questions (Merrill and Wood, 1974; Merrill, 1980). The student must set his learning goals and decide how to achieve them. His decisions are given to the program through a command set which enables him to browse, at various levels of detail, through the topics which make up the curriculum. Thus, he can decide on the content sequence to be followed. This learning strategy is not only affected by sequence but by type of material (rules, examples and test questions) and by its difficulty. In TICCIT the content varies on a hard-easy dimension by altering the formal-thematic terms in which it is expressed. The commands (made available through function keys) allow learners to manipulate these dimensions and an elementary Advisor can comment on progress in relation to the students' previous decisions and performances.

Merrill has given a clear educational rationale of his methods, and provided a language (TAL) for teacher-authors who wish to prepare materials following his schemes. During 1975–76 an independent and large-scale evaluation was carried out (Alderman, 1978), and in the mathematics area 5000 community college students were involved. All had completed at least one term's work using TICCIT and since the materials were used as a direct replacement of the teacher, an equivalent groups comparison was made against conventional lecture-discussion methods. The results were interesting and perhaps unexpected. For the conventional teaching, the course completion rate was 50 per cent, for TICCIT it dropped to 16 per cent and the TICCIT students showed less favourable attitudes to mathematics. The interpretation was that 'programs which allow each student to proceed at his or her own pace, risk losing students unable to manage their own learning.' However, post-test data for all the participating students showed the TICCIT groups were more than 10 per cent better than those conventionally taught, and data on problem-solving tests showed even greater benefits.

Other research teams developing learner-controlled systems have followed somewhat different representational schemes (Pask and Scott, 1973; Hartley 1981), but have again found building advisory aids extremely difficult. Pask proposed adaptive methods which allowed more competent learners to set more complex goals. Butcher (1982) has taken a similar view. The subject matter was chemical thermodynamics, and his program could provide explanations and feedback following either a 'molecular' or 'work done' approach. It could also detect the student's preferred style and kept records of this. Further, the decision-maker had data on each individual's performance and on the 'best' or 'expert' approach for each problem. For competent undergraduates the program followed their preferred schemes, but if they performed badly in their explanations or acted in an inconsistent way then the computer was more likely to direct and change them to the 'expert' mode.

In science subjects the ways concepts are linked are often well-defined and able to be expressed as a quantitative model. When programmed, this model can serve as a simulator and help develop the students' understanding of its underlying relations. Usually learners cannot edit or amend the model itself, but they can select and input values of variables and observe their effects through the output displays. Such simulation exercises have proved a popular and useful development, and most of current micro-based CAL has followed this approach. For example, there are Mendel-like genetic breeding simulations, pollution-effects exercises, and programs on geographical decision-making. One such program computes crop acreages on farms located in different parts of the country. The model statistically chooses weather patterns which influence crop yields and profits. By placing similar choices in the regional farms and/or considering the effects of several years' weather, a qualitative understanding of the interrelating variables can develop. In many programs the results can be displayed graphically. Thus computer-based simulations can provide a learning experience not easily obtained by other means.

However, students need careful preparation for their use, as the value of simulators comes from the ways they encourage learners to translate their knowledge into hypotheses and then test them out in systematic ways. Accordingly, when Bork and Robson (1972) used a rope-wave simulation program with physics students, they provided pre-stored advice within the program for those students whose decisions were haphazard. These hints became progressively stronger. Even so ratings showed that half the students liked the program, half did not. It became clear that for weaker students the program did not sustain interest long enough for them to make sufficient discoveries about the behaviour of the rope. When more advanced students used the program (many of whom understood the basic physics, and so had a frame of reference), they became more involved and enthusiastic, and were much more successful with the program.

Sometimes it is useful to discuss the underlying model, its supposed structure and its deficiencies with the class; or it may be an interesting exercise to see the effects of using different relations within the model. Unfortunately such amendments can only be made (even if permitted) by those with some computing expertise. However, there are spread-sheet programming systems now available on microcomputers (e.g., VISICALC, SUPERCALC) which allow the ordinary user to build his own data structures. The systems work using an array of row-column cells to which numbers, text or arithmetical relations or expressions can be attached. Since these expressions can reference other cell expressions, an interconnected chain of calculations is easily specified. As values are changed in one cell, their effects ripple through to the others as an automatic recalculation takes place. The farm simulation, referred to above, is one example which can be handled well by this method.

For verbal materials, corresponding data structures which can be readily manipulated by programs are more limited. Educational data bases though can be set up by the teacher, using languages such as MICRO-QUERY. Conditional statements on the values contained under the data headings allow a subset of class members to be specified, and selected information relating to them can be printed. For example, the census data of a medieval village, or socio-economic data showing the changing employment patterns of a locality during the last century (as well as more obvious instances of biological taxonomies), have been used in a variety of classroom projects. The exercise of setting up such classification systems, as well as considering the implications of the data, can be made into stimulating class/group sessions. Another development, which is likely to be even more significant, is the use of logic language such as PROLOG (or micro-PROLOG). In this language particular statements or assertions can be made (e.g., fertile Denmark) and so can more general rules which define these attributes (e.g., x is fertile if x has rain and x has warmth). Relations might be used (New Zealand competes with Denmark) or more generally (*x* competes with *y* if *x* produces *z* and *y* produces *z*). In this way an information base on climates and commodities could be developed, where the higher-order relational rules are defined by the user himself (perhaps the teacher or a student group). There can be a creative querying of this data base, e.g., which country produces meat? or which countries compete with each other? The questions will be worked out by the system using the specified rules, and it can also be asked to give logical explanations of its answers. Subsidiary or further questions may then follow. The syntax of micro-PROLOG is rather ungainly, but teachers who are interested in the variety of simulations and projects which can be developed are referred to Ennals (1982).

Programming Tools for the Learner

The interest in these differing modes of CAL has led to the development of software tools so that teachers, as well as using published programs, can produce a variety of other materials which suit their wishes and curriculum needs. A bolder approach has been taken by Seymour Papert (1980). He proposed that programming tools should be designed for the learners, i.e., for children themselves to develop their own learning. The aim is to allow pupils to become active builders of their own intellectual structures, and this process must be strongly influenced by the language tools that control the communication between the learner and the computer. Papert used the language LOGO to exploit these ideas and perhaps the best illustration occurs in the teaching of geometry to young children. The drawing instrument, an extension of the child, is a 'turtle' — an elementary moving robot connected to a microcomputer — which is able to mark out the route it travels by inking its path on a piece of paper. Alternatively it can be the cursor on the screen of the terminal. The turtle has two properties, a 'position' and a 'heading', and through LOGO the pupil can issue commands, e.g., FORWARD 100 (length units) RIGHT-TURN 90 (degree units). Sequences of commands teach the turtle how to perform actions (e.g., draw a square or a triangle). Papert describes such learning as 'body syntonic' because the child is using knowledge about his own body movements for instructing the turtle. From studying the visual results, the pupil can debug, amend and improve his programs. From simple procedures, more complex programs can develop (e.g., drawing a house may incorporate the procedures from drawing a square and a triangle). The child will realize that the command-values may have to be changed independently of the commands — thus he appreciates the notion of a variable. The pupil may instruct the turtle to move FORWARD a little (small *X* units), RIGHT TURN a little (small *Y* units) and repeat these instructions recursively. By altering *X* and *Y* and studying the shapes produced, the learner may, for example, discover the approximation between a circle and a many-sided polygon. Putting in additions on the FORWARD step-length will cause spiralling; using tests to control the sequence of commands will allow shapes to roll along or round themselves. Such programs can be extended or generalized so that a child can develop his notions of the properties of shape and symmetry.

Although geometric examples show Papert at his most persuasive, he has extended and demonstrated the use of LOGO more widely (Papert and Solomon, 1972; Papert, 1980) in, for example, physics, music and poetry/ grammar. A more extensive discussion of LOGO for exploring mathematics is provided by Abelson and de Sessa (1980), while du Boulay (1981) has used these techniques with student-teachers. However, although illustration and case studies have been provided, there is a lack of detailed recorded evidence on the use of LOGO in the working classroom, and an absence of studies which show how pupils' cognitive processing has been influenced and their mathematical thinking improved by using the language. Exceptions are the evaluative studies of Howe *et al.* (1981), the Brookline project in the USA, and current work which is exploring the use of LOGO with groups of pupils in the Chiltern region (Noss, 1983). The idea of building software laboratories for learning has also been taken up in statistics, in algebra/calculus and in language writing skills (Sharples, 1981).

Knowledge Representation and Intelligent Teaching Systems

All of the CAL materials considered thus far are limited by their lack of general knowledge about the learning topic, about the student and about the teaching/learning process. For example, in tutorial programs using pre-stored material, the learner has to respond to specific questions imposed by the program in ways expected by the program. If he asks, 'Why?...', 'How?...' sensible replies will be given only if such questions have been anticipated by the author. The program does not have the knowledge to work out explanations. Again, simulation programs rarely keep records of the individual student, and do not have the capability to offer advice on the problem or what to do next. Typically these matters have to be left to the teacher. However, workers in artificial intelligence and cognitive science have studied ways of representing such knowledge systems and are developing reasoning programs which can manipulate them. Such formulations and techniques are becoming of increasing interest to CAL practitioners (see, for example, Sleeman and Brown, 1983).

A first requirement for programs to become teachers is for them to have the knowledge to undertake the teaching/learning task and be able to explain and justify their working. For example, MYCIN (Shortliffe, 1976) can give consultative advice on infectious diseases. The program interviews the doctor about a particular patient, and from this information proposes diagnosis and therapy. The general medical knowledge base is a set of approximately 200 decision rules (If — then) statements. When interlinked in a reasoning chain they may suggest action to be taken (e.g., a drug treatment proposed), request more information be gathered, or enable a conclusion (about the particular organisms) to be drawn. The consultant can question WHY? is that information needed and HOW? was it decided (i.e., what rule sequence was used in making the inference). As well as being a working tool, the teaching capabilities of MYCIN are being developed (Clancey, 1979).

Intelligent teaching systems, rather than storing summary performance data from specific tasks (such as number done or number right) represent the students' knowledge in more general terms — usually as rules and mal-rules. These are expressed in the form: If < these task conditions hold > then < perform action X >, and the mal-rules represent the students' misconceptions. Brown and Burton (1978) have designed a program that can infer mal-rules from responses made to specific arithmetic tasks. Expressing mistakes in this form (as rules) not only identifies errors but provides a mechanism for explaining them. Consequently the system has been used in teacher training. After selecting a mal-rule, the program provides instances of consistently wrong responses to arithmetic questions. The student-teacher can have further examples by typing additional items which the program will answer incorrectly following the same mal-rule. When the student has a diagnosis, he uses his version of the mal-rule to work out answers to test-questions supplied by the program. Feedback either confirms he is right and states the mal-rule, or redirects his efforts. In other contexts Sleeman has developed programs which describe performances in solving, or not solving, algebraic equations. Again his work shows that the majority of pupil errors are not erratic behaviour but come from a consistent application of mal-rules. On a more elaborate scale Newell and Simon (1972) have analyzed students' talk-aloud protocols as they worked through problems in logic, cryptarithematic and chess. From these data they represent complex strategies as sets of ordered If ⟨task conditions⟩ then ⟨action⟩ rules. Larkin (1981) has applied their techniques to problems in mechanics and was able to make interesting comparisons between the rule systems of experts and novices.

Having a model of the students' knowledge structures, and a capability to perform the teaching/learning task, allows the system to give more intelligent coaching and advice. Burton and Brown (1979) developed such a program for arithmetic tasks with primary school children. The aim was to develop their understanding of number expressions, and to do this the program played a type of 'snakes and ladders' game. At each turn a pupil has three random numbers which are used to make any valid arithmetic expression. The move on the display board is the value of that expression, but it is not always the best strategy to work out the biggest number. As well as snakes and ladders, an opponent can be 'taken' and sent back. From comparisons with worked out 'expert' moves, the program can diagnose and discriminate between optimal moves, valid moves, and incorrect working of the arithmetic expressions. Correspondingly the coach can then advise (and/or tutor) on strategy (best moves), allowable moves, and arithmetical evaluation. A classroom study between coached and uncoached versions of the game showed clear advantages for the former group in numerical accuracy, variety of number-patterns and in attitude.

These comments refer to only a small proportion of ongoing work (interested readers should consult Barr and Feigenbaum (1982) for comprehensive coverage of applications). Although these programs usually require significant computing resources, their ideas and formulations should be a continual stimulation even to CAL which is based on more modest equipment.

A common aim of all the workers referenced in this article has been to release the educational potential of the computer. Hopefully this focus will encourage practitioners from different disciplines to undertake a wider interest in each other's work.

References

ABELSON, H. and DE SESSA A. (1980) *Turtle Geometry*, Massachusetts, MIT Press.

ALDERMAN, D.L. (1978) *Evaluation of the TICCIT Computer Assisted Learning System in the Community College: Final Report*, Princeton, N.J., Educational Testing Service.

ANDERSON, R.C. and BIDDLE, W.B. (1975) 'On asking people questions about what they are reading', in BOWER, G. (Ed.) *Psychology of Learning and Motivation*, Vol. 9, New York, Academic Press.

ANDERSON, R.C. *et al.* (1971) 'Feedback procedures in programmed instruction', *J. Educ. Psychol.*, 62, pp. 148–56.

AUSUBEL, D.P. (1968) *Educational Psychology: A Cognitive View*, New York, Holt, Rinehart and Winston

BARR, A. and FEIGENBAUM, E.A. (1982) *The Handbook of Artificial Intelligence*, Vol. 2, London, Pitman.

BORK, A.M. and ROBSON, J. (1972) 'A computer simulation for the study of waves', *American Jour. of Physics*, 40, pp. 1288–94.

BROWN, J.S. and BURTON, R.R. (1978) 'Diagnostic models for procedural bugs in basic mathematical skills', *Cogn. Sci.*, 2, pp. 155–92.

BURTON, R.R. and BROWN, J.S. (1979) 'An investigation of computer coaching for informal learning activities', *Int. J. Man-Machine Stud.*, 11, pp. 5–24.

BUTCHER, P. (1982) 'A CBL study of the understanding of chemical thermodynamics', unpublished MPhil thesis, University of Leeds.

CLANCEY, W.J. (1979) 'Dialogue management for rule-based tutorials', *IJCAI*, 6, pp. 155–61.

CRAIK, F.I.M. and LOCKHART, R.S. (1972) 'Levels of processing: A framework for memory research', *J. Verb. Learn. Verb. Behav.*, 11, pp. 67–684.

DU BOULAY, B. (1981) 'Re-learning Mathematics through LOGO 69–81', in HOWE, J.A.M. and ROSS, P.M. (Eds) *Microcomputers in Secondary Education*. London, Kogan Page.

ENNALS, R. (1982) *Beginning Micro-PROLOG*, London, Ellis Horwood.

Roger Hartley

Eysenck, M.W. (1978) 'Levels of processing: Critique', *Br. J. Psychol.*, 69, pp. 157–69.

Frederiksen, C.H. (1975) 'Acquisition of semantic information from discourse: Effect of repeated exposures', *J. Verb. Learn. Verb. Behav.*, 14, pp. 158–69.

Gagné, R.M. (1974) *Essentials of Learning for Instruction.* Hillsdale Ill., Dryden Press.

Gentner, D.R. (1976) 'The structure and recall of narrative prose', *J. Verb. Learn. Verb. Behav.*, 15, pp. 411–18.

Grundin, H. (1969) 'Response mode and information about correct answers in programmed instruction', in Mann, A.P. and Brunstrom, C.K. (Eds), *Aspects of Educational Technology III*, London, Pitman.

Guthrie, J.T. (1971) 'Feedback and sentence learning', *J. Verb. Learn. Verb. Behav.*, 10, pp. 23–8.

Hartley, J.R. (1981) 'Learner initiatives in Computer Assisted Learning', in Howe, J.A.M. and Ross, P.M. (Eds) *Microcomputers in Secondary Education*, London, Kogan Page.

Hartley, J.R. and Bostrom, K. (1982) 'An evaluation of micro-CAL in schools', *Int. J. Man-Machine Stud.*, 17, pp. 127–43.

Howe, J.A.M. *et al.* (1981) 'Teaching mathematics through LOGO programming: An evaluative study', in Lewis, R. and Tagg, E.D. (Eds), *Computer Assisted Learning*, London, Heinemann.

Kulhavy, R.W. *et al.* (1976) 'Feedback and response confidence', *J. Educ. Psych.*, 68, pp. 522–28.

Larkin, J. (1981) 'Enriching formal knowledge: Model for learning to solve textbook physics problems, in Anderson, J.R. (Ed.), *Cognitive Skills and Their Acquisition*, New York, Lawrence Erlbaum Associates.

Mayer, R.E. and Greeno, J.G. (1972) 'Structural differences between learning outcomes produced by different instructional methods', *J. Educ. Psychol.*, 63, pp. 165–73.

Merrill, D.M. (1980) 'Learner control in Computer Based Learning', *Computers and Education*, 4, pp. 77–96.

Merrill, D.M. and Wood, N.D. (1974) 'Instructional strategies: Preliminary taxonomy', Columbus: Ohio ERIC Information Centre.

Meyer, B.J.F., *et al* (1980) 'Use of top-level structure in text', *Reading Res. Quart.*, 16, pp. 72–103.

Morris, C.D., *et al.* (1977) 'Levels of processing versus transfer appropriate processing', *J. Verb. Learn. Verb. Behav.*, 16, pp. 519–33.

Newell, A. and Simon, H.A. (1972) *Human Problem Solving*, New York, Prentice-Hall.

Noss, R. (1983) *Starting LOGO: Interim Report*, Hatfield, Chiltern MEP Office.

Papert, S. (1980) *Mindstorms*, London, Harvester Press.

Papert, S. and Solomon, C. (1972) 'Twenty things to do with a computer', *Educational Technology*, 12, pp. 9–18.

Pask, G. and Scott, B.C.E. (1972) 'Learning strategies and individual competence', *Int. J. Man-Machine Stud.*, 4, pp. 217–53.

Pask, G. and Scott, B.C.E. (1973) 'CASTE: A system for exhibiting learning strategies and regulating uncertainties', *Int. J. Man-Machine Stud.*, 5, pp. 17–52.

Sharples, M. (1981) 'Microcomputers and creative writing', in Howe, J.A.M. and Ross, P.M. (Eds), *Microcomputers in Secondary Education*, London, Kogan Page.

Shiffrin, R.M. and Atkinson, R.C. (1969) 'Storage and retrieval processes in long-term memory', *Psychol. Rev.*, 76, pp. 179–93.

Shiffrin, R.M. and Schneider, W. (1977) 'Controlled and automatic human information processing', *Psychol. Rev.*, 84, pp. 155–71.

Shortliffe, E.H. (1976) *Computer Based Medical Consultations: MYCIN*, Amsterdam, North Holland.

Skinner, B.F. (1954) 'The science of learning and the art of teaching', *Harvard Educ.*

Rev., 24, pp. 86–97; reprinted in ENTWISTLE, N.J. and HOUNSELL, D.J. (Eds) (1977) *How Students learn*, University of Lancaster.

SKINNER, B.F. (1968) *The Technology of Teaching*, New York, Appleton-Century Crofts.

SLEEMAN, D.H. and BROWN, J.S. (Eds) (1983) *Intelligent Tutoring Systems*, New York, Academic Press.

SUPPES, P. and MORNINGSTAR, M. (1972) *Computer Assisted Instruction at Stanford*, New York, Academic Press.

TAIT, K. (1974) 'Development of an adaptive CBL system for teaching arithmetic', unpublished MPhil thesis, University of Leeds.

TAIT, K. (in press) 'The building of a Computer Based Teaching System', *Computers and Education*.

TAIT, K. *et al.* (1973) 'Feedback procedures in computer assisted arithmetic instruction', *Br. J. Educ. Psychol*, 43, pp. 161–71.

WICKENS, D.D. (1970) 'Encoding categories of words: An empirical approach to meaning', *Psych. Rev.*, 77, pp. 1–5.

Index